THE BUSINESS GUIDE
TO
TAIWAN

This book is dedicated
to the memory of
David Bonavia

THE BUSINESS GUIDE
TO
TAIWAN

Michael Clancy
http://virtualtaiwan.com

Asia,
a division of Reed Elsevier (Singapore) Pte Ltd
1 Temasek Avenue
#17-01 Millenia Tower
Singapore 039192

ISBN 981–00–80824

Cover design by Fred Rose
Typeset by Big Picture Communications
Printed and bound in Great Britain by
Biddles Ltd, Guildford and King's Lynn

CONTENTS

	Preface	vii
	About the Author	xi
1	An Historical Perspective of Current Conditions	1
2	Taiwan in Transition	19
3	Taiwan as a Trading Nation	51
4	Industry and Investment Policies	83
5	Foundations for Successful Business	121
6	Some Practical Issues	139
7	The Labour Market and Employment Issues	155
8	Taiwan's Regulatory Environment	179
9	Working With The Market	207
10	Winning Friends and Influencing People	229
11	The ROC Tax System	243
12	Individual Income Tax in the ROC	253
13	Corporate, Business and Other Taxes	261
14	Money and Banking	289

15   Taiwan's Capital Market   325
16   Living in Taiwan   343
        Appendix—Taiwan A to Z   375
        Readers Reply Coupon   387
        Index   389

PREFACE

In approaching the task of writing this book, I have set out to write a practical guide rather than an academic treatise. Drawing on both my consulting and public speaking experience, I therefore wrote from the standpoint of a business person who has been 'through the hoops'. Within the text is the information I wish I had known when first I set out to do business in Taiwan.

Believing the adage that 'a picture is worth a thousand words' I have included many charts and diagrams as well as tables for those who like to see actual numbers. In this manner I have tried to balance the often conflicting requirements of breadth and depth.

A further problem with any printed book of this nature is the timeliness of the information within its pages. This is especially true given the rambunctious pace of Asia in 1998. I have approached this problem from two standpoints. Firstly, during the first quarter of 1998 I set out to completely revise the text to bring it up to date with current developments. Most of the tables and charts therefore provide information to the end of 1997 at least. Secondly, I have taken advantage of the new multimedia opportunities to establish an Internet website for this Guide. This site is located at http://virtualtaiwan.com.

Readers who have access to the Internet and who require the most up-to-date information available are invited to complete and return the enclosed Reader Reply Coupon at the end of the book and send it to me. By return e-mail you will receive your password allowing you to access the restricted area of the website. As well as providing updated information as it becomes available, the website includes additional material that space has prevented from appearing in the printed book. This includes industry sector reviews, major legislation referred to within the book and of interest to foreign companies and also many additional tables and charts. Regrettably, I am not yet a charitable institution and this service has to be confined to *bona fide* purchasers.

For me, the last eight years have been focused primarily on Taiwan and in working both with Taiwanese seeking to invest overseas as well as with major corporations seeking entrée to the local market. It has been a fascinating period, not only from the standpoint of establishing and maintaining a business presence, but equally for watching a country shake off the burden and trauma of an extended period of martial law and to emerge as one of Asia's very few truly democratic countries.

In the very first chapter of the book I refer to Taiwan's past as a haven for pirates and smugglers. This fiercely independent spirit must have become embedded in the genes for these traits have carried through today—much to the chagrin of government and legitimate business alike. Outward bravado often masks an inherent insecurity. In the case of Taiwan, this is rooted both in the rapid modernisation that has taken place over the space of a single generation as well as in its ambiguous international standing as Taiwan fights to maintain an identity separate from the PRC.

The Taiwanese are not sophisticated international players. For many, especially among the older generation, exposure to the outside world has been limited and they are often at a loss outside their own cultural environment.[1] Indeed a whole industry has been spawned in Taipei through cigar and wine clubs which cater to a pseudo-sophistication. Yet, while unsure of their position in the world at large, the alternative—to become absorbed into the Chinese Mainland as an integral part of the PRC (albeit with special status similar to that accorded to Hong Kong)—is unthinkable to the vast majority of the population.

I am not an apologist for the government but I do believe Taiwan needs better understanding by the outside world. This in part is one of the objectives of this Guide. I owe this much to my Taiwanese friends. As frustrating as they can be at times to foreigners not used to their ways, the

---

[1] Although, with an increasing number of Taiwanese now studying overseas for extended periods, this is slowly waning.

people of Taiwan are at heart warm, compassionate, friendly and generous and they deserve a bright future.

There are many people I should thank for providing advice and assistance in the writing of this book. However, should any errors, either of fact or omission, be found within their pages then I can only cry *mea culpa*. It is invidious to single out any individuals for acknowledgment though a special mention should be given to two people. Firstly I wish to thank Ms Rosemary Peers, the Editorial Production Manager within Reed Academic Publishing Asia for her patience and support during the final throes of this project. Secondly I wish to thank and acknowledge the work of my editor, Ms Isabel Partridge, for all her effort and for her tolerance with my last minute changes as some new snippet of information came my way and needed to be included.

Finally, I have dedicated this book to the late David Bonavia, former China correspondent for the *Times* of London and the *Far Eastern Economic Review*. David taught me to appreciate China in all its facets. His first words to me upon my arrival as a diplomat in Hong Kong were "Asia: you're either into it boots and all, or you're out of the picture". Nobody has summed it up better. David was a great writer as well as a dear friend until his untimely death. This is the least I can do to honour that friendship.

Michael Clancy
Taipei, May 1998

Email: clancy@ozinfo.com
Personal Website: http://ozinfo.com
This Guide at: http://virtualtaiwan.com

ABOUT THE AUTHOR

D r Michael Clancy has lived in Asia for more than 20 years; first as an Australian diplomat and later as an independent business person. After obtaining his doctoral degree from Adelaide University, Dr Clancy spent a period in Hong Kong in 1976 as Head of the Political and Economic Affairs Section at the Australian Consulate General, a position which required him to monitor and report to the Australian Government on developments not only in Hong Kong but also in Taiwan and Southern China. Later he spent four years in Seoul, Korea as Deputy Chief of the Australian Embassy.

Resigning from the (then) Australian Department of Foreign Affairs in 1987, Dr Clancy was recruited to lead a Sydney-based team dealing in technology transfer between Australia and Asia. In 1990, realising that there was a need for more Australian consulting companies to base themselves within Asia, Dr Clancy established his own company and moved the focus of his business operations to Taipei.

In addition to managing a company which is engaged in developing a range of on-line business services based around a hub in Taiwan, Dr Clancy is a senior partner within the Asian Business Information Services Group, specialising in Asia-wide market research, projects, acquisitions and mergers. He is a consultant to the Economist Intelligence Unit and a senior adviser to the Asian Credit Information Industries Association.

CHAPTER 1

AN HISTORICAL PERSPECTIVE OF CURRENT CONDITIONS

"To show its present condition and prospects, and to afford the world at large an opportunity of becoming acquainted with the potentialities of a little known but much misunderstood island is the object of the following pages."

PREFACE TO "FORMOSA"
J. D. CLARK, M.J.I.,
EDITOR OF THE *SHANGHAI MERCURY*
1896

Taiwan, also known officially as the Republic of China on Taiwan, is a country of 21 million people. In terms of population and GNP it is the second largest of Asia's mini-dragons. Isolated diplomatically by Beijing, which (officially at least) still seeks to resolve the civil war it failed to completely win almost half a century ago by incorporating Taiwan into the PRC on its own terms, the Taiwanese have prospered in adversity. Yet today's economic prosperity of the island is no accident. The people of Taiwan were by nature seafarers and traders with centuries of commercial experience and business networks behind them. The country was occupied by the Japanese for a little more than half a century and at liberation in 1945, despite the devastation of war, it retained a relatively well organised infrastructural base.

Always more prosperous than the Chinese mainland, Taiwan did not suffer from the tyrannies of distance and social revolution that, until recently, have hampered both the social and the economic development of China proper.

It is more than a century since the editor of the *Shanghai Mercury* published what was possibly the very first 'business guide' to Taiwan and his book makes for fascinating reading. Unfortunately, to many people, Taiwan remains to this day 'little known and much misunderstood'. The world at large may use and know Taiwan's products but it understands little of the background to Taiwan's current economic prosperity and political adversity.

Taking a cue from Clarke writing a century ago, this introductory chapter is devoted to providing an essential thumbnail picture of this fascinating island—*Isle Formosa*—which in 1950 was one of the world's poorest countries but which by the present decade had prospered to the extent that it now holds the world's third largest currency reserves (valued at more than US$83 billion in April 1998).

TRAVELLERS' INFORMATION

Doing Business in Taiwan

Normal business hours are from 09:00 until 17:30 Monday to Friday and from 09:00 until 12:00 noon on Saturday. Government office hours are from 08:30 until 17:30 from Monday to Friday and from 08:30 until 12:30 on alternate Saturdays. Private companies are increasingly following government practice.

Retail establishments—especially the larger stores—often open from 11:00 until 21:30 although opening times vary between districts and individual stores. Supermarkets are generally open from 09:00 until 22:00. Convenience stores are now widespread throughout the island and provide a 24-hour shopping service for many basic necessities.

Business cards are essential in Taiwan and should preferably be in Chinese as well as English. Great store is given to names in Chinese and advice should be taken before selecting a Chinese company or personal name. Literal translations are less important than appropriateness of meaning.

Business visitors should avoid major national holidays such as the lunar New Year, and mid autumn festivals during which business virtually ceases. In the case of the lunar New Year holiday especially, little attention is paid to new work in the month-long run-up to the holiday. At this time the main emphasis is on clearing up outstanding work from the old year and partying with friends and established business associates.

Other times to avoid are the July holiday period as well as August (Ghost month) during which little new business is likely to be written or major decisions taken.

Postal Information

Postal agencies are open from 09:00 until 17:30 from Monday to Saturday. (Since January 1998 post offices and agencies have followed the practice of other government agencies of working only alternate Saturdays.) The Taiwan postal service is generally quite reliable though envelopes with English addresses should be written in a clear hand to ensure prompt delivery.

Red postal boxes are for airmail (usually the left hand slot) and prompt delivery items (right hand slot) while green boxes are for local mail (left hand slot is generally for local mail only).

Telephones

The basic local telephone rate from public phones is NT$1 for two minutes. Coin phones accept NT$1, NT$5 and NT$10 coins.

Public pay phones are also widespread throughout Taiwan and separate phones are available for coins or cards. Local telephone cards are widely available at kiosks and convenience stores. Cards cost NT$100 and permit 100 call units.

International Direct Dial (IDD) phones as well as credit card phones are now being installed in many locations and offer much cheaper international phone rates than available in hotels.

All Taipei area (02) phone numbers have changed to eight digit code since January 1998. A '2' should be prefixed to any seven digit Taipei number in addition to any long distance or international dial codes.

Table 1.1. Useful phone numbers

Service	Phone number
English Speaking Police	(02) 2555 4275
English Speaking Phone Operator	(02) 2311 6796
Fire Department	119
CKS (International) Airport	(03) 398 2143
Sungshan (Domestic) Airport	(02) 2717 3737
Radio Taxi Service	(02) 2301 4567; (02) 2746 9988
International Dial Code	002

Table 1.2. Taiwan: basic facts

Area	36,006 sq km
Population	21.68 million as of December 1997
Population Growth	<1% annually
Government Title	The Republic of China on Taiwan. (Most countries recognise the Government of the Peoples Republic of China as the sole legal government of China. Consequently, all dealings with the Republic of China on Taiwan are unofficial in nature.)
Language	Mandarin Chinese is the official language and the language of instruction in schools; Taiwanese (Hokkien) remains the first language of approximately 80% of the population and is especially prevalent in the centre and south of Taiwan.
Religion	Buddhism, Taoism, some Christianity
Capital	Taipei

Table 1.2 cont'd

Currency	New Taiwan Dollar (NT$)
Time Zone	GMT + 8 hours (no daylight saving)
Fiscal Year	1 July to 30 June

THE ORIGINS OF CHINESE SETTLEMENT

Taiwan today is a part of China, but not part of the Peoples Republic. Its people are predominantly Chinese. Its culture and philosophic traditions are those of the Han people. But it was not always so.

Taiwan was not formally annexed to China until 1863 at the start of the Ch'ing Dynasty. Indeed until the 15th century, the Chinese barely paid any attention to Taiwan at all. China's annexation of Taiwan, following a brief period of Dutch colonisation, has to be seen in the context of the general southward expansion of the Chinese people over the centuries as available land in the heartland of China became over-populated. If the movement of the Chinese to Taiwan has a single distinctive feature it is that, for the first time, it involved settlement across open water rather than being a landward expansion.

From its earliest days, Chinese society in Taiwan developed features quite distinctive from the prevailing norm. Geographically, Taiwan is part of an island chain that stretches from the Kuriles in the north through to the Philippines in the south. Its coastline was considered hazardous by the early mariners: the western coast facing the mainland of China consists of a narrow coastal plain stretching the length of the island but which quickly gives way to high and inhospitable mountains in the east. It is terrain that held scant attraction for people who were used to farming fertile river valleys.

Since historic times, China has always had a population problem. By the 15th century, the problem of over-population had already become acute in the coastal province of Fujien. According to contemporary Chinese records, by the year AD1500, the amount of arable land per head of population in Fujien was only half the national average. The Fujienese had little option but to turn away from farming and towards the sea where they became first coastal traders and, later, colonisers as well. Coinciding with the move of European seafarers into the East Asian region a flourishing trade quickly developed with the Dutch and Portuguese, trading in sugar, textile, metalware and porcelain.

Taiwan quickly became a haven for pirates and a base for smuggling foreign goods into China. Under imperial edicts of the time, Chinese were prohibited from trading in their own ships and Imperial law required all trade to be carried in foreign vessels—an edict the Fujienese were happy to ignore.

It was the Dutch who, looking for a base to rival the Portuguese settlement in Macau, first formally colonised Taiwan in the 17th century. The Dutch, needing labour and other support, brought with them the first true Chinese settlers from Fujien province. Quickly however, the Europeans stationed on Taiwan became overwhelmed by the people brought in to assist them.

For the next two centuries Taiwan remained at the outer limits of the Chinese empire. It was China's 'wild west'—a frontier area lacking coordinated government and controlled by local chieftains who based their support largely on clan loyalties and lineage. Imperial control was exercised spasmodically and was confined to the administrative area of Tainan in the south of Taiwan. Tainan and the nearby fishing village of Kaohsiung became the focus of Chinese control.

At the time of its formal annexation to China in the 19th century, Taiwan was still a crude and lawless place. The merchant society that had developed in Taiwan, and which had been honed on the values of foreign trade and commercial profit, was often at odds with the more traditional Confucian traditions of agrarianism and self-sufficiency dominant on the mainland of China.

This situation continued until the start of the present century when the Japanese, encouraged by Chinese weakness, incorporated Taiwan into the Japanese empire and shifted the capital and the port from the south of the island to Taipei and Keelung in the North, closer to Japan.

Taiwan has a rich and unique history. A part of China it may well be but (and as the Chinese in Taiwan are quick to point out) Taiwan has never been part of the Peoples Republic. In considering Taiwan as a part of China, 'China' needs to be considered in continental and historical rather than in politically convenient nationalistic terms. As at least one commentator has previously pointed out, 'China', in its historical context, has far more in common with the Holy Roman Empire than it does with a modern nation state. Viewed in this light, Taiwan today is but one of the many faces of China.

THE PEOPLE OF TAIWAN

Until recently, for statistical purposes all citizens of the Republic of China were classified into one of three distinct ethnic groups: Taiwanese, Mainland

Chinese and Aboriginal. Although now formally abandoned, people still associate themselves with one or other of these ethnic groups.

The vast majority of the population (around 70%) are Taiwanese who by definition are people of Chinese cultural background and whose family had settled in Taiwan prior to the arrival of the Kuomintang (KMT) at the end of World War II. The predominant language of this ethnic group is Taiwanese—one of the Chinese language groups closely related to Fujienese from which it originated.

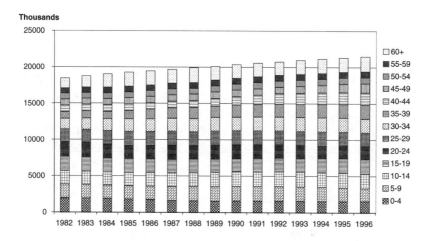

Figure 1a. Age distribution of the Taiwan population

Those Chinese who arrived after World War II are simply known as 'Mainlanders' although these days there is so much intermarriage between the two groups (not to mention the passing of 50 years) that differences are no longer clearly defined. The Hakka, another group from Southern China who today comprise around 5% of the population, have also intermarried and are no longer a visible minority although Hakka communities remain in Judong, Hsinchu, Miaoli and Pingtung.

It is Taiwan's aboriginal community that provides a cultural contrast to the overwhelming influence of Chinese norms in modern Taiwan. Taiwan's Aborigines are distinguished by darker skins and rounder eyes than Chinese but today comprise less than 2% of the island's population.

The Aborigines who in past times retreated into the mountainous areas of the island under the pressure of Chinese settlement are today found mostly along the eastern coast of Taiwan and in the central mountain areas of the island. There are 10 recognised tribes, of which nine have continued to maintain their own language and cultural identity. (These tribes are known as the Ami, Atayal, Bunun, Paiwan, Rukai, Shao, Saisiat, Tsou and Yami. The 'Pingpu' or 'plain dwellers' are now extinct as a separate tribe.) Total aboriginal numbers are claimed to be around 350,000.

Intermarriage between Aborigines and Chinese certainly occurs but with far less frequency than between Taiwanese and Mainlanders. Like native people in other countries, the Aborigines in Taiwan were, in earlier times, badly treated at the hands of the Chinese colonisers. During the period of martial law, while an official policy of assimilation prevailed, the Aborigines were for the most part neglected and much tribal land was appropriated. The situation is now changing with more recognition of aboriginal culture and the need to preserve traditional ways of life.

Overall, Aborigines have had less access to education and would certainly constitute a less privileged socio-economic group. Their relatively small number and isolation from the mainstream of Taiwanese life has left the aboriginal communities without any political advocates except for the Christian church. As a consequence, many Aborigines have converted to Christianity.

POLITICAL FOUNDATIONS

Under the Yalta Agreement, signed between the Great Powers in the closing days of the Second World War, China (then led by Nationalist General Chiang Kai-shek) regained the sovereignty over Taiwan it lost during the period of Japanese occupation. In 1949, as the Chinese Civil War drew to a close and the Chinese Communist Party led by Mao Zedong wrested control of the Mainland from Chiang's Nationalist Kuomintang Party, the latter fled to Taiwan with his army intending to regroup and resume the fight.

Altogether around one and a half million people, including some 600,000 soldiers as well as their families, fled to Taiwan during the closing days of the Civil War. As a result, the island's population increased rapidly from around 6 million people in 1946 to 7.5 million by 1950.

The Nationalist Kuomintang troops were able to hold the battle lines at two small islands, Kinmen and Matsu, just off the Fujien coast, an advance position still occupied today. An invasion of Taiwan itself by the Communist troops was fully expected but fate intervened. The outbreak of the Korean War in 1950 and the bogging down of PLA troops in the Korean conflict, not to mention the dispatch of the US 7th fleet into the Taiwan (Formosan) Straits gave the Nationalists the time they so desperately needed.

From the outset, the Kuomintang leadership maintained that their stay in Taiwan would be temporary and until such time as they regained control of the Mainland from the Communist forces. For this reason, and in order to maintain law and order under a restive local population, the island was governed under martial law and no opposition to the martial government was tolerated. Such policies further alienated the Mandarin Chinese-speaking KMT from the native Taiwanese (who predominantly spoke a local dialect related to that spoken in Fujien). Relations between the two Chinese groups remained tense for many years and only now is this tension beginning to disappear as the government moves to repair past wounds and injustices. The healing process remains painful for many.

Nevertheless, the KMT—with American aid—proved itself capable of repairing Taiwan's war shattered economy. An excellent and far-reaching land reform program was introduced in the 1950s which resulted in a far more equitable income distribution than is found in many other Asian countries and which is the foundation of much of the wealth of the native Taiwanese population today. Rapid industrialisation, which followed the land reform program, saw Taiwan emerge from being one of the poorest to one of the wealthiest places in Modern Asia. Taiwan was on course to become the first of the Asian mini-dragons.

In October 1991, the Republic of China (Taiwan) lost its seat in the United Nations. A further blow to local esteem came in January 1979 when the United States withdrew its recognition from the ROC in favour of the Peoples Republic of China in Beijing. In the face of pressure from Beijing, which has sought to isolate Taiwan diplomatically, most countries within the developed world have withdrawn their diplomatic recognition from Taipei in favour of the PRC. However, because of the strength of its economy and its transition from martial law state to a multi-party democracy, this lack of formal recognition has not prevented most countries from maintaining close unofficial links with Taiwan (see below).

President Chiang Kai-shek died in 1975 from a heart attack at the age of 87. His son, Chiang Ching-kuo became President of the ROC in 1978 and, in the context of Taiwan being a single-party state at the time, was re-elected for a second term. For a while it appeared that a pattern of dynastic succession could be emerging but, to his credit, it was Chiang Ching-kuo who laid the foundation for the present multi-party state that exists today.

In 1986, after almost forty years of being a single-party state governed by martial law, a group of dissident politicians banded together to form a new political party—the Democratic Progressive Party (DPP). The DPP was allowed to form despite a ban on the convening of new political parties.

After much debate the KMT, on the specific orders of Chiang Ching-kuo, decided not to interfere. The first DPP candidates were elected to the Legislative Yuan (Taiwan's Parliament) in 1986 and were permitted to take their seats in the Legislature. The ground had been laid for development of a multi-party state.

The first free elections permitted after the DPP was formally recognised by the authorities came in 1989. In that election, which was marred by many claims of vote buying (a claim that is still common in local elections well into the 1990s) the KMT took approximately 70% of the vote with the remainder going mostly to the DPP.

In 1987, thirty-eight years of martial law were formally ended in one of the last important acts by President Chiang Ching-kuo before his untimely death in January 1988. He was succeeded by Dr LEE Teng-hui, a University professor and agricultural scientist. Lee became the first native Taiwanese to hold the Presidency and retains the position to this time, having become the first person to be elected to the office by popular vote in March of 1996.

THE FOUNDING FATHERS

Wherever one travels in Taiwan, two major Chinese figures of the 20th century are never far from view. Chiang Kai-shek, the Nationalist General who lost the civil war on the Mainland and fled to Taiwan is still honoured in Taiwan (particularly among the older generation and KMT stalwarts) as having saved China (or at least one province of it) from Communism. However it is Dr Sun Yat-sen who is seen as the real father of the nation and is revered as having overthrown the Ch'ing dynasty and founded the Republic of China in 1911. In Taiwan, official dates are still numbered from the founding of the Republic so that 1998 is year 87 in the Chinese system. Indeed, while Chiang remains a controversial figure now reduced from his previous god-like position to a flawed leader of human dimensions, Sun Yat-sen remains revered on both sides of the Taiwan Straits as the founder of modern Chinese nationalism.

The political doctrine of the KMT (which until the end of the martial law period was a political party organised on Leninist principles) is in fact based on the writings of Dr Sun and in particular on his *Three Principles of the People*. The book—still compulsory study in Taiwan's schools—is not easy reading. The Three Principles of 'Nationalism', 'Civil Rights' and 'Peoples Livelihood' are pervasive in daily life, having been drilled into people since an early age. In addition to being studied in schools, candidates for civil service positions must still pass an examination specifically on the subject of the Three Principles.

The National Anthem of the ROC carries the same message and virtually every town in Taiwan has its Mintzu (Nationalism) Road, its Min Shen (Livelihood) Road and Min Chuan (Civil Rights) Road. Chung Shan (Sun Yat Sen) Road and Chung Cheng (Chiang Kai Shek) Roads are also common in just about every town and city. Just to add to the confusion, some towns and districts even have more than one road carrying the same name!

THE FOUNDATIONS OF WEALTH

Taiwan today is above all else an economic engine—the first of the 'mini-dragons' to emerge as newly industrialising powers within the Asian Pacific region. With its economy for the most part in ruins at the end of the Second World War, the island has since experienced an extended period of rapid economic growth. The people of Taiwan—Mainlanders and native Taiwanese alike—have created one of Asia's truly prosperous societies and, with some justification, claim to be the first Chinese democratic state.

In crude statistical terms, per capita GDP has increased from a mere US$196 in 1950 to more than US$13,000 by 1997.

The foundations of the economic success of Taiwan are not dissimilar to those of Korea and Singapore—although Taiwan started on its course of economic modernisation somewhat earlier—and are rooted in two basic factors. First, the economic and rural reforms of the 1950s placed land in the hands of a large number of native Taiwanese. The recovery of the global economy during the 1950s and 1960s and the demand at the time for cheap consumer goods led to the establishment first of cottage industries and later of fully fledged factories upon the land that had been given to the Taiwanese by the earlier reform programs.

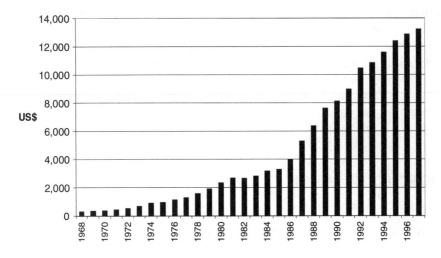

Figure 1b. Growth in per capita GNP in US dollars

Table 1.3. Basic economic indicators

Year	Economic Growth Rate at 1991 prices	GNP in US$ million at current prices	GDP in US$ million at current prices	Per capita GNP (US$)
1966	8.9%	3,148	3,151	237
1976	13.9%	18,492	18,624	1,132
1986	11.6%	77,299	75,434	3993
1987	12.7%	103,641	101,570	5,298
1988	7.8%	126,233	123,146	6,379
1989	8.2%	152,565	149,141	7,626
1990	5.4%	164,076	160,173	8,111
1991	7.6%	183,736	179,370	8,982
1992	6.8%	216,254	212,150	10,470
1993	6.3%	226,243	222,604	10,852
1994	6.5%	243,934	240,986	11,597
1995	6.1%	263,554	260,746	12,439
1996	5.7%	275,144	273,050	12,872

Certainly, industrial growth was aided by the support of the United States during the cold war period for the 'free economies' of Asia. But full credit is due to the indigenous Taiwanese who, denied active participation in government, were able to channel their creative industries back into commerce and trade as their forebears had done.

The second factor which aided the emergence of a strong industrial economy was the existence of martial law and the 'external threat' from the Mainland which (as it did in Korea) acted very effectively to cap dissent and prevent the emergence of organised labour which could nurture political aspirations. With a legal system anchored in Confucian tradition and containing none of the usual (Western) limits and restrictions placed upon commerce, a free-wheeling yet dynamic enterprise system emerged in Taiwan. This was, until recently, a system which gave scant regard to personal values and quality of life but which ensured that those with the ability to do so were able to prosper.

Until recently, it was foreign trade rather than domestic demand that was the mainstay behind Taiwan's engine of growth. Taiwan's total exports in 1997 were valued at more than US$122 billion, exceeding those of the PRC. In the same year Taiwan imported US$114 billion in goods from world markets.

Taiwan is currently seeking admission to the World Trade Organisation as an independent customs area, as a result of which it is under significant pressure to liberalise its domestic markets and redress the ongoing trade imbalance Taiwan has enjoyed, particularly with the United States. Improved access and a growing maturity within the domestic market will provide many new opportunities for overseas companies. This has already had a noticeable effect within the services sector.

Taiwan maintains the third largest foreign currency exchange reserves of any country in the world (exceeded only by Japan and China). In recent years, the sheer magnitude of these reserves has led to inflationary pressures in the local economy. With too much money and, until recently, too many restrictions on overseas investment, many Taiwanese have in recent years turned from traditional manufacturing industries to speculative ventures such as stocks, futures trading and real estate.

During the period 1988–90 real estate prices in metropolitan Taipei more than doubled and the local stock exchange came to have all the attributes of a gambling casino. Prices soared throughout the island and many workers left their jobs seeking speculative fortunes from the stock market or from trading real estate. The effects of this period have fundamentally affected the island's economy to the present time. Much new investment, particularly in the housing sector, was wasted—there were reputedly more than 600,000 vacant housing units at the end of 1997. Many of the more traditional industries, particularly those in rural areas, have been forced to close through scarcity of labour. A large number of these industries have relocated to elsewhere in Asia, particularly the low labour cost countries such as Mainland China and Indonesia.

The response of the government to changing economic circumstances has been to encourage the transformation of Taiwan into a high-tech manufacturing centre as well as offering the prospect of replacing Hong Kong as a regional 'operations' centre; lofty aspirations that have not yet been fully achieved.

While outwardly and to the casual observer, Taiwan appears to have a thoroughly capitalistic free market economy much like that of Hong Kong, government involvement in the economy and particularly in a number of strategic industries remains strong. The financial market in particular remains over-regulated and subject to more cumbersome and arbitrary bureaucratic controls than many foreign visitors realise at first glance. Nevertheless, long-time observers note that the situation today is a vast improvement on what is was only a few years ago.

Despite the aversion to dealing with the government bureaucracy, an aversion deeply rooted in all Chinese people, a career as a modern day Mandarin is still seen as a desirable objective pursued by many of the young elite. The government apparatus itself operates at the national level (and was originally set up to operate on behalf of the whole of China), the provincial level (for managing the day to day affairs of Taiwan province) and the local level. There is also a plethora of large government-owned monopolies which control industries such as tobacco and liquor, sugar, telephones, bus and rail transportation and much of the banking sector.

Changes are in the wind. There are moves afoot to 'downsize' the provincial government and to privatise or corporatise many of the government monopolies. Whether this amounts to window dressing or real reform remains to be seen. Many of the privatised monopolies still maintain their cumbersome bureaucratic ways. Real change continues to be slow.

In recent years, and particularly in regard to the financial sector, there has been a gradual process of liberalisation and deregulation, but overall the process has been far slower than most people would like. The price of democracy has seen the national legislature become far more concerned with political infighting and protecting vested interests than with getting on with the business of legislative and economic reform.

THE ROC GOVERNMENT SYSTEM

The Government in Taiwan is still structured to reflect the historic claim by the Republic of China on Taiwan to sovereignty over all of China; both the island of Taiwan as well as the Chinese Mainland. The ROC claim—formally at least—even extends to Mongolia. Although this claim is now allowed to languish in ambivalence, the three tier system of government on Taiwan: central, provincial/municipal and local, is a reflection to this claim to China as a whole. The basic constitution of the ROC dates from 1911 and many of the laws and statutes in force in Taiwan have their origins in the Chinese Republic of Dr Sun Yat-sen.

The Central Government

The Central or National Government is, politically, the most important of the three government levels. The head of state is the President who, until the advent of direct presidential elections in 1996, was elected by the National Assembly (an electoral college whose sole remaining role is to approve amendments to the constitution).

The central government has a five branch (*Yuan*) structure. The *Executive Yuan* is the executive arm of government. It is headed by the Premier and his Cabinet. The Executive Yuan consists of eight ministries and a number of other cabinet level bodies.

The *Legislative Yuan* is the unicameral parliament of the ROC. It has general legislative powers and supervises the work of the Executive Yuan including consideration of the annual budget. The Legislative Yuan also confirms the appointment of the premiers who are nominated by the president. Until recently, Lien Chan held both the Premier and Vice President positions, the legality of which provoked a spirited constitutional debate in the aftermath of the 1996 presidential election. Matters were finally resolved in August 1997 with the replacement of Lien Chan as premier by the popular Vincent Siew.

The *Judicial Yuan* consists of a President, Vice President and 15 Grand Justices. It supervises the work of the Ministry of Justice, the Supreme Court, Administrative Court, High Court and District Courts. Although nominally independent, the judiciary still retains a reputation for being partisan and open to influence especially where powerful local interests are involved.

The *Examination Yuan* is responsible for all official examinations and professional licensing procedures. It is directly responsible for the examination, employment and management of the civil service at all levels of government in Taiwan as well as the licensing of professional personnel such as doctors, lawyers, architects and engineers who wish to enter independent practice. The Examination Yuan consists of a council, a secretariat and two ministries: the Ministry of Personnel and the Ministry of Examination.

The *Control Yuan* is the highest supervisory organ in Taiwan. It exercises powers of consent, impeachment, censure and audit. The Control Yuan consists of a council, secretariat and a standing Ministry of Audit—the latter having particular responsibilities for the examination of government tenders.

The Provincial/Municipal Governments

The second tier of government in Taiwan consists of the Taiwan Provincial Government and the Taipei and Kaohsiung Municipal Governments. Each of these three governments has a range of administrative departments responsible for such matters as finance, budget and accounting, transport, land administration, urban planning, public utilities, infrastructure development, police, education, social affairs, labour affairs, public health and housing.

In early 1997 and following a constitutional review conference (the outcome of which seems to have been pre-determined), President Lee Teng-hui announced a rationalisation of the government system which effectively sidelined the provincial government with the intent of abolishing it. James Soong, the popular governor of Taiwan, was to be the first and only elected governor in the island's history. While undoubtedly there is ample room for improvements in government efficiency, there remains a nagging feeling that removal of the provincial legislature had little to do with rationalisation and was aimed at preventing the emergence of an alternative elected power-base that could challenge the President's authority over Taiwan's affairs.

For the moment, the provincial government agencies remain intact although Soong's replacement will undoubtedly be an appointed official rather than an elected representative.

Local Government

The final level of government in Taiwan consists of the sixteen counties and five cities within Taiwan Province, two counties within Fujien Province (the offshore islands controlled by Taiwan) and 21 districts within the municipalities of Taipei and Kaohsiung. Each of these local government units has a range of administrative departments similar to those at the provincial/administrative level.

Appointment to legislative bodies at each level of government is by direct election. Local government has a notorious reputation for being dominated by hoodlums and gangsters with long-standing ties to the KMT. Despite attempts by the Ministry of Justice to remove such elements from the body politic, the reform movement has been stunted by fear in some quarters of the KMT losing dominance at the local level to an emergent DPP. Dealing at the local level remains a problem for many foreign companies not used to the rough and tumble and the central authorities often appear impotent or unwilling to intervene.

The special municipalities of Taipei (DPP controlled) and Kaohsiung (KMT controlled) are exceptions to the rule. Both mayors enjoy wide popularity and are generally regarded as running 'clean' administrations.

KEY GOVERNMENT AGENCIES

The Control Yuan
>2 Chunghsiao East Road, Section 1, Taipei
>Tel: (02) 2341 3183
>Facsimile: (02) 2341 3761

Ministry of Audit
>1 Hangchow Road, Taipei
>Tel: (02) 2397 1366
>Facsimile: (02) 2397 7889

The Central Trust of China
>49 Wuchang Street, Section 1, Taipei
>Tel: (02) 2311 1511
>Facsimile: (02) 2311 0772

Taiwan Provincial Supply Bureau
>Taipei Office: 3 Kaifeng Street, Section 1, Taipei
>Tel: (02) 2371 3281
>Facsimile: (02) 2371 7854

CHAPTER 2

TAIWAN IN TRANSITION

S ince the late 1980s, Taiwan has come a long way towards becoming a modern democratic state. Taiwan now ranks 16th in the World Competitiveness Yearbook and is about to be granted observer status at the Paris-based 'rich-man's club'—the Organisation for Economic Cooperation and Development (OECD). The country has formulated plans and policies to become an Asian Pacific Regional Operations Centre (APROC) and has weathered the recent Asian financial turmoil with minimal disruption to its domestic economy. Taiwan has required no international bailout. Indeed, it is in the process of bailing out several of its neighbours.

Taiwan's future should look bright. But not quite. Taiwan, or to use its formal title, The Republic of China on Taiwan, still has to come to terms with the last vestiges of the Cold War. China, like Korea (albeit for different historic reasons) remains a country divided by two competing ideological systems. Taiwan, democratic and more prosperous than the Mainland of China (per capita GNP in Taiwan is more than seventeen times that of the PRC) is a country of only 21 million people and faces a neighbour intent on reunification on its own terms.

Having removed past shackles from the domestic press, the imperfections of local society have become blatantly evident. Nevertheless, any fair-minded observer would have to agree that were a political and economic ledger to be drawn up, Taiwan has so far been well served. Yet a simple projection of current policies and attitudes into the future may not be sufficient for Taiwan to achieve its ambitions. Forces are at work—particularly in regard to the China issue—that will call for some innovative footwork and political initiative if Taiwan is not to be caught flat-footed in its quest for survival as an independent political entity. Whether the leadership is up to the task remains to be seen.

OLD CUSTOMS DIE HARD

For the people of Taiwan, the recent high profile kidnapping and murder of the teenage daughter of a local TV celebrity was a brutal reminder that all was not well within the fabric of society. The subsequent manhunt for the three kidnappers and their accomplices lasted almost six months and at times the fumbled (and televised) attempts to apprehend Taiwan's most wanted would have taken on all the aspects of a Keystone Cops saga were it not for the gravity of the crime, further compounded by subsequent rapes and murders committed by those on the run.

Eventually, two of the three died during attempted arrests; one was shot by police and the other committed suicide. The drama thrust Taiwan reluctantly into the world's media focus in November 1997, when the remaining kidnapper and alleged ring-leader, CHEN Chin-hsing, apparently fearing that the police would rather take him dead than alive, took a South African diplomat and his family hostage in order to negotiate his surrender.

Subsequently Chen received five death sentences for his crimes while on the run, which were both brutal and shocking. Unfortunately though, while conducting the most intense rampage of violence that many people can remember, his crimes were far from an isolated occurrence. Extortion, kidnappings and the gangland-style murder of local politicians have become almost commonplace and the police and political leaders have appeared at times weak and ineffectual in dealing with the violence.

Indeed, there is a real fear that, at the local level at least; politics is becoming dominated by the hoodlum element within local society. According to local reports, at least one-third of local mayors, township chiefs and local deputies have gangland connections and some have even been sufficiently brazen to (successfully in some instances) run their election campaigns from inside Taiwan's prisons.

Pingtung mayor, HUANG Ching-hang, recently received 13 years in gaol for bribery in relation to construction projects in Taiwan's southern-most county and, as 1997 ended, evidence was unfolding of a major land scandal in Taipei county involving kickbacks to the Land Administration Director totalling a staggering NT$340 million (US$10 million approx).

Large scale corruption in both the military and the judiciary has been uncovered and sadly, even the Taipei Symphony Orchestra has been tainted by scandal with allegations that its director and senior manager had falsified invoices.

For Taiwan's ruling political leaders their inability to deal with growing problems of law and order despite making public commitments to do so was compounded by political infighting and jockeying for positions ahead of the late 1998 legislative elections and the year 2000 presidential elections. 'Pork Barrelling', it seems, is too often taking precedence over genuine electoral concerns and the people are not happy.

The one bright spot appears to be Taiwan's economy. While shaken by the Asian financial crisis that emerged in late 1997, Taiwan was seen to be down but not out and, relatively speaking, is weathering the storm better than many.

TAIWAN'S DIPLOMATIC ALLIES

South Africa's switch of diplomatic recognition from Taipei to Beijing as of January 1 1998 has deprived Taiwan of its last remaining major diplomatic ally and has reduced the number of countries that formally recognise the Republic of China to 28.

While Taipei, in recent years at least, has been more flexible on the issue of dual recognition, Beijing, which is seeking to isolate Taiwan from international contacts, has remained adamant that any country seeking diplomatic ties with the Peoples Republic must withdraw recognition to Taipei and restrict ties to unofficial and non-governmental contacts. Resolving its relationship with the Mainland in a manner that preserves Taiwan's *de facto* independence is the most critical issue Taiwan faces.

Despite its lack of formal ties, most countries maintain 'unofficial' offices in Taiwan staffed by trained diplomatic personnel able to perform the usual range of trade and consular functions. Taiwan maintains 92 representative offices in sixty countries performing similar functions. 'Unofficial' ministerial visits both into and from Taiwan are growing as part of Taiwan's newfound international respectability, which stems from its emergence as a modern democratic country.

Taiwan is not a current member of the United Nations but participates in twelve international governmental organisations. It has applied for admission to the World Trade Organisation as an independent Customs Territory and for observer status at the OECD on similar terms. Taiwan is also a member of 852 non-governmental organisations in an effort to influence opinion at the grass-roots level.

Government policy is to pursue what has been termed a 'pragmatic diplomacy', a policy that is coming increasingly into question as Taiwan seeks, often through financial aid, to bolster its diplomatic numbers and the ego of policy makers. It is a policy that many would agree is ultimately doomed to failure, especially as China is now—publicly at least—displaying a more conciliatory attitude towards the reunification question. Many believe that Taiwan has a just claim for recognition, if for no other reason than that the people of Taiwan, who have had *de facto* independence for the past 50 years, want this situation to remain. However, some major readjustment to Taiwan's foreign policy will be needed if it is ever to get the message across effectively that Taiwan is not another Hong Kong.

A TIME OF TRANSITION

Taiwan remains a society in transition. Having achieved a laudable degree of economic prosperity on the basis of developing its industrial sector during the extended period of martial law (and built on low labour costs and a tightly regulated labour market), the situation in Taiwan in the late 1990s is markedly different from that of only a decade earlier. Taiwan ten years ago was still shaking off the effects of forty years of martial law.

When ROC President Lee Teng-hui was returned to office in March 1996, the event was hailed locally as marking the first democratic election of a Chinese leader in more than 5,000 years of history. A slight exaggeration perhaps, but it did serve to underscore (and to contrast with the Mainland, which was then bringing overt military pressure to bear in an unsuccessful bid to influence the election outcome) that Taiwan had come of age politically. Despite its ambiguous international status Taiwan had become one of Asia's truly democratic countries.

Democracy has not come without a price and possibly at an inconvenient time in terms of the economic pressures now facing this small island powerhouse. Economic rationalists and technocrats in the key government ministries are keen to open the Taiwanese economy to world forces. Blueprints and programs for achieving the status of an East Asian Regional Hub are published with an almost depressing regularity: depressing because the Legislature is no longer the tame arm of the Executive ready to rubber stamp government plans and proposals.

Unfortunately in this age of global news coverage, the international media attention given to the regular displays of pugilism in the National Assembly, not to mention the other unwanted publicity, has not served to bolster Taiwan's image as a mature democracy even though the people of Taiwan have shown themselves to be quite mature in their ability to weigh the campaign issues and cast a rational vote.[1] More unfortunate for Taiwan, the acrimony in the Assembly often remains more concerned with self-serving issues than it does with the merits of rational economic debate and national interest. In this regard, while the President, through the executive arm of government, has vowed to clean up politics, one result of the democratisation of Taiwan has been the transfer of the pork barrel from the executive to the legislative arm.

Alongside the issue of Mainland relations and that of achieving greater international recognition for Taiwan, as Taiwan moves towards the millennium, another key issue is whether Taiwan will be able to achieve the basic economic reform it claims to seek and which is a necessary precursor to becoming part of the global market and achieving new investment into the domestic economy.

Taiwan wishes no more than to develop its own national identity free from any interference from the Mainland of China or elsewhere but the window of opportunity it now has to attain this goal is slowly closing. Regrettably, some of the world's leading democracies, in their efforts to appease the PRC sometimes appear willing to sacrifice the 21 million people on Taiwan. It is a return to what, in Australian foreign policy terms, used to be known as the 'Timor Solution' for Taiwan.

---

[1] With the overbearing military force displayed by the Chinese PLA during the 1995 and 1996 election campaigns, designed to bolster pro-China candidates at the expense of the Taiwan Independence Movement, there was a clear danger of a polarised electorate; in the event the extremes of both sides lost ground and moderate politicians—on both sides—gained most from the result.

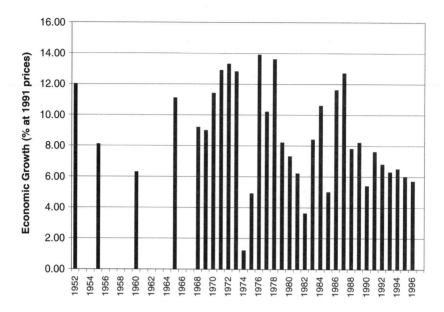

Figure 2a. Annual economic growth 1952–1996

The development of Taiwan as one of East Asia's regional hubs, if it can be achieved, will serve to internationalise the island and this in turn will provide some measure of protection from outside—or PRC—interference. Yet the success of this policy depends on Taiwan's ability to sell itself to the world as the platform for multinationals and others seeking to tap the vast and growing (if somewhat overstated at times) Mainland China market. Taiwan needs not only change but a rate of change that will keep it ahead of other aspirants to this role—most notably, Shanghai—while at the same time allowing direct trade and communications links with the Mainland which will give it a credible regional role. At this time, the eventual success of this policy is by no means clear.

Taiwan is no longer a country dependent on low cost, low value-added manufactures. Rising affluence, labour shortages in traditional manufacturing industries and scarcity of industrial land for new growth (not to mention the high cost of land acquisition) have forced the relocation of much traditional manufacturing to elsewhere in Asia, particularly the Chinese Mainland. Since the late 1980s Taiwan's economy has undergone a fundamental structural change as the government has pursued a policy of developing sophisticated technologies that will lead to high value-added exports.[2] Overall this policy has been successful. Sophisticated manufactures such as electronics products have overtaken more traditional items such as textiles as principal export items.[3] However, while Taiwan's export sector has generally performed well, domestic demand has remained sluggish, leading to an economy which has generally under-performed in recent years. More worrisome still is the lack of overall consumer confidence; a direct result of the uncertainties surrounding Taiwan's future status with China, as evidenced by a lack of domestic re-investment, high capital outflows and emigration rates which are high by historic standards. By early 1998, and despite a currency that had fared better than many, the Asian financial crisis had been added to the growing list of uncertainties worrying consumers.

THE POLITICAL ENVIRONMENT IN THE LATE 1990s

The December 1995 elections for the national legislature were something of a watershed. It saw the Kuomintang Party (KMT) returned to power but with only a slim majority over the opposition parties. The KMT lost 5 seats in the election to hold 84 of the 164 legislative seats contested. Traditionally the party that has advocated Taiwanese independence from China, the Democratic Progressive Party (DPP) is considered to be the main opposition party with 54 seats in the national legislature. The DPP has enjoyed widespread support among native Taiwanese, particularly those in the central and southern regions of Taiwan where ethnic rivalries between native Taiwanese and Mainland Chinese have remained the most strong. But it was the smaller New Party, a conservative grouping which promoted greater accommodation with Beijing (in contrast to the polices of the DPP) and which broke away as a factional grouping from the KMT in 1994 that gained the most in the December 1995 run-off. Overnight, the New Party increased its representation from seven seats to 21 and was seen at the time as being a possible alternative opposition grouping to the DPP. This was not to be.

The 1995 elections were held against a backdrop of escalating tensions with Beijing and a breakdown of political talks between the two sides which had followed President Lee Teng-hui's visit in June that year to the United States. The visit was seen at the time as a diplomatic victory for Taiwan, as

---

[2] See 'Mapping a Path to the Future' (p 34) for a discussion of current government policy issues.

[3] See Chapter 3 for further discussion of Taiwan's exports.

Lee is the first ROC President ever to set foot on US soil—albeit only in a private capacity and after considerable vacillation on the part of Washington. However, after an initial delay, the response from Beijing was quite unexpected. It came in the form of breaking off quasi-official channels of communication and escalating military tensions in the Straits of Taiwan, including live missile firings in Taiwan's territorial waters.

Had Beijing ceased its intimidation at that point, it might have walked away from a confrontation with a sense of victory. However between December 1995 and the March 1996 Presidential election, the geriatric military leaders who were then widely considered to be handling Chinese policy towards Taiwan chose instead to step up the level of confrontation. This included at one point a public threat, later withdrawn, to use nuclear weapons against Taiwan. The policy was clearly aimed at discrediting Lee among Taiwan's electorate in the (possibly accurate) belief that he harboured pro-independence sentiments.

Lee, the incumbent President and leader of the Kuomintang (KMT)—the party that has ruled the Republic of China on Taiwan for the last fifty years—went into the election with real problems. Relations with Mainland China had been on a slide since the first round of Chinese missile tests held in the wake of Lee's US visit. Tensions with the Mainland had been mounting since then and Taiwan's economy had paid the price. Investor confidence dropped sharply as did the local currency, faced with large-scale capital flight.

But Beijing miscalculated badly with its campaign of personal vitriol against Lee and the belief that it could intimidate Taiwan's 15 million voters with a show of force, designed to dissuade from voting for candidates which Beijing saw as 'pro-Taiwan independence'. The Taiwanese are made of sterner stuff.

So, of course, the reverse happened. On the eve of the March 23 poll, Lee Teng-hui was fighting for 50% of the vote—the minimum he judged necessary to claim a fresh mandate. He faced a tough challenge with three other presidential hopefuls against him. On polling day Lee predicted he would garner between 46% and 52% while his chief rival, the pro-independence Democratic Progressive Party (DPP) candidate, PENG Ming-min, was hoping for between 35% and 38%.

The results came as a surprise to all. Voter turnout was particularly heavy—more than 76% of eligible voters cast their ballot—and polling went smoothly across the country. Victory came swiftly to Lee with the nationwide swing to the incumbent president evident. With the final tally counted, Lee had grabbed 54% of the total vote, more than double the votes cast for Peng Ming-min. The New Party's conservative 'third force' in politics, which was generally regarded as being pro-Mainland China, only managed to muster a quarter of the votes and this was split between two candidates. No longer could anybody in Taiwan openly regard himself or herself as 'pro-Mainland'.

In the end, the vote was a victory for common sense and the middle ground. Lee drew votes away from both the pro-Mainland lobby as well as the pro-independence camp. Whether Beijing likes it or not, Taiwan is not Hong Kong and Taiwan's democratic political institutions are here to stay.

While victory has been sweet, Lee and his Vice-President, (and then Premier) LIEN Chan, have faced some tough issues and at times have seemed somewhat inept at dealing with them. March 1996 was perhaps Lee's finest moment. His popularity and that of his government has dropped considerably since that time.

While the government has expressed a willingness to repair relations with the Mainland, Beijing itself remains in no mood for talks although the level of tension has been markedly reduced and working level visits between the two sides (which were never really interrupted) have continued.

The Mainland however is not the major issue; certainly in so far as the electorate is concerned. Although Lee had promised continued reform and clean government, the Cabinet picked by KMT leaders following the inauguration (behind closed doors and without reference to its legislative members) did not augur well. Most of the key portfolios changed hands in the reshuffle including the ministries of Foreign Affairs, Finance, Education, Economic Affairs and Communications. However, the big losers were those such as the former Justice Minister, MA Ying-jeou, who had been most vocal in fighting corruption and underworld influence in government. Ma was demoted to the position of a Minister without Portfolio (having refused a demotion to Head of the Government Information Office) and subsequently retired from politics altogether—and in doing so received huge support island-wide for his stand. He remains one of the most popular and charismatic figures and is seen by all, except those in government, as a future leader. Another prominent corruption fighter, former Transport and Communications Minister LIU Chao-shiuan, was moved sideways to become Chairman of the National Science Council.

The failure to consult the Legislature over the appointments and Lee's decision to retain Lien Chan as Premier concurrently with his new Vice-Presidential role angered lawmakers from all parties, including many within the KMT. Constitutional issues and the President's supposed hidden agenda—to consolidate the power base of his own faction within the KMT—

further muddied the prospects of a clear focus on the agenda for economic reform.

The appointment of the former Head of the Council for Planning and Economic Development, Vincent Siew, to the Premiership in mid 1997 cleared the air on this particular issue and has allowed the government to press ahead with its economic agenda, but valuable time had been lost, as well as the popularity of the government. Corruption scandals, especially in the military and judiciary, appear regularly in Taiwan's (now) free press as do reports of government links to organised crime and plain ineptitude (evidenced most recently—at the time of writing—by a series of aviation disasters), all of which have diverted attention from the government's reform agenda. This is an unfortunate and unintended consequence of democratic reform. Taiwan is certainly less corrupt now than before when a previously shackled press would have prevented such stories from ever seeing the light of day.

Nevertheless, this penchant for action and manoeuvring without consultation has produced other adverse consequences for Lee. At the constitutional review conference at the end of 1996 it emerged that a deal had been worked out ahead of time between the KMT and the DPP to downsize the Provincial Government. As good an idea as this might be, nobody it seems had told Taiwan Governor, James Soong, about the proposal. Soong has always been a popular politician and enjoys considerable support at the grass-roots level. Indeed he has subsequently emerged as Taiwan's most popular politician—a December 1997 poll put his approval rate at 82%.

There was a widespread feeling that the move had less to do with rationalisation of government than it did with neutralising Soong as a political force likely to receive the KMT nomination for the year 2000 presidential race. It is an open secret that Lee has been grooming Lien Chan for this post, although it is increasingly unlikely that Lien will ever get the top job. He remains a politician lacking any charisma and even within the KMT enjoys less popularity than Soong. At the time of writing, the stand-off between Soong and the leadership remains a festering issue and despite the best of public faces, behind the scenes there appear to be some real divisions within the KMT. This has not been lost on the voters at large. Lien himself has become embroiled in a corruption scandal involving loans to other politicians.

TAIWAN'S 'LOYAL OPPOSITION'

Having moderated its position, at least publicly, on the issue of independence for Taiwan, the DPP has made significant progress towards becoming an alternative governing party. In the December 1997 elections for mayoral and county seats, the DPP won 12 of the 23 contested positions and for the first time ever, its share of the popular vote exceeded that of the KMT—43% compared to the KMT's 42%. If the party can maintain its position it is well placed to wrest the majority position from the KMT in the late 1998 legislative elections and, on present indications, could well take the presidency by the year 2000 if a charismatic candidate can be found. Current Taipei Mayor, CHEN Shui-bian, who enjoys a 76% approval rating, has been widely tipped to be the DPP's Presidential nomination and, barring unforeseen circumstances, would be expected to easily out-poll Lien Chan.

So far, Chen appears content to serve out another term as Taipei's mayor and if he does so, while it may cost the DPP the Presidency, it may also prove to be in Taiwan's best long term interest. Certainly the KMT appears unwilling to field a strong candidate against him (the mayoral elections are due at the end of 1998) and may have decided that as Taipei mayor he is effectively neutered in any presidential race.

In the KMT camp, only Soong and former Justice Minister Ma Ying-jeou, now retired from politics (see above), would have had any chance of defeating Chen—either as a Taipei mayor or as a national President. However, with Lien Chan having already declared himself a candidate for the Presidency, the emergence of any rival candidate from within the KMT camp would cause major problems for the party. There is still plenty of time for further manoeuvring to occur before the die is finally cast.

The influence of the New Party has been on the wane in recent times. In the initial period following its breakaway from the KMT, the New Party was seen as a rallying point for intellectuals and the middle class. Many hoped that it would become a real 'third force' occupying the middle ground and with sufficient numbers to become a moderating influence. However, with a policy that advocates reunification with the Mainland, Beijing's confrontationist stance towards Taiwan left the party without any advocates. Although the New Party has so far rejected recent KMT calls for a merger, it is looking increasingly likely that its members will eventually be brought back into the KMT fold leaving Taiwan with, effectively, a two party system of government.

TAIWAN AND THE MAINLAND

Like it or not, Taiwan's future is inextricably bound to Mainland China. Taiwan is the second largest investor in Mainland industry (after Hong Kong) and fences will have to be mended eventually if Taiwan is to go forward with its plans to transform itself into a regional operations centre and transportation hub. Some common ground needs to be reached, and quickly, between the various political camps.

In his inauguration address, Lee Teng-hui sought to calm Beijing's fears and reassure its leaders that Taiwan was committed to the reunification process and was not seeking independence from the Mainland. In what was considered to be a significant departure from previous policy, he indicated that he would be prepared to travel to the Mainland to meet with Chinese leaders in an effort to secure peace. The offer has not been taken up.

Nevertheless, while characterising the dispute with Beijing as one over systems and ways of life rather than of national identity, Lee also made plain his intention to continue to seek greater international recognition for Taiwan. While the heat has gone out of the fire and while high level talks remain on hold,[4] working-level arrangements and agreements—one noteworthy example being the post-handover air services pact with Hong Kong, which has seen the introduction of indirect 'direct flights' to the Mainland (after a change of flight number)—continue to be put in place.

In the meantime, and having previously excoriated the DPP for its pro-independence stance, China has now softened its attitude. Visits to China by DPP leaders are no longer banned and China has signalled that it wants to initiate a dialogue with the DPP. With real power now within its grasp, the Party also appears determined to soften its stand lest its fiercely pro-independence image damage it electorally. Current DPP Chairman HSU Hsing-liang has gone on record as declaring that the DPP must show that it can co-exist peacefully with China.[5] In fact Hsu has gone somewhat further than the government in advocating that Taiwanese should continue to invest in the Mainland and that Taiwan proceed immediately with the three direct links—trade, communication and transportation. So far the ROC government has been unwilling to negotiate.

---

[4] Political discussions resumed tentatively in April 1998 but without any matters of substance decided.

[5] Peng Ming-min had resigned in 1995 to take responsibility for the party's poor performance in the presidential race.

Nevertheless, resolving its position on the China issue is possibly the least of the DPP's problems if it is to produce a credible alternative government. With only 600,000 claimed members to the KMT's claimed 3 million,[6] the DPP does not have anything resembling the Kuomintang's network that pervades every level of society. Neither should it be forgotten that the KMT is the world's richest political party. The KMT owns more than 100 corporations involved in retailing, trading, finance, construction, manufacturing and petrochemicals. The net worth of its business empire in 1997 was placed at NT$57.1 billion (US$1.7 billion) and the pre-tax profits on those investments amounted to NT$15.9 billion (US$480 million) in the same year. Whether or not it retains government the party will continue to influence Taiwan for some time to come.

There is a growing belief that China will wait until after the year 2000 presidential election before re-engaging in any meaningful and high level dialogue. For the present, both sides seem content to probe each other's positions. This suits Taiwan well.

SIGNS OF ECONOMIC REVIVAL

The final estimate of Taiwan's economic growth rate for 1996 came in at 6.1% (higher than the 5.8% expected in the final quarter but considerably less than the 6.5% target hoped for earlier in that year). Economic growth in that year was largely a reflection of strong export performance assisted by a modest depreciation of the local currency. Domestic demand languished in the aftermath of the brouhaha with Beijing.

Provincial estimates released so far suggest that Taiwan fared better in 1997 than in 1996, although the aftermath of the Asian currency meltdown which finally hit Taiwan in late October 1997, following the abandonment of support by the Central Bank, meant Taiwan headed into 1998 with a greater air of uncertainty than it would otherwise have hoped for. Real economic growth in 1997 came in (provisionally) at around 6.81%—a performance considered to be significantly better than that recorded the previous year. Price inflation at 1.1% was the lowest in a decade.

The outlook for 1998 is less certain and will depend as much on regional factors as it will on domestic performance. Growth estimates for the coming year range from a high of 6.7%, forecast by the Council for Economic

---

[6] There are no published membership figures and both claims should be treated with caution.

Planning and Development, to a low of 4.9% predicted by some of the foreign bank analysts. Price inflation of around 3% is expected as higher import prices work their way through the economy.

With the winding back of the political heat, the local stock market which had been in the doldrums in the early years of the decade finally rallied following the Presidential election, and by June 1996 had climbed back above the 6000 point mark—though government intervention prior to the election, in the form of a NT$200 billion stock stabilisation fund, played a significant role in under-pinning stock prices in the early part of that year. By early 1997 investor confidence had been sufficiently restored that the market really took off and by mid year had surged past the 10,000 mark, although it dropped significantly in the final quarter to below the 7,000 level. Since then it has again rallied. Most people, it seems, are remaining liquid; retailing is booming.

In his first major public statement on the economy and one designed to project a leadership role, Lien Chan called for Taiwan to increase its competitiveness and become one of the world's 'top five' by the year 2000. The call was dismissed locally as empty rhetoric in the absence of any accompanying major new reform proposals announced by the government so far. As a future leader, Lien remains a relatively unknown quantity. His current high profile in government is said to be due more to his family's wealth and influence than any innate leadership ability.

A recent report by the Swiss-based International Institute for Management Development has ranked Taiwan 16th in its latest worldwide survey of international competitiveness. Administrative reform, financial market controls, problems of land availability and acquisition, power shortages and other infrastructural bottlenecks were singled out as problem areas that will all take time to overcome even assuming the government has the will to do so.

A recent OECD forecast has also sounded alarm bells suggesting that Taiwan's economic growth in the immediate future will be the lowest of the 'Asian dragons'. Of course, all of this came before the emergence of Asia's financial crisis and some reassessment of positions is no doubt taking place.

Taiwan's currency remained relatively stable throughout most of 1997, for the most part trading at around 28.5 New Taiwan dollars to the US dollar—a slight depreciation on its 1996 value. This changed overnight on October 28 following the global stock sell-off. Taiwan's own stock index, always volatile, fell by 5.9% in one day and the currency also started its own slide. By year-end there had been an almost 20% fall in the value of the New Taiwan dollar which breached the 34.0 mark in December 1997 and was widely predicted to drop below 35.0. So far this has not happened and the currency appears to be holding up in the 33–34 range although the Central Bank has announced that, barring intervention into the market by currency speculators, it will allow market forces to determine the currency level. The general prognosis is that unless there is further slippage in other regional markets or a worsening of Japan's position, the local dollar is expected later in the year to settle in the range between 31.0 and 33.0.

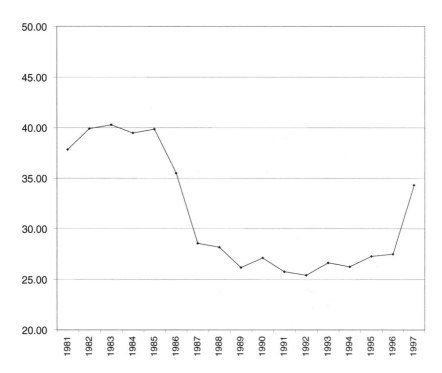

Figure 2b. Exchange rate movements to the US dollar 1981–1997

MAPPING A PATH TO THE FUTURE

The ROC Government has adopted an aggressive approach to industrial upgrading and improvement of Taiwan's overall investment climate. The *Statute for Industrial Upgrading* and the *Act for Accelerating Investment and Upgrading of Manufacturing Industries* are among the best known examples. The Six-Year National Development Plan announced in 1991 first called for the development of Taiwan into a regional operations centre for the Asian-Pacific region. Although the Plan itself no longer exists, having proven itself too grandiose for even a government with the reserves of the ROC, individual elements of the plan have now been incorporated into national policy.[7]

Taiwan as a Regional Operations Centre

In formulating its plan to build Taiwan into an Asian Pacific Regional Operations and financial Centre (known as APROC), the ROC Government hopes to build on what it believes are the comparative advantages of Taiwan's island economy. These include its substantial economic and financial resources which, in fact, enable Taiwan to play an increasingly important role as a regional financing centre. Other perceived advantages are its strategic geographic position in East Asia (and especially its proximity to the Chinese Mainland), its record and networks as a trading nation and its highly skilled human resources.

At the macroeconomic level, the stated intention on the one hand is to foster policies which encourage deployment of the labour force in new emerging science- and technology-based industries, and on the other to use Taiwan's strategic location within East Asia as a transhipment and communications centre for the region and, although mostly unstated, for business with the Mainland of China.

To the international business community these policies translate into a strategy for encouraging inward investment into the new manufacturing industries while serving at the service industry level to attract companies that wish to use Taiwan as their communications or distribution hub for Asian operations.

Giving practical effect to these policies has proven harder than lofty statements of principle. To its credit, the national government of Taiwan is pursuing an omni-directional policy aimed at economic liberalisation, albeit at a pace which sometimes leaves foreign companies gasping with frustration.

Key areas of macroeconomic adjustment announced by the ROC and incorporated into current policy initiatives include:

- A liberalisation of trade and investment measures through a progressive lowering of tariffs, removal of non-tariff trade barriers and a general opening up of the service sector to international competition;

---

[7] These issues are discussed in greater detail in Chapter 4.

- Simplifying the entry and exit formalities for foreign personnel and easing work restrictions on foreign professionals and specialists who are required to work in Taiwan;
- A progressive easing of the restrictions on capital movements and the staged liberalisation of foreign exchange controls;
- Establishment of a modern legal code suited to an information-based society. This includes allowing the free circulation and dissemination of information, use of government information including the collection and publication of statistical information and the protection of intellectual property.

Although these measures are desirable in themselves, they form the central underpinning of government plans for the development of sector-specific operations centres where Taiwan is judged to be able to compete internationally. Six areas have been designated for primary attention: manufacturing; sea and air transportation, financial, telecommunications and media.

Taiwan as a Manufacturing Centre

Manufacturing has been at the heart of Taiwan's economic development from the outset and the government firmly believes it will continue to play a strategic role in the future. Considerable effort is put into the education of engineers and technicians who are expected to play a crucial role in transforming Taiwan's manufacturing base.

A number of areas have been singled out for specific incentives (see Chapter 4). Work has already commenced on building a second science-based industry park in the south of Taiwan and the government has already formulated plans to establish between 20 and 30 'intelligent industrial parks' with specific inducements for private sector investment.

Taiwan as a Sea Transportation Centre

Although publicly the emphasis is on the potential of Taiwan as a cargo transhipment centre for South-East Asia, the real motivation behind the proposal is the prospect of future large scale direct trade with China which will be able to handle both local and transhipment traffic. Direct shipping links between Taiwan and the Mainland have been on the table for some time but slow progress has been made in their implementation. China, which is a staunch advocate of early cross-straits shipping links—more for political reasons than anything else—wishes to restrict cross-straits traffic to Chinese vessels (whether ROC flag vessels would be allowed access to Chinese ports has so far gone unsaid), while Taiwan wishes to begin the trade with third country vessels. Most Taiwanese ships fly flags of convenience, and because of Taiwan's ambiguous international status, such flags are truly convenient.

In late 1994, Taiwan proposed as a first stage the development of offshore transhipment zones whereby third country goods could be transhipped direct to China from Taiwan ports provided they did not go through ROC customs clearance and were carried in third country vessels. The plan represented a practical first step that was intended to serve as a confidence building measure but progress in the cross-straits transhipment proposals was an early casualty of the soured political atmosphere.

The bulk of Taiwan's seaborne traffic is handled through the two container ports of Keelung, in the north of Taiwan, and Kaohsiung in the south. While Kaohsiung is by far the larger of the two, its overall traffic volume remains only about half the volume of Hong Kong measured on a TEU basis. Measures to upgrade facilities at both ports are underway while a third port, Taichung Harbour in central Taiwan, is being developed specifically for the expected surge in cross-straits shipments, which will occur once an accommodation is reached. Although some point-to-point services have been permitted for transhipments since early 1997, China has so far licensed only two ports—Xiamen and Fuzhou—for such services. Domestic cargoes, in either direction, still have to travel via third country ports increasing costs by up to 50%. Overall the policy to develop sea-borne transhipments is going more slowly than expected and a full opening of cross-straits shipping routes remains as distant as ever.

Taiwan as an Air Transportation Centre

Civil aviation traffic has grown rapidly over the past ten years. International passenger traffic has increased by an average of 23% annually between 1986 and 1997 while, aided by low ticket prices, domestic aviation traffic has increased on average by 55% a year. The strain has taken its toll on the domestic aviation industry which has been hit recently by a number of tragic, and in many instances fatal, accidents.

Taiwan has a total of 17 civilian airports (of which several are combined with military installations) including two international airports: Taipei–CKS in Taoyuan County, south of Taipei, and Kaohsiung Airport in the south of the island. Three of these airports—Taipei Domestic Airport, Taipei International Airport and Kaohsiung International Airport—together account for more than 75% of all aviation traffic in Taiwan. In terms of international traffic, by far the largest volume of both passenger and freight is handled by Taipei–CKS International Airport.

International passenger volumes, measured in both absolute passenger numbers as well as passenger-kms, have increased more than three-fold in the last ten years. The number of international passengers has grown from 4.8 million in 1986 to 17 million in 1997 while international passenger-kms increased from 11.6 billion in 1986 to 34.5 billion in the same period.

By contrast; transit passenger traffic has grown at less than 6% in the same period suggesting that Taiwan remains reliant on end-to-end services and has failed to capture the fifth and sixth freedom passenger markets.

The greater use of domestic aviation services has made Taipei Domestic (Sung Shan) Airport the busiest terminal. In 1996, traffic through Sung Shan Airport surpassed that of Taipei–CKS International Airport for the first time.

Freight traffic—by far the greater proportion of it being international—has also increased greatly by more than 18% a year. In terms of metric tonnage, the total volume of airfreight traffic more than doubled in the period 1986–1997 from 424,000 to 1.3 million metric tonnes.[8] The same three airports account for almost 100% of all freight traffic, of which 84% is handled by Taipei–CKS International Airport and a further 10% by Kaohsiung Airport. Taipei–CKS has been designated as the first airport to be developed as an express cargo transportation centre with other airports following as circumstances require.[9]

All freight at CKS airport is handled by Taipei Air Cargo Terminal Ltd, which at the present time is a government-owned agency with a monopoly on all air cargo services at the airport. The facility has been modernised in recent years, is fully computerised and is generally considered to be efficient in its operation. The air cargo operations are in the process of being corporatised and will eventually be privatised before the year 2000.

---

[8] Measured in ton-kms the increase was smaller—only 34% indicating a greater use of air freight for short haul traffic—probably associated with the China market.

[9] See Chapter 3 for a discussion of recently introduced measures to facilitate cargo clearances.

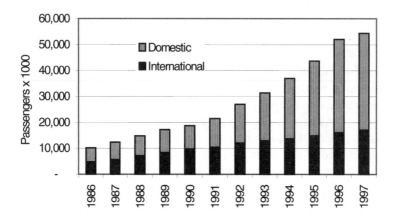

Figure 2c. Growth in aviation passenger traffic

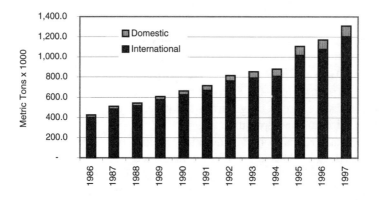

Figure 2d. Growth of airfreight traffic

Taipei as a Financial Centre

Given Taiwan's capital reserves—the third largest in the world—and its willingness to play a role as a capital source for investment into the Asian region, the prospects for Taipei developing as a regional financial centre are probably better focused than some of the other operational concepts being mooted. Continued reluctance to introduce a freely convertible currency is probably one of the major impediments facing Taiwan although the government has announced a plan to free remaining controls 'at an appropriate time'.

There appears to be on-going debate within the executive arm of government over the desirable pace of financial liberalisation, with the Central Bank of China consistently taking a more cautious line than other government agencies.[10] As a first step the financial market has already been divided into a domestic segment and an offshore segment, and while the domestic market remains under firm control, the offshore market has been totally freed. The foreign exchange and currency markets have been steadily liberalised while at the same time (and in the wake of a series of financial scandals in 1995), regulatory control over the domestic banking sector is in the process of being rationalised. While Taipei clearly has some way to go and many foreign banks operating in Taiwan complain of the restrictive environment, all acknowledge both the importance of the market and the fact that the government appears serious in its intent to open the market to international competition.

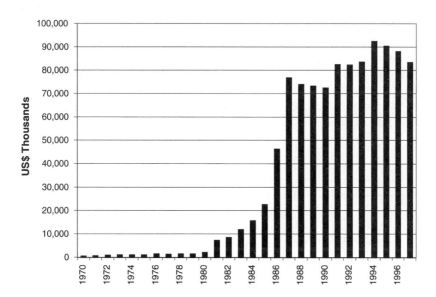

Figure 2e. Growth of Taiwan's Forex reserves

---

[10] See Chapter 14.

For its part, the government has signalled in its most recent statements that despite the current volatility of the region, Taiwan remains committed to establishing a framework for 'free capital flows' by the year 2000. The emergence of Taipei as a regional financial centre may be the first success of government policy in this area.

Taiwan as a Telecommunications Centre

The August 1996 break-up and corporatisation of the old Directorate General of Telecommunications (DGT), and the emergence of Chunghua Telecom as the new local telecommunications operator, mark the most important steps in government plans to free the domestic telephony market and develop a telecommunications centre in Taiwan. Chunghua Telecom remains for the present a government-owned corporation, although it is intended to be privatised in the longer term. Current plans call for this to occur by June 2001.

Taiwan has a sizeable telecommunications industry by Asian standards with 586 phone lines per 1,000 of the population. For the present Chunghua Telecom remains the sole local carrier with a monopoly over all wired local and trunk services; however the market is slowly opening for so-called value-added (VAN) services in a manner similar to that followed by Japan. Although the government has a stated intention to make Taiwan an Asian telecommunications hub, with foreign participation still restricted or denied in many aspects of the telecommunications industry, overall the quality of services remains poor by OECD standards.

Table 2.1. Growth of communications traffic

	1986	*1991*	*1997*
Local Telephone Circuits	136,469	296,842	571,523
International Telephone Circuits	1,639	4,945	15,037
Total Telephone Circuits	**138,108**	**11,787**	**586,560**
Telephone Subscribers	4,540,359	6,853,080	10,862327
Radio Paging	97,710	1,078,487	2,496,090
Mobile Phones	n/a	299,690	2,083,000
Population (thousands)	19,455	20,557	21,683

Despite expectations of an early relaxation of restrictions on foreign investment into local telephone services, the government has in fact reconfirmed its tough controls on the level of overseas investment permitted into the local industry. At the present time there is a cap of 20% total equity allowed to foreign investors in the telecommunication sector, which covers both direct and indirect investments. Licence applications which breach the 20% ceiling are not being approved for the present, although the government has pledged to both the USA and Europe in recent WTO negotiations that the market will eventually be opened to the extent of allowing foreign ownership of up to 60% in local telecommunication firms.

Taiwan as a Media Centre

The media in Taiwan is a thriving industry. As of 1998 Taiwan boasted a total of 351 newspapers, 5,643 domestically produced magazines, 8,878 publishing houses, 256 news agencies, 180 audio publishing houses, 74 radio stations, 4 broadcast television networks, 146 cable TV channels, 395 film production companies and 663 movie theatres.

Taiwan now has a free press although the quality of reporting in many areas remains quite poor. Competition for advertising dollars is fierce and, as is common practice throughout much of Asia, journalists double as sales representatives for their media bosses. Invariably much reporting is influenced by advertisers. It is common practice for articles to be placed in the press by companies or their promotional agencies without any indication of it being other than a news item. Aside from this bias, editorial content, political cartoons and letters to the editor are free of any government control.

The three national television stations are controlled respectively by the Taiwan Provincial Government, Kuomintang Party and the ROC Military with no prospect of ownership being changed or of other investors being allowed a stake in existing channels. Claims of biased news coverage over the television network remain common, especially by opposition politicians. In fairness to the stations concerned, reporting appears for the most part to be unbiased without overt interference. A new public television channel (PTV) financed by government but supposedly free of government control has existed since 1994 but curiously has yet to be licensed to go to air. Trial programs commenced as far back as November 1996 following an (even more curious) agreement with the Government Information Office not to broadcast 'news programs' but only 'news magazines'. There things remain.

The introduction and subsequent legalisation of the cable television industry (commonly referred to as the 'fourth channel' to distinguish it from its three rivals) has seen an explosive growth in the number of cable broadcasters with quality ranging from world-class to mediocre. News services on the cable channels appear to have a much greater impartiality and willingness to deal with controversial issues than the traditional broadcasters.

Two groups, both affiliated with the KMT, dominate the cable distribution industry to the detriment of consumer choice. Their monopoly position is now coming under the scrutiny of the Fair Trade Commission. Poor programming and lack of international content has produced widespread media criticism, especially from the foreign community, though the situation remains far from satisfactory. In this regard Taiwan lags behind much of Asia.

Yet proposals to develop Taiwan as a media centre are aimed less at traditional media outlets and more at using the industrial and cultural base of Taiwan to develop media-based industries. At one level this translates into satisfying the demand in Asia for Mandarin-language television programming (Taiwan is re-inventing the soap opera) while at the other extreme, it is the development of Chinese language software programming and other forms of publishing services. [11]

With its well-educated workforce and high level of computer literacy, Taiwan is well placed to provide foreign firms with opportunities to develop Chinese language software and multimedia. In terms of developing a Chinese language media centre on Taiwan, Taiwan appears well on its way to achieving its objectives.

THE ROLE OF THE STATE SECTOR IN THE ECONOMY

While committed to a free-enterprise system, Taiwan has not yet dismantled the network of government-owned corporations and monopolies that still control, or at least retain influence, in many sectors of the economy. Established during the martial law period, government has dominated many of the strategic industries such as power, petroleum, transportation and significant areas relating to financial services.

---

[11] One amusing if unintended consequence of using Taiwan as a base for Chinese software development was the release of Microsoft's Windows 95 software package on the Chinese Mainland with a Chinese language dictionary carrying such politically charged phrases as 'Communist bandits' and 'Taiwan Independence'.

Employees of State-owned services have traditionally been regarded as public sector employees and have enjoyed many of the benefits extended to public servants. Over-staffed and often inefficient, there has been a move in recent years to sell off government interests in many of these agencies and to place others on a more commercial footing through corporatisation. Overseeing the government's privatisation plan is the responsibility of the Council for Economic Planning and Development.

Generally, the pace of privatisation has proceeded more slowly than the government had originally forecast. Weak stock prices, until the resurgence of the market in 1997, have led the government to resist sale of its stock for fear that such sales would not realise the true asset value of the company being sold. In other instances, staff resistance to privatisation and fears (well founded, given the inefficiencies and bloated payrolls of many such companies) have forced the government to slow its progress rather than face industrial confrontation.

So far twelve companies have been partially privatised including China Steel, China Airlines and Yang Ming Marine. A number of Acts before Taiwan's legislature will pave the way for further privatisation measures.

Taipower has already lost its monopoly in the production of electrical power although not, so far, in its distribution. Taipower has already been corporatised in anticipation of full privatisation once the revised *Electric Utilities Act* is passed—possibly by early 1999.

As noted previously, Chunghwa Telecom remains a State-owned corporation and maintains its monopoly position in wired services. In other areas, particularly the lucrative cellular market, the market is slowly opening to other service providers.

The accident-prone Chinese Petroleum Corporation is to sell 51% of its stock by the end of the century and the Bank of Taiwan, together with several other of the State-owned banks, is also slated for privatisation by this date.

Nevertheless, despite some progress, the government appears reluctant to withdraw totally from its involvement in business—if for no other reason than the loss of revenue it would suffer. Privatisation in Taiwan for the most part simply means reducing the government's stock by less than 50%. In many instances, as is the case with China Steel, cash-rich and KMT-controlled investment funds and corporations will replace the government as significant stockholders. Following the examples of Europe, America and Australia in truly privatising the State-controlled corporations is likely to remain on the wish list for some time to come.

Table 2.2. Major State-owned or State-invested corporations

Sector	Company	Agency
Industrial Corporations		
Agricultural Products	Taiwan Sugar	Provincial
Ammonium Sulphate	Kaohsiung Ammonium Sulfate Co. Ltd	Central
Appliances	Chung Hsing Electric and Machinery	Central
Chemicals	Taiwan Fertiliser Corporation	Provincial
Construction	BES Engineering	Central
	Ret-Ser Engineering	Defence
Machinery Manufacturing	Taiwan Agricultural and Industrial Development Corporation	Provincial
	Taiwan Machinery Manufacturing Corporation	
Oil and Gas	Chinese Petroleum Corporation	Central
Paper Manufacture	Taiwan Chung Hsing Paper	Provincial
Petrochemicals	China Petrochemical Development Corporation	Central
Salt	Taiwan Salt Works	Provincial
Semiconductors	United Microelectronics	Central
Shipbuilding	China Shipbuilding Corporation	Central
Wine, Spirits and Tobacco—Supply and Distribution	Taiwan Wine and Tobacco Monopoly Bureau	Provincial
Steel	China Steel	Central
	Tang Eng Iron Works	
Financial Services		
Banking	Bank of Taiwan	Provincial
	Chang Hwa Commercial Bank	Central
	Bank of Kaohsiung	Kaohsiung City

Table 2.2 cont'd

Banking cont'd	Taipei Bank	Taipei City
	Co-operative Bank of Taiwan	Central
	Export–Import Bank of China	Central
	Farmers Bank of China	Central
	First Commercial Bank	Central
	Hua Nan Commercial Bank	Central
	Land Bank of Taiwan	Provincial
	Medium Business Bank of Taiwan	Provincial
	Postal Remittances and Savings Bank	Central—MOTC
Procurement	Central Trust of China	Central
	Taiwan Provincial Supply Bureau	Provincial
Bills Instruments	Ching Hsing Finance	Central
	Chung Hwa Bills Finance	Central
Development Banking	Chiao Tung Bank	Central
Insurance	Central Trust of China Life Insurance	Central
	Central Reinsurance Corporation	Central
	Life Insurance Department of the Ministry of Transport and Communication	Central
Investment Services	Central Investment Holding Company	Central
Transportation		
Air Transport	China Airlines	Central
Railways	Taiwan Railway Administration	
Bus Transport	Taiwan Motor Transport	Provincial
Shipping	Taiwan Navigation	Provincial
	Yangming Marine Transport	Central

Table 2.2 cont'd

Communications, Broadcasting and Television		
Communications	Chunghwa Telecom	Central— MOTC
	Hinet (ISP)	Central— Chunghwa Telecom
	Seednet (ISP)	Central— Institute for Information Industries
Broadcasting[12]	Central Broadcasting System	Central
Television[13]	China Television Services (CTS)	Central (ROC Military)
	Taiwan Television Enterprises (TTV)	Provincial
Postal and Courier Services	Directorate General of Posts	Central
Utilities		
Electricity	Taiwan Power Company (Taipower)	Central
Water	Taiwan Water Supply	Central

[12] The Broadcasting Corporation of China is KMT-controlled.

[13] The third rediffusion channel, CTV, is controlled by the Kuomintang and is in effect a government channel.

KEY GOVERNMENT AGENCIES

Ministry of Economic Affairs
15 Foochow Street, Taipei, Taiwan ROC
Tel: (886 2) 321 2200
Fax: (886 2) 391 9398

The Ministry of Economic Affairs has overall responsibility within the ROC Government for administering investment policy. Within the Ministry specific agencies dealing with investment and licensing matters include:

Investment Commission (MOEA)
8F, Yumin Building, 7 Roosevelt Road, Section 1, Taipei, Taiwan ROC
Tel: (886 2) 738 0007
Fax: (886 2) 735 2656

The Investment Commission approves all inwards and outwards investments according to MOEA guidelines. Foreign companies seeking assistance in making an application may contact the:

Industrial Development and Investment Center (MOEA)
19F, 4 Chunghsiao West Road, Section 1, Taipei, Taiwan ROC
Tel: (886 2) 389 2111
Fax: (886 2) 382 0497

Patent and licensing applications should be referred to the:

National Bureau of Standards (MOEA)
3F, 185 Hsinhai Road, Section 2, Taipei, Taiwan ROC
Tel: (886 2) 738 0007
Fax: (886 2) 735 2656

Companies wishing to set up in one of the industry parks should contact the:

Industrial Development Bureau (MOEA)
41–3 Hsinyi Road, Section 3, Taipei, Taiwan ROC
Tel: (886 2) 754 1255
Fax: (886 2) 703 0160

Companies seeking to set up operations in one of the export processing zones should contact:

Export Processing Zone Administration (MOEA)
    600 Chiachang Road, Nantze, Kaohsiung, Taiwan ROC
    Tel: (886 7) 361 1212
    Fax: (886 7) 361 4348

Companies wishing to set up science- or technology-based manufacturing operations should contact:

Science-Based Industrial Park Administration
    2 Hsin Ann Road, Hsinchu, Taiwan ROC
    Tel: (886.35) 773 311
    Fax: (886 35) 776 222

All applications for investment or company licencing involving the banking or financial sectors must be approved by the:

Ministry of Finance
    2 Aikuo Road, Taipei, Taiwan ROC
    Tel: (886 2) 322 8000
    Fax: (886 2) 321 1205

Enquiries concerning portfolio investment or qualifications as a foreign equity investor should be made to the:

Securities and Futures Commission
    12F, Yangteh Building, 3 Nanhai Road, Taipei, Taiwan ROC
    Tel: (886 2) 341 3101
    Fax: (886 2) 394 0714

Other important government agencies include:

The Fair Trade Commission (Executive Yuan)
    8F, 150 Tunhwa North Road, Taipei, Taiwan ROC
    Tel: (886 2) 545 5501
    Fax: (886 2) 545 0107

Directorate General of Customs
85 Hsinsheng South Road, Taipei, Taiwan ROC
Tel: (886 2) 741 3181
Fax: (886 2) 711 4166

CHAPTER 3

TAIWAN AS A TRADING NATION

T aiwan is at heart a nation of traders. Having enjoyed uninterrupted trade growth for more than a decade and having weathered a global recession relatively well in the mid-nineties, there are now genuine fears that Taiwan's exporters could well come unstuck by problems elsewhere in Asia and especially Japan.

1997 actually proved to be a better year for Taiwan's international trading position after a difficult year in 1996. In that year, depressed domestic demand led to a downturn in imports while export growth was the lowest for a decade.

The previous year had started well enough but weak demand elsewhere in Asia, damaging typhoons during the summer season and the crisis in cross-straits relations that slowed trade with the Chinese Mainland and which spilled over into general political uncertainty, quickly stalled early strong growth prospects. Imports in 1996 actually went into a decline, seeding fears that the economy was heading into recession.

In absolute terms, total trade value in 1996 reached US$218.31 billion placing Taiwan in 14th place in the world as a trading nation. Exports were valued at US$115.94 billion (US$215.21 in 1995) while imports amounted to US$102.37 billion (US$103.56). Total trade growth in 1996 amounted to less than 2% overall—the lowest in a decade.

The global recovery that took place in 1997, as well as the slow depreciation of the New Taiwan dollar against the US dollar that had taken place throughout 1996 and the first three quarters of 1997, also played their part in making 1997 a better year. The local currency dropped from NT$27.27 to the US$ at year end 1995 to 27.49 in 1996 and had fallen further by mid-1997 to around 28.5. This represented an overall depreciation of around 5% over the period.

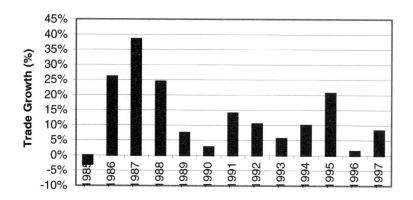

Figure 3a. Year on year trade growth 1985–1997

As 1996 drew to a close, signs of the recovery were already becoming evident although it had come too late to influence the result for that year. However, export and import growth during the first quarter of 1997 amounted to 5.6% and 9.1% respectively. Taiwan's foreign trade volume continued to show strong growth throughout that year with exports provisionally slated to have reached US$122 billion and imports US$114.4 billion over the period. By the year's end, Taiwan's annual trade surplus stood, provisionally, at NT$7.6 billion (US$230 million), a reduction of 44% from the previous year's surplus (NT$13.6 billion).[1]

---

[1] Measured in US dollar terms at historic rates.

While a strong reserve position and the intervention of the Central Bank of China has so far insulated Taiwan from the worst effects of the currency instability that affected much of Asia in the latter part of 1997, it has also eroded Taiwan's competitive performance in relation to other Asian competitors, especially in the lower value-added items. It remains to be seen, however, what long term effects recent Asian currency realignments may have on Taiwan's future trade growth. Thanks both to its reserves and a mature domestic market, Taiwan's currency has fallen by only 20% as compared against 50% falls for the Indonesian rupiah and the Thai baht. South-East Asian countries were already making inroads into Taiwan's markets for traditional export items such as textiles and the realignment can be expected to reduce further Taiwan's competitive position in these market segments. Against this can be weighed the fact that Taiwan, increasingly, is reliant on value-added and high-tech manufactures for much of its exports and export growth. The devaluation that occurred in the latter months of 1997 should therefore make Taiwan more competitive in key market niches. Developments in Japan are being monitored closely.

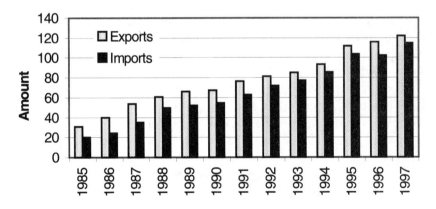

Figure 3b. ROC foreign trade statistics (US$ billions)

TAIWAN AND THE WORLD TRADE ORGANISATION

Taiwan's application to join the World Trade Organisation remains outstanding eight years after originally applying for membership of the WTO's predecessor, the General Agreement on Tariffs and Trade (GATT), as an independent customs territory.

Progress has been made. Trade negotiations have been concluded with 22 of the 26 counties that requested bilateral talks, and the only country with which significant issues remain outstanding is the United States. Discussions with the EU are all but concluded with only residual issues remaining to be resolved in areas such as excise duties on wines and spirits, maritime transport and in legal services.

The most vexing issue of recent concern to EU members—certainly the most high profile—has been the discriminatory duties applied to certain spirits. Currently Scotch and Irish whiskies are taxed in Taiwan at NT$440 (US$13.30 approx.) per litre, considerably higher than the levy charged on whiskies from elsewhere. A discriminatory tariff is also applied against French Cognac which is taxed at NT$1,000 (US$30) per litre. Taiwan has proposed to amend its Tobacco and Wine Tax Law to remove these tariffs within five to seven years and draft amendments to implement this proposal have been passed to the legislature.

Problems with the United States have proven more vexing with the US demanding that Taiwan further improve its market access for agricultural items as well as meat and livestock products. Other issues of concern to the US, relating to government procurement and the lifting of remaining restrictions on insurance and other professional services, appear to have been resolved. In recent talks with the US, Taiwan has agreed:

- To open more of its industrial procurement requirements to foreign bidders within two years of WTO entry;
- To open its market to foreign-made motorcycles (150cc or larger) within two years of WTO entry;
- To revise its insurance law and allow those foreign mutual companies with more than NT$2 billion (US$60 million) in net worth to operate in Taiwan;
- To overhaul its coal purchasing arrangements; and
- Reform its commercial port construction surcharge.

While Beijing has not sought to prevent Taiwan's membership of this particular body (as long as it abides by its application as a 'customs territory' and not a 'state'), Beijing is insisting that Taiwan not be allowed to join ahead of China whose own negotiations are taking longer to conclude. The majority of WTO members would like to see the applications of both countries considered at the same time. Taiwan has sought to separate its own membership application from that of the PRC and, officially at least, is pushing for its membership application to be considered as quickly as

possible. However, given the considerable structural adjustments necessary
—particularly in the politically sensitive area of agricultural products—
Taiwan may well appreciate a delay not of its making.

EXPORT MARKETS AS THE KEY TO PROSPERITY

Taiwan's economic success and present prosperity are due in large measure
to its success as an exporter. Based originally on a strategy which relied on
supplying developed market economies (principally the United States) with
low cost industrial and manufactured goods, the value of Taiwan's two-way
trade has soared from a mere US$300 million at the start of the economic
reconstruction period to its present levels—more than US$236 billion in
1997. Taiwan only recorded its first trade surplus in 1971.

Since the beginnings of the Nationalist Government on Taiwan at the end
of the Chinese Civil War, the development of a strong manufacturing base
for the world market was at the cornerstone of the government's economic
program. Prosperity has been built on the twin pillars of import substitution
and export expansion. Factory conditions in these early years were appalling,
use of child labour was common,[2] and both wage levels and safety
conditions went largely unregulated. With martial law in place until the mid-
1980s the concept of organised labour was totally foreign to Taiwan (and
largely remains so—the workforce in Taiwan shares none of the militancy
shown in other newly developed countries such as Korea despite the
similarity of their growth regimes). Such social justice as did exist in those
early years was largely dispensed in accordance with Confucian norms.

Yet Taiwan and the Taiwanese prospered. As national income grew, so
did the individual incomes of the workforce—to the point that, by Asian
standards, the Taiwanese now enjoy one of the most egalitarian societies in
Asia. The majority of the population would regard themselves as middle
class and disposable incomes are on a par with OECD standards. The high
level of discretionary spending enjoyed by the youth of Taiwan today is
based solidly on the hard work and sacrifice of the older generation. Among
some commentators at least, there are quite genuine fears that the greatest
problem facing Taiwan today may be the loss of the work ethic among
younger people.

---

[2] Although this is no longer the case and employment conditions are now strictly
regulated by the *Labor Standards Law* which bans children from the workforce.

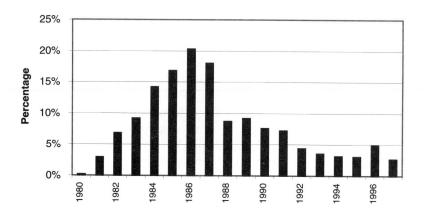

Figure 3c. Taiwan's trade surplus relative to GNP

With per capita GNP having broken the US$10,000 level in 1992, Taiwan is no longer a low-labour cost centre and many of the traditional low-cost labour intensive industries have already relocated to elsewhere in Asia. The government is pinning future expectations of economic growth more on increased domestic demand than it did in the past, yet export income—derived increasingly from high value-added products and components—will continue to play an important role well into the 21st century. At the same time, as part of its effort to internationalise its own economy and with early membership of the World Trade Organisation a prime government objective, Taiwan is increasingly opening its own markets to import competition, thereby providing new market opportunities for traders.

According to the World Trade Organisation, Taiwan accounted for some 2.0% of total world trade in 1996, making the ROC the 14th largest exporter and 15th largest importing nation in the world. Within Asia and in terms of domestic exports, Taiwan is positioned only behind Japan, the PRC and South Korea (although in total trade volume terms, both Hong Kong and Singapore rank ahead of Taiwan). However, of the four Asian mini-dragons, only Taiwan has been able to claim a consistent surplus in foreign trade.

Table 3.1. 1996 ranking of world exporters

Rank	Exporting Country	Total Exports	World Share	% Growth (YOY)
1	United States	624.8	11.9	6.8
2	Germany	521.2	9.9	-0.3
3	Japan	412.6	7.9	-6.9
4	France	290.3	5.5	1.3
5	UK	259.1	4.9	7.0
6	Italy	250.7	4.8	7.1
7	Canada	201.2	3.8	4.7
8	Netherlands	197.1	3.8	0.9
9	Hong Kong (Total)	180.9	3.4	4.0
	(Domestic)	27.4	0.5	-8.4
10	Belgium/ Luxembourg	166.7	3.2	-1.8
11	P.R. China	151.1	2.9	1.5
12	R.O. Korea	129.8	2.5	3.8
13	Singapore (Total)	125.1	2.4	5.8
	(Domestic)	73.6	1.4	5.7
14	Republic of China	116.0	2.2	3.9
15	Spain	102.1	1.9	11.4
16	Mexico	95.9	1.8	20.6
17	Sweden	84.2	1.6	5.8
18	Switzerland	80.0	1.5	-2.0
19	Malaysia	78.4	1.5	5.8
20	Russia	70.4	1.3	8.6

Units: US$ billions; %

Source: World Trade Organisation

Table 3.2. 1996 ranking of world importers

Rank	Importing Country	Total Exports	World Share	% Growth (YOY)
1	United States	817.8	15.2	6.1
2	Germany	456.3	8.5	-1.5
3	Japan	349.6	6.5	4.1
4	UK	278.6	5.2	5.0
5	France	275.3	5.1	-0.2
6	Italy	207.0	3.8	0.4
7	Hong Kong (Total)	202.0	3.7	3.0
	(Domestic)	48.5	0.9	-7.0
8	Canada	175.0	3.2	3.9
9	Netherlands	174.1	3.2	-1.0
10	Belgium/ Luxembourg	154.6	2.9	-0.4
11	R.O. Korea	150.3	2.8	11.2
12	P.R. China	138.8	2.6	5.1
13	Singapore (Total)	131.5	2.4	5.6
	(Domestic)	79.9	1.5	5.4
14	Spain	121.9	2.3	6.1
15	Republic of China	102.5	1.9	-1.1
16	Mexico	90.3	1.7	23.6
17	Malaysia	78.6	1.5	1.0
18	Switzerland	78.5	1.5	-2.1
19	Thailand	68.3	1.3	-3.5
20	Austria	66.0	1.2	1.0

Units: US$ billions; %

Source: World Trade Organisation

THE CHANGING COMPOSITION OF TAIWAN'S TRADE

Until the mid-1980s the Taiwan market was largely insulated from international competition. However, significant internal and external imbalances were emerging during this period. In 1987 Taiwan's trade surplus had grown to US$18.7 billion. The external trade imbalance that had become evident in the first part of the 1980s was mirrored domestically by a situation of excess savings over investment and pressures were building in the economy.[3]

At the same time that Taiwan politically shed martial law and embarked on its policy of domestic political reform, it also sought to open its economy to international competition and commence the economic restructuring process that would ensure continuing competitiveness on world markets.

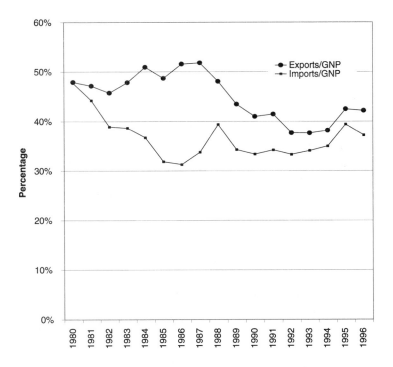

Figure 3d. External trade imbalance 1980–1996

[3] See Chapter 4 for a discussion of the internal imbalance.

Import Patterns

Reduced to the most basic level, Taiwan is an importer of raw materials and an exporter of finished or semi-finished goods. The same basic pattern of trade that has existed for the past forty years holds well today albeit with a change of focus. Agricultural and industrial raw materials account for around 72% of Taiwan's total imports; capital goods account for a further 16% with consumer goods providing the balance.

Table 3.3. Gross composition of imports by sector

Year	Capital Goods	Agricultural and Industrial Raw Materials	Consumption Goods
1995	16.3	72.0	11.7
1990	17.5	70.4	12.0
1985	14.1	76.9	9.0
1980	23.4	70.8	5.8

The most significant overall trend to emerge in recent years has been the rise in the import of consumption goods—from only 5.8% of total imports in 1980 to reach around 12% of total imports in the current decade.

Crude sector comparisons disguise the fundamentally changed pattern of Taiwan's import trade. When broken down by product group and comparing the current import patterns with those of a decade previously, the significance of higher value-added imports becomes immediately apparent.

Whereas in 1985 crude petroleum, chemicals and machinery were the dominant imports, by 1995 electronic products had become the dominant item accounting for 16% of total imports and registering (in US dollar terms) a ten-fold increase over the past decade. This change is a reflection of Taiwan's own changed industrial structure whereby electronic information products such as integrated circuits, personal and laptop computers and peripheral equipment are becoming Taiwan's mainstream export products. The increase in imports of precision instrumentation is another facet of this changed structure.

In 1996 and in terms of the two-digit HS codes, electrical machinery and mechanical appliances accounted for 35% of all imports. With emphasis now placed on the rapid development of the semiconductor and information technology industries in Taiwan both of these product groups can expect strong growth prospects into the medium term.

Table 3.4. ROC current major import categories (1995 and 1996)

Product	HS	1996		1995		Change	
		Units	*% of Total*	*Units*	*% of Total*	*Units*	*% (+/-)*
Electrical Machinery	85	21.32	20.8	22.37	21.6	-1.05	-4.7
Mechanical Appliances	84	14.66	14.3	13.29	12.8	1.37	10.3
Mineral Fuels, Oils	27	8.26	8.1	7.14	6.9	1.12	15.7
Organic Chemicals	29	5.63	5.5	6.60	6.4	-0.97	-14.7
Optical Instruments	90	4.99	4.9	3.75	3.6	1.25	33.3
Iron and Steel	72	4.90	4.8	6.43	6.2	-1.53	-23.8
Transport'n Equipment	87	3.39	3.3	4.64	4.5	-1.24	-26.8
Plastics and Articles	39	2.79	2.7	2.82	2.7	-0.03	-1.1
Special Products	98	2.74	2.7	1.97	14.5	0.77	39.1
Copper and Articles	74	2.00	2.0	2.41	2.3	-0.41	-16.8

Units: US$ billions; %
Source: ROC Board of Foreign Trade

In terms of the full 10 digit HS codes, refining oil is still the major single import commodity but this is now followed by such items as machinery for the manufacture of integrated circuits and other high-value machinery items. Taiwan's current top 20 import items are shown in Table 3.5 below.[4]

---

[4] 1997 data not yet available.

Table 3.5. ROC 20 leading import items (1995 and 1996)

Rank	Product	HS Code	1996	1995	Change	
			Amount	*Amount*	*Amount*	*YOY %*
1	Oil (for refining purposes)	2709001000	4,852.70	3,781.90	1,070.80	28.30
2	Other Integrated Circuits	8542809090	3,084.40	3,099.80	-15.40	-0.50
3	Other Machinery (individual functions)	8479899090	1,751.80	1,076.90	674.90	62.70
4	Colour High-Res CRT	8540110010	1,712.00	1,758.10	-46.10	-2.60
5	Bituminous Coal	2701120000	1,437.60	1,352.90	84.70	6.30
6	Other Machinery	8419899000	1,381.60	1,242.30	139.30	11.20
7	Sedans (exceeding 1500cc)	8703231000	1,359.70	1,902.30	-542.60	-28.50
8	Chip & Wafer of other IC	8542801000	1,179.00	915.00	264.00	28.9
9	DRAM Circuits	8542809010	949.60	1,046.80	-97.30	-9.30
10	Other IC and Micro-assemblies (without software)	8542809040	862.30	188.80	673.50	356.70
11	Hard Disk Devices	8471931010	850.30	562.40	287.90	51.20
12	Chips & Wafers of Digital IC's	8542111000	847.80	600.40	247.40	41.20
13	P-xylene	2902430000	770.40	972.30	-201.90	-20.80

Table 3.5 cont'd

14	Other Hybrid IC	8542200010	667.70	417.60	250.10	59.90
15	Other Parts of Data Processing Machines	8473301090	659.30	551.80	107.50	19.50
16	Styrene	2902500000	582.40	771.80	-189.30	-24.50
17	LNG	2711110000	499.60	436.70	62.90	14.40
18	Ethylene Glycol	2905310000	435.40	506.80	-71.40	-14.10
19	Other Semi-finished Products of Iron	7207120000	432.50	610.50	-177.90	-29.10
20	Parts for Motor Vehicles	8708999000	429.90	638.20	-208.30	-32.60

Units: US$ millions; %

Source: ROC Board of Foreign Trade

Export Patterns

Taiwan's export trade has also been changing. While industrial products have for many years accounted for the bulk of exports, increasingly the trend is towards higher value-added goods and away from labour intensive manufactures. In 1997, exports of industrial products were valued at US$119.522 billion and accounted for almost 98% of the export total. Whereas 10 years ago garments were the major export item, by 1995 this category has slipped to 11th place. Increasingly, Taiwan is shipping heavy industrial items rather than light industrial goods. Machinery is now the dominant single export item accounting for more than 22% of Taiwan's total exports and registering a ten-fold increase over the last decade. Mechanical appliances, electrical machinery, plastics and their derivative products, transportation equipment, synthetic fabrics and steel fabricated items together account for more than 60% of Taiwan's total exports.

Export of agricultural items and processed agricultural products has been in continuous decline for many years in keeping with the overall shift of domestic production. Present production levels are only sustained through massive production subsidies, tariff protection and outright ban of imports in some agricultural commodities such as rice. A further decline in both production and exports in this area can be expected once Taiwan joins the WTO and opens its markets to agricultural imports. In the future Taiwan will be largely reliant on imports to feed its population.

Table 3.6. Export trade by sector (%)

Year	Agricultural Products	Processed Agricultural Products	Industrial Products
1997	0.3	1.8	97.9
1996	0.4	3.1	96.5
1995	0.4	3.4	96.2
1990	0.7	3.8	95.5
1985	1.6	4.5	93.9
1980	3.6	5.6	90.8
1970	8.6	12.8	78.6
1960	12.0	55.7	32.3

In recent years, Taiwan's information industry has grown rapidly and this is reflected in the overall export figures. Broken down into their full ten-digit codes the importance of Taiwan as an exporter of computer and related products is immediately apparent. Export of data processing equipment has been growing most rapidly as shown by Table 3.8.[5]

Table 3.7. ROC current major export categories (1995 and 1996)

Product	HS Code	1996		1995		Change	
		Units	% of Total	Units	% of Total	Units	% (+/-)
Mechanical Appliances	84	28.83	24.9	24.89	22.3	3.9	15.8
Electrical Machinery	85	24.9	21.5	23.94	21.4	1	4

---

[5] Data for 1997 not yet available.

Table 3.7 cont'd

Plastics Articles	39	6.69	5.8	7.1	6.4	-0.4	-5.8
Transportation Equipment	87	4.77	4.1	4.87	4.4	-0.1	-2
Man-Made Filaments	54	3.53	3	3.85	3.4	-0.3	-8.4
Articles of Iron or Steel	73	3.48	3	3.48	3.1	0	-0.1
Toys and Sports Equipment	95	2.67	2.3	2.75	2.5	-0.1	-2.8
Articles of Apparel	60	2.6	2.2	2.29	2.1	0.3	13.5
Furniture	94	2.39	2.1	2.47	2.2	-0.1	-3
Textiles for Industrial Use	59	2.27	2	2.13	1.9	0.1	6.6

Units: US$ billions; %

Source: ROC Board of Foreign Trade

Table 3.8. ROC 20 leading export items (1995 and 1996)

Rank	Product	HS Code	1996	1995	Change	
			Amount	Amount	Amount	YOY %
1	Other parts of Data Processing Machines	8473301090	5,459.9	5,895.0	-435.1	-7.4%
2	Digital Auto Data Processing Machines	8471200000	5,447.9	3,568.2	1,879.7	52.7%
3	Other Integrated Circuits	8542809040	3,181.1	1,152.8	2,028.3	175.9%
4	Terminals	8471921000	2,831.5	2,632.1	199.4	7.6%
5	Chips and Wafers	8542801000	1,657.0	1,244.1	412.9	33.2%
6	Parts of Word Processing Machines	8473302100	1,481.2	947.7	533.5	56.3%

Table 3.8 cont'd

7	Colour Video Monitors	8528102000	1,458.4	1,597.1	-138.7	-8.7%
8	Other Plastics Articles	3926909090	1,386.1	1,297.2	88.9	6.9%
9	Parts of Other Motor Vehicles	8708999000	1,020.8	954.5	66.3	6.9%
10	Other Input or Output Units	8471929090	999.9	846.9	153.0	18.1%
11	Bicycles	8712001000	982.1	1,066.4	-84.3	-7.9%
12	Electrical Parts	8548000000	967.7	785.9	181.8	23.1%
13	Cathode Ray Tubes	8540110010	857.5	589.9	267.6	45.4%
14	Printed Circuit Boards	8534000013	818.7	694.2	124.5	17.9%
15	Other Parts of Radios	8529909000	814.7	713.0	101.7	14.3%
16	Other Articles of Iron or Steel	7326909090	791.7	750.8	40.9	5.4%
17	Acrylonitrile Butadiene	3903300000	757.9	829.7	-71.8	-8.7%
18	Parts of Data Processing Machines	8473302900	701.7	464.5	237.2	51.1%
19	Textured Filament Yarn	5402330000	664.9	808.8	-143.9	-17.8%
20	Integrated Circuits	8542809090	637.1	2,309.0	-1,671.9	-72.4%

Units: US$ millions; %
Source: ROC Board of Foreign Trade

EMERGING TRADE PATTERNS

The United States, Hong Kong and Japan together absorb over 60% of Taiwan's exports. The USA has traditionally been the dominant market for Taiwan's products although Taiwan's reliance on the USA has decreased steadily over the years (from 48% of all exports in 1985 to 24% in 1997).

This has come about as a direct result of Taiwan's attempts to diversify its export markets. While exports to Japan, as a percentage of the total, have been on an upward trend, export growth to that country has not kept pace with imports resulting in an ongoing source of friction in Taiwan's relationship with Japan.

The most important shift that has occurred in recent years is the pattern of Taiwan's trade with Asia and especially the emergence of the PRC market. All trade with the Peoples Republic remains indirect and by far the major portion flows through Hong Kong. In 1996 Taiwan's exports to Hong Kong accounted for 23.4% of total exports, making it on a par with the USA as a destination for Taiwan's exports. In 1996, Hong Kong actually became the dominant market for Taiwan's exports though preliminary figures released for 1997 suggest that the USA is still the main export market.

Much of the indirect trade with China (as with trade with the rest of Asia) flows to ROC-owned factories that have relocated to the Chinese mainland. While the primary motive behind relocation has been economic—a desire (as well as the need) to take advantage of the lower land and labour costs—nevertheless there has also been a strong cultural pull among many of Taiwan's Chinese and the desire by many to play a philanthropic role in their former home-towns or ancestral homes.

For the most part, the goods shipped to China are semi-finished products that subsequently will be re-exported. Many of these goods produced in Taiwanese-owned factories using Chinese labour will enter the USA and other countries as Chinese origin goods thereby avoiding any quota restrictions imposed on goods of Taiwanese origin. To a lesser extent the same holds true of the export growth to ASEAN countries and Vietnam. Although the shifting focus of trade is a reflection of comparative advantage at work, as long as much of the finished product still ends up in America the United States market industry remains as important to Taiwan as ever.

In global terms, intra-Asian trade now accounts for more than half the total, providing 53% of Taiwan's imports and taking 54.5% of its exports.[6] North America is the second most important market followed by Europe. Trade with the rest of the world is insignificant by comparison.

---

[6] Based on 1996 figures.

The United States

In 1986 Taiwan's two-way trade with the United States accounted for 38% of its total trade. As a market for Taiwan's export goods, almost 50% was destined for the USA. A decade later, the trade imbalance had shrunk noticeably. While total two-way trade had almost doubled in this period to US$47 billion, Taiwan's export growth to the United States had grown on average by only 4.2% annually over the 11 year period, compared to an annual growth rate of 27% for imports from the US market.

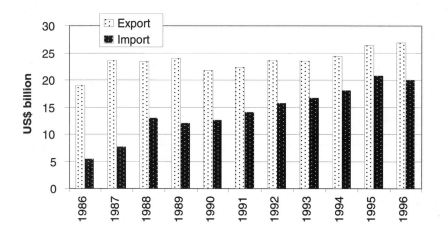

Figure 3e. ROC–US trade

Labour-intensive export products have over recent years been replaced with products from Taiwan's high value-added manufacturing sector. Export items now include mechanical appliances (32%), electrical machinery (24%), articles of iron or steel (5%) and transportation equipment (4%). Within these overall categories the most important export items for the ROC are digital data processors, data processing accessories, terminals, integrated circuits and electronic components.

Major import items from the USA include electrical machinery (21%), mechanical appliances (15%), organic chemicals (8%) and cereals (7%). The single most important import items in recent years have included integrated circuits and electronic components, chips and wafers and factory machinery and equipment.

Taiwan recorded a surplus of US$6.3 billion in its trade with the United

States in 1997 out of a total bilateral trade value of US$52.8 billion.[7] The weakened Taiwan dollar is expected to lead to increased competitiveness in the US market for Taiwanese goods during 1998 and this will mitigate to some extent the anticipated reduction in demand from some of the Asian markets.

Japan

After the United States, Japan remains Taiwan's most important trading partner. In contrast to the surplus Taiwan has enjoyed in the US market, Taiwan has had a consistent and indeed growing trade deficit with Japan.

Overall two-way trade with Japan reached US$41.2 billion in 1996, a reduction of 5.2% compared to 1995 but still a 222% increase over 1986 levels. While exports to Japan have increased by an average of 20% annually over the period, imports have been increasing at a much faster rate—more than 23% annual growth. In 1997, there was a further slight decline in US dollar terms to US$40.7 billion although, at US$17.3 billion, the trade deficit was largely unchanged from the previous year.

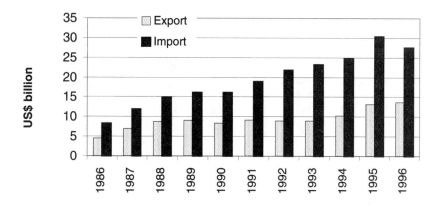

Figure 3f. ROC–Japan trade

---

[7] Provisional statistics for January–December 1997 show that exports to the USA amounted to US$29.557 billion while imports were US$23.243 billion.

The European Union

In recent years the countries of the European Union have been among Taiwan's fastest growing trading partners in line with an overall expansion of economic and trade relations between Taiwan and the EU member countries and as part of the ROC's trade diversification policy. Two-way trade has doubled over the last decade with imports increasing by more than 20% a year.

Senior ROC political leaders have made a concerted effort to court their EU counterparts through a series of discrete high level political visits and through cultural promotion. Trade with the UK, the Netherlands and France has been growing while trade with Germany has weakened in recent years as a result of slackened demand for German motor vehicles in Taiwan and a reduction in the competitiveness of traditional ROC export products. The recent award of the high-speed rail contract to a European consortium composed primarily of German and French interests will ensure a continued expansion of trade with Europe into the medium term.

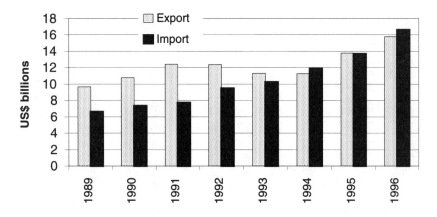

Figure 3g. ROC–EU trade

Hong Kong and China

As discussed above, a redirection of much of Taiwan's basic manufacturing industries to the Mainland of China and especially to the southern coastal provinces of Fujien and Guangdong has led to a rapid expansion of Taiwan's trade with and through Hong Kong. Direct trade with the Chinese Mainland is still banned although it is now included in ROC customs statistics.

Overall trade between Taiwan and Hong Kong reached US$28.5 billion in 1996, a 19% increase over 1995 levels.[8] Despite the tension in the political relationship between Taipei and Beijing, export trade still recorded a 2.6% overall growth although imports fell 7.5% in the same period. Overall, ROC exports far outweigh imports. Total value of this export trade in 1996 was placed at US$26.79 billion while imports in the same period amounted to only US$1.70 billion.

Official estimates count 70% of the ROC's exports to Hong Kong as being destined for the Chinese Mainland and the true volume is probably even higher than this amount. The increasing dependency of Taiwan's economy on its private sector investments in the Mainland is a dilemma for ROC officials, which so far they have been unable to solve.

Major export items to Hong Kong include electrical machinery, synthetic fibres and mechanical appliances, and all items destined for offshore ROC-owned factories on the Mainland, which comprised 35% of the total. The remainder was largely comprised of raw and semi-finished materials for processing. Imports from China consist mainly of lumber, farm products and consumer goods.

TRADE INCENTIVES AND RESTRICTIONS

Taiwan's Exim Bank

The Export-Import Bank of the ROC (Exim Bank) provides the traditional range of financial support services to locally registered companies in order to finance their overseas trade and investment activities. The Exim Bank is a government-owned banking institution capitalised through the national treasury and with annual appropriations to fund specialised operations from other government agencies including the Development Fund of the *Executive Yuan* and the Small and Medium-Sized Business Development Fund of the Ministry of Economic Affairs. Foreign companies registered in the ROC can apply for assistance from the bank on the same basis as locally-owned companies.

Principal activities of the Exim Bank are the provision of medium- and long-term trade support facilities in the form of financing of merchandise

---

[8] Exports to Hong Kong in 1997 were valued at US$28.7 billion compared with US$2.6 billion to the USA.

trade, guarantees and export insurance. The bank acts to support government policy in specific areas such as the provision of assistance in the export of turnkey plants, machinery, equipment and new products. Also, and in keeping with government policy of industrial upgrading, the Exim Bank finances overseas construction projects and investments into overseas factories.

On the import side the bank is particularly active in support of activities designed to bring in foreign technology. In certain circumstances, bank credit facilities can be used to finance the importation of specialised equipment, strategic raw materials as well as foreign technology and components. Indeed, at a time when Taiwan is seeking to upgrade its local industry infrastructure, Exim Bank facilities are regarded as an important source of funds for companies seeking to upgrade their production capabilities.

Fixed rate re-lending facilities, in the form of credit lines, are provided to both domestic and foreign financial institutions for customers who wish to purchase ROC-sourced equipment and facilities. The re-lending program has existed for many years and application procedures have now been greatly simplified.

Currently the Exim Bank has in place re-lending relationships with 76 banks in 25 countries as follows: local (ROC) banks—7; other Asia—17, Europe—17, North America—15, Central and South America—13, Africa—4, Australia—3. The most common items purchased through the aid of credits in 1995 included industrial equipment, machine tools, telecommunications and electronic products as well as essential industrial raw materials.

Other facilities offered by the bank include guarantee services of which Overseas Construction Guarantees account for the largest share. Guarantee facilities can be extended to cover actual overseas construction work as well as a full range of exports ranging from individual parts and components to complete turnkey plants.

The provision of export insurance is another of the bank's key functions. The bank is able to provide insurance services to local exporters when transactions are made by L/C, D/P, D/A or medium- or long-term credit facilities. The bank will also insure against losses in overseas investments and provides limited underwriting facilities for overseas construction projects.

The Exim Bank currently (FY1997) has a net worth of NT$12.582 billion made up of fully paid in capital of NT$10 billion and retained earnings of NT$2.582 billion. Outstanding loans as of end FY1997 amounted to

NT$95.171 billion as compared to NT$81.228 billion the previous year. This represented an increase of 17.2% over the period. Medium- and long-term import credits accounted for 49.1% of total loans outstanding while medium- and long-term export credits accounted for a further 27.7%.

Table 3.9: Medium- and long-term Exim loan structure (NT$1000s)

	1997		1996		1995	
	Amount	*%*	*Amount*	*%*	*Amount*	*%*
Total Loans Outstanding	95,170,675	100	81,227,744	100	64,331,372	100
Of which:						
Medium- and Long-Term Import Credits	46,714,372	49.1	39,822,335	49.0	31,221,511	48.5
Medium- and Long-Term Export Credits	26,330,809	27.7	21,035,377	25.9	18,198,462	28.3
Short-Term Export Credits	200,879	0.2	378,988	0.5	977,897	1.6
Shipbuilding Credits	2,605,176	2.7	3,912,849	4.8	3,683,617	5.7
Overseas Construction Credits	2,933,650	3.1	2,483,650	3.1	1,500,000	2.3
Overseas Investment Credits	9,695,620	10.2	8,728,614	10.7	4,898,376	7.6
Fixed-Rate Re-lending Facilities	1,803,073	1.9	1,922,181	2.5	1,477,817	2.3
Syndicated Loans	4,887,096	5.1	2,873,750	3.5	2,373,692	3.7

Guarantee services in 1997 amounted to NT$4.16 billion, representing 63.4% of the total.

Total export insurance facilities extended in FY1997 amounted to NT$11.35 billion after having fallen the previous year (NT$9.59 billion in 1996, down from the NT$10.45 billion recorded in 1995). D/P and D/A export insurance accounted for 78% of the total. The export volume covered by the insurance program amounted to NT$8.85 billion with 55.1% of all insurance directed at covering exports to North America (down from 63% the previous year). Metal products were again the leading category and accounted for 63% of the total.

Taiwan's Exim Bank has observer status within the International Union of Credit and Investment Insurers (The 'Berne Union') and maintains overseas offices in Jakarta, Mexico City and Budapest.

Export Processing Zones

Taiwan currently has four export processing zones under the control of an Export Processing Zone Administration (EPZA) which is an agency within the Ministry of Economic Affairs. The headquarters of the EPZA is based in Kaohsiung and all enquiries regarding zone facilities are routinely referred to the Kaohsiung Office. In addition the Hsinchu Science Park also operates as an export zone under special regulations.

There are two export processing zones located in the Kaohsiung area and one in Taichung. A new zone in the Nankang area of Taipei for the production of computer software was finally opened in early 1997 after a delay of several years.

Under government regulations governing the operation of the export processing zones, any enterprise establishing a factory within an EPZ must invest a minimum of NT$20 million in new or underdeveloped industries and all production must be for export. Raw material imports for processing within the zone are exempt from payment of normal Customs dues (though in certain circumstances, other restrictions such as import licensing still apply—see below) and factory output is exempt from payment of the Commodity Tax.

The combined area of the existing zones totals about 140 hectares. All land within the zone is government-owned and leased back to qualifying manufacturers. Government-constructed factory buildings are available with annual rental costs for factory space costing between NT$5,684/m^2 and NT$7,234/m^2.

Exports from Taiwan's export processing zones in 1997 amounted to US7.9 billion, or 6.5% of the total. This represents an increase in output, measured in value terms, of 28% over the previous year. Japan and the US were the dominant suppliers of materials for zone factories.

Bonded Warehouses and Factories

The *Customs Act* provides for the establishment and operation of both bonded warehouses and bonded factories. The operating regulations governing the establishment and management of bonded warehouses were last revised in January 1996. Except for those operated by government agencies, any bonded warehouse must take the form of a company limited by shares; if it is going to act as a distribution centre its paid up capital must be greater than NT$100 million. Bonded warehouses can be established at locations specified in the regulations including at harbours, airports, export processing zones, at the science-based industrial park or in areas approved by the Customs authorities. Business operators are required to pay a guarantee deposit which for an ordinary bonded warehouse is NT$300,000. Government bonds, banker's guarantees or a negotiable bankers' certificate of time deposit may be used as security in lieu of a deposit.

Bonded warehouses may be classified as 'ordinary bonded warehouse' for the storage of general purpose goods, 'exclusive bonded warehouse' for the storage of special purpose goods such as fuel and materials for transportation, repair of ships or aeroplanes, mineral oils, hazardous materials etc. or a 'distribution centre' which imports on its own account and provides materials to other factories.

The *Regulations Governing Customs Bonded Factories* fall under separate provisions of the *Customs Law* and were last amended in October 1995. Under these Regulations, any company manufacturing for export, irrespective of its location, may apply to the Customs Bureau to have one or other of their factory sites designated as bonded factories as part of their manufacturing operations. A number of companies, especially those operating within the Science Industrial Park at Hsinchu, have taken advantage of the bonded factory facility. In order to operate a bonded factory a company must have a valid factory license issued by the Ministry of Economic Affairs, minimum paid-up capital of NT$20 million (foreign branch companies which have remitted into the ROC capital of at least NT$20 million may also apply for registration as a bonded factory), all production must be for export and a bonding agent must be appointed to supervise the use of bonded materials. A number of the banks fulfil the role of bonding agents. The role of the bonding agent is to finance and administer imports as well as assuming responsibility for the settlement of all taxes and duties levied on the goods for a period of two years.

An export processor utilising this system can use the raw material itself as collateral to obtain the foreign exchange necessary for their purchase. The bonding agent provides the finance for the raw materials and purchases on consignment. Goods can be sold from one bonded factory to another for further processing upon application to the Customs Bureau but goods made available to the local market are classified as 'imported goods' and become dutiable items.

Larger companies utilise the bonded factory system and can import directly or obtain supplies from a designated bonded warehouse distribution centre. Such centres provide a means whereby smaller export processors can obtain raw materials for export processing. From time to time the Customs Bureau publishes a list of those materials and components that are covered by bonding agents.

CONTROLS ON TRADE

Since the onset of the government's trade liberalisation policy and with (indirect) trade now allowed between Taiwan and the Chinese Mainland, controls on the free flow of trade are rapidly disappearing.

A small number of items remain listed as prohibited imports into the ROC including items made of ivory, Chinese-made liquors, lethal chemicals, pornographic literature and narcotics. A number of other items, particularly those in the agricultural sector, remain subject to import control largely exercised through quotas. In other areas, the tariff is now used as the favoured means of controlling imports.

The list of controlled items includes weapons and ammunition, certain drugs, endangered animal species and currency paper, as well as some agricultural and marine products. Controlled items are subject to import licences issued by the Board of Foreign Trade. General trade items that appear on the 'permitted' list but which require prior approval are generally licensed by the BOFT or authorised banks as set out in the Customs Regulations.

In certain commodities, import into the ROC is limited to specific designated geographic areas or countries although these controls are rapidly being phased out as Taiwan prepares for WTO membership. Quantitative restrictions remain on many items, particularly those in the agricultural sector. Other items where import is permitted but requires prior authorisation include:

- Animal, vegetable or fisheries products: subject to quarantine;
- Pharmaceutical products: regulated by the Department of Health of the *Executive Yuan*;

- Toxic chemicals: Environmental Protection Administration of the Executive Yuan;
- Certain fertilisers: Council of Agriculture;
- Gold: import is limited to the Central Trust of China or registered jewellery companies or factories;
- Tobacco, wines and spirits: import is controlled through approval from the Taiwan Tobacco and Wine Monopoly Bureau.

The English language edition of the Customs Import Tariff and Classification of Import & Export *Commodities* is published annually by the China External Development Council and contains both the applicable import tariffs as well as details of any import or export regulations in relation to the item in question.

MARKET OPPORTUNITIES

While recent rates of economic growth in Taiwan have not matched those of previous years, overall levels are still quite healthy by OECD norms. As the Taiwan economy matures so opportunities change. For the trader seeking to sell to Taiwan the opportunities are enormous: not only are there the large ticket items offered by the development of new technologies and economic restructuring, as well as large scale infrastructure projects, there is now in Taiwan a large and affluent middle class with high levels of disposable income and a propensity to spend. The massive surge in real estate prices which occurred towards the end of the last decade has on the one hand produced an extremely affluent population—especially those who were fortunate enough to be in the market at the time—while on the other hand, the high buy-in price and predictions of a flat (even falling) market for some years to come have switched spending patterns from long term investment into short-term consumer spending.

For the trader seeking to buy from Taiwan, it is no longer the source of cheap low cost commodities (though many local traders will have access to factories in Mainland China or elsewhere who can ship the low cost/low value items). Rather, Taiwan is now gaining a reputation for higher value-added manufactured products and this is where the real opportunities lie.

In Taiwan as in any foreign market, certain ground rules apply of which the most basic is the need to do the necessary homework before entering the market.

Some basic rules for buying from Taiwan

1. Know the market; is Taiwan currently manufacturing the item in question? A number of trade directories are available—of varying quality—to help the buyer identify companies and products; CETRA provides (for a fee) computerised printouts broken down by CCC (Customs) code of export statistics and companies involved in exporting commodities. Other private companies such as Asian Company Profiles Inc (ACP) and China Credit Information Services (CCIS) also provide computerised listings;
2. For a variety of reasons, industry lists often have no more than a 60% accuracy rate. It is a wise move to filter potential suppliers before your arrival to ensure you do not waste valuable time;
3. If you are dealing with a trading company in Taipei which claims to 'own a factory', try and visit the factory yourself; more often than not there will be no direct relationship between the trading company and the actual manufacturer—especially if the industry is small scale. Traditionally the trading companies were an interface between small manufacturers and foreign buyers and added a margin accordingly; increasingly factories are seeking to by-pass trading companies in the export trade and deal direct with customers. Remember, though, language may be a problem;
4. Always remember the first price offered is seldom the final price, though best prices are built on the assessment of long term relationships;
5. Visit the trade fairs. The Taipei trade exhibitions are among the best in Asia and are natural meeting points for beginning a business relationship. A trade fair will certainly provide an overview of what is available;
6. Make contact with the appropriate industry association. In Taiwan virtually all manufacturing companies belong to associations; the association will have name lists and directories of companies involved in producing items of interest to you (though generally these will be in Chinese);
7. In cases of OEM manufacturing, if transfer of any form of intellectual or other property is involved then beware! Whether it is a technical drawing, a mould or any similar item seek proper legal advice; do not rely on oral assurances from your local business partner or professions of friendship which appear to render written assurances unnecessary: The rule of 'buyer beware' applies as much in Taiwan as it does in every other country of the world;

8. If potential business volume warrants, consider the establishment of a registered liaison office independent of your local business partner. A liaison office is *your* agent who will not only monitor the performance of your supplier but will be able to provide you with ongoing feedback as to market conditions, alternative sources of supply as well as acting as an expediter;

9. Above all do your homework before you arrive in Taiwan. Engaging a reputable market analyst or research company to undertake the initial market research can save you both time and money. Often the cost of such research will be less than the price of a plane ticket and accommodation.

Some basic rules for selling to Taiwan

1. Research the market; know the potential of the market for your product;
2. Understand how current market needs are being met. Is the item in question manufactured locally? To what extent is the market reliant on imported products?
3. Who is the ultimate end-user of the product? What are the factors influencing purchasing decisions? To what extent is price a determining factor for your product?
4. Who is currently purchasing similar products? Industry lists are available from CETRA and other sources, including industry associations;
5. Are you selling direct to the end-user or through a local agent? If the end-user is not an established importer then most probably you will need to appoint an importer to handle customs clearance and other formalities;
6. Obtain informed views of your own product; be ready to sell its advantages with specification sheets and other relevant data presented in Chinese;
7. Use existing networks to build your contacts. Usually if you are an exporter, your country's local trade office will be able to assist in identifying suitable companies in Taiwan who can assist your market entry;
8. Foreign banks as well as chambers of commerce are another valuable source of local knowledge which can be tapped;
9. Do not expect one visit to change established buying patterns. Most probably it will take several visits and establishment of personal relationships of trust before any business is done—especially if you are looking for substantial and repeat orders;

10. Ensure that your local import agent or buyer is fully supported in terms of product manuals, performance reliability etc.;
11. If you are tendering for government contracts, work with a reliable local partner who can deal with the local bureaucracy and who knows local customs;
12. Above all else, give the market the attention it deserves and ensure that your own management is working at optimum efficiency. Unless especially trained, do not send in your engineer to close the sale nor expect your sales person to explain the technical specifications of your product. In any event, if you are the team leader or head person of your organisation ensure that you take the time to build the relationship of confidence with your counterpart.

Whether buying or selling, keep a flexible attitude towards achieving your objective but always be ready to walk away from a bad deal. Chinese are not as impatient as many foreign (especially Western) business people to close a deal and will take the time to probe the other's position. Do not fall into the trap of being pressured by time.

KEY GOVERNMENT AGENCIES

China External Trade Development Council
4–8F, 333 Keelung Road, Section 1, Taipei
Tel: (02) 2725 5200
Fax: (02) 2757 6653

Bureau of Commodity Inspection & Quarantine MOEA
4 Chinan Road, Section 1, Taipei
Tel: (02) 2343 1700
Fax: (02) 2393 2324

Board of Foreign Trade
1 Hukou Street, Taipei
Tel: (02) 2351 0271
Fax: (02) 2351 3603

Export Processing Zone Administration
600 Chiachang Road, Nantze, Kaohsiung
Tel: (07) 361 1212
Fax: (02) 361 4348

The Export-Import Bank of the Republic of China
3 Nanhai Road, Taipei
Tel: (02) 2321 0511
Fax: (02) 2341 5297

CHAPTER 4

INDUSTRY AND INVESTMENT POLICIES

Taiwan is entering the Year of the Tiger in better shape than many of its regional competitors. In no small measure, credit for insulating Taiwan from the worst of Asia's upheavals goes to Taiwan's economic planners and their unswerving commitment over several decades to sound macroeconomic policies implemented through a series of national development plans.

ECONOMIC PLANNING AS THE CATALYST FOR DEVELOPMENT

Taiwan's first Medium-Term Economic Development Plan was launched as early as 1953 and ran for four years. This four year planning cycle lasted until 1976 when the world's first oil crisis triggered the need for a quick response to the dislocations caused by rapidly escalating oil prices.

Responsibility for overseeing the early plans was given first to an Economic Stabilisation Board created as a body under the *Executive Yuan* and then to a Council for US Aid, since it was the United States that supplied the bulk of the assistance to Taiwan in the early years and especially until 1965.[1]

As the country stabilised so the scope of the early plans increased. Early plans were project-orientated and were coordinated with the US aid program. With the winding back of such aid during the 1960s the focus was enlarged to cover all aspects of economic and social development.

The present Council for Economic Planning and Development was established in December 1977 and replaced the Council for International Economic Cooperation and Development, a reflection that Taiwan was no longer reliant on international assistance for its economic growth.

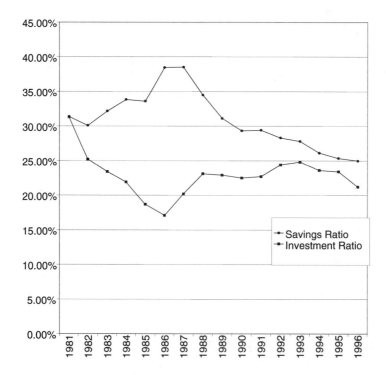

Figure 4a. Savings and investment ratio as a percentage of GNP

---

[1] US Aid terminated in 1965 but projects under the aid program continued until 1968.

The two decades from 1965 to 1985 saw a period of rapid advancement during which time per capita GNP increased more than ten-fold. However, by 1987 major problems were emerging for the Taiwan economy that forced fundamental changes in the planning processes. It was the period of the 'bubble economy'. The growing trade surplus had led to a rapid increase in savings of which public and private investment was not soaking up the excess. An excessive increase in the money supply, rapidly increasing foreign exchange reserves and a dramatic appreciation of the local currency led to soaring stock and real estate prices and a rapid expansion of real wages. The consequence was a reduction of export competitiveness coupled with a deterioration of the investment climate. Export growth slowed, there was a general unwillingness to invest and many of Taiwan's traditional light industries began to move offshore to lower cost centres elsewhere in Asia.

Problems on the economic front were exacerbated by changes taking place within the social order. The lifting of martial law and the ban on political organisation ushered in a period of political uncertainty for Taiwan as rival political groups came to terms with the changed environment. Labour disputes, previously unheard of in Taiwan, began to emerge and there was a sharp increase in the crime rate. Taiwan's political and social institutions were proving themselves outdated and unable to cope with the new situation.

A period of structural adjustment was emerging and dominated economic policy from the mid-eighties to the mid-nineties. The policy of economic and trade liberalisation introduced with the 9th Economic Development Plan in 1987, called for stimulation of private sector investment and sustainable economic growth through the underpinning of the private sector with major public investments. Plans were introduced for a progressive deregulation of the financial institutions and the foreign exchange market. At the same time a major overhaul of Taiwan's outdated—and highly protectionist—regulatory environment began.

These policies had an immediate effect in improving both Taiwan's internal and external position. The share of domestic demand as a percentage of GDP rose from 80.2% in 1986 to more than 95% by 1990. Excess savings were reduced to less than 4%. While many labour intensive industries have continued to move offshore, this is being compensated for by a significant inflow of new foreign investment into Taiwan. More than 80% of all foreign investment into Taiwan has occurred since 1987.

Table 4.1. Taiwan's Economic Development Plans

Period	Planning Targets	Average Growth	Per Capita GNP[2]
1953–1956	1st Economic Development Plan	7.9%	US $167
	• Increased agricultural and industrial production • Promoted economic stability • Improved the balance of payment situation		
1957–1960	2nd Economic Development Plan	6.9%	US $160
	• Increased agricultural production • Accelerated industrial development • Promoted export expansion activities • Created job opportunities • Improved the balance of payments situation		
1961–1964	3rd Economic Development Plan	9.8%	US $152
	• Maintenance of economic stability • Acceleration of economic growth • Strengthening the industrial base • Improvement of the investment environment		
1965–1968	4th Economic Development Plan	9.6%	US $217
	• Promotion of economic modernisation • Maintenance of economic stability • Promotion of sophisticated industries		
1969–1972	5th Economic Development Plan	12.6%	US $345

---

[2] At commencement of the planning period.

Table 4.1 cont'd

5th Plan cont'd	• Maintenance of price stability • Promotion of export expansion • Strengthening Taiwan's infrastructure • Improving the industrial base • Promotion of agricultural modernisation		
1973–1976	6th Economic Development Plan	6.0%	US $695
(The 6th Plan was superseded by the 7th Plan as a result of the first oil crisis)	• Industrial modernisation • Infrastructure construction • Manpower quality improvements • Export expansion		
1976–1981	7th Economic Development Plan	9.8%	US $1,132
	• Promotion of energy efficiency • Improvements to the industrial structure • Manpower development • Promotion of balanced economic and social development • Completion of ten major construction projects		
1982–1985	8th Economic Development Plan	7.4%	US $2,673
	• Maintenance of price stability • Coordination of industrial development • Full employment • Improved income distribution • Balanced regional development		
1986–1989	9th Economic Development Plan	9.3%	US $3,993
	• Trade liberalisation • Expansion of public investment		

Table 4.1 cont'd

9th Plan cont'd	• Strengthening of the fiscal and monetary systems • Modernisation of the services sector • Development of 'key technologies' • Introduction of pollution control		
1990–1993	10th Economic Development Plan	–	US $8,111
(The 10th Plan was superseded by the *Six-Year National Development Plan* in 1991)	• Expansion of public expenditure • Streamlining of laws and regulations • Economic liberalisation • Improving the investment environment • Acceleration of transportation and communications development • Strengthening environmental protection measures • Improvements to social welfare		
1991–1996	Six-Year National Development Plan	6.5%	US $8,982
	The Six-Year plan incorporated the projects introduced in the 10th Plan and in addition gave priority to: • Balanced development including regional development; • Infrastructure development and modernisation; • Improving the quality of life.		
1997–2000	Plan for National Development into the Next Century	6.7%[3]	US $12,971
	• National modernisation • Increased competitiveness • Sustainable development • Improving the quality of life		

---

[3] Target.

Industrial upgrading, through the promotion of capital and technology-intensive industries, has been the cornerstone of the macroeconomic adjustment process. A *Statute for Upgrading Industries* was introduced in 1991 providing tax and other incentives for companies engaged in industrial upgrading. An important provision of the Statute was the establishment of a Development Fund to invest in major projects that were beyond the capability of individual private investors as well to provide development loans to industry through the banking sector.

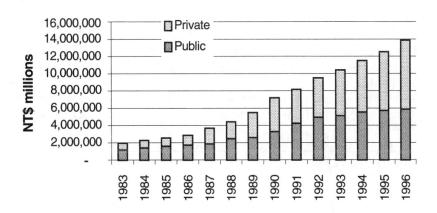

Figure 4b. Expenditure on research and development

Expenditure on research and development has increased dramatically in recent years with industry being required—through both tax incentives and tax penalties—to contribute to the process. As a result, while manufacturing as a percentage of GDP has declined from previous levels, it has stabilised in recent years at around 30% of GDP. Much of the excess labour has been taken up by the growth in the services sector. Furthermore there have been some fundamental changes within the manufacturing sector itself. The output of heavy capital-intensive industries such as chemicals and chemical products, as well as technology-intensive manufacturing—of which the growth in electrical and electronic items has been the most spectacular—has been increasing while the more traditional industries have been allowed to wither.

The gross output of Taiwan's 'sunset' industries has gone from 40% of the total in 1986 to 26% of the total 10 years later and a further decline is expected. The difference has been made up by technology-intensive manufactures, which have risen from 24% to 38%. In 1983, Taiwan was a world leader in ship-breaking, and in the manufacture of such items as footwear, electric fans, umbrellas and water heaters. A decade later it leads the world in such items as PC monitors (56% global market share), motherboards (80%) and scanners (61%).

The Six-Year Plan introduced in 1991 was an ambitious attempt to leapfrog into the 21st century. Cobbled together hurriedly to jump-start an economy that was again showing signs of slipping into recession, the massive infrastructure development program announced in 1991 proved overly ambitious and beyond the means of Taiwan to implement even with its vast reserves. The plan was hurriedly revised mid-term with more realistic targets and time frames. The philosophy behind the plan has proven more enduring.

In addition to embarking on a major program of public sector construction and administrative reform, it was during this period that the government first advocated the development of Taiwan as an 'Asia-Pacific Regional Operations Centre'. The APROC initiative was formally announced in January 1995.

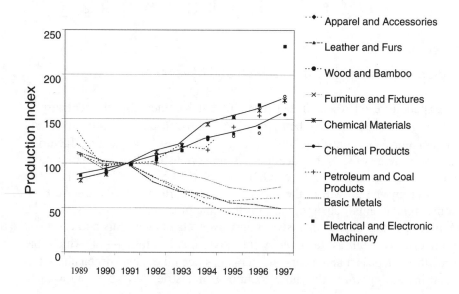

Figure 4c. Output of sunrise and sunset industries (1991 = 100)

Taiwan has increasingly taken a global view of its future and, while much remains to be accomplished, even the critics would acknowledge that Taiwan has opened its economy far more quickly than many others in Asia have.

A number of problems remain to be addressed. The pace of legislative reform has not proceeded as quickly as Taiwan's economic rationalists would have wished. Cumbersome bureaucratic procedures and a civil service that in many areas has proven itself resistant to change have hampered administrative reform. Corruption and ineptitude, especially at the lower levels and in the Taiwan Provincial Government structure, remain major headaches.

At the economic level, the deterioration of the political environment has had an ongoing impact on domestic investment. Taiwan's investment ratio has fallen well below that of other regional economies. Scarcity of land has forced prices to escalate and has made (in US dollar terms) millionaires out of many of Taiwan's agricultural labourers. There is many a farmer in Taiwan driving a plough during the week and a Mercedes at the weekend. Illegal encroachment of land and land-use outside of its designation has undermined both planning systems and protection of the environment.

All of these issues are being addressed by government but even the most optimistic planners concede that past neglect will mean that it will be well into the next century before Taiwan achieves its goal of becoming a modern state with adequate standards of quality of life, social security and welfare.

SCIENCE AND TECHNOLOGY

Total spending on research and development has risen from 0.96% of GNP in 1984 to an expected 2.15% in 1997 and 2.5% by the year 2000. In 1993 Taiwan's private sector replaced the government as the primary source of R&D funds. This trend is expected to continue with current government programs whereby research projects deemed of importance to Taiwan's industrial effort are contracted out to private corporations.

Almost 60% of all R&D in Taiwan is conducted by private sector firms with the bulk of the remainder taking place within the science and technology institutes. The universities and colleges are primarily teaching institutions with very little research capability.

As more effort has gone into research so has a greater allocation of manpower, with the total number of research workers increasing from 18,000 in 1982 to 63,000 in 1995. In per capita terms this represents a three-fold increase in numbers.

By far the greatest research effort goes into applied research and product development with less than 20% of the total research budget allocated to basic research tasks. Product development accounts for almost 60% of the total R&D effort and this is likely to continue for the foreseeable future.

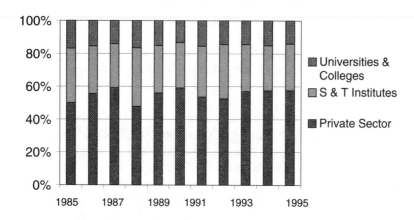

Figure 4d. Research expenditure by sector

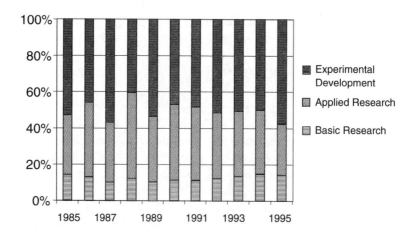

Figure 4e. Research expenditure by research type

Companies with a majority local ownership are required under the *Statute for Upgrading Industries* to allocate a portion of their total annual revenue to research and development activities. This can take the form of in-house or cooperative research or a contribution to development projects sponsored by the government.

Expenses recognised by the government as legitimate R&D expenditure include the following:

1. Research and development leading to new products;
2. Upgrading of production or management technologies;
3. Acquisition of technologies from overseas;
4. Investments into energy-efficient facilities;
5. Investment into pollution-control equipment;
6. Market survey work designed to promote sales.

For a number of industries, the government has specified minimum acceptable levels of R&D expenditure as a percentage of total annual tax-reported revenue. Companies in other industries are reviewed on a case by case basis and any company not meeting its required contribution level must pay the balance into a special fund designed to promote the technological upgrading of local industry.

The release in December 1997 of the government's first ever *White Paper on Science and Technology* is intended as a blueprint for Taiwan's scientific and technological development into the next century. Increasingly, the planning of S&T development activities is being seen as a necessary adjunct to economic planning. The report, prepared by the National Science Council of the ROC, reaffirms the government's intention to grow the sci-tech budget, to improve both international collaboration in specific areas of basic and applied research and to develop the necessary mechanisms so that research findings can be used to improve the living environment and grow the high-tech industries of the future.

Among the more important of the strategies and measures outlined in the paper are the following:

- Increase R&D expenditure to 2.5% of GDP by the year 2000 and 3.0% by 2010;
- Support for basic research at a level not less than 15% of total R&D expenditure, and the provision of long term funding for selected programs in a number of areas: number theory; non-linear systems; strong correlation electro-systems; new chemical materials and chemical dynamics; glycobiology; gene expression and control; neuroscience; the mechanism of ageing; structural biology and inter-disciplinary cognitive science;
- The further identification of additional 'key technologies' for industrial development including: multimedia and communications;

biotechnology; aerospace; precision machinery, special materials, electric vehicles and battery technology;

- Accelerate Internet use towards a goal of three million domestic subscribers by the year 2000 and establish Taiwan as an 'Asia–Pacific regional Internet hub' through further deregulation of the telecommunications industry and the accelerated establishment of network lines;
- The drafting of additional statutes to cover intellectual property rights, personnel rules and the development of industrial technologies;
- A stepped up program of bilateral science and technology cooperation agreements and the active participation in international research projects.

THE ROLE OF FOREIGN INVESTMENT

Taiwan welcomes foreign investment. Investment restrictions are rapidly being lifted in many areas.

Cumulative inward private investment during the period to 1997 totalled US$28.4 billion, of which 89% is accounted for by foreign investors and the remainder by overseas Chinese (for whom slightly different rules apply—see below). Official records date from 1952 and include only those funds approved under the various statutes and laws governing foreign investment. Not included in official totals are those funds, the bulk of which would probably be from overseas Chinese, brought into the country for small scale domestic enterprises that do not attract specific incentives from government.

Large-scale inward investment is a relatively recent phenomenon. More than 80% of all inward investment has occurred in the last ten years. Indeed, the level of inward investment in 1997 was on a par with the total received between 1952 and 1983. Overseas Chinese investment has always been a small part of the total and has been declining in recent years. Eighty-nine per cent has been approved under the *Statute for Investment by Foreign Nationals* (see below). Importantly, when measured in year-on-year terms, inward investment slowed in 1996 and the total for the year was 16% below the 1995 level. In 1997, there was strong growth—up by 50% over the previous year.

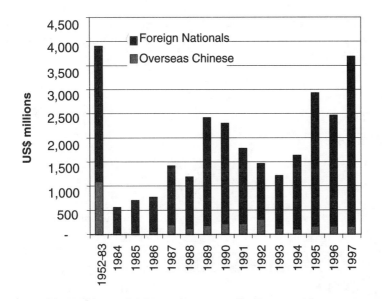

Figure 4f. Approved overseas inwards investment 1952–1997

Investment By Origin

Japan and the US are the major foreign investors in Taiwan. The US alone accounts for 27.6% of all direct overseas investment while Japan accounts for a further 26.4%. Hong Kong accounts for 10.6% and Singapore almost 6%.

European investors have contributed around 12% of the total, of which the UK and the Netherlands are the two largest sources of European investment funds. The pattern of investment, in terms of its origin, has been remarkably consistent over the years.

Total US approved investment in 1996 and 1997[4] was well below previous levels and amounted only to US$935 million—only 15% of the total for these two years. This contrasted with a level of more than US$1.3 billion (or more than 46% of total approved foreign investment) in 1995 but was still higher than the US$293 million approved in 1994.

---

[4] Data only to the end of November is available at the time of writing.

Japan, Singapore and Australia have been the other major investors in recent years. In the last two years, Japan has kept to its previous levels with total remittances of US1.35 billion (22%) while Singaporean investments have risen to 10% of the total, slightly ahead of Australia at 9%.

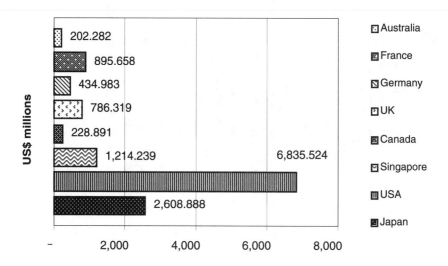

Figure 4g. Overseas investment by origin

Investment by Sector

Some 25% of all foreign investment has been directed into the manufacture of electronics and electrical items, followed by the chemical industry (13%), service industries (10.7%) and the banking and insurance industries (8%).

Foreign investment is generally governed by the *Statute for Investment by Foreign Nationals* (or in the case of Overseas Chinese, the *Statute for Investment by Overseas Chinese*). These are discussed in the following section which deals with government incentives for overseas investment into the Taiwan economy.

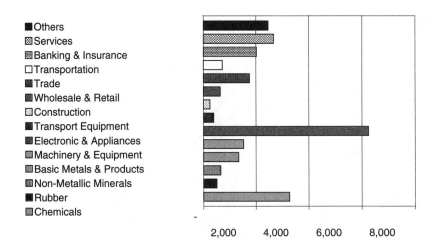

Figure 4h. Approved overseas investment by industry 1952–1996

OUTWARDS INVESTMENT FROM TAIWAN

In recent years Taiwan has emerged as a significant source of investment funds. Statistical data (reproduced below) compiled by the Investment Commission show levels of outward investment from Taiwan in roughly consistent proportion to the capital inflow.

Taiwan's own outward investment policy encompasses two clear strategic objectives. On the one hand there has been a clear emphasis on the acquisition of key technologies through the purchase of, or investment in, established high-tech corporations in Europe and America. On the other hand, Taiwan has adopted a 'go south' policy whereby it has become a large scale investor in South-East Asia and into the Chinese Mainland as a means of claiming a stake in the emerging regional economy.

More than 55% of all outward investment has gone to the Americas and almost half of that to the USA. The bulk of the remainder has gone chiefly to Taiwan's allies in Central America as a means of shoring up political and diplomatic support. Almost 40% has gone to Asia of which, outside the Chinese Mainland, Malaysia has been the most significant beneficiary followed by Hong Kong, Singapore and Thailand. More recently, Taiwan has started to invest in Vietnam and the Philippines, and Taiwanese companies are among the most prominent engaged in the development of the Subic Bay area.

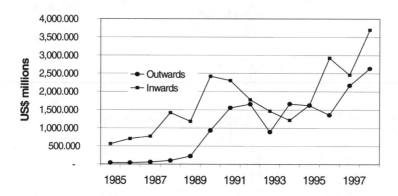

Figure 4i. Comparison of inward and outward investment flows

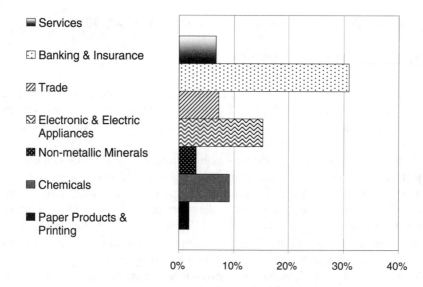

Figure 4j. Outward investment by sector 1952–1986

Official statistics relating to Taiwanese investment into the Mainland of China have only been compiled since 1991. According to ROC data, a total of US$8.2 billion in approved investments have gone to the Mainland in the past six years. This is generally regarded as a highly conservative figure, with the true level of investment believed to be well in excess of US$20 billion. Taiwan is now the second largest investor in Mainland China, ahead of Hong Kong and exceeded only by Japan.

TAIWAN'S CURRENT PLAN: PROSPECTS FOR SUCCESS

Undoubtedly Taiwan has come a long way in the last decade and its achievements have been well publicised. Working alongside the economic planners is a highly effective public relations machine that seizes on every opportunity to reassure potential investors that liberalisation efforts are on track and that Taiwan is the best place in Asia for their money. Bodies such as the US-based Heritage Foundation, the Business Environment Risk Intelligence Unit (BERI) and the Geneva-based World Economic Forum are regularly quoted as extolling the virtues of Taiwan. They are probably right, as far as they go. However, foreign business associations operating in the local environment are less sanguine in their assessments. A *White Paper* published by the influential American Chamber of Commerce in Taiwan (AMCHAM) in September 1997 drew some much needed attention to the unfair treatment many foreign companies still experience in Taiwan. In far too many instances, 'actions by ROC Government appear arbitrary, non-transparent and discriminatory in nature'. These are tough words from a body that is well known as one of Taiwan's most effective lobby groups in Washington.

The European Council of Commerce and Trade (ECCT) has echoed similar sentiments in its own reports and has cautioned that time is running out for the government's plan to transform Taiwan into an Asian-Pacific Operations Centre. The nub of the issue here is that of cross-straits links; direct sea, air and communications services that would be the impetus to launching Taiwan as a centre for companies engaged with the Mainland.

Despite calls for a reassessment of the 'Three Links' issue, even from within the ruling Kuomintang, the ROC Government has ruled out any movement on direct links with the Mainland for the time being. Pressure is building, though. On the issue of discriminatory treatment and bureaucratic procedures, the government claims it is aware of these obstacles and is addressing them, but is it moving fast enough?

It is hoped that the current Four-Year Plan for National Development into the next century will address these questions in a serious manner. Commenced in January 1997, the current plan will run to the end of the year 2000. In broad terms the plan will continue and consolidate the liberalisation processes already under way. At the same time, an embryonic ten-year strategy has been mapped out covering the broad national goals to the year 2006. Major elements of the current plan include:

- Consolidation of the Asia-Pacific Regional Operations Centre concept;
- An Economic Revitalisation Program aimed at overcoming investment barriers and stimulating further domestic and foreign investment into the local economy;
- An Administrative Reform Program aimed at upgrading the integrity and efficiency of the public sector;
- Ongoing commitment to twelve major construction projects to provide further infrastructure development programs using both public and private sector finance (in reality, these represent a larger number of smaller projects grouped into twelve broad theme areas);
- The National Information Infrastructure Project, aimed at bringing Taiwan to the forefront in the use of information and Internet technologies.

Specific initiatives as well as targets have been made public. At the macro level the current period will be a time for introduction of new legislation (as well as amending the old regulations) to bring Taiwan into line with international practice; trade and investment controls are to be further liberalised as are the entry and exit controls on foreign nationals. A further easing of remaining restrictions on capital movements will see Taiwan's currency fully convertible by the year 2000.

Table 4.2. National development targets: 1997–2006

Item		Actual		Targets	
Description	Units	1995	1997	2000	2006
Economic Development					
Economic Growth Rate	%	6.0	6.7	6.7	6.2
Per Capita GNP	US dollar	12,396	13,971	18,438	30,608
CPI Increase	%	3.7	3.0	3.2	3.0
Manufacturing Output	US$ billion	228.1	-	300.0	410.0
Manufacturing Exports	US$ billion	109.2	-	150.0	220.0

Table 4.2 cont'd

Budget Deficit at all levels	US$ billion	154.9[5]	125.0	Bal-anced	-
Average Nominal Tariff	%	8.6	-	7.9	6.3
Unemployment Rate	%	1.8	2.5	2.5	2.8
Labour Force Participation	%	58.7	58.5	59.1	61.4
Total Energy Demand	MLOE	70,110	78,470	95,340	115,550
Total Energy Supply	MLOE	79,150	86,650	106,100	126,880
Installed Generating Capacity	MW	23,960	29,920	34,610	49,040
Transport and Communications					
Road Density	Km/km^2	0.90	0.9	0.94	-
Railway Density	Km/km^3	0.038	0.038	0.038	
Number of Air Passengers	1,000 pax	27,607	33,167	57,513	
Fibre Optical local loops	Lines x km	57,941	132,179	234,679	
Internet Hosts	1,000 pax	-	2	5	
Science and Technology					
R&D as % of GDP	%	1.8 (1994)	2.15	2.5	2.8
R&D as % of sales	%	1.06	1.5	2.0	3.0
Researchers[6]	Person	40,684	-	52,500	64,000

[5] Fiscal Year 1996.

[6] Bachelors Degree or higher.

Table 4.2 cont'd

Technicians as % of mfg w'force	%	11.2	12.0	15.0	-
Culture and Education					
Pupil/Teacher Ratio (Primary)	Students per teacher	22.42	21.95	20.0	-
Pupil/Teacher Ratio (Secondary)	Students per teacher	20.12	20.06	18.71	-
Population with higher education[7]	%				28.2
Literacy Rate	%	93.8	95.0	98.0	100

NATIONAL DEVELOPMENT TARGETS: 1997–2006

While direct links with China remain on hold, the government has moved ahead with its efforts to develop warehouse transhipment centres in Taiwan. In October 1996, the *Executive Yuan* approved new regulations offering tax incentives to companies that developed cargo transhipment services within the export processing zones. Aimed at attracting more multinational companies into the EPZs, the revised *Statute Governing the Export Processing Zones* will see such companies paying tax at a rate of only 10% of total income while preserving other privileges and incentives available to companies operating in such zones.

Privatisation of commercial ports is under way with private stevedoring and berth management services now allowed at Kaohsiung, Taichung and Keelung harbours. Total private sector contracts at these three ports are expected to exceed NT$5.4 billion (more than US$160 million) annually. Ground services at Taipei's international airport are also to be privatised.

The domestic transportation market is also to be opened to foreign investment. Initially this will cover the car rental business, truck freight and container services. In addition to allowing foreign car rental companies into the market, more importantly, foreign shipping lines will be able to improve their competitive position by offering integrated door-to-door transportation services. Broadcasting, gas and power generation are other areas to be

---

[7] As a percentage of the population aged 15 and over.

opened to foreign investment while import of oil and aviation fuel are to be liberalised in 1999.

Ongoing transformation of the manufacturing centre is a key element of current strategies. 'Ten Emerging Industries' and 'Eight Major Key Technologies' have been singled out for special attention. The government is especially keen to attract investment into these areas. In addition to the investment incentives available to general foreign investors, there are specific incentives offered under the *Statute for Industrial Upgrading* for investments into these areas. Taiwan's Ministry of Economic Affairs is providing seed funds for private sector involvement into related research projects. A total of NT$286 million (US$8.7 million) was allocated to this program during 1987 and this amount is slated to increase to NT$600 million (US$18 million) for 1998 and to NT$1.5 billion (US$45 million) by the year 2000.

Table 4.3. Key areas for investment

The Ten Emerging Industries	*The Eight Key Technologies*
• Communications	• Opto-electronics
• Information	• Software
• Consumer Electronics	• Industrial Automation
• Semiconductors	• Material Applications
• Precision Machinery and Automation	• Advanced Sensing
• Aerospace	• Biotechnology
• Advanced Materials	• Resources Development
• Specialty Chemicals and Pharmaceuticals	• Energy Conservation
• Medical and Health Care	
• Pollution Control and Treatment	

A total of twelve new industrial parks are to be opened within the next decade, of which eight are already under construction. Four of these parks are to be located within the economically depressed eastern seaboard of Taiwan in Ilan, Hualien and Taitung counties. Government incentives are already in place for companies that relocate to these areas and the establishment of the new industrial parks will improve development opportunities in the area while at the same time removing some of the pressures along the western corridor. A new Science-Based Industry Park has been established at Tainan in the south of Taiwan, specialising in semiconductor and information technologies and in biotechnologies.

Table 4.4. Current Four-Year Plan: 12 major construction projects

#	Project Name	Completion Date	Funds Required	
			NT$ billion	US$ million
1	Improvements to Junior High and Elementary School Facilities	Jun 1997	60	1,818.18
2	Recreation Facilities, Metropolitan Parks and Stadiums				
	Development of Recreation Facilities				
	East Coast Scenic Area	Jun 1996	1.68	50.91
	Penghu Scenic Area	Jun 2001	3.46	104.85
	Matsu Scenic Area	Jun 2000	0.32	9.70
	Kinmen National Park	Jun 2001	2.2	66.67
	Yue-mei Recreation Resort	Jun 2003	9.93	300.91
	Development of Metropolitan Parks				
	Taichung Metropolitan Park	Jun 1998	5.55	168.18
	Kaohsiung Metropolitan Park	Jun 1997	4.72	143.03
	Stadium Construction				
	Domed Stadium in Taichung	Jun 1997	1.7	51.52
	Domed Stadium in Taipei	Jun 1998	6.93	210.00
	Modern Gymnasium in Kaohsiung	Jun 1998	3.32	100.61
3	Improvements to Cultural Facilities				
	Taiwan History Museum	Jun 2001	5	151.52
	County/City Cultural Facilities	Jun 2000	5.25	159.09
	Community Cultural Development	Jun 1999	3.65	110.61
	Conservation of Cultural Assets	Jun 2000	5.43	164.55

Table 4.4 cont'd

4	New Town Development and Public Housing Construction			
	Tanhai New Town Development	Jun 2007	147.8	4,478.79
	Kaohsiung New Town Development	Jun 2007	131.4	3,981.82
	Public Housing Construction	Jun 1997	209.86	6,359.39
5	Improvements of Public Transportation, Construction of Road Systems and Parking Lots			
	Upgrading the East Coast Railway	Jun 2002	48.65	1,474.24
	Purchase of Rolling Stock	Jun 1998	25.42	770.30
	Extensive Road Systems for living perimeters	Jun 2006	475.13	14,397.88
	Public Parking Lots	Jun 1999	65.98	1,999.39
6	Construction of Industrial-Commercial Zones	undecided		
7	Construction of Incineration Plants and Sanitary Landfills			
	Incineration Plants	Jun 2001	101.99	3,090.61
	Sanitary Landfills	Jun 1998	13.2	400.00
8	Improvements to Development and Management of Water Resources			
	Chi-chi Common Diversion	Jun 2000	32.65	989.39
	Nanhua Reservoir Phase 2	Jun 1998	2.79	84.55
	Shilin Hydro Power Project, Liyutan Reservoir	Sept 2001	12.03	364.55
	Diversion Embankment along the Kao-pin River	Jun 1999	3.8	115.15
	Hsingchu Paushan Second Reservoir	Jun 2003	17	515.15
	Management and Conservation of Water Resources	Jun 1998	2.2	66.67
9	High Speed Rail Construction	Jun 2003	441.92	13,391.52

Table 4.4 cont'd

10	Construction of the Kaohsiung MRT System and underground rail systems in Taichung, Tainan and Kaohsiung			
	Kaohsiung MRT System, Phase 1	Dec. 2005	195.2	5,915.15
	Underground Railways in Taichung and Tainan	Jun 2005	97.5	2,954.55
	Underground Railway in Kaohsiung	Jun 2007	123.2	3,733.33
11	Construction of Second Freeway Extension and East-West Expressway			
	Second Freeway Extension	Dec. 2003	525.198	15,915.09
	East-West Expressway in the Western Corridor	Jun 2001	198.52	6,015.76
12	Planning of Central Cross-Island Expressway	Jun 1998	0.64	19.39

In the area of infrastructure development, the government is increasingly moving to involve the private sector in major construction projects on the Build, Operate and Transfer (BOT) system and using a mix of public and private sector funds. The most notable examples of this practice so far are to be found in the energy and transportation sectors. A number of independent power producers are already building privately owned power generation stations in Taiwan while the long-delayed contract to build a High Speed Rail Link providing a very fast train service between Taipei and Kaohsiung has recently been let to a European-backed consortium. A number of other such projects are in the pipeline including the building and operation of a rapid transit rail-link between Taipei and the CKS International Airport in Taoyuan County (projected cost US$1.8 billion).

In a further move to stimulate private sector involvement in public sector construction, the government announced in November 1997 that it would offer special incentives—including tax rebates—to companies that undertook such projects. Furthermore, it would in future be open to the private sector to put proposals for such development direct to government and negotiate terms for construction and operation of facilities on a case by case basis.

GOVERNMENT ASSISTANCE AND INCENTIVES

The Ministry of Economic Affairs is the central government agency that administers Taiwan's macro-economic policy and monitors overall growth targets. Within the Ministry are a number of specialised agencies charged with specific responsibilities for the various aspects of economic planning and implementation.

The Industrial Development Bureau is responsible for the overall coordination of economic development of the major industry sectors including the operation of industrial estates other than the science parks and the export processing zones (which are under separate administrations). The Investment Commission of the MOEA is responsible for administering the *Statute for Investment by Foreign Nationals* and the corresponding statute governing overseas Chinese investment and reviews, and approves all applications for inward investment into the ROC under these statutes.

The Industrial Development and Investment Center and the Technology Transfer Service Center are two organisations also under the MOEA which provide general and introductory consultancy services to foreign companies seeking to invest in Taiwan or who wish to transfer technology to Taiwan.

The government has recently announced that it intends to set up a new office under the Industrial Development Bureau to provide streamlined processing for investment proposals by large-scale corporations that entail a capital commitment of more than US$7 million. In order to stimulate the small and medium business sector, the same facilities will be accorded to smaller firms with investment proposals exceeding US$700,000. This proposal was announced in October 1997 and is expected to be introduced in early 1998.

General Incentives

Foreign invested companies (FIC) established under the SIFN have the same access to local incentives and privileges provided to domestic companies under other statutes and additionally enjoy a number of privileges not accorded to companies without such status:

- Generally, a right of up to 100% foreign ownership. Although this is restricted in some industries, the trend has been towards liberalisation of the restrictions on foreign investment and ownership;
- A waiver of the requirement that the Chairman, Vice Chairman and half the shareholders be Taiwan citizens;

- Full convertibility and the right to remit all profits or interest payments from the local investment;
- The right to repatriate up to 100% of the approved investment capital should ownership of the company be transferred or sold, or upon dissolution of the company;
- A government guarantee against requisition or appropriation by the ROC government within 20 years, provided 45% or more of the shares in the business are held by foreign or overseas Chinese investors. If the foreign investment component is less than 45% of the total, the statute provides for 'reasonable compensation' should appropriation become necessary.

In addition to the specific incentives and protection accorded under the various Statutes for Investment, an FIC company is also accorded preferential status under other acts and statutes including the tax law of the ROC.

Foreign investments in Taiwan are protected from appropriation by government. The Statutes provide for appropriation only in case of national defence needs and after compensation has been paid. In fact, no cases of appropriation have ever been recorded and the risk of such appropriation in the future is considered highly unlikely.

Tax Preferences

Tax preferences for FIC companies include:
- For foreign and overseas Chinese investors in FIC companies, the with-holding rate of income tax on dividends is reduced to 20% (from 35% otherwise);
- Companies operating in the Hsinchu Science-Based Industrial Park are provided with a five-year tax holiday;
- R&D or production equipment not manufactured in Taiwan is exempt from import tariffs in the case of an FIC company;
- Accelerated Depreciation provisions include a two-year depreciation on instruments and equipment for research and development, experimentation and quality inspection, as well for machinery and equipment used for energy conservation or energy substitution. A 50% reduction in depreciation rates is offered for machinery and equipment used by certain designated industries which are being encouraged in order to adjust the local industrial structure and which improve operating scales or production methods;

- Investment tax credits are available for investments made in certain designated areas of Taiwan which are judged to be poor in resources or backward in economic development. Investment tax credits are available for investment or capital increases amounting to NT$25 million (US$900,000), or for the hiring of fifty or more additional personnel. In addition a 20% credit on business income tax is offered on the value of new machinery, equipment or structures;
- A tax credit of 20% is available for investment into important high-tech enterprises designated by the ROC government as the 'Ten Emerging Industries'. These credits are available for new investment or capital increase amounting to NT$200 million (US$7.3 million) or more, or the procurement of NT$100 million or more of machinery and equipment, provided that any project undertaken pursuant to the investment must be completed within three years and the investment maintained for a minimum of two years. For projects within the technical services sector, a reduction of 50% on the above investment or procurement amount applies.
- A tax credit of 20% is available for investments into major investment enterprises where the investment amount is NT$2 million or more, or for procurement of NT$1 million or more of machinery and equipment. Any investment claiming such credits must benefit industrial upgrading and conform to environmental quality standards, New projects must be completed within three years and investments must be maintained for at least two years;
- Tax credits and preferences are available for investments into venture capital enterprises: a tax credit of 20% is allowed for investments made for at least two years and 80% of the income from the investment is exempt from income tax.

Investment Tax Credits

Investment tax credits are allowed in a number of areas, including the procurement of at least NT$600,000 worth of automated production and pollution control equipment or technology (within a single year), for the spending of NT$3 million or more on research and development within a single year, for spending on personnel training or for spending on the establishment of an international brand image. Actual rates of credit are as follows:

- Procurement of automated production equipment attracts a credit of 20% for domestically manufactured equipment or 10% for imported equipment;
- Procurement of automated production equipment attracts a 10% investment tax credit;
- A 20% credit is available for pollution control equipment manufactured locally or 10% for an imported product. In addition acquisition of pollution control technology attracts a 5% credit;
- For spending of more than NT$600,000 a year on personnel training, a credit of 15% is allowed;
- For spending of more than NT$3 million or more per year on establishing an international brand image, a 10% tax credit is given while if the amount is above NT$5 million a year and the label 'It's Very Well Made In Taiwan' is used, the rate is 15%.

A proposal is currently before government to amend the *Statute for Industrial Upgrading* to allow a five-year tax holiday for high-tech companies that float shares in order to raise funds for expansion. This is to be introduced in the context of revisions to the tax law that are intended to consolidate business and personal income taxes while taxing retained earnings at 10%. The tax holiday, as well as other measures, is designed to offset the effects of the changes for firms that are prepared to re-invest.

A further planned measure is the introduction of an investment tax credit for the shareholders of companies that allocate funds for production automation, pollution control and research as well as those investing in government designated industries and/or large scale investment projects.

Loans and Financial Subsidies

In addition to the general financial credits provided by the banking system, a range of specific subsidies and preferential loans are provided for industries and industrial projects which are judged to be integral to the government's efforts at industrial upgrading.

- Loans are available for the development of new products and for the upgrading of traditional industries;
- Preferential loans at low interest rates are available for the purchase of automation facilities and for pollution control facilities;

- Financial subsidies are provided from government funds through the banking system for a number of commercial projects directed at industrial upgrading:
- A 50% subsidy can be requested for the development of new products with a zero interest loan extended to cover the remaining 50% of development cost;
- A subsidy of up to 60% can be approved for whole-plant automation up to a maximum of NT$1million;
- Subsidies amounting to 50% of the cost are available for acquisition of automated production technology up to a maximum of NT$1 million;
- For the acquisition and application of strategic technologies, a subsidy of 50% of the cost is available up to a maximum of NT$1 million;
- For the technological upgrading of traditional industries, up to NT$300,000 is available in the form of a subsidy per project, while for the upgrading of traditional technologies, a 60% subsidy is available to a maximum of NT$2 million.

Table 4.5. Preferential loans

Type of Loan	Max. Finance (NT$)	Max. Repay't Period	Interest Rate
Procurement of Pollution Control Equipment	Up to 100 million: 80% 100–500 million: 60% > 500 million: 50%	10 years, including a 3 year grace period	Chiao Tung Bank's basic interest rate minus 2.875%
Industrial Upgrading	80% or 40 million	10 years, including a 3 year grace period	The Medium Business Bank of Taiwan's basic interest rate minus 2%
	Up to 100 million: 80% >100 million	10 years, including 1–2 years grace period	Bank of Taiwan's basic interest rate minus 0.25%
Procurement of Taiwanese Automated Machinery and Equipment	Up to 100 million: 80% 100–200 million: 75% > 200 million: 70%	7 years, including a 2 year grace period	Rediscount rate plus 0.875%–1%

Table 4.5 cont'd

Procurement of Imported Automated Machinery and Equipment	Up to 100 million: 80% 100–200 million: 75% 200–400 million: 70%	7 years, including a 3 year grace period.	Chiao Tung's basic interest rate minus 2.125%–2.25%
Economic Revitalisation Program	80%		Bank of Taiwan's basic interest rate minus 2.125%–2.25%
Encouragement of Private Participation in Infrastructure Projects	70% or 400 million	10 years, including a 2 year grace period.	Chiao Tung's basic interest rate minus 2.125%–2.25%
Reaccommodation of Foreign Exchange Funds	30%–80%	5 years	Tantamount to the interest rate on US dollars in the inter-bank foreign exchange call market.

Arranging an Investment

Foreign companies or individuals wishing to invest in Taiwan, either to take advantage of the incentive provisions afforded to FIC invested companies or for other reasons, must first obtain government approval. Some of these approvals—such as those pertaining to the banking and insurance industries—are sector specific. Fortunately, a number of Central Government agencies, most noticeably the Industrial Development and Investment Center, provide general guidance to those contemplating an investment, including application forms and processing.

The actual application process itself is not complicated, although the local bureaucracy can be intimidating to the foreigner. Most of the large law and accounting firms maintain specialists able to guide a foreign company through the ROC bureaucracy, and foreign companies contemplating a large-scale investment into Taiwan would certainly be guided by professional advice.

The Investment Commission of the Ministry of Economic Affairs is the body responsible for processing all investment applications. All applications must be accompanied by a statement furnishing details such as:

- Project capital;
- Goods to be sold;
- The names of the shareholders, directors and supervisors.

The processing of investment applications has been steadily streamlined with most applications now processed within two weeks of receipt. The Chairman of the Investment Commission has the delegation to approve investments amounting to NT$200 million or less.

As part of its effort to attract multinational corporations to Taiwan, and especially those that are prepared to establish a regional 'hub' in Taiwan, the Ministry of Economic Affairs has since 1993 maintained a specific program in order to provide special assistance to such companies. The 'strategic alliance' program is coordinated by IDIC and is open to global corporations that sign 'letters of intent' with the Ministry. As of January 1998, a total of 51 multinationals had signed up for the program of which 31 were US-based. With the exception of one company from Canada and one from Australia, all others were Europe-based. No Japanese or other Asian companies had joined the program.

Assistance and services to such companies provided under the 'letter of intent' include joint consultations with government relating to their investment in Taiwan, assistance in resolving any problems or bureaucratic bottlenecks that develop, relaxed visa restrictions on company personnel, including those of residents of the PRC, and courtesy VIP facilities for senior officials at Taipei's international airport. Companies participating in the program must be involved in investments of more than NT$200 million (US$6 million).

As of January 1998, there had been forty investments valued at US$3.4 billion initiated under this program, including an investment of US$1 billion by Texas Instruments and Acer for the establishment of an eight-inch wager fabrication plant, and an investment of US$330 million in the construction of a high resolution CRT plant by Philips.

Table 4.6. Multinational companies signing 'letters of intent' with the Taipei Ministry of Economic Affairs

#	Company	Country	Area of Cooperation
1993			
1	Lucent Technologies Telecommunications Co. Ltd (AT&T)	USA	Communications products and services, network equipment and computer systems
2	General Electric	USA	Nuclear power generation, medical systems, transportation equipment, information and financial services
3	Carpenter Technology Corporation	USA	Manufacture and marketing of specialty metal products
4	Motorola Inc.	USA	Electronic equipment systems and services
5	General Motors Corporation	USA	Design and manufacture of automobiles, parts and components
6	Hicks, Muse Co. Inc/Mills & Partners	USA	Mergers and acquisitions, efficient management
7	ABB Limited	Sweden	Electrical power generation and transmission, transportation, financial services, electronics-related engineering
8	Philips Electronics N.V.	The Netherlands	Consumer electronic products and components, lighting, communications and medical equipment
9	CSR Ltd	Australia	Construction materials, sugar and aluminium production

Table 4.6 cont'd

10	Westinghouse Electric Corp.	USA	Electrical power generation systems, electronic systems, environmental protection services, temperature-controlled transportation, broadcasting
11	Ciba-Geigy Ltd (Novartics)	Switzer-land	Dyestuffs, pharmaceuticals, agricultural chemicals, plastics, additives, pigments, contact lenses, measuring equipment
1994			
12	Ansaldo Volund A/S	Denmark	Incinerator equipment design, production, construction and operational management
13	Texas Instruments Inc.	USA	Semiconductors, computers, defence electronics, metallurgical materials, industrial automation equipment
14	Nalco Fuel Tech	USA	Air Pollution Control Equipment technology, design and manufacturing
15	Hewlett Packard Co.	USA	Hardware manufacturing and marketing; software services, instruments for medical and chemical analysis, electronic testing instrumentation
16	Framatome S.A.	France	Nuclear energy, connectors, mechanical engineering, industrial information technology
17	Du Pont Co.	USA	Chemical fibres, petrochemicals, polymers, agricultural products, electronics, imaging systems, medical products

Table 4.6 cont'd

18	Raychem Corporation	USA	High technology electrochemical materials, special-purpose electric wire and cable for use in aerospace, mass rapid transit, marine industries
19	Finmeccanica	Italy	Aerospace, defence, energy, transportation and automation industries
20	Siemens AG	Germany	Power generation, telecommunications, transportation and medical care equipment, lighting and semiconductor production
21	IBM Corporation	USA	Computer equipment, networking services
1995			
22	Digital Equipment Corporation	USA	Computer equipment, networking services
23	Olivetti	Italy	Personal computers, printers, bank branch automation systems, self-service bank terminals, multivendor services, integrated building systems
24	Bayer AG	Germany	Polymers, organic products, health care, agrochemicals, imaging technologies
25	Northern Telecom Ltd	Canada	Switching networks, multimedia communication systems, transmission equipment, cellular wireless communications systems
26	United Defense L.P.	USA	Armoured combat vehicles and components

Table 4.6 cont'd

27	Electronic Data Systems	USA	Management consulting, systems development, systems integration, systems management, process management
28	Allison Engine Co.	USA	Aerospace engines, industrial engines
29	Allied Signal Inc.	USA	Aerospace, automotive, engineered materials
30	Lockheed Martin Corp.	USA	Aerospace, electronics, information services
31	Northrop Grumman International Inc.	USA	Military aircraft, aerostructures, systems integration, electronics and data systems
32	Dassault Industries Group	France	Aviation, Falcon jets, electronics, automation, telecommunications, investment
33	Southwestern Bell International Inc.	USA	Mobile communications, international telecommunication operations, network services and equipment, yellow pages directories
34	Landis & Gyr	Switzer-land	Optical pay phones and optical stored value cards, electronic building control systems, electricity meters for industrial use
35	Chemetall GMBH	Germany	Lithium compounds
36	Bell Communication Research Inc.	USA	Telecommunications network services
37	Lam Research Corp.	USA	Semiconductor manufacturing equipment

Table 4.6 cont'd

1996			
38	Senecma Corp.	France	Military and civil aircraft engine manufacturing
39	University of Southern California	USA	Establishment of the Asia-Pacific Institute which provides opportunities for partnerships between US and ROC companies through its education, partnership and technology programs
40	Applied Materials Inc.	USA	Semiconductor manufacturing equipment
41	Ferrostaal AG	Germany	Steel products manufacturing
1997			
42	Rockwell	USA	Industrial automation, avionics, semiconductor systems
43	Avesta Sheffield AB	Sweden	Steel products manufacturing
44	Compaq Computer Corporations	USA	Computers
45	Enron	USA	Power generation
46	Tanox Biosystems	USA	Biochemistry
47	Barco	Belgium	Electronics
48	Degussa AG	Germany	Petrochemicals
49	Sikorsky	USA	Aerospace
50	Merck KgaA	Germany	Chemicals for the electronics industry
1998			
51	Textron	USA	Aircraft, industrial, automotive, finance

Investment Restrictions

There are now few areas in which foreign investment is prohibited outright or otherwise limited. The ROC Government maintains two lists—a 'negative' and a 'restricted' list—which detail broad areas where limitations apply. Overt limitations on overseas capital have been reduced substantially in recent times, along with measures to internationalise the local economy in preparation for Taiwan's entry to the World Trade Organisation. Some areas of the economy that remain off-limits to foreigners are open to overseas Chinese. The Industrial Development and Investment Center of the MOEA freely distributes copies of these lists but because of the dynamic nature of the local economy they are constantly changing and specific information should be sought from the IDIC regarding any proposed investment at the time.

In general, there is a blanket prohibition on any foreign investment that threatens public safety or security or which threatens to undermine public morals. Industries which discharge significant quantities of industrial waste are now subject to environmental impact studies and community scrutiny before approval, and highly polluting industries are unlikely to be approved without stringent guarantees relating to waste treatment. Certain publicly owned industries such as oil refining and core telecommunications services, as well as the tobacco and wine monopolies, are also off-limits to foreign participation. The government has, however, indicated its intention to privatise these industries and open them up to international competition, although specific timetables or targets have been set in few cases.

At the end of 1996, foreign equity participation was subject to government restrictions in some 55 industry categories (44 for overseas Chinese) including mining, construction, fertiliser manufacture, domestic aviation, coastal water transport, container terminal operation, professional services, and the banking, insurance and securities industries. Restrictions are being eased progressively, although vested local interests have in many cases slowed the pace of liberalisation.[8] A revised, and much shortened, list is due to be published early in 1998.

---

[8] Perhaps the most notable example of this is the construction industry, areas of which are widely reported to be under gangland influence. Despite the shoddy nature of much construction activity in Taiwan, local influence and political kickbacks have served to keep foreign engineering and construction companies from gaining any kind of independent foothold in Taiwan.

In keeping with local aspirations to develop Taipei as a regional operations centre, liberalisation of the financial, services, transportation and telecommunications sectors has been given top priority.

Foreign banks, insurance companies and securities brokerage firms can operate in Taipei subject to approval from the Ministry of Finance and, where required, the Securities Exchange Commission. Since early 1997 individual foreign investors have been able to purchase local stocks along with foreign institutional investors.

CHAPTER 5

FOUNDATIONS FOR SUCCESSFUL BUSINESS

Whether coming to Taiwan on assignment with a major corporation or as a small business person requiring a local presence, an understanding of the way business is organised and conducted in Taiwan and approaching the market accordingly is fundamental to long-term business success. Like all countries, Taiwan has its own way of doing things and traps abound for the unwary. The wise business person will approach with caution and with a clear understanding of the available options. Establishing an appropriate local business structure and obtaining an understanding of prospective business partners and colleagues should be at the top of the priority list.

While establishing a legal presence in Taiwan requires the services of a trained accountant or lawyer (and there are many firms specialising in such services) a basic understanding of both local custom and practices is essential, as is a basic knowledge of the practicalities of 'setting up shop'. These issues are the topic of this and the following chapters.

Perhaps one of the most noteworthy features of the local business scene in Taiwan is its dynamic and fluid nature. This is a country dominated by small business and entrepreneurs.[1] Anyone who has dealt with the small business sector over any period of time will have noted the rapidity with which new companies are established, some to prosper, others to wither in a matter of months and (while often remaining as legally registered business enterprises) to disappear.

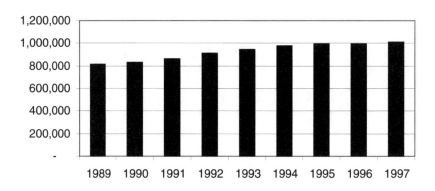

Figure 5a. Total number of registered business units in Taiwan

While Taiwan has its share of large corporations and State-owned enterprises, the economy is largely driven by Taiwan's small and medium business sector. As of December 1997 there were over one million registered business units—in a nation of only 21 million people. More than 50% of the total (600,000) were engaged in general commerce. This group was four times larger than the next largest sector—manufacturing—with 148,908 registered units.

Small and medium businesses have underpinned Taiwan's economic development from the outset and unlike Korea (and to some extent, Thailand), the risk is far more broadly spread in Taiwan. It is sometimes said that the Taiwanese became rich in spite of the KMT and not because of it. Certainly, in enfranchising the Taiwanese population economically in the

---

[1] As is noted in Chapter 9, only 55% of all income received in Taiwan is in the form of wages and salaries. The balance of income received represents various forms of entrepreneurial income.

1970s, the government opted for a strategy of 'managed liberalisation'. One facet of that strategy was that the KMT itself became a large-scale investor and often a proxy for the government. The extent of this business empire which persists until today has already been noted in Chapter 1. Secondly, Taiwan's business incorporation laws were designed to ensure that small enterprise remains just that. The requirements for minimum numbers of shareholders, and the requirement to establish separate companies for different business activities, were part of a deliberate 'divide and rule' strategy to put hurdles in the way of local business people who might otherwise grow to challenge the power of the elite. Some have certainly prospered and grown; companies such as Evergreen are prime examples. However, Taiwan remains at heart a nation of small business.

Most businesses are established by individuals and often for a specific purpose. Small businesses are often undercapitalised, there being little correlation between registered capital (as recorded on the business licence) and true asset value of a company. Entrepreneurs abound in Taiwan but separating the good from the bad, let alone the downright ugly, can sometimes be a difficult task. A starting point is to understand the legal requirements that govern Taiwan's business sector and this is the subject of the following section.

THE LEGAL REQUIREMENTS

The majority of licensed local businesses can be categorised into three general classes that correspond to sole proprietors, limited (proprietary) companies and companies limited by shares (limited liability companies). Companies are structured in compliance with the *Companies Act of the ROC* and come under national (ROC) law, while sole proprietorship businesses fall under Taiwanese provincial and local regulations.

The Taiwanese depend closely on family and kinship groups and by far the majority of companies registered in the ROC are the local equivalent of proprietary companies. In many cases, especially within the small business sector which accounts for the overwhelming majority, the officially reported shareholdings will be notional, as will be the registered capital. Neither is a reliable guide to the asset value or control of a company. Because of the minimum numbers of shareholders prescribed by statute (see below) it is common practice for local business people seeking to register a new company to do so by distributing shares among immediate family members and/or close friends. These may or may not have any genuine role in the business. Traditional seals (chops) are routinely used on business documents rather than signatures and, in many instances, the person who holds the chops holds the company. Often, especially in companies that subcontract to government or to one of the major corporations, the true owner may be a government official or an employee of the corporation, but this will be disguised.

The exclusion of outsiders—other than trusted employees—from the business often serves to limit the accumulation of business capital. It is also common in Taiwan (and the system unwittingly promotes it) for employees with aspirations to operate a business of their own to acquire knowledge within an existing and successful business and to take the first available opportunity to separate from their employer and establish their own entity in direct competition. Foreigners are often accosted by employees who offer to cut side deals. Such practices are common in any society, of course, but in Taiwan they are more pronounced than in many other places. Taipei and Taiwan are both characterised by whole streets and indeed whole communities based on a single industry and in almost all cases, this situation has been seeded by one successful business in the area which all others have tried to emulate.

There are therefore sound commercial reasons for any circumspect business person to keep tight control both on the shareholdings of their company as well as the key decision-making personnel within it. This often means that the second in charge of a company will either be another (albeit) junior member of the family or a close friend where a bond of mutual trust and mutual loyalty has already been established. In any event it will be rare among private companies that this family or kinship bond does not exist among the top personnel.

For foreigners seeking to do business with such Taiwanese companies the major implication is the need to be assured of the *bona fides* and credit-worthiness of the local business partner. Claims should never be accepted at face value. Credit checking agencies are available in Taipei and are able to perform appropriate checks on potential business associates. This is discussed further later in this chapter. For major business dealings, while legal remedies are often limited, international law firms and legal consultants can advise on additional precautions that can be taken to ensure business dealings commence—and continue—on a sound footing.

For foreigners or foreign companies seeking to establish their own legal presence, forming a local company often appears at first sight to be an attractive option. While this is certainly allowed under ROC law, provided the foreign entity (who can be an individual or local person) has a majority of local partners, it should be borne in mind that for domestic companies the

Responsible Person (defined below) must always be an ROC national and that person has ultimate control over the company and the disposition of its assets. Unless one is dealing with Taiwanese partners who are well known and totally trusted, internal business disputes can often bring down such business arrangements—usually to the detriment of the foreign party who is often unfamiliar with the intricacies of ROC law and its requirements.

COMPANY DEFINITIONS

ROC Company Law recognises and governs four classes of domestic companies as well as foreign companies authorised to do business in the ROC as follows:

- An Unlimited Company denotes a company organised by two or more shareholders who bear unlimited joint liability for the company;
- A Limited Company denotes a company organised by no less than five and no more than 21 shareholders with each shareholder being liable for the company to an amount limited to the capital contributed by him/her;
- An Unlimited Liability Company with Limited Liability Shareholders denotes a company organised by one or more shareholders of unlimited liability and one or more shareholders of limited liability,
- A Company Limited by Shares denotes a company organised by seven or more shareholders with the total capital of the company being divided into shares and each shareholder being liable in the amount of the shares subscribed by him/her;
- A Foreign Company is a company organised in accordance with the laws of a foreign country and authorised to transact business within the ROC.

Sole Proprietors

For ROC nationals, a sole proprietorship is the simplest type of business to establish and operate. Sole proprietors require only a minimal capital base and do not require formal registered shareholdings. Sole proprietors are required to carry a business licence issued by the provincial or city government administration within the area in which the business is located. The business licence specifies the permitted lines of business, which have to be in conformity with any zoning restrictions within the area of business. Most retail establishments as well as much of the service industry in Taiwan are operated as sole proprietorship businesses and often these can be of substantial size.

Foreigners cannot operate sole proprietorship businesses legally in Taiwan. Sole proprietors can only be established by ROC nationals who must submit to the local business administration body the national identity card of the business proprietor, articles defining the business scope (similar to the articles of association required of companies but less complex), evidence of title or rental contract for the business premises—to ensure the business falls within the scope of zoning restrictions—as well as any special or professional licences required of a particular business (medical, architectural and engineering services are all examples where such licences are required).

Sole proprietors are required by law to display their business registration certificate within their business premises. Any foreign company dealing with a sole proprietorship (as with any other form of business) on a regular basis should as a first precaution sight the appropriate licences held by the business and, as an added precaution, take a copy of the licence—especially in contractual situations.

Registered Companies—ROC Company Law

ROC Company Law as amended in 1990 recognises four classes of domestic company although in practice only two are of importance. These are, firstly, the Limited Company governed by Chapter III of the Law (and which broadly equates to a Proprietary Limited Company in the Australian system). Secondly there is the Company Limited by Shares which is governed by Chapter V of the same Law (and which broadly equates to a Limited Liability Company in Australia).

A Limited Company is required to have a minimum of five shareholders and a maximum of 21. The liability of any individual shareholder is limited to the amount of their contributed capital (*Article 2.2*). A Company Limited by Shares requires a minimum of seven shareholders with no maximum set down in law; total subscribed capital must be divided into shares with each shareholder liable in the amount of shares subscribed (*Article 2.4*).

Two other forms of Unlimited Liability Company provided for in the *Company Law* are not common and are not dealt with here. In the case of Limited Companies, *Article 98* requires that at least one half of the shareholders should be Chinese nationals domiciled within the territory of the ROC and that such shareholders should together contribute more than half of the total capital of the company. In the case of a Company Limited by

Shares, *Article 128* requires that more than half of the founder shareholders ('promoters') must be domiciled within the ROC.

Companies are required under *Article 8* of the *Company Law* to nominate a Responsible Person who must be an ROC national and who is legally liable for the conduct of business operations of the company. For limited companies, the Responsible Person must be one of the directors of the company, while for Companies Limited by Shares the definition is usually broader and includes promoters, managers and supervisors of the company.

The means of appointing managerial officers of a company are set out in *Article 29*. In the case of a Limited Company, managerial officers are decided by a majority of shareholders while for a Company Limited by Shares the managers are appointed by a majority of the directors.

Limited Companies must have at least one and no more than three directors (who must also be shareholders) while Companies Limited by Shares must have a minimum of three directors as well as a supervisor appointed by the shareholders. The role of the supervisor is to protect the interests of the shareholders at the board level. The supervisor is empowered to review the company's books and to report independently to the shareholders and, if necessary, to the regulatory authorities should any discrepancies be found in the conduct of company business. In practice, unless the company is listed on the Taipei stock exchange or has significant external corporate shareholders, the role of supervisor is often an honorary one. It is, however, a potentially powerful position designed to protect shareholders who are not represented at the board level.

Companies are required to notify the appropriate ministry of any changes to the scope of operations of the company, business address, shareholdings, responsible person or directors. In the case of the central government, the Ministry of Economic Affairs administers the regulatory requirements of the *Company Law* while at the provincial and local level this task is delegated to the Department of Reconstruction and the Bureau of Reconstruction respectively. Directors are normally nominated for a term of three years.

Table 5.1. ROC companies: a quick comparison

	Limited Company	*Company Limited by Shares*
ROC Company Law	Chapter 3	Chapter 5
Shareholders	Minimum of 5	Minimum of 7
	Maximum of 21	No maximum

Table 5.1 cont'd

Directors	Minimum of 1 Maximum of 3	A Board of Directors is required with a minimum of 3 directors plus a supervisor
Authorised Capital	Minimum of NT$500,000	Minimum of NT$1 million
Public Subscriptions	Not allowed	Allowed
Share Certificates	Not compulsory	Required to be issued within 3 months of incorporation
Share Transfer	Not permitted without the written consent of a majority of the other shareholders	Share certificates may be transferred; certain limitations apply to directors.
Company Documentation Required to be Filed	Articles of Association Shareholders Roster Name of Director	Articles of Incorporation Shareholders Roster Issued shares 'In-kind' contributions Expenses of incorporation Total number of special shares Directors and supervisors

CAPITAL REQUIREMENTS

Article 100 states that the minimum capital of a company shall be as decided by decree and according to the nature of business operations. These amounts are stipulated for a number of specific company operations in *Article 2* of Appendix 1 of the Law and are as follows (approximate US dollar amounts at current exchange rates are given in brackets):

A limited company or a company limited by shares which operates an enterprise engaged in any one of the following businesses, shall have the minimum amount of paid-in capital as indicated respectively herein below:

1. *Public housing, construction for selling or rent: NT$25 million (US$750,000);*
2. *Business building construction for selling or rent: NT$35 million (US$1.06 million);*

3. *Off-shore fishery: NT$4 million* (US$120,000);
4. *Automobile production: NT$100 million* (US$3 million);
5. *Tourist hotels: international tourist hotel: NT$65 million* (US$2 million); *and general tourist hotel: NT$26 million* (US$790,000);
6. *Management of construction business: NT$50 million* (US$1.5 million).

Where a company operates a business other than those listed in the preceding paragraph, the minimum amount of paid-in capital shall be NT$500,000 if it is a limited company or NT$1million if it is a company limited by shares. However, if a higher amount of minimum paid-in capital is prescribed by the competent authority in charge of enterprises, such criterion shall govern.

It is important to note that while the *Company Law* sets out a number of specific capitalisation requirements, these are not the only specifications. Where specific types of company operations are regulated by other codes and government agencies, additional regulations may apply. This is particularly true in the financial services sector: banks, insurance and securities companies are all subject to specific capitalisation requirements.

BUSINESS DOCUMENTATION

The formal documentation required of ROC registered companies will depend on the nature of the business being conducted. All businesses whether or not they are incorporated as companies are required to obtain business registration certificates and the business certificate can only be issued once all other formalities have been completed.

Company and Business Licences

All registered companies must obtain a company licence issued by the Ministry of Economic Affairs or its delegated agency. In areas under the control of the provincial or municipal governments, the quaintly named provincial or municipal Bureau of Reconstruction handles registrations and issues corporate licences on behalf of the Ministry of Economic Affairs. The company licence specifies the scope of business operations of the company and its permitted business lines. Company activities regulated under separate laws (including those of foreign companies) must obtain additional licences from the regulatory authority administering the law. Banks and other financial institutions are required to obtain such licences from the Ministry of Finance and, in certain instances, from the Securities Exchange Commission (if dealing in securities); foreign trading companies are licensed by the Board of Foreign Trade, educational institutions are licensed by the Ministry of Education, etc.

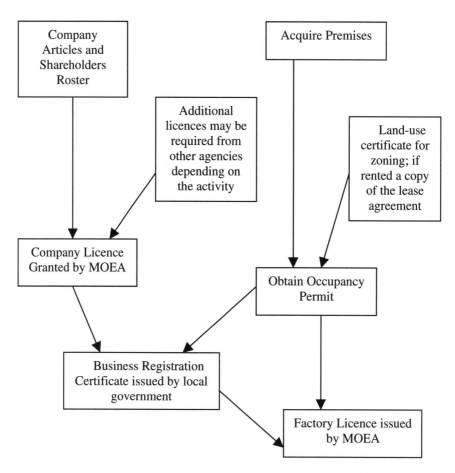

Figure 5b. Flow chart of documents required for company registration

Companies engaged in manufacturing are, in most instances, exempt from specific licensing requirements but must ensure that their activities are conducted in a designated industrial zone. Generally, manufacturing activities are prohibited in commercial and residential areas. Likewise companies not engaged in manufacturing are (in theory) prohibited from establishing offices in industrial areas.

The business registration certificate (business licence) is issued not by a central government ministry but by the provincial or (in the case of Taipei and Kaohsiung) municipal governments. Business licences will not be granted unless the business is operating in conformity with local zoning requirements.

Company and business licences in Taiwan generally include details of the date of legal incorporation of the business, the name of the Responsible Person, the level of capitalisation and the purpose for which the licence is granted, as outlined in the articles of the company.

Company and business licences may be re-issued from time to time and always when there is a change in the registered capital, Responsible Person or business address. At such times old licences are surrendered although registration amendment cards, detailing changes to the shareholders and directors, are generally retained and company histories can be traced in this manner or through copies of these documents filed with and retained by the Bureau of Reconstruction.

The business licence is also the basic document through which a 'unified taxation number' is granted to a business. This number is used on all invoices and receipts as a means of identifying (provincial) business and (national) company tax payable.

Factory Licences

Manufacturing companies operating in legally defined industrial zones are also required to obtain a factory licence issued by the Ministry of Economic Affairs. However, such licences can only be granted if the factory is operating in such a zone. If a factory is located on land officially zoned for other purposes (which is often the case, especially in rural areas) the business operates without the benefit of a factory licence and is technically operating illegally. In theory such businesses could be forced to relocate or close their operations, although in practice this rarely happens if the business is otherwise operating within the law.

As of December 1997 there were more than 96,000 registered factories in Taiwan. Estimates of unregistered factories vary widely but the number could be as high as 40% of the total.

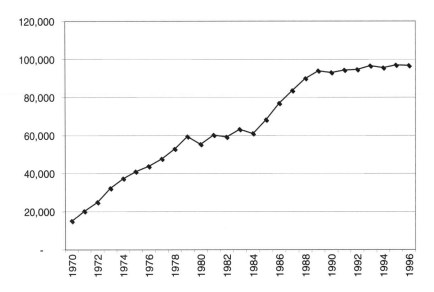

Figure 5c. Total registered factories in Taiwan area

Professional Licences

Proprietors of businesses of a professional or semi-professional nature (such as engineering consulting companies, health clinics and hospitals, etc.) are also required to hold an appropriate professional licence issued by the *Examination Yuan* of the ROC. Unlike a special business licence, which is issued to a corporate entity engaging in specific business lines regulated by law, the professional licence is issued to an individual on the basis of a government examination and corresponds to professional registration required of certain professions in other countries. Obtainment of a professional licence is mandatory for any professional seeking to set up an independent business practice, although it is not uncommon in Taiwan for entrepreneurs to rent the professional licences of others in order to engage in business. Although illegal, this practice is quite widespread in some areas such as pharmacies. The druggist behind the counter proffering advice and dispensing OTC drugs may hold no more than a high school diploma. Any foreigner doing business with a professional firm such as an architectural or engineering consultancy should, as a basic precaution, identify the names on the professional licences to ensure that those contracting for work are suitably qualified.

Roster of Directors and Shareholders

This document is required of all Limited and Share Limited Companies and records details of all formal shareholdings within the company. As the issue of share certificates is not common practice, it is often the only formal record of the company structure.

A complete shareholders roster is usually included with or appended to the articles of association or incorporation of a company. Additionally, a Registration Establishment or Registration Amendment Card has to be filed with the Ministry of Economic Affairs or its delegate upon any change to the Roster of Directors and Managers, share capital or registered business address.

Foreign Companies

Chapter V11 of *ROC Company Law* governs the operation of foreign companies in Taiwan that wish to establish a local presence in one form or another. No foreign company can apply for recognition in Taiwan without being incorporated and having operations in its own country. Foreign companies may only operate in Taiwan upon being granted recognition and certification in Taiwan (*Article 371*).

In practice, a foreign company wishing to establish an identifiable and legal presence in the ROC for commercial purposes can do so in one of three ways.

The simplest form of legal presence takes the form of a Representative or Liaison Office. A Liaison Office is established in accordance with *Article 386* of *ROC Company Law* and is registered with the Ministry of Economic Affairs. A Liaison Office may undertake legal acts on behalf of its parent company such as contract quotation, negotiation, acceptance of orders or purchasing activities, but it is not empowered to hire staff or to undertake domestic commercial activity on its own behalf. Any local invoicing must be done through the overseas parent company or through a local agent acting on behalf of the liaison office.

Applications to establish a legal representation are to be filed by a Board or Management Committee member or shareholder of the home company along with the necessary documentation appointing the Representative, who should be either an ROC citizen or a person holding an Alien Residence Certificate.

Article 386—Representative Offices

A foreign company which, having no intention to set up a branch office to transact business within the territory of the Republic of China has not applied for recognition in the Republic of China, but designates a representative for the performance of juristic acts relating to its business in the territory of the Republic of China, shall file a report for record with the central authority setting forth the following particulars:

1. *The name, class of company, nationality and location of the company;*
2. *Its authorised capital and the date of its incorporation;*
3. *The business of the company and the juristic acts relating to its business to be done by its representative in the territory of the Republic of China; and*
4. *The name, nationality and domicile or residence of its designated litigious and non-litigious representative in the Republic of China.*
5. *The aforesaid representative shall, from time to time, be required to reside in the territory of the Republic of China, the company shall establish a representative's office and report its location in accordance with the aforesaid provisions.*
6. *The documents filed for record, as specified in preceding paragraphs 1 and 2, shall be notarised by the authority of its own country or by a consular officer or a designated agency at the place where its representatives shall perform the juristic acts to do business or at the place where its representative office is located.*
7. *A foreign company may not set up a representative office within the territory of the Republic of China unless an application is filed for designation of the representative for record.*

Foreign nationals cannot obtain an Alien Registration permit on the basis of their status as a representative of a foreign company unless the overseas company was registered in the ROC prior to 1981.

An overseas company that requires a full commercial presence in the ROC can establish either a Branch Office or a Branch Company. A Branch Office is a company established under ROC law which is a wholly owned subsidiary of the parent company.

A company established as a branch of a foreign company must obtain a licence from the Ministry of Economic Affairs as well as comply with any licensing conditions specific to the class of company (see above). Once licensing formalities are completed, a Branch Company is permitted to trade under the same basic terms and conditions as a locally owned company. A

Branch Company is taxed on its earnings in Taiwan but earnings of the parent company or other Branch Companies of the parent are not subject to local tax.

A third means by which an overseas company may undertake business in Taiwan is through establishing a Joint Venture Company with a local partner. Joint Venture Companies operate much the same as local companies and in normal circumstances, foreign equity is limited to 50% of the total capital. Joint ventures are most appropriately established in situations involving the licensing of technology in Taiwan for local manufacture where the existence of a legally registered joint venture provides a means of protecting intellectual or other property rights.

As explained elsewhere, foreign invested companies established under certain other ROC statutes enjoy certain privileges not afforded companies in general.

In spite of aspirations to become a regional operations centre, Taiwan has no special regulations in place to govern regional management companies at the present time, although (as discussed in Chapter 4) the Ministry for Economic Affairs has, since 1993, operated a program designed to provide administrative assistance to foreign multinationals seeking to establish a regional operating base in Taiwan.

Foreigners or foreign companies requiring a formal presence in the ROC would be well advised to consult with either an international law or accounting firm as to their requirements and not rely on any local advice that might be offered.

CONDUCTING BUSINESS, CREDIT AND OTHER INFORMATION CHECKS IN TAIWAN

The adage 'buyer beware' certainly applies as much to the conduct of business relationships in Taiwan as it does anywhere and in an age of global business where prospective partners may be half a world away, the conducting of basic background checks on a prospective supplier or business partner is part of the necessary 'due diligence' process.

Many Chinese will not deal with people they do not know and trust. Family and kinship groups as well as other long-term relationships, often extending back to childhood, play a much more important role in the Chinese business sphere than they normally do in Western societies.

Foreign business people commencing business in Taiwan do not have this luxury. There are a few precautions that can be observed to minimise business and/or employment risks.

Employees

Resumés can look impressive as can business reference letters. There is a thriving local industry in writing resumés and forging employment reference letters. In the hiring of staff, especially for important or sensitive positions, many companies will use the services of an outside employment agency. However, if for one reason or another this is not practicable, there are a few basic rules to follow.

- Always ask to see originals of certificates; especially educational certificates;
- Most employees, especially those in clerical or manufacturing positions, will have had labour insurance paid for by their employer for many years prior to the introduction of the national health insurance scheme. Each such employee will have a 'labour insurance card' that they take from position to position and which records the name of the employer and the period of employment (or, more accurately, the period during which the company insured the person). Such cards provide a useful cross-correlation with claimed employment experience;
- If reference letters are produced which speak in glowing terms of the applicant's capabilities it is always a good idea to cross-check with the company and person that issued the letter. Sometimes, even when the letterhead is genuine, the name on the letter may be false. Be especially cautious of letters that carry a chop but no name or signature;
- For NT$250, any ROC national can obtain a Certificate of No Criminal Conviction, in English and from the local police department. For some positions, it may be appropriate to ask for such a record;
- Credit checking on individuals without their knowledge is not permitted in Taiwan under the *Consumer Data Protection Law*; however, as credit cards are becoming increasingly popular, most applicants, especially those in the younger age group, will have at least one credit card. A government-sponsored national credit agency does exist and is one of the best in Asia. Banks have access to credit data but individuals do not. However, it may be possible for the applicant to obtain such a personal check through the bank that issued them with the credit card, provided there is a valid reason to do so.

Businesses

There are a number of companies in Taiwan that offer 'credit reporting' or 'business investigation' services. In fact many of these are not what they seem. A number of such companies deal primarily in property appraisals for the banks—with varying degrees of professionalism—while others are primarily engaged in debt collection or private detective work.

Five companies or organisations offer genuine business checking and/or credit information services.

Asian Company Profiles

FBR Building,
No. 5, Lane 190, Chung Shan North Road, Section 7
Taipei, Taiwan
Tel: 886 2 28754355
Fax: 886 2 28754360; 28735502

Asian Company Profiles (ACP) is a subsidiary of the FBR Group, which is Australian–American-owned and which has been engaged in the provision of on-line credit information services in Asia for almost 20 years. ACP maintains a database of more than 500,000 companies in 18 Asian countries. Database information can be obtained at varying levels including 'basic', 'detailed' and 'in-depth'. Within Asia, access to the database can be obtained through the Asian Credit Information Services network and globally through the on-line data carriers such as DIALOG, FT, Reuters and Lexis-Nexis. Cost of access depends on the type of report selected but is relatively inexpensive.

Customised off-line services are also available from the FBR Group, as are market research and other services.

China Credit Information Services

5F, 115 Tung Hsin Road, Taipei
Tel: 886 2 27653266
Fax: 886 2 27656033

China Credit is a well-established company that has offered credit and investigatory services for more than 30 years. The company specialises in commercial credit reporting, real and moveable property appraisals and market research. Credit reports are custom-prepared and relatively expensive.

China Credit also has an established reputation for the conduct of consumer behavioural studies and market research.

CETRA (China External Trade Development Council)

International Trade Building
333 Keelung Road, Section 1, Taipei
Tel: 886 2 2725 1111
Fax: 886 2 2725 1314

CETRA is the government-owned and operated trade promotion bureau based at the Taipei World Trade Center. The trade database maintained by CETRA is based on information held by the government on those companies that hold export licences. Computerised data printouts are inexpensive but limited in terms of information available.

Dun & Bradstreet Taiwan

12F, 188 Nanking East Road, Section 2, Taipei
Tel: 886 2 2756 2922
Fax: 886 2 2749 1936

Dun & Bradstreet is relatively new to Taiwan, having set up its Branch Office in 1992. Lacking in-depth local knowledge, and having terminated contracts with its previous country partners, D&B has concentrated so far on educational and debt collection services, though it is now moving into the more traditional credit services at the high end of the market in terms of price.

Edwards International Limited

188 Fu Hsing South Road, Taipei, Taiwan
Tel: 886 2 2709 8981
Fax: 886 2 2708 3563

Edwards International is another well established local company that specialises in corporate credit checking services and investigative work on behalf of export insurance groups and other international clients, mainly in Europe and Asia. Edwards reports are also custom-produced and this is reflected in their price.

CHAPTER 6

SOME PRACTICAL ISSUES

Taiwan, and especially Taipei, is a relatively high-cost centre both for general living and for business operations. Any company considering establishing an office in Taipei will need to be aware of current market conditions as they affect expatriate business operations.[1]

The cost of living for expatriates in Taiwan is among the highest in Asia, and foreigners living in Taiwan believe that the general rate of inflation experienced locally by the foreign community is about double the rate of inflation in the community as a whole. The influx of foreign businesses into Taiwan continues, placing a strain on an already crowded office accommodation problem in Taipei's central business areas (see below). This,

---

[1]Issues relating to employment conditions, and in particular expatriate working conditions in Taiwan, are summarised here while local labour market conditions are dealt with in the following chapter. General issues relating to living in Taiwan are dealt with in Chapter 16.

139

when added to the high cost of maintaining expatriates in Taiwan, has forced many overseas companies to localise their operations as quickly as possible.

Conditions in Taipei are changing rapidly and for the better, although it still lacks many of the amenities that would be expected in a truly international city. Generally speaking (and leaving aside the very large Japanese community which tends to merge into the local population), the Western community is small and specialised. While Taiwan is seeking a role as a regional centre, it has not yet achieved this and is therefore neither a natural focus nor meeting ground for foreign business people (except for missionaries and teachers). The foreign community profile in Taipei is very different from that which would be found in places such as Hong Kong or Singapore. This places particular strains on families who lack many of the normal support mechanisms found in a truly international city and who have to cope with daily problems of dealing with tradespeople etc. Foreign spouses in Taiwan generally require a lot of support.

The shortcomings of life in Taipei are felt even more acutely once outside of the main metropolitan centre. Life styles in the provincial cities (and even in some areas of Taipei City and County) are still very traditional.

The selection of an expatriate executive who can cope with the local environment should therefore be given very careful consideration by companies seeking to post staff to Taiwan. With care and an attitude attuned to the local environment, life in Taiwan can be most enjoyable—but it requires a willingness to adapt and overcome challenges as well as sympathy for, and patience with, a culture that is quite different to that experienced in most Western countries (or in Hong Kong for that matter).

An appropriate allowance package (see below) can go some way to cushioning the impact of a totally different lifestyle, but unless the expatriate is attuned to and accepts the local way of life, monetary compensation alone cannot produce a desirable result.

GENERAL EXPATRIATE WORKING CONDITIONS IN TAIPEI

Conditions of service in Taiwan differ widely, between companies with general managers of Branch Companies generally enjoying the highest conditions while technical and personnel and engineers often fare less well. The following are the major elements of a typical package for an expatriate living in Taiwan.

Cost of living adjustment

There are companies and organisations that regularly monitor conditions locally and throughout the Asian region, and which recommend appropriate salary packages. The larger accounting firms offer similar services. A general 'cost of living/location' allowance in Taiwan can often amount to between 20% and 25% of base salary.

Housing allowance

Unless dictated by work location, most expatriates live in one of four communities in the Taipei area: Yang Ming Shan, Tienmou, Wellington Heights (Peitou) or East Taipei (in the vicinity of the World Trade Centre). The first three locations are all co-located in the northern suburbs of Taipei and are conveniently located near the American and European schools as well as shops which cater for expatriate personnel. For families with young children, these really represent the only choice.

According to local realty companies specialising in expatriate placements, the cost of accommodation can vary widely. Generally, for a Chief Executive with a family, between NT$100,000 and NT$250,000 per month should be budgeted. For a single person the range would generally be between NT$80,000 and NT$130,000. Three months' deposit is the norm and a commission is payable to the realty company—usually half of one month's rental. At present, apartment rental costs are reasonably stable and in some instances have even declined slightly.

Engineers employed by the MTR and similar government projects fare less well and are often co-located with the project. Their base housing allowance is generally between NT$25,000 and NT$80,000 depending on the area of Taipei. Generally, much better value for money can be had by relocating to one of the outlying or newer residential areas of Taipei. A number of residential community estates have been established which offer single unit houses, often with small gardens, and with recreation facilities such as swimming pools and tennis courts. However, these estates really cater to professional Chinese rather than to foreigners and people new to Taiwan or not understanding the language may feel isolated by moving to such areas, even though the quality of life offered is often better than in other places.[2]

---

[2] Housing is discussed in more detail in Chapter 16.

Education

Most English-speaking families send their children to either the American School in Taipei or to the British Section of the European School. Typical costs are given in Chapter 16.

Club memberships

Most expatriate packages include at least one club membership. The most popular are the American Club (with sports and family facilities) or the Bankers Club. Both clubs operate a minimum monthly billing fee. Again current membership prices are provided in Chapter 16.

Car and driver

Most companies provide a car for their executive and some companies also employ a driver who is available to assist families when not required by the company. A driver typically costs around NT$40,000 per month, depending on hours worked. Self-drive in Taipei is not really a problem aside from parking in the city during working hours.

Leave entitlements

Most expatriates enjoy between four and six weeks' annual leave. Return economy class air fares to base for all family members are usually provided.

Miscellaneous

Home help is available in Taipei. Many families recruit Filipino domestic helpers who live within the family home, while others recruit part-time help from the local market. Labour costs for live-in Filipino domestics are around NT$16,000 per month plus board and accommodation. For daily household help, the cost is typically between NT$1,800 and NT$2,000 per day.

Visas

Confusion about the granting of visas for expatriate staff continues to be a source of conflict between foreign businesses and the government. Foreign business groups often complain that rules are difficult to understand and inconsistently applied. The Council of Labour Affairs has in the past been particularly hostile to the employment of foreigners in Taiwan, although attitudes are slowly changing and, as noted in the previous chapter, a relaxation and streamlining of foreign professional employment procedures is high on the government agenda. Matters will hopefully improve although many expatriates continue to face difficulties in obtaining long term visas for Taiwan.

For the present, visas routed through the Ministry of Economic Affairs for top company officials tend to be the least problematic and there is usually little difficulty in obtaining a residence visa for a chief executive. Work visas for officials below that level require negotiation with government officials; in practice, there are no fixed guidelines.

THE COMMERCIAL PROPERTY MARKET

Despite a year of political uncertainties and an economy which has still not totally emerged from a near recession in 1996, the commercial real estate market in Taipei is again starting on an upward trend. That is good news for landlords or developers with property for sale; bad news however for any overseas company seeking to set up or expand operations in Taipei.

Since the end of 1996, demand for prime office space has becomes strong and vacancy rates in Taipei's dispersed central business district appear to have fallen dramatically over the past two years. Continued economic liberalisation, particularly within the financial sector, has played a major role in soaking up available space as new banking, insurance and securities companies seek to stake their claim in the local market. A number of existing players, particularly those with retail operations such as Citibank and the Standard Chartered Bank, have been expanding quickly while there is still space to do so.

With little new building activity under way at present, a squeeze is definitely coming. Office vacancy rates at the end of 1997 had dropped to around 3.5% overall. At the end of 1996 it was a little under 7% and stood at 18% two years before that. Crude numbers do not tell the full story however. Within this total, vacant Grade A office space has fallen to less than 2% of the available total and just over 1% is available for lease (compared to 4.4% at the end of 1996). The remainder is offered for sale only. Some prime locations, particularly those in Eastern Taipei, have zero vacancies.

With current demand for prime space running at a little over 1.44 million square feet (40,000 pings) per year the situation will worsen before it gets better. [3] Supply of quality office space in Taipei in the immediate future will not only be well below current anticipated demand, but the space that is expected to become available in the short term will generally be in less

---

[3] All measurements in Taiwan are in the Chinese unit of 'ping'. One ping is equivalent to 35.58 square feet (approximately 3.45 square metres).

favoured and highly congested areas. In 1997 only 17,600 pings of Grade A office space became available and much of it was in secondary or suburban locations. A further 19,000 of lower graded space was also added.

Commercial property rentals are already creeping upwards. Prime rentals peaked in 1990, the height of the boom years, before falling sharply in subsequent years. By 1994, space which in 1990 would have rented for an average NT$2,800 per ping per month, had fallen to a low of NT$2,200. Prices are now rising back towards 1990 levels. Lease terms are also moving in favour of landlords: whereas only two years ago the standard deposit (key money) on new office space was the equivalent of between two and four months' rent, six months' deposit is now common. For long-term leases, rental escalation clauses have also tended upwards—from 5% per annum to between 6% and 8% now being asked. The asking price for Grade A space varies considerably from area to area within the central business district.

Generally, highest prices are to be found on Tun Hua North Road in the eastern area of Taipei close to the domestic airport. Rentals in this part of the city run from between NT$2,000 to as high as NT$3,000 per ping per month. The lowest prices are to be found in the older properties along Keelung and Nanking East Roads. The space available in these (generally congested) areas is to be had for between NT$1,700 to NT$2,200 per month.

Nevertheless, by comparison with other Asian markets, Taipei still appears to offer value for money. In its third quarterly market survey for 1997, Richard Ellis ranked Taipei eighth among twelve Asian cities in terms of 'total occupation costs'.

The Taiwan property market has always been driven by short-term speculation rather than long-term capital gain or income return. Nothing has changed in this regard and the real crunch is yet to come.

Apart from a small number of isolated blocks, mostly in inconvenient locations, only the new Hsinyi development area adjacent to Taipei's World Trade Centre offers the prospect of a high-grade integrated development. It is the sole remaining area of Taipei with significant tracts of land still available. However, many of the development companies owning this land are thought to have paid prices in the boom years which remain well above current market levels. Developers have therefore been prepared to play a waiting game, letting demand outstrip supply so that prices can rise still further before bringing new buildings onto the market.

Table 6.1. Asian office market indicators (annual survey Sept. 1997)

Market	Occupation Cost[4]	Yearly Change[5]	Prime Yield	Capital Value[6]
Mumbai	13.1	-17.0	8.2	608
Hong Kong	10.1	42.9	4.1	2,062
Delhi	7.6	-13.3	8.0	359
Singapore	6.3	-3.9	4.1	1,435
Tokyo	5.4[7]	22.9	5.5	643
Beijing	5.2	-4.4	12.7	302
Shanghai–Puxi	4.5	-4.3	12.0	233
Taipei	**4.2**	**0.0**	**5.3**	**350**
Bangalore	3.4	-14.3	8.1	166
Manila–Makarti	2.7	15.3	11.5	234
Jakarta	2.0	1.0	8.0	232
Bangkok	1.4	-7.7	9.0	149

Source: Richard Ellis Research. Used with permission.

Fortunately, during 1997 a number of new developments in this area were commenced, including the groundbreaking for the new 101-storey World Financial Centre. A serious attempt is being made by town planners to avoid many of the planning disasters that have been the blight of other areas of the city and over the next few years this area will emerge as a development showpiece for the city.

Companies now entering the Taiwan market appear to have limited options for the time being. Many of the buildings constructed during the boom years by inexperienced local developers are simply not suited to large corporate operations. Many are wasteful of interior space with large atriums or service areas that cut down on useable space. Others lack the flexibility to reconfigure interior space to tenant requirements.

The secondary market offers little scope for alleviating the problem. Most of the secondary market is taken up with older buildings of inferior

[4] In US$ per square foot per month including management, air-conditioning charges and local property taxes.
[5] From end third quarter 1996 in %.
[6] US$ per square foot gross; based on net prime rents and prime yields.
[7] Central areas—non prime.

construction and multiple ownership on each level offering no chance for either space consolidation or redevelopment. While smaller businesses may consider taking such space it is not really an option for major corporations.

Really prime space is a matter of 'catch as catch can'. When IBM moved out of its building on Tun Hua South Road in mid 1996, the four floors that become available were immediately snatched up by Bank of America, Chase Manhattan and others already in the market. At a price of a little over NT$2,000 per ping this building offered exceptional value, and despite its unprepossessing appearance is generally regarded as one of the most efficient buildings in Taipei.

Many companies, such as IBM, are solving the problem by moving non-core operations to secondary space outside the main commercial area. Some of the industrial zones surrounding Taipei offer excellent accommodation and at reasonable prices, but because of the corporate licensing system in Taiwan, only companies that are licensed to manufacture are strictly speaking allowed occupancy within these areas. However, as with many things in Taiwan, the finer legal points are often overlooked, especially by local authorities eager to attract employment opportunities and big name companies into their area.

While Taiwan's other major urban centres of Taichung in Central Taiwan and Kaohsiung in the South appear to offer much better value for money (and have quality office space available equal to any in Taipei), for most MNCs relocation from the capital is simply not feasible because of the lack of communication and other facilities in these centres. This situation could of course change dramatically should direct transportation and communication links be established with Mainland China. Both Taichung and Kaohsiung are expected to play major roles in any cross-straits trade, and much of the building and infrastructure being put into these cities has this in mind. Companies considering Taiwan as a hub for Greater China can find real bargains by looking at places other than Taipei as a centre for their operations. Already the Taoyuan area south of Taipei (and about one hour's commuting along the congested freeway) is attracting a number of international companies with major warehousing and distribution operations because of the availability of relatively cheap space and its location adjacent to the main north-south artery.

For most companies that require a presence in Taipei, the only alternative to a compromise on quality and location is to buy space. Regulations governing investment into the property market have recently been relaxed, and although foreign companies are still precluded from purchasing land (ostensibly to prevent speculation, but in reality to protect local developers) purchase of office space for own use is now an option. Asking prices are often high. Space in the new Sunrise Building on Nanking East Road, Section 5, is being offered for rent at NT$3,000 per ping—generally regarded as being 50% above current market rates for the area. The same premises are also offered for sale at NT$600,000 per ping. Although this is still considered to be 20% above a realistic asking price, there would appear to be room to negotiate a deal and, with many developers strapped for cash, there may still be bargains to be had. One thing is for sure; any such bargains will not last long in the current climate.

Table 6.2. Grade A office accommodation—market comparisons

Location	Vacancy Rate	Rental (NT$/ping/month)
Taipei	1–2%	2,200–3,000
Taichung	30%–35%	400–650
Kaohsiung	25%–30%	600–850
		Source: Richard Ellis, Taiwan Branch.

Commercial terms vary greatly from building to building and with time. In a dynamic situation, companies seeking to set up operations in Taipei should seek professional advice. A number of international property consulting firms are available in Taiwan to assist overseas companies in their search for accommodation and in the negotiation of lease conditions, and most major companies seeking to establish or expand facilities would use a professional consulting firm.

The following may be considered a general guide to local market practices:

1. All premises, whether business or residential, are normally leased on a 'gross' basis which includes not only the useable area of the lease but also a pro-rated portion of the common areas of the building as a whole;
2. As previously noted, the standard unit of measurement for area in Taiwan is the 'ping'. One ping is equivalent to 3.45 square metres or 35.58 square feet. One square metre is 0.29 ping;
3. The majority of office buildings in Taipei are multi-ownership and are strata titled. This can often lead to management and maintenance problems, especially in older buildings. Each tenancy will be separately registered with the government land office. Split tenancies are not generally permitted;

4. Taipei has a zoning system which dates from the 1960s and which often causes problems for a city which has expanded and evolved considerably since that time. Activities listed on the company business licence must be compatible with the uses specified on the land title certificate. Much of Taipei is zoned as a high-density residential area although general office use is permitted in such areas. Banking is only permitted in commercial zones and manufacturing is only permitted in industrial zones. (As a corollary: general business activities are not allowed in industrial zones);

5. Rent is generally determined on the basis of 'per ping per month'. Rent is paid in advance on either a quarterly or monthly basis. Other charges such as Rental Withholding Tax, Value-Added Tax, utilities, management fees and air-conditioning/heating charges are payable separately;

6. Leasing terms are generally written for periods of between two and five years although there is a current trend towards shorter lease terms. Break clauses can usually be negotiated. Security of tenancy and most commonly accepted international practices are protected by legal statute;

7. Lease deposits are generally required and can vary from between two to six months' rent and are in theory refundable upon lease expiry. It is not uncommon, especially for tenants in multi-owned buildings, to have difficulty in obtaining lease refunds. Generally, lease deposits bear no interest or benefit to the lessor;

8. Most office buildings are under professional management contracts which, together with air-conditioning, parking and other fees, form an additional monthly charge paid separately from the main lease. Generally such charges are levied on a 'per ping' basis;

9. Tenants are required to withhold a portion of the rent and pay it directly to the local tax bureau. Where an individual owns leased premises, a 10% withholding tax applies; where a company owns premises, a Value-Added Tax of 5% is withheld;

10. Cost of office decoration is generally a charge to the tenant and some leases stipulate that any furnishing and internal partitioning must be removed at the conclusion of a lease.

Rental of Factory Space

Foreigners and foreign-owned firms may purchase or lease land only for their own use. The maximum term permitted for land leases is twenty years. However, for most companies, rental of facilities is more usual, especially during the start-up phase.

Rental of factory space does not present insurmountable problems. Probably the most difficult task would be locating the land on which to establish the factory. There is no shortage of industrial areas to choose from and a number of incentives exist for companies establishing factories in industrial or export processing zones (see previous chapter).

There are two main options when considering factory rental in Taiwan. They are (1) rental of vacant land where the owner builds a factory to specifications provided by the lessor; and (2) rental of land with a vacant factory already built on it.

A third option would be to rent a 'greenfields' site and build a customised plant from scratch. Because of the complexities involved and the difficulties with language and culture, this is often not considered to be a viable option initially. However, once a company is established and has had experience operating in the country for a while, this alternative could be considered once the company has outgrown its first plant.

In either of the first two options the rent paid is based on the value of the land. Factory buildings in Taiwan have a minimal value and so have very little effect on the total cost of rent.

In order to establish a 1,500 square metre factory, it would be necessary to rent as much as 2,150 square metres of land. Factory buildings in Taiwan, on average, occupy 70% of land area. The local unit of measurement for land in Taiwan is also the ping.

Rental Costs

The rental costs of well located and serviced industrial land are generally around NT$150–NT$175 per square metre per month (NT$500–NT$600 per ping per month).

Lease Conditions/Lease Periods

Normally, a land owner will accept a lease for five years with an option of renewal for a further three years. An initial five-year lease with an option of renewal for five years is less common though possible in some cases. Periods of less than five years are generally unacceptable to owners because they want the security of assured income. This is especially so if they are going to construct a factory building for the tenant. Similarly, landowners are unwilling to tie up their property for periods over eight years, because in the past there have been wild fluctuations in the price and availability of land. While these fluctuations will continue to occur it is not as likely that they will be as radical as they have been in the past.

Rental Escalation

Rental escalation can be handled in one of two ways. Rent increases are either (1) linked to an economic indicator such as the Consumer Price Index, or (2) fixed in the contract for the term of the contract.

Both alternatives are used and it is generally up to the parties concerned to negotiate the formula best suited to their needs. Inflation is relatively low at the moment and is expected to be held at around 3% for the immediate future. (A number of informed sources believe that the real underlying rate of inflation is understated in the CPI figures.) Fixed rate contracts generally specify between 4% and 5% annual escalation during the term of the contract, though the eventual figure will be negotiated between the parties.

Location Parameters

Industrial land in close proximity to Taipei is most readily found in the adjacent areas around Linkou, Taoyuan, Yangmei, Hsinchu and Miaoli. These are all industrial areas in northern Taiwan and accessible from Taipei by freeway. People do commute daily to these areas from Taipei. The opening in 1997 of a second north-south freeway with access to the south and east of Taipei, as well as a new extension to the international airport, has not only relieved peak congestion on the main truck route but has also opened up new residential options for commuters.

Insurance

Comprehensive insurance cover for plant and equipment is available from a large number of both local and foreign insurance agencies in Taiwan. Indications of the loss or damage risks that can be insured against are:
1. Fire, Lightning Strike, Electrical Fault, Explosion, Impact by Aircraft;
2. Flood, Inundation by Rain, Snow or Snow Slide;
3. Typhoon, Cyclonic Winds, Hurricane;
4. Earth Quake, Tidal Wave, Earth Collapse, Avalanche and falling rocks and stones;
5. Robbery and Theft or the unsavoury actions of third parties;

6. Other accidents and occurrences.

Companies generally do not quote rates other than against specific proposals. Factors that would be likely to affect the final insurance rate include:

- Location of risk property;
- Its nature, e.g. age, construction material etc;
- Value;
- Type and nature of safety protection systems installed;
- Age, type and nature of equipment installed;
- Period of insurance;
- Nature of risks to be insured against.

INTERNATIONAL PROPERTY FIRMS IN TAIWAN

The following are well known and well established companies dealing in the commercial property market.

Richard Ellis, Taiwan Branch
7F, Cosmos Building, No. 134, Section 3,
Min Sheng East Road, Taipei
Tel: (02) 2713 2266
Fax: (02) 2712 3065
Managing Director: Mr David Pitcher

Pan Asia Real Estate Group
12F, #25, Jen-Ai Road,
Section 4, Taipei
Tel: (02) 2777 4567
Fax: (02) 2777 1618

C.Y. Leung & Company Limited
3F, Taipei Financial Center,
62 Tun Hua North Road, Taipei
Tel: (02) 2778 1296
Fax: (02) 2778 1543

UTILITIES

Charges for electricity, gas and water are considered to be generally high.

Electricity

Taipower remains the sole distributor of the electricity supply to the national grid although a number of the independent power producers are in the process of building co-generation plants and using part of the output for their own industrial needs.

Supply is normally 60 Hz, Single Phase (2 wire) or 3 Phases (3 wire) at 220 or 380 volts. Three phase (4 wire) 220 volt and 380 volts are also available although users are only able to select one of the above choices. While industry generally works on 220 volt supplies, domestic electricity is supplied at 110 volts.

Industrial consumers have a number of choices when applying for an electrical power connection. There are options within options within options, as summarised below:

Low tension services

- Lighting Only:
  - Metered Rate, or
  - Flat Rate
- Combined Lighting and Power:
  - Installed Capacity Contracts, or
  - Maximum Demand Contracts:
    - Regular Service Rate, or
    - Time of Use Rate
- Power Only:
  - Installed Capacity Contracts:
    - Regular Service Rate, or
    - Time of Use Rate
  - Maximum Demand Contracts:
    - Regular Service Rate, or
    - Time of Use Rate

High tension and extra high tension services

- High Tension:
    - ◆ Time of Use Rate (A), or
    - ◆ Time of Use Rate (B)
- Extra High Tension:
    - ◆ Time of Use Rate (A), or
    - ◆ Time of Use Rate (B)

Within this multiplicity of choices are time and seasonal variants to the charges. The summer period is from June 1 to September 30. This is the time of greatest demand as domestic and office air-conditioning add a considerable additional load to an already over-stretched supply. The non-summer rate applies to all other periods.

Off-peak hours generally apply from 10:30 p.m. to 07:30 a.m. Monday to Saturday and on Sundays and National holidays. Peak hours are from 10:00 a.m. to 12:00 a.m. Monday through Saturday and from 01:00 p.m. to 05:00 p.m. Monday through Friday. All other hours are regarded as semi-peak hours.

There are complex formulas for establishing the 'Installed Capacity' amount, but basically this is the sum of the horsepower rating of all installed electrical components (including lighting and small appliances) at the site. The 'Contracted Supply' amount is an amount negotiated between Taipower and the end-user. For contracts with no allowance for peak and off-peak rates, the amount is fixed as the highest expected electricity requirement for any 15-minute period, calculated for the non-summer zone.

Certain discounts are applicable to customers using off-peak heating and cooling storage systems and in other special instances.

Water

Water supplies are under the jurisdiction of the municipal or provincial governments. Within the Taipei area a minimum monthly fee as well as a progressive rate applies, which is dependent upon the size of the water pipe installed and amounts consumed.

Natural Gas

Commercial natural gas supplies are available only through contractual arrangements with the Chinese Petroleum Corporation, and pro-rata price increments are charged if actual consumption is in excess of the amounts stipulated in the contract.

CHAPTER 7

THE LABOUR MARKET AND EMPLOYMENT ISSUES

Foreign companies establishing themselves in Taiwan will have access to a workforce that is well-educated and well-motivated. The Chinese have a will to succeed and employment opportunities with foreign companies are keenly sought after. Strikes are rare in Taiwan, not because they are illegal—Chinese workers generally enjoy the right to strike with few exceptions—but because the Chinese disposition towards harmony predisposes labour and management alike to resolve potential conflicts through dialogue and compromise.

Labour turnover rates, especially in foreign companies, are very low among general clerical staff and a recent survey conducted by the Council of Labor Affairs indicated that worker job satisfaction island-wide stood at 65%. While the cost of labour in Taiwan is highest among Asia's four mini-dragons, a US Department of Labor Survey ranked Taiwan in 22nd place in terms of labour costs among the world's 25 most industrialised nations.

Wage growth has been rapid in recent years while increases in labour productivity have not grown apace, thereby increasing real labour costs. In some sectors in Taiwan a shortage of workers is causing serious problems which could serve to restrict future growth. In part the labour problem has been overcome through the legalisation of foreign guest workers—chiefly from Thailand and the Philippines—who are employed on two-year contracts. Among the sectors hardest hit by labour shortages are the manufacturing and construction industries, although in the case of the latter, the recent downturn in construction activity has meant that a number of construction employees have been laid off, contributing to the recent rise in unemployment levels.

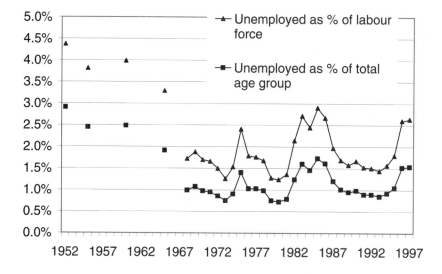

Figure 7a. Taiwan's unemployment rates

LABOUR MARKET OVERVIEW

As of February 1998 the labour force consisted of some 9.488 million workers, or about 44% of the total population (and 57% of the population aged 15 years and above[1]). In recent years the labour market has been growing at around 2% annually. The official unemployment rate has

---

[1] The legal minimum working age.

156

averaged only about 1.5% in recent years and in 1993 reached a 12-year low of 1.45%. Since then the rate has tended upwards. As of February 1998 the official unemployment rate had reached 2.57%. The real rate is thought to be somewhat higher, since many people classified as part of the labour force are actually in unpaid family work, chiefly in rural areas. There is little incentive for unemployed workers to report to the government, as Taiwan has not yet introduced unemployment compensation.

Salaried employees make up 70% of the total workforce, a percentage that has been steadily increasing over the years (in 1966, the same group accounted for only 45% of the total). Private sector employment has gone from 30% in 1966 to 58% in 1996. All other occupational groups—with the exception of those categorised as employers—have been in decline. Self-employed personnel numbers have gone from 28% in 1966 to 17% thirty years later. In the same period, unpaid family workers have declined from 25% to 8% and government employees from 15% to 11%. The only other employment category to increase—the employer—has more than doubled, from 2.3% in 1966 to 5.35% in the late 1990s. This reflects the strength of the small business sector in Taiwan and the strength of the entrepreneurial spirit that exists in the society. It is one of Taiwan's great assets.

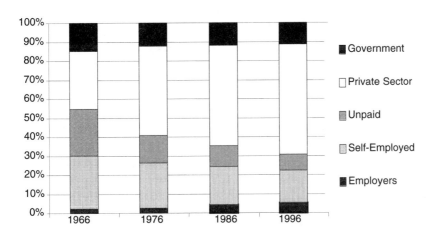

Figure 7b. Employment by sector

Structure of the Workforce

The structure of Taiwan's workforce is changing. Not only is the workforce now more mature—the bulk of employees are now those in the age brackets between 25 and 39—but female participation is also much higher with women now comprising almost 40% of the total workforce. Considerable effort is being expended by government to increase the female participation rate as one means of overcoming current labour shortages. This includes paid maternity leave and subsidies that are available for workplace nurseries. However, women do not yet enjoy full equality in the workplace. They are generally paid less than their male counterparts, nor do they enjoy the same career prospects.

While in recent years total employment in the manufacturing and service industries has been remarkably stable—at around 58% of the total workforce—there has been a noticeable shift away from the manufacturing and into the service sector. In 1997, within these industrial groupings manufacturing accounted for 52% of the total and the service industries contributed 48%. As recently as 1989, these figures were 62% and 38% respectively.

Agricultural employment continues to decline to a mere 10% of the total. There has been little promotion of modern agricultural techniques in Taiwan and little attempt to encourage higher level agricultural training. As a result, rural employment is not sought after by Taiwan's younger and better-educated workforce.

The service sector—particularly in large urban centres—is emerging as the preferred area of employment for recent graduates. As a result of the loss of jobs in rural centres, the gap in disposable incomes between urban and rural dwellers is widening. Wage rates are highest in Taipei. Households in the capital now have nearly double the disposable income of their rural counterparts—NT$955,000 per annum, or 94% higher than in some country areas. The three largest cities, Taipei, Kaohsiung and Taichung, account for more than 55% of total annual disposable income on the island. Average wages of Taipei residents rose by 41% between 1990 and 1993 and average annual per capita income now stands at around NT$300,000.

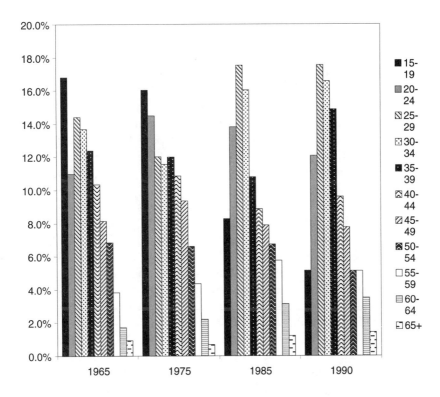

Figure 7c. Age distribution of the workforce

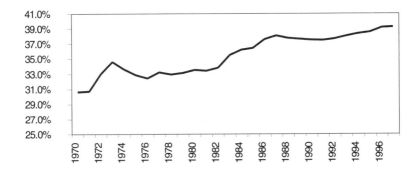

Figure 7d. Female participation in the workforce

159

Faced with ongoing urbanisation, rural areas are also facing a rapid demographic ageing. Real incomes in the countryside have been in continual decline since 1989, when the traditional family-based manufacturing industries started moving overseas. Beyond offering certain industry incentives to firms establishing themselves in rural areas, there appears to be no coordinated government policy able to reverse this trend.

Even though the pool of skilled labour has expanded rapidly in recent years, demand has generally far exceeded supply, particularly in skilled areas and in commerce. Skilled foremen and managers have continued to move to high paying jobs at factories on the Mainland and elsewhere in Asia which are owned and operated by Taiwanese investors. Many recent college graduates are interested in management positions, but lack hands-on experience. Among white-collar workers, 'job-hopping' is becoming increasingly common, especially in local companies. Clerical staff working for foreign companies generally expect conditions well above what they would obtain working for a local company, including a five-day week. Under-utilisation of the female labour force is exacerbating the problem.

Although Taiwan is undergoing a transition to more advanced technology and heavier industries, reducing its dependence on labour-intensive, simple-process manufacturing will take years. By the year 2000 the number of engineers should grow from the current 10% to 15% of the workforce, and the proportion of unskilled workers is expected to decline from 50% to 35%.

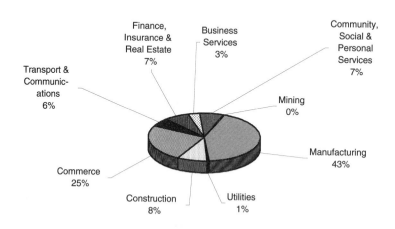

Figure 7e. Employment by industry—1997

Educational Levels

Nine years of schooling is now compulsory in Taiwan, giving the island an overall literacy rate of more than 94%, and among younger workers the rate is 100%. Because Taiwanese are staying at school longer and increasingly seeking higher education qualifications, people are entering the workforce later.

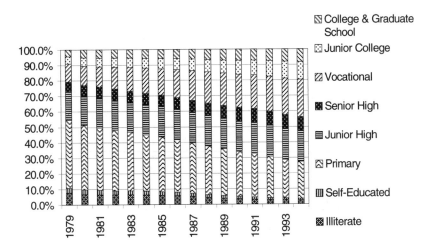

Figure 7f. Education level of the workforce

Twelve years of education is now almost universal with many students —especially those who do not intend to seek higher education—attending vocational training schools in place of senior high schools, where they receive basic trade or clerical skills. Others enter the junior college system which offers two-year post secondary diplomas equivalent to advanced trade certificates. Since 1993, more than 50% of the total workforce has received at least the equivalent of twelve years' schooling with 20% having a post-secondary qualification. Among the new entrants to the workforce, this ratio would be even higher.

THE LEGAL AND REGULATORY FRAMEWORK

The Council of Labor Affairs (CLA), a body under the ROC *Executive Yuan* (Cabinet), is the highest administrative body dealing with labour matters at the national level. The CLA is responsible for drafting and enforcing the regulations dealing with all employment issues including labour conditions, welfare, insurance, industrial safety and health. Similar bodies exist at the provincial and municipal levels to deal with local issues or to act as the local arm of the CLA in inspection and enforcement of labour conditions.

The 13-member cabinet level CLA, made up of academics, government officials, and representatives of labour and management, is playing an increasing role in the protection of workers' rights and in the mediation of labour disputes.

Labor Standards Law

As originally drafted, the 1984 *Labor Standards Law* pertained only to those working in specified industries: manufacturing, construction, transport, communications, mining and quarrying, utilities, agriculture, forestry, fishing, livestock farming and the mass media. The law is in the process of being extended to cover additional industries including retailing and department stores, restaurants, financial, insurance and banking institutions, law firms and information service providers.

The *Labor Standards Law* grants workers certain rights, including the right to fair wages, to compensation for occupational injuries, the right to strike and retirement benefits. The law prescribes such things as contract arrangements, working hours, mandatory benefits, retirement programs and severance pay.

Key sections of the *Labor Standards Law* and the associated *Enforcement Provisions* include the following:

- Wages should be paid at least twice a month (*Article 23*);
- Overtime shall be paid at the regularly hourly rate plus one third for overtime not exceeding two hours, at the regularly hourly rate plus two-thirds for overtime between two and four hours, and at double the normal hourly rate for overtime in excess of four hours (*Article 24*);
- Regular work hours shall not exceed eight hours per day or 48 hours per week (*Article 30*);
- Holidays and leave entitlements are specified in *Articles 37* and *38*;

- Female workers are generally not permitted to work between 10 p.m. and 6 a.m. unless a three-shift system is in operation and certain specified health and safety criteria are met (*Article 49*);
- Female workers are entitled to maternity leave before and after childbirth (*Article 49*);
- Retirement provisions are specified in *Articles 53* to *58*;
- Compensation for occupational accidents is specified in *Articles 59* to *63*.

Other important laws and regulations relating to employment conditions include the *Employment Services Act (1992)* which regulates the conditions under which aliens may work in Taiwan, including foreign labourers, the *Labor Inspection Law (1993)*, and the *1991 Labor Safety and Health Law*, which prescribes conditions for working with toxic substances or in hazardous conditions.

GENERAL EMPLOYMENT CONDITIONS

Slowing population growth, a restructuring of the manufacturing sector towards higher valued-added products, and a reduction of working hours have all contributed to Taiwan's current labour market imbalances. These issues have also had a dampening effect on efforts to further liberalise general working conditions in the absence of marked productivity improvements. Nevertheless, there is a definite long term commitment on the part of government to improving general labour conditions through the wider application of the *Labor Standards Law*. Such measures as shorter working hours, improved insurance and unemployment programs as well as retirement benefits are all part of the agenda. The introduction in 1998 of a five-day alternate working week (see below), introduced as a compromise package given the stand-off between the Cabinet and the CLA over a full five-day working week, has exacerbated conditions for many companies.

Working Hours and Conditions

In accordance with the *Labor Standards Law*, the working week in industrial plants is normally six eight-hour days. A draft proposal from the legislature to amend the Labor Law and shorten the working week to 44 hours has so far been blocked by the ROC legislature, and the Cabinet has proposed instead to phase in the 44-hour work week over five years. By contrast, the

Council for Labor Affairs is pushing to have the working week cut to forty hours by the turn of the century. Overall working hours vary between different industry sectors but both the downward trend and the convergence towards a common standard are clear. Working hours are generally shortest in the service industries and highest in the manufacturing sector. While foreign companies generally adhere to the five-day working week, local companies and factories generally work five and a half days. The government is seeking to encourage employers to move more quickly to the five day week, and in January 1998 introduced a system whereby government employees (including employees in State-owned companies) work only alternate Saturdays. The private sector has been encouraged to follow suit but results have been patchy with only the banking sector opting universally to follow the government lead. The system is seen as cumbersome and unworkable by many within industry and has been criticised for further eroding Taiwan's competitive position.

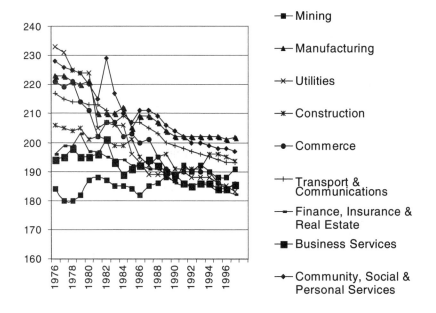

Figure 7g. Trend in monthly working hours by industry sector

Female employees may work on night shifts if the company has adequate facilities for them (e.g. women's dormitories, transport to and from work, good security and reasonable sanitary conditions). Plants employing women on night shifts must use a three-shift system. Employees under the age of 16 may not work overtime or between 8 p.m. and 6 a.m. Employment below the age of 15 is not permitted.

All workers are entitled to a 30-minute break after every four hours of work. Mothers of infants may take two additional 30-minute breaks daily for nursing.

Workers may take up to a month of paid sick leave at half pay each year. Employers are expected to grant eight days' leave for marriage or death of the employee's spouse or parents, and six days' leave for death of the employee's grandparents. Employees can also take up to fourteen days' leave (without pay) annually to attend to personal business, but not more than five days at a time. Factories may write their own codes for unpaid leave provided they include the above provisions.

Leave with pay must be granted to employees receiving short term military training, attending military roll-calls or undergoing draft processing. During military service (two or three years, starting at age twenty) the employee's pay is suspended but his position is (in theory) retained. Women get up to eight weeks' paid maternity leave, though only at half pay if they have been employed for less than six months.

In addition to a minimum of one day off per week, workers are also entitled to fourteen annual commemorative holidays as specified in the *Enforcement Rules* of the *Labor Law* and to annual leave (see below).

Remuneration Levels and Workers Benefits

As of the end of 1997 the minimum adult monthly wage stood at NT$15,840 (US$480 approx). In practice, the minimum wage is seldom used except for calculating the insurance contributions of employers and only legally working Filipino and Thai labourers are paid at the minimum rates. Market rates for locally recruited staff are considerably higher than the minimum.

Any employment package, irrespective of industry sector, will normally include three components:
1. **Regular earnings**. This refers to regular salary or wages that in Taiwan are paid monthly. It consists of basic pay, regular allowances and awards such as housing and transportation allowances, meals etc;
2. **Overtime pay**. This represents rewards paid for working in excess of standard contract hours. The rate of overtime pay is stipulated in the *Labor Standards Law* (see below) or in other industry regulations;
3. **Irregular Earnings**. Specialised payments common in Taiwan include incentive payments for performance and/or full attendance as well as

bonuses paid at year end (Lunar New Year) and at other festivals; 'irregular' earnings also includes *per diem* rates paid for official trips and job transfer allowance.

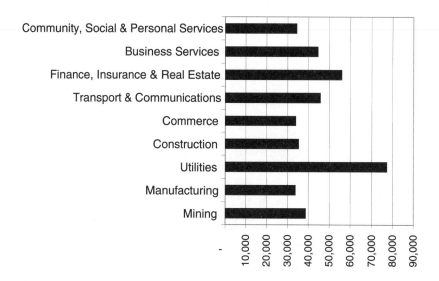

Figure 7h. Average monthly earnings by sector (in NT$) 1996

Average wages are highest in the utilities sector (US$1830 per month)—a reflection of the disproportionate number of engineering personnel employed in comparison to general clerical workers. Rates are lowest in the manufacturing and general commerce sectors (around US$985 per month).

There remains a considerable disparity in many industries between salary levels for male and female workers, with females paid on average only 65% of equivalent male rates. The difference is most marked in the financial, insurance and real estate sectors. The official explanation for the difference is that female workers exhibit a higher turnover rate and therefore are not paid at rates commensurate with their skills and work experience. This would be surprising. Most employers, Taiwanese and foreign alike, generally regard female employees as more stable and work conscious than their male counterparts, and less likely to blow the corporate entertainment budget. Lingering cultural and sexual bias probably has a lot to do with wage differences.

Overtime, which is common, is limited under the *Labor Standards Law* to three working hours per day for men and two for women. Office workers generally adhere to a five and a half day working week, although in foreign companies a five day week is not uncommon.

Paid annual leave entitlements for larger domestic companies and for foreign companies operating in Taiwan are generally based on *Article 38* of the Labor Law. Minimum prescribed leave entitlements are as follows:

- Seven days annual leave for workers with more than one year's service but less than three;
- Ten days annual leave for workers with more than three years service but less than five;
- Fourteen days for those with more than five but less than ten years service; plus
- One additional day per year for each year of service over 10 years up to a maximum of thirty days.

The above entitlements are based on continuous employment with the same employer or business entity. While many smaller companies do not strictly adhere to these standards, any employer of standing is expected to do so.

Any foreign employer entering the market and wishing to attract and retain quality personnel will be expected to offer rates of pay and general working conditions well above average market conditions. Recent surveys have shown that remuneration levels are only one of a number of factors sought by Taiwanese when considering a career move. Other important factors include job security, potential transportation problems (living convenient to the workplace is important for many Taiwanese, especially in Taipei's chaotic traffic conditions) and compatibility with lifestyle and personal interests.

Calculations in the table below are based on regular salary and allowance payments paid 14 times per year (including a customary two-month New Year Bonus). While a two-month bonus payment is considered the norm, bonuses are linked to profitability and vary from company to company and from year to year. For a multinational however, it represents the minimum expected payment.

Table 7.1. Typical remuneration levels in the Taipei area (1997)

Position	US$/month
General Manager	7,720
Financial Manager	5,900
Sales/Marketing Managers	5,100

Table 7.1 cont'd

Factory Manager	5,300
Senior Engineer	1,850
Engineer	1,500
Junior Engineer	950
Senior Accountant	1,700
Accountant	1,200
Accounting Clerk	900
Executive Secretary (bilingual)	1,700
Clerk (bilingual)	1,300
Factory Foreman	1,200
Skilled Computer Operator (PC Network)	850
Electrician	1,000
Mechanic	1,100
Unskilled Factory Worker	700

The importance of fringe benefits and working conditions is growing. Workers in labour-intensive jobs, particularly younger workers, often change jobs to obtain better employment conditions. Factors such as cleanliness, air conditioning and the availability of transport may be critical to maintaining a trained labour force. When plants are located far from community centres, it may be necessary and desirable to provide dormitory facilities and company buses for transport to and from the plant. Nearly all modern factories provide eating space and facilities for warming lunches. Many supply hot meals at a nominal cost to workers.

Part-time and Temporary Workers

The use of part-time and temporary workers is permitted in Taiwan. The minimum wage, calculated on an hourly basis for part-time workers, currently stands at NT$62 (since August 1995).

The *Labor Standards Law* determines base conditions of employment in a wide variety of industries including agricultural, mining, manufacturing, construction, utilities, transportation, warehousing, and communications industries. This law covers both fixed and undefined term contract employment. All temporary, short-term, seasonal and special work contracts may be made in the form of fixed-term contracts. By contrast, any recurrent work assignments must be in the form of undefined term contracts. The maximum period for contracts for temporary and short-term work is six months. The maximum periods for seasonal work and work for a specific purpose are nine months and one year respectively. The law prohibits an employer from hiring an employee on a repeated short-term basis.

There are no restrictions on part-time work. Most industries not directly covered by the *Labor Standards Law* incorporate the terms of the law in their employment contracts.

Labour insurance must be provided for all employees from the first day of employment.

Insurance Provisions

All workers must be insured under government-administered policies covering injury, disability, sickness, retirement, and deaths and births in the family. Benefits are in cash payments, except for sickness (in which case the benefit is in the form of hospitalisation).

Under the *Labor Insurance Law*, any establishment employing three or more workers must have contracts with the Labor Insurance Bureau. Coverage consists of two types. Ordinary insurance provides benefits in relation to maternity, injury, sickness, old age and death, while occupational injury insurance provides four specific types of benefit—injury and sickness, medical care, disability and death. The second category of insurance is applicable only to certain types of industries and at rates determined by the government. Employers pay 70% of the insurance premium while employees pay 20% with the government paying the balance.

In July 1994 Taiwan's parliament, the *Legislative Yuan*, passed legislation providing for the establishment of a compulsory and universal national health insurance scheme. The scheme was finally implemented in March 1995. The medical insurance components of the labour insurance scheme have now been incorporated into the new national health scheme which has also provided for the 41% of the population that previously were not insured.

The cost of premiums to the national health insurance fees are split between employees, employers and government. Employers pay 60% of the fee, workers pay 30% and the government pays the balance. The insurance premium to be paid is calculated on a fixed rate which is currently set at 4.25% of a worker's reported salary (which in Taiwan is often lower than the actual salary paid—especially in the small business sector) and has a cap of

6%. Foreign nationals with valid Alien Residence Certificates employed in Taiwan are eligible for insurance, as are their family members.

The health care program pays between 70% and 95% of the cost for patients admitted to hospitals but not for outpatient care.

Termination of Employment

Under the law, minimum dismissal notice requirements for blue-collar workers are ten days for those employed consecutively for three months to one year; twenty days for those employed for between one and three years; and thirty days for those employed longer than three years. Workers are entitled to two paid working days off per week during the notice period in order to seek new employment. Under the *Labor Standards Law*, severance pay is calculated on the basis of one month's pay for each year of service, at a rate equal to the worker's average monthly income (including overtime) during the previous six months. Workers employed for specific periods or fired for misconduct or similar reasons are not entitled to severance pay. In practice, dismissal terms are often more generous.

A contract employee may be dismissed only if proven unable to meet responsibilities or if there are major changes in the firm's circumstances (i.e. it closes, changes ownership, suffers huge financial losses, is forced to cut production, suspends operations for more than a month or changes the nature of its business).

Although it is illegal to dismiss women when they marry, this practice is fairly common owing to lax enforcement of the law. The ongoing labour shortage, however, is pushing more firms to welcome married women who wish to remain employed.

The Council of Labor Affairs is developing a general unemployment insurance system. As currently envisioned, the system would replace the present severance pay provisions of the *Labor Standards Law*, permitting laid-off employees to draw benefits for up to eight months at half their average pay during the three to six months prior to their loss of employment. Both employers and participating employees would contribute to the program, which would offer benefits only to workers employed for at least two years and with paid-up premiums. The draft program reportedly also stipulates that those drawing benefits would have to actively seek job placement assistance and take advantage of all vocational training opportunities. Benefits would be denied to those dismissed for violations of contract. Some 4.6 million full-time workers on the island would be eligible to participate initially.

Employee Welfare and Retirement Benefits

All companies with fifty or more workers must establish funds for employees' welfare. When an enterprise is founded, between 1% and 5% of its registered capital must be set aside for the fund, and amounts equal to between 0.05% and 0.15% of monthly revenues must be added periodically. Deductions of 0.5% from each employee's wage (including any subsidies or special allowances) must be paid in, as well as between 20% and 40% of the proceeds from any plant waste and sweepings sales. Welfare funds must be devoted to providing mess halls, housing, clinics, reading rooms, bathrooms and similar amenities, or to setting up training, recreational and educational facilities for workers and their families.

The *Labor Standards Law* provides for separate funds under joint labour/management control for pensions, settlement of outstanding wages and wage arrears. Retirement pensions are set at two months' wages for each year of service, with a ceiling of 45 months' wages. Pensions must be paid in a lump sum unless special exemption is granted by the authorities. The government collects some NT$30 billion annually in retirement reserve funds. Employers covered by the law contribute a maximum of 0.1% of workers' wages to the outstanding wage settlement fund each month; in addition, they must set aside 0.05% of the firm's total insured value for use as back-pay clearance funds.

The normal retirement age is sixty for all workers except miners, who retire at 55. Those covered by the 1984 *Labor Standards Law* are entitled to retire after 25 years' employment by the same company (fifteen years for those over the age of 55).

INDUSTRIAL RELATIONS

There has been virtually no labour unrest in recent years, mainly because the ongoing labour shortage has ensured continued wage growth. Of Taiwan's 3,725 unions registered in 1996, 1,213 are industrial and a further 2,408 are craft based. The remainder consists of federated bodies. Membership of unions totals 3,278,416 workers, or about 36% of the working population. Indeed, foreign companies establishing themselves in Taiwan are probably more likely to be held to ransom by local government councillors than they would by their workers.

Taiwan has no works councils or representation of workers on corporate boards. The country does not recognise Western-style labour rights, and wages are set unilaterally by employers. Unions, traditionally dominated by

171

the government and enjoying good relations with company management, usually confine their activities to bread-and-butter issues such as working conditions and fringe benefits. But the power and influence of workers are growing as a result of increased democratisation and political and legal reforms.

Strikes may be called if endorsed by at least half the members of a union and reported to employers and labour officials seven days in advance. Politically motivated and sympathy strikes remain illegal.

Disputes

Serious labour disputes are uncommon in Taiwan. The workforce, although far from docile, does not display the same level of militancy as workers, for example, in Korea. A number of the more prominent recent labour disputes receiving attention in the local press have resulted from foreign labourers rather than their Chinese counterparts.

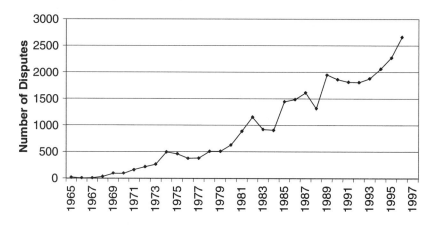

Figure 7i. Labour disputes 1965–1995

Nevertheless, the number of industrial disputes has been rising. More than 2,500 disputes were registered at the end of 1997 (later data is not available) although when viewed in terms of the percentage of the workforce in dispute, less than 0.20% of the entire workforce is exposed to industrial action.

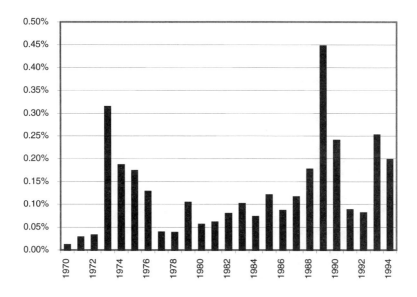

Figure 7j. Disputing workers as percentage of the workforce

Contract and wage arrangements account for the overwhelming majority of industrial disputes—more than 75% of the total—while occupational safety issues and retirement/severance benefits make up the bulk of other issues.

Disputation in Taiwan seldom involves strike action and even more rarely involves foreign companies. Although strikes are not banned as such, except for government and military employees, there is not the necessity. Taiwanese prefer compromise, and conciliation and mediation are the preferred means of settling industrial disputes.

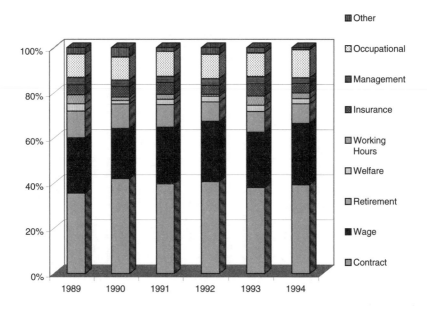

Figure 7k. Disputes by category 1989–1995

EMPLOYMENT OF FOREIGNERS

Some of the more acute labour shortage problems—particularly affecting the manufacturing and construction sectors—have been alleviated by allowing legal foreign guest workers into Taiwan (chiefly from Thailand and the Philippines). The government has permitted six key industries to import foreign labourers for fifteen different job classifications. The industries are textiles, basic metals, metal production manufacturing, machine equipment, electrical and electronic goods, and construction. Imported workers are not permitted to stay longer than a year and female workers who become pregnant are deported immediately. All foreign workers must report for regular medical check-ups including HIV tests.

The Council of Labor Affairs has streamlined procedures for the introduction of alien workers, who are drawn only from countries that are friendly towards Taipei and appropriately regulate outbound employment seekers. Currently, workers from Indonesia, Malaysia, the Philippines and Thailand are permitted to enter Taiwan.

The council currently takes four working days to respond to an application for the importation of foreign workers, who may begin work within three weeks of approval. All legal foreign workers are protected by Taiwan's labour laws, receive minimum monthly wages on the same basis as local workers and must be covered by labour insurance. It is this provision that has sometimes given rise to industrial action as often Taiwanese workers receive benefits well above the legal minimum.

As of December 1997, a total of 282,000 legally contracted foreign workers were employed in Taiwan—an increase of 74% on the level just two years previously. Most foreign workers are employed in manufacturing and in the construction industry, with 56% of all foreign labourers employed in the electronics sector and a further 10% in the metal fabrication industries. Many such factory workers are highly skilled with post-secondary qualifications but are attracted to Taiwan by the comparatively high wage rates offered.

Labour shortages have led to an influx of illegal foreign labourers, including from Mainland China, entering Taiwan. Illegal foreign workers from the Asian region are estimated at around 50,000. There also appears to be a small but growing trend of workers leaving their registered employment and going underground or overstaying their work permits.

Foreign Professional Workers

Separate laws from those pertaining to industrial labour regulate employment of foreign white-collar workers in Taiwan. Two key laws in this area are the *Regulations Governing the Entry, Exit, Residence, and Stay of Foreign Nationals (1996)* and the (rather long-winded) *Rules Governing the Approval and Administration of Foreign Specialist and Technical Personnel Employed by Public or Private Enterprises and Ranking Executives Employed by Overseas Chinese or Foreign National Invested Enterprises.* The Rules are part of the *Employment Service Law* and were last updated in 1996.

The Rules define the circumstances under which any public or private enterprise may apply for the employment of foreign nationals. Generally, three circumstances are foreseen:

- Ranking Executives of Branch Offices of foreign companies or enterprises approved under either the *Statute for Investment by Overseas Chinese* or *the Statute for Investment by Foreign Nationals*;

- Specialised work relating to business promotion, market surveys, personnel training, operational management and relevant research work;
- Technical work relating to the installation or maintenance of machinery or equipment, upgrading, special operation or control procedures, etc.

All such employment applications are handled either by the Investment Commission of the Ministry of Economic Affairs or (in the case of enterprises operating in the export processing zones) by the Export Processing Zone Administration.

All applications are handled on a case-by-case basis and the number and duration of foreign nationals to be employed is assessed on the basis of the business category, scale of operations, personnel development program and contribution to domestic economic development.

Article 11 of the *Rules* describes the form of any application for employment of a foreign national required to perform specialised or technical work:

1. One copy of the business plan. With regard to applications filed for extension of employment, the performance certificate and tax payment certificate of the foreign national for the period of employment in Taiwan should also be attached;
2. One photocopy, according to the nature of each Employer's business, of the Employer's ROC company licence, profit-seeking enterprise registration certificate, foreign company recognition certificate, foreign company registration card, association establishment registration documentation, foundation registration certificate, export/import firm registration card, and/or factory establishment registration documentation respectively;
3. One photocopy of the passport or another identification certificate of the foreign national to be employed;
4. One photocopy each of the foreign employee's academic certificates, professional training certificate or certification of passing a professional examination, and working experience certificates. (These certificates are not required in the case of applying for extension of employment);
5. Four copies of the personal data sheet of the foreign national to be employed;
6. Two duplicates of the employment contract;
7. One photocopy of the practicing licence or certificate as required to be possessed by the person performing work in Taiwan in accordance with the provisions of any other applicable laws;
8. Other documents as required by the competent authority.

If documents are in a foreign language, Chinese copies are normally required together with attestation by the competent ROC consular or other relevant authority in the applicant's home country.

Additional documents must be provided under *Article 14* after the person enters the country and before commencing work. These must include, together with a copy of the employment contract, the following documents:

1. Name, address, telephone number, and scope of business of the employing enterprise;
2. Name, sex, date of birth, nationality, domicile in the foreign country, and residence in Taiwan of the foreign national employed;
3. Title of the post and contents of the work to be assumed by the foreign national at the said enterprise in Taiwan;
4. Amount of the monthly or yearly salary and allowances;
5. Dates of beginning and expiration of the duration of employment.

Once again, all documentation submitted must be in the Chinese language or a Chinese copy provided by an accredited translator.

Confusion about the granting of visas for expatriate staff continues to be a source of conflict between foreign businesses and the government. Foreign business groups often complain that the rules are difficult to understand and are inconsistently applied. The Council of Labor Affairs has been particularly hostile to the white-collar employment of foreigners in Taiwan. Visas routed through the Ministry of Economic Affairs for a top company official tend to be the smoothest. Work visas for officials below that level require negotiation with government officials. There are no fixed guidelines.

It is estimated that there are up to 50,000 illegal white-collar foreign workers in Taiwan, many of whom are young foreign students able to obtain (illegal) office and teaching jobs in Taipei because of their language skills but unable to obtain proper professional employment.

CHAPTER 8

TAIWAN'S REGULATORY ENVIRONMENT

In keeping with Taiwan's efforts to internationalise its economy and conform to WTO and other international standards, Taiwan is now seeking to develop a proper legal code for commercial operations. A number of areas of regulation governing commercial conduct should be carefully considered by any company seeking to do business in Taiwan. Of particular importance among these are the *Fair Trade Law* and the *Consumer Protection Law* (designed respectively to regulate competition and protect consumers), the *Commodity Labelling Law*, the various environmental protection laws, those governing intellectual property protection and the law protecting personal data from unauthorised computer processing. A brief review of these areas of legislation is the subject of this chapter.

TAIWAN'S FAIR TRADE LAW (FTL)

Taiwan's *Fair Trade Law* was promulgated in 1991 and came into force a year later. Together with the Enforcement Rules they provide the regulatory framework for defining acceptable market practices and the protection of consumers' interests in line with WTO standards. The Law also provides a catalyst for modifications and extensions to other legislation that restricts market competition. A further consideration is that the FTL also provides a measure of protection for unregistered symbols and marks not covered by normal intellectual property laws.

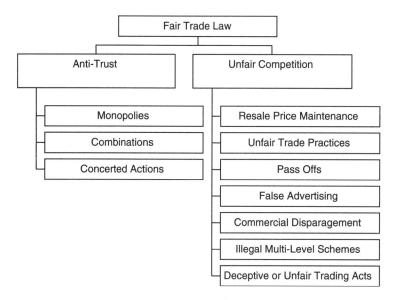

Figure 8a. Regulatory framework of the *Fair Trade Law*

The Fair Trade Commission, established as a body under the *Executive Yuan* in 1992, is charged with implementation of the FTL and, while having limited powers of enforcement, has a broad mandate to investigate complaints and recommend action to the government. At the Provincial (Municipal) Level, the functions of the Fair Trade Commission are handled by the Department (Bureau) of Reconstruction while at the county (city) level they are handled within the county or city government.

Until the mid 1980s and under the martial law regime, Taiwan maintained a very tightly controlled environment that was, nevertheless, largely left to bureaucratic and political discretion and had little to do with the rule of law.

In recent years, as the domestic market has liberalised so the government has sought to bring Taiwan into line with international trading practices. With a slow but steady dismantling of Taiwan's monopoly industries and with Taiwan's application for membership of the World Trade Organisation still pending, the government has moved to increase the applicability of the *Fair Trade Law* and the powers of the Commission. This has been particularly evident in the services sector of the economy, an area that is generally opening to international competition at a fast rate.

The Fair Trade Commission

The Fair Trade Commission is the watchdog body established pursuant to Chapter 4 of the *Fair Trade Law* as a body under the direct control of the *Executive Yuan*. The Commission's functions are to review and report to government on issues relating to competition policy, to administer the *Fair Trade Law* and to investigate the activities of business enterprises and to dispose of any cases violating this Law. The organisational structure of the Commission is governed by a separate statute, *The Organic Statute of the Fair Trade Commission*, promulgated on January 13 1992.

Activities of the FTC are under the daily control of the Chair who is responsible to the nine full-time commissioners who meet weekly and who are each appointed for a term of three years. Commissioners can be re-appointed for a second term. Organisational and administrative control is vested in the Secretary-General but the Secretariat has no decision-making power.

As of early 1998, two of the current commissioners (including the Chair) were members of the ruling Kuomintang party while the remainder were without party affiliation. No more than half of the members of the Commission can belong to the same political party and are required to exercise their authority independently. The Commission operates by majority decision of the commissioners. The Commission is composed of five departments and five supporting divisions, as shown in Figure 8b.

The First and Second Departments are responsible for investigations into monopolies *(Article 10)*, combination *(Article 11)*, horizontal collaboration *(Article 14)* as well as vertical restraints *(Article 19)* while the Third Department investigates unfair competitive practices such as false and misleading advertising *(Articles 20, 21 and 24)* as well as multi-level sales *(Article 23)*.

The Planning Department is concerned with compliance and education. It conducts in-house studies and formulates competition policies on behalf of the ROC Government as well as developing plans for strengthening the enforcement provisions of the *Fair Trade Law*. It is this department which serves as the main contact point for all international affairs of the Commission.

The Legal Affairs Department deals with all matters of law arising from investigations of the FTC and provides assistance to the other departments in the interpretation and application of the law and penalties to be levied. Where criminal activities are concerned, the Legal Affairs Department is responsible for liaison with the relevant judicial authorities.

It is important to recognise that although the FTC has powers to investigate, it has no judicial police powers. It does not have the power to order searches of premises nor can it impel organisations to surrender records. In this respect it is reliant on, and receives cooperation from, the Ministry of Justice. Increasingly there is a trend towards reaching an amicable administrative settlement in many disputes in order to reduce the heavy workload of the Commission.

While the Commission aims to make its decision-making procedures as transparent as possible, the procedures followed are somewhat different from American and other Western practice. Lawyers in Taiwan are not subject to the same level of client confidentiality as elsewhere and this limits the Commission's power of disclosure.

Parties to an investigation can apply for access to the relevant files held, but release by the Commission is on a case-by-case basis. In general, Taiwanese administrative law allows people the right of access to their files subject to considerations of confidentiality and the rights of other parties that derive from other laws such as the *Trade Secrets Law*. There are no unfettered rights of access enshrined in law or in 'freedom of information' codes. In general the FTC seeks to be as forthcoming as possible in such situations and is currently drafting guidelines for access to files.

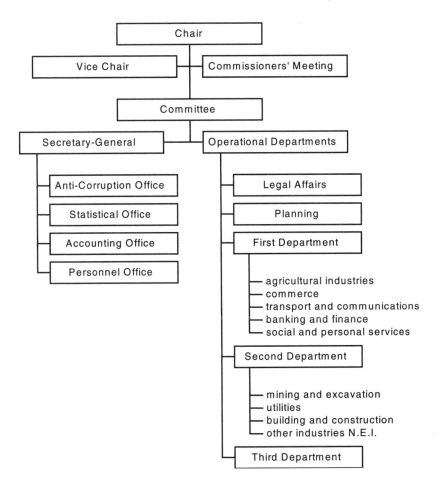

Figure 8b. The Fair Trade Commission of the ROC

Anti-Competitive Practices

The *Fair Trade Law* covers a broad range of anti-competitive business activities and unfair trade practices.

Article 10 of the FTL concerns the prevention and abuse of monopoly power—most prevalent in Taiwan among the State-owned corporations, many of whom have monopolies enshrined in legislation dating from the martial law period. One of the first acts of the Fair Trade Commission was to compile and publish a list of those firms identified to have monopolistic powers in Taiwan.

The term 'monopoly' is defined in *Article 5* as 'referring to a condition in which a business enterprise faces either no competition at all or has such a dominant position that it is able to exclude other competitors from the market'.

Table 8.1. Taiwan's monopolies

Organisation	Monopoly Area
Taiwan Sugar Corporation	Refining and distribution of sugar
Taiwan Salt Works	Salt manufacture
China Petroleum Corporation	Refining and distribution of gasoline
Chunghwa Telecom (basic services)	Wired phone services
Taiwan Wine and Tobacco Monopoly Bureau	Production of alcoholic beverages and cigarettes

Note: Taiwan's monopoly industries are all currently undergoing 'privatisation' which will remove their monopoly privileges—at least on paper. The sheer size of many of these companies will ensure a dominant position in the marketplace for some time to come.

Mergers and acquisitions also fall within the scope of the *Fair Trade Law*. Circumstances in which such mergers and acquisitions have to be brought to the attention of the Fair Trade Law include those in which:

- the surviving enterprise acquires a market share of at least one third;
- the two enterprises in combination hold a market share of at least one quarter;
- the annual sales volume exceeds a prescribed level.

In such circumstances, the FTL requires companies to file an application for approval from the Commission, which then conducts a review to ensure that market competition will not be unduly affected as a result of the merger.

As far as foreign businesses are concerned, *Article 11* of the FTL applies not only to 'combinations' within Taiwan in which foreign businesses are involved, but also to mergers of headquarters and parent companies occurring abroad which—after the merger—may affect market conditions within Taiwan. If an overseas merger triggers the definitions described under *Article 6* of the Law, then the companies involved in the merger will need to file applications with the FTC for merger approval.

The FTC is in the process of simplifying its merger application forms and procedures in order to reduce processing times.

In general, evaluation of mergers and business combinations is given priority over other responsibilities of the FTC. Applications are decided on the principles of *Article 12*; i.e. when the economic benefits to society as a whole exceed that of the restraints to competition, the FTC will generally approve the merger.

In cases involving foreign businesses participating in local mergers, the calculation of sales for the purpose of meeting definitional requirements is based only on transactions conducted in Taiwan, but also includes the sale of subsidiaries and branches as well as the cash amount of goods imported from overseas.

The FTL is not applied to mergers of foreign parent companies occurring outside Taiwan unless the merger occurs among subsidiaries or branches of the foreign parent company and falls within the definition provided in *Article 11*. When a merger abroad triggers the merger of subsidiaries within the ROC (and where such a merger falls within the definitions of *Article 6* of the FTL) the parties involved are required to apply for merger approval from the FTC.

In situations where a multinational corporation (MNC) restructures outside the ROC and shares are transferred between groups of companies, the merged foreign company may end up owning more than one-third of the shares in a local company. In such situations, the requirement to seek prior approval for the merger from the FTC is based on two considerations: firstly, whether the business involved falls within any of the circumstances provided for in *Article 11* of the FTL, and secondly, whether the merger caused by a transfer of shares outside the ROC falls within the definitions provided for in *Article 6*.

In principle, concerted actions and collusions are banned under *Article 14* of the FTL although exceptions are granted on a case-by-case basis where such collusion can be proven to be beneficial to the national economy and to public interests.

The Commission has a particular concern to take action against illegal concerted actions which have in the past often included bid rigging, price fixing agreements and certain practices organised by trade associations which serve to restrict competition. To a lesser extent these practices continue to cause concern.

Resale price maintenance is regarded as unfair competition and is generally banned under *Article 18*. Exceptions are currently made for certain types of 'daily products' if the Commission decides that sufficient similar goods exist so that price fixing does not interfere with free competition. However, it is planned to abolish this practice in the near future.

Article 19 regulates a number of practices that may be considered to hinder fair and open competition. These include refusal to deal (vertical restraints), discriminatory treatment, elimination of price competition, infringement of trade secrets and undue vertical restrictions such as tying arrangements and engagement in exclusive dealings.

The practice of 'pass-offs'—using names, trademarks, product packaging and other symbols in a manner designed to cause confusion with another person's goods or services—is regulated under *Article 20*, false advertising is regulated by *Article 21* and commercial disparagement by *Article 22*. Counterfeits and deceptive advertisements are common practice in Taiwan.

The FTC has formulated a number of principles to handle cases of pass-offs and counterfeiting generally. Importantly, it is not sufficient for a complainant to establish that their product, name or trademark is used overseas; it must be established that the complainant has taken reasonable steps to acquaint the relevant public with their product, brand name or symbol. In general, well known international brand names and symbols are automatically protected under the Law.

Use of symbols, marks and names as defined in *Article 20* of the FTL can refer to a variety of situations including a personal or corporate name, a trademark or logo as well as specially designed containers and packaging. Owners of symbols or marks which are not internationally recognised have to demonstrate the use of their symbol or mark in Taiwan. In determining whether a certain symbol is known in Taiwan the Commission takes account of such factors as the local advertising and other promotion afforded to the symbol, the length of time goods or services marked by the symbol have been marketed in Taiwan, and whether the volume of sales marked by the symbol has been sufficient to have made an impact on the market.

Any company wishing to make a claim for redress under *Article 20* is required to submit a written report detailing the specifics of the complaint and furnishing the correct name and address of the complainant. The complainant is required to provide the Commission with evidence as to the symbols under dispute, to establish that they are commonly known and to furnish concrete evidence of violations by the other party. Thus the onus is on the complainant to establish the claim. The FTC will not initiate its own investigations, although it may seek to substantiate claims from experts through independent advice obtained by means of public hearings as well as from representatives of enterprises and consumers.

While *Article 20* governs the use of symbols, *Article 21* is concerned with the advertising of symbols and the misrepresentation of goods or services. In fact misrepresentation through advertising or other promotions is much more endemic in Taiwan than outright pass-offs. Any overseas company advertising in the local market or designing promotional material for use in Taiwan should be fully aware of the situations in which presentations can be construed as false, untrue or misleading:

1. A presentation or symbol that causes people to wrongly assume the enterprise in question is the (sole) agent, (sole) distributor, branch, maintenance centre or service station of other enterprises and therefore has certain qualifications, credibility and other qualities that can persuade trading counterparts to do business with it;

2. A presentation or symbol that greatly exaggerates the scale of business operations;

3. A presentation or symbol that causes people to wrongly assume the names of other enterprises or certain brand name products have changed or are no longer in circulation;

4. A presentation or symbol that causes people to wrongly assume that government agencies or public welfare organisations are sponsors or co-sponsors of an enterprise or that it is related to government agencies or public welfare organisations;

5. List prices that are significantly different from selling prices for an extended period;

6. An offer of minimum prices in situations where there are no or too few goods available at the minimum price;

7. Where the figures or instructions contained in the presentation or symbol are inconsistent with the quality of goods or services actually available, and the discrepancy between the claim and reality is generally too large to be generally acceptable to trading counterparts;

8. Where a presentation or symbol claims to provide certain services or certain grades of service, but the discrepancy between the claim and reality is too large to be generally acceptable to trading counterparts;

9. Where a presentation or symbol makes certain claims of quality for a commodity or service and the discrepancy between the claim and reality is too large to be generally acceptable to trading counterparts;

10. A presentation or symbol that falsely claims foreign technology (cooperation) or authorisation by a foreign firm;

11. A presentation or symbol that causes people to wrongly assume certain goods or services have been awarded prizes, in order to enhance the reputation of the goods or services;

12. A presentation or symbol that causes people to mis-identify the actual

presenter or author of publications or the people involved in preparing them;

13. A presentation or symbol that causes people to wrongly assume the producer of the presentation or symbol has certain patent rights, trade mark authorisation or other intellectual property rights;

14. Where a presentation or symbol causes people to wrongly assume a certain commodity fulfils certain functions or conforms to certain specifications, but it actually does not or the discrepancy between the specifications claimed and reality is too large to be generally acceptable to trading counterparts;

15. A presentation or symbol that fails to make clarifications on conditions, undertakings, expiry, and other restrictions;

16. A presentation that shows the place of origin of a commodity which causes people to wrongly assume the commodity was manufactured in the place of origin (this provision does not apply if the name of the place of origin is commonly used to refer to certain special products);

17. A presentation or symbol by a multi-level sales organisation that causes people to wrongly assume participants earn high incomes;

18. A presentation or symbol by an enterprise engaged in the marketing of investment products or services which causes people to wrongly assume its trading counterparts earn high incomes;

19. Any one of the following conditions in the case of presentations or symbols associated with buildings:

    (a) The discrepancy between the location claimed by a presentation or symbol and the actual location is too large to be generally acceptable to trading counterparts;

    (b) A presentation or symbol that causes people to wrongly assume a building permit has been issued;

    (c) A presentation or symbol that is liable to cause people to wrongly assume delivery includes certain facilities;

    (d) The discrepancy between the size claimed and the actual size is too large;

    (e) The construction materials and design are not what the presentation or symbol claimed;

    (f) Where a part of the building is reserved by law for certain specific purposes, but a presentation or symbol causes people to wrongly assume that it can be used for other purposes;

    (g) Where a building is located in an industrial zone and, as such, cannot be used for residential purposes, but a presentation or symbol causes people to wrongly assume it can be used for residential purposes;

(h) Where the use of a building as an office is prohibited by law, a presentation or symbol causes people to wrongly assume it can be;

(i) Any other presentations or symbols sufficient to cause misunderstanding among the general or relevant public;

20. Other false, untrue, or misleading presentations or symbols that are sufficient to prevent trading counterparts from making reasonable judgments and transaction decisions.

Multi-level sales schemes are regulated separately by *Article 23* to ensure the protection of the rights of participants. In addition to the *Fair Trade Law* such schemes are also covered by the 1992 *Supervisory Regulation of Multi-Level Sales* which have been enacted pursuant to *Article 23* of the *Fair Trade Law*.

Article 24 is a catch-all clause designed to cover unfair trade practice situations not covered in *Article 20*. In particular, two situations that are considered to be covered under *Article 24* and are of particular importance to foreign companies are the following:

1. 'Imitation of the symbols of goods and services provided by others which, albeit confusion is not yet caused, constitutes an attempt to benefit from the corporate reputation of others';

2. 'Imitation of the symbols of goods or services provided by others which being an attempt to exploit the fruits of the hard work of others, is obviously an unfair act against competitors that is sufficient to affect transaction order'.

Application of the FTL to Government Operations

The FTC has not limited the scope of its investigations to private companies. It has also initiated a number of investigations into the practices of government enterprises where there is a belief that their practices may be contrary to the spirit of the *Fair Trade Law*. While the FTL is limited in its applicability to government procurement activities, it does include those State-owned enterprises which operate in a commercial environment through the supply of goods and services which can be assigned a market value. By way of example, police and military functions of government are outside the scope of the Law while transportation services operated by government are within the Law's area of authority.

The FTC has intervened in a number of instances of government procurement practices that have been found to fall within the scope of the

Fair Trade Law and has identified four types of specification which, in broad terms, are inconsistent with the FTL.

In general, the Commission regards the setting of specifications to be unjustifiably discriminatory in situations when the consequences of such actions may lead to impediments to fair competition. Examples of discriminatory activities include the announcement of such things as specifying standards, geographic location, brand names, etc. as part of the procurement bid process.

Firstly, where qualifying standards are set with the deliberate intention of disqualifying certain competitors, such practices are judged to be discriminatory unless justified on other grounds. A further instance of discriminatory effect is where bidders, in dispute with a procurement agency, are automatically disqualified from participating in further tenders. The FTC has found that such dispute should not necessarily affect the bidder's capability of performing subsequent contracts.

Secondly, where technical specifications are set in a manner to favour a particular bidder, such practices have also been found to be discriminatory. Such specifications include the designation of a specific brand or the setting of specific standards such as the Chinese National Standards.

The third type of specification judged to be discriminatory involves 'favouritism', where priority rights to bid have, in the past, been granted to particular organisations such as those operated by ex-servicemen.

The final area found open to abuse is in the setting of specifications which require a certain level of market power. The FTC has determined that in normal circumstances, qualifying bidders for major contracts should need no more than a market share of 10% in order to qualify.

Table 8.2. Examples of FTC intervention in government procurement

Government Agency	Situation
Tobacco Wine and Monopoly Bureau	During a machinery procurement process the Bureau was accused of restricting market competition by specifying the brand name of an imported product in the bidding process to the detriment of other machines of similar function.

Table 8.2 cont'd

Provincial Housing and Urbanisation Council	The Council was accused of improper bidding procedures by pre-setting the qualification of manufacturers for the bidding process during the construction of one of the rapid transit lines. The Department had discriminated against private bidders while favouring offers by State agencies.
Tainan Municipal Council	The Council was accused of setting improper restrictions on the procurement process for the construction of a garbage burial site. The Commission found in favour of the Council because, although it had placed restrictions on the products to be used by the successful bidder, the specified product was available from multiple sources and so did not inhibit the spirit of competition.
	Source: FTC

Discriminatory provisions considered and accepted by the Commission as justifiable include specifications related to assurances of product quality and experience of the contractor as well as those which take account of specific and more general government policies.

The Council for Economic Planning is currently drafting a new *Statute Governing Government Procurement* that will provide a comprehensive legal framework for all government procurement activities. It is envisaged that the new Statute will provide an independent avenue for private parties to seek redress from government independent of the FTC and will be broadly consistent with the WTO Agreement on Government Procurement Activities.

THE CONSUMER PROTECTION LAW

While the *Fair Trade Law* governs general policies relating to competition and fair trade, the 1994 *Consumer Protection Law (CPC)*, sets out the rights of consumers, the protection of their interests and the penalties relating to non-compliance. Specific measures and issues covered by the Law relate to 'standard contracts' (contracts unilaterally prepared by business operators for entering into contracts with non-specific and multiple parties), mail order purchases, door-to-door sales and instalment sales. The Law also sets out the rights of consumer protection groups.

Under *Article 40* the Consumer Protection Commission, also a body directly under the *Executive Yuan*, is responsible for the development and coordination of basic policies relating to consumer protection and for the enforcement of the *Consumer Protection Law*.

In general, business operators are required by law to have regard for the health and safety of consumers. Where any injury is caused to a consumer through use of a product, unless the business operator responsible for the product can demonstrate that they were not negligent, the consumer has the right to compensation. Importantly, under *Article 8* businesses engaged in sales and distribution activities are jointly and severally liable together with those engaged in design, production and manufacture. Under *Article 9* this liability is also extended to the importer of foreign goods.

In relation to 'standard contracts', *Article 11* requires such contracts to be based on the principles of 'equality and reciprocity' and where such contracts contain terms and conditions that are ambiguous in nature, the interpretation more favourable to the interests of consumers shall govern. *Article 17* allows the government to regulate such by authorising it to designate certain industries in terms of the mandatory and prohibitory provisions of such contracts.

In relation to mail order or purchases resulting from door-to-door sales, *Article 19* gives the consumer the right to rescind the purchase contract within seven days of receiving goods without reason or need for compensation.

In some areas the *Consumer Protection Law* extends obligations of businesses under both the *Fair Trade Law* and the *Commodity Labelling Law* (see below). *Article 22* of the CPC requires business operators to ensure the accuracy of their advertising and states that any obligation to consumers shall be not less than that stated in the advertisement.

Article 24 extends the packaging and labelling obligations relating to imported goods and services with the requirement that labels and instructions in Chinese 'shall not be less comprehensive than the contents of labels or pamphlets from the place of origin'.

THE COMMODITY LABELLING LAW

Taiwan's *Commodity Labelling Law* was revised in 1991. Administered by the Ministry of Economic affairs, the Law requires the labelling of all goods sold on the domestic market to be primarily in Chinese. However, for imported commodities sold on the domestic market, the addition of labelling or a descriptive leaflet in Chinese is deemed to be sufficient to meet the intention of the Law.

Any product sold in Taiwan in packaged form is required to include the following particulars:

- The name of the commodity;
- The name and address of the manufacturer or trader and (in the case of imports), the name and address of the importer;
- Major components/ingredients;
- Weight, volume or quantity;
- Specifications or grade;
- The dates of manufacture and expiry— in either Chinese calendar form or in Gregorian calendar form;
- Any other particulars specified by the competent government authorities in relation to specific products.

Where any information affixed to a label indicates patent rights held for the item in question, the label is required to include the title of the patent and patent certificate number.

ENVIRONMENTAL PROTECTION

Concern for quality of life issues has come late to Taiwan and the country is now counting the environmental cost of decades of rapid and unfettered industrialisation. Indeed, even by third-world standards, Taiwan (which increasingly sees itself as being a fully industrialised nation) has one of the most heavily polluted living environments on the planet. Population densities throughout much of the island rank among the highest in the world, yet only 3% of Taiwan has an adequate sewerage system. Ninety-seven per cent of all effluent is discharged untreated into the island's rivers and waterways.

The Environmental Protection Administration (EPA) is the sole agency at the national level responsible for developing environmental standards, drafting legislation and coordinating action among the other various agencies of government at national, provincial and local levels. The EPA has been pro-active in developing a proper legislative basis for environmental management in Taiwan.

There are more than three registered factories and 460 motor vehicles for each square kilometre in Taiwan. Not surprisingly, air quality in Taiwan is also amongst the world's worst. Taiwan's Pollution Standard Index—or PSI (an index which provides a benchmark for measuring air quality standards)—records levels of pollution which are typically six times greater than those of the US. The worst levels of air pollution are usually recorded in the south of Taiwan—in the industrialised areas of Kaohsiung and Pingtung counties—where daily PSI readings of more than 100 are common. Suspended particles contribute some 70% of total pollutants, followed by ozone at 20%. Vehicular exhaust is the main cause of air pollution in Taiwan.

Until recently, Taiwan's Environmental Protection Administration appeared to be fighting a losing battle. Despite a number of legislative and administrative remedies, concern for economic development at minimal costs resulted both in a failure of proper infrastructure planning as well as lax enforcement of any form of pollution control measures. This situation is now changing but it will take Taiwan many years to clean up. In a number of areas the environment has been degraded to such an extent that damage is likely to be permanent.

The affluence of Taiwan's middle class and the demands for a quality of life commensurate with purchasing power have forced a radical shift in attitudes at the policy level. Measures to improve both water and air quality have been strengthened, as have waste disposal systems. It is not overstating the case to realise that until as recently as 1996, official attitudes to waste disposal at the local government level appeared to be for garbage trucks to dump their refuse in the nearest riverbed. Sadly this still sometimes happens, although these days such activities prompt immediate investigation.

Of particular importance to companies establishing factory operations in Taiwan is the landmark 1994 *Environmental Impact Evaluation Law* developed and administered by the EPA, which requires the screening by government of all new development projects including, as appropriate, public hearings and community consultations. Stiff penalties, including fines and prison terms, can be imposed on developers who refuse to put projects on hold during the screening process.

The EPA also maintains Taiwan's air quality monitoring network (which only commenced operations in 1993) and monitors river and stream water quality, ocean water quality and airport noise.

Table 8.3. Taiwan's principal environmental legislation

Year	Legislation (revision)
1972	Drinking Water Management Act (1997)
1974	Waste Disposal Act (1997)
1975	Air Pollution Control Act (1997)
1988	Toxic Chemicals Control Act (1988)
1991	Water Pollution Control Act (1991)
1992	Rules for Promoting the Use of the Taiwan Ecolabel (1992)
1993	Hazardous Industrial Waste Import, Export, Transit and Trans-shipment Management Measures (1993, 1997)
1993	Emergency Response Measures for Serious Deterioration of Air Quality (1993)
1993	Law for the Settling of Public Nuisance Disputes (1993)
1994	Oceanic Effluent Standards (1994)
1994	Industrial Waste Water Pollution Control Measures and the Management of Urban Effluent (Sewerage)
1994	Environmental Impact Evaluation Law (Pending)
1995	Program for Implementing Air Quality Improvement Plan and for Levying Air Pollution Control Fees
1996	Measures for Encouraging Publicly or Privately Owned Organisations to Construct and Operate Incinerators

Air Quality Standards

As part of its strengthened measure to improve air quality and establish emission control standards, the ROC Government in 1995 introduced a *Program for Implementing Air Quality Improvement Plan and for Levying Air Pollution Control Fees*. Measures include a tax of NT$0.375/litre on unleaded gasoline and NT$0.75/litre on leaded gasoline. Leaded gasoline still accounts for more than 60% of all gasoline sales in Taiwan.

Industrial Effluent

Because of the immediate impact on an already overcrowded (and highly degraded) environment, the greatest attention of the government so far has been placed on improving water quality standards, on improving standards of toxic waste disposal and on general solid waste management issues.

The 1991 *Water Pollution Control Act* stipulates daily fines for individuals or companies found to be polluting waterways. Water pollution control measures were strengthened in 1994 with the passage of two additional Acts governing ocean effluent standards and waste water management. New companies or those entering into new projects must ensure adequate treatment of both solid and liquid wastes and submit their management control programs to public scrutiny as part of the environmental impact screening procedures.

All companies managing toxic substances or which discharge waste water, gas or other industrial waste are responsible for managing their waste products and are required to file plans with the EPA for the proper disposal of their output. Individual companies are then assigned deadlines for the establishment of proper disposal systems and management programs. Provided a company meets its deadline for action, no penalty is levied. However, for companies which have not submitted such a plan and which are found to be polluters, the penalties can be severe. Companies or individuals found dumping hazardous waste resulting in loss of life can be sentenced to imprisonment for life.

INTELLECTUAL PROPERTY PROTECTION

In recent years Taiwan has made a concerted effort to conform to international trading practices and to shake off its former image as a haven for commercial piracy and counterfeiting. Although precluded by its anomalous international position from joining many international organisations and diplomatic conventions, Taiwan has gone to great lengths to act as a modern responsible member of the international community.

Table 8.4. Taiwan's bilateral IP agreements

Country	Agreements
Australia	Patents, Trademarks
France	Patents, Trademarks

Table 8.4 cont'd

Germany	Invention Patent, Petty Patent
Japan	Patent
Switzerland	Patent
United States	Patent, Trademarks
	Source: National Bureau of Standards

Within the government, patent and trademark protection matters are handled by the National Bureau of Standards within the Ministry of Economic Affairs while copyright matters are the responsibility of the Ministry of the Interior.

Of particular importance to Taiwan is its admission to the World Trade Organisation, an application which has been pending since 1990 when it filed for membership of the WTO's precursor, the General Agreement on Tariffs and Trade (GATT). As part of its effort towards membership (and in the face of much international pressure, particularly from the US) Taiwan has accorded high priority to strengthening its intellectual property protection laws.

All major legislation dealing with IP issues has now been enacted and further amendments are before the Legislature which would bring Taiwan into line with the provisions of the Trade Related Aspects of Intellectual Property (TRIPS) Agreement. One consequence of WTO accession will be the increased level of protection afforded to foreign nationals. At present, Taiwan generally operates on the basis of reciprocity: nationals of those countries that accord intellectual property protection to ROC nationals receive protection in Taiwan. After accession to the WTO, nationals of all WTO member states will receive equal protection.

Table 8.5. Taiwan's IP legal framework

Year	Legislation
Pending	Omnibus Amendments in order to comply with TRIPS Agreement
1996	Trade Secrets Law
1995	Integrated Circuit Layout Protection Law
1994	Patent Law (Revised); Copyright Law (Revised)
1993	Trademarks Law

THE TRADE SECRETS LAW

Although the ROC Civil Code, Criminal Code and the *Fair Trade Law* provide some measure of protection for trade secrets, Taiwan has recently enacted explicit regulations governing this aspect of intellectual property protection. A 'trade secret' is held to be something that is not generally known to the public and that has commercial value which the owner has sought to protect. Penalties under the Law are limited to civil damages which include punitive damages up to three times the amount of injury proven in court. The Commercial Business Department of the Ministry of Economic Affairs is responsible for administering the *Trade Secrets Law*.

Criminal action for the infringement of trade secrets may be instigated under the ROC Criminal Code. Under this code, any person who is required by law, order or contract to preserve commercial or industrial secrets and who discloses such secrets without legitimate reason may be imprisoned for up to one year.

COPYRIGHT PROTECTION

The *Copyright Law* was substantially amended and expanded in 1992 to bring ROC copyright provisions into conformity with the Beme Convention. Copyright matters are under the jurisdiction of a Copyright Committee within the Ministry of the Interior. Works subject to copyright include oral and/or literary works, musical, dramatic and choreographic works, photographic and pictorial works, audiovisual works and sound recordings, architectural works and computer programs. Original productions adapted from pre-existing works are classified as Derivative Works and are protected independently of the *Copyright Law*.

Generally, economic rights enjoyed by an author of a copyrighted work endure for the life of the author plus fifty years. In situations of joint authorship, economic rights continue up until fifty years after the death of the last surviving author. Photographs, audiovisual works, sound recordings and computer programs are protected for fifty years from the date of public release. The same fifty-year rule is applied in situations where the author of a work is a juridical person

The amended *Copyright Law* also makes provision for copyrighted works to be reproduced in Braille and authorises the use of sound recordings, computers or other means to make any publicly released work suitable for exclusive use by the blind.

Copyright can only be assigned upon completion of a work. Procedures for registering a copyright are outlined in the *Implementation Rules of the Copyright Law 1992*. Registration is not compulsory.

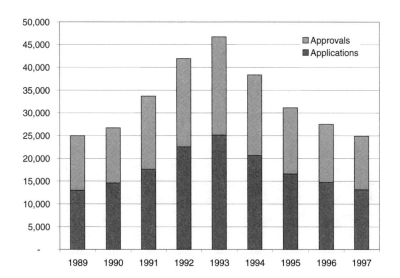

Figure 8c. Copyright applications and approvals

Table 8.6. Copyrights registered

Year	Total		Nationals		Foreigners	
	Applications	*Approvals*	*Applications*	*Approvals*	*Applications*	*Approvals*
1989	12,974	11,992	12,230	12,263	744	729
1990	14,578	12,131	14,170	11,787	408	344
1991	17,620	16,069	17,412	15,940	208	129
1992	22,529	19,399	21,775	18,811	754	588
1993	25,111	21,574	24,294	20,937	817	637
1994	20,637	17,713	20,067	17,247	570	466
1995	16,571	14,547	15,973	14,044	598	503
1996	14,728	12,769	14,155	12,354	573	415
1997	13,116	11,784	12,817	11,488	299	296

Protection of foreign works is, at present, based on the principle of national treatment. Nationals of those countries which offer reciprocal protection to ROC nationals are afforded protection under ROC law without the requirement of registration. At present however, only nationals of the US, the UK, Hong Kong, Switzerland and (in limited circumstances) Spain and the Republic of Korea can benefit from this reciprocal treatment. In all other instances, protection is based on first publication in Taiwan or local publication within 30 days of being published in the home country.

REGISTRATION OF TRADEMARKS

The *ROC Trademark Law* was revised in December 1993 and the enforcement provisions were adopted in July 1994. These broadly follow the international classification system for goods and services. The Trademark Office within the National Bureau of Standards handles all applications for trademarks and trade-service mark licences.

Applications for trademark protection are, in principle, available to all foreign nationals but may be rejected if the foreign national's own country does not accord reciprocal treatment to the ROC. The Law also provides for registration of associated and defensive trademarks as well as certification and association marks.

The registrant of a trademark has exclusive rights to the mark for a period of ten years from the date of registration (*Article 21*). However, the Law also recognises prior use and any third party who, prior to the filing, had been using in good faith the same or similar trademark retains some *a priori* rights of continuance (*Article 23*). After the expiry of the ten-year period, the mark should be renewed for further ten-year periods. Unregistered marks are afforded limited protection under the *Fair Trade Law* (see above).

Rights are granted on the basis of class of products and/or services and on priority of registration in the ROC, not on the basis of use. However, for an overseas mark, priority may be claimed provided the application is filed in the ROC within six months of the date of first application. Failure to make the priority claim at the time of filing or to submit supporting documents within the time limit leads to forfeiture of the priority claim. Priority filing rights are only extended to nationals of countries that grant similar rights to Taiwanese nationals. However once Taiwan joins the WTO, nationals of all WTO member states will automatically enjoy priority rights under Taiwan law.

Applicants for trademarks who are neither domiciled nor have a place of business in the ROC must appoint a 'trademark agent' to act on their behalf.

Trademark agents are generally qualified attorneys whose qualifications and activities are governed by a separate law.

The international classification system for goods and services was adopted by the ROC in July 1994 as the minimum standard.

The principal requirement for registration of a mark is that it is distinctive. Words, designs, letters, numerals or combinations thereof may qualify for registration for use with goods within the scope of the relevant business. Secondary marks can also, in principle, be registered although attorneys involved with trademark registration claim that in practice it is often difficult to persuade examiners that a secondary mark has acquired sufficient distinctiveness to qualify.

Trademark rights may be assigned or pledged in whole or in part to third parties and assignment of rights must be registered with the Trademark Office. Once pledged, the pledgee may not use the trademark without the permission from the owners of the right of exclusive use.

In addition to specific penalties imposed for infringement of registered trademarks, the owners of a trademark may apply for damages under the ROC Civil Code. *Article 66* of the *Trademark Law* specifies a number of formulas that may be applied for calculating damages including compensation based on an amount equal to between 500 and 1,500 times the unit retail price of the commodities seized. Owners may also claim for additional compensation should it be shown that their business reputation has suffered damage as a result of the infringement.

A number of further changes to the *Trademark Law* have been foreshadowed and will bring Taiwan into line with the TRIPS Agreement. Among the proposed changes *Article 5* (which defines items capable of protection) is to be broadened to include marks incorporating colour combinations. It will also make explicit the ability to protect such things as descriptive, family and geographic names where it can be shown that these have met the requirement of distinctiveness through use.

The proposed amendments will also extend the grace period for renewal of registrations. Under the current Law, an application for renewal of a trademark registration must be filed during the twelve-month period preceding expiry. On the one hand, the renewal period will be shortened to six months prior to expiry; however, it will also add a six-month grace period following expiry so that, provided the renewal is effected during the grace period, the registration will be considered to be continuously effected.

Additional protection is also to be given to famous marks through denying registration to any mark that is either identical or similar to the famous mark, unless the applicant has obtained prior consent from the owner of the mark.

Registration will also be denied to designs that are the same or similar to marks previously used and where the applicant has some ongoing or former association with the owner of the previous mark and where it appears a mark is being misappropriated.

PATENT PROTECTION

The *ROC Patent Law* was last revised in January 1994 when it was brought broadly into line with international conventions. Patents are classified under three categories: invention, new utility model (petty patent) and new design (*Article 2*). For new inventions, protection is generally provided for twenty years although in the case of inventions covering pharmaceuticals and agrochemicals, a two- to five-year extension may be granted. Micro-organisms as well as food and beverages are in the process of being added to the items classified as being patentable subject matter.

For new utility models protection is given for twelve years, and for new designs the period is ten years. Protection is deemed to commence on the date of filing of an application. The usual tests for novelty, usefulness and non-obviousness are applied to applications for patents.

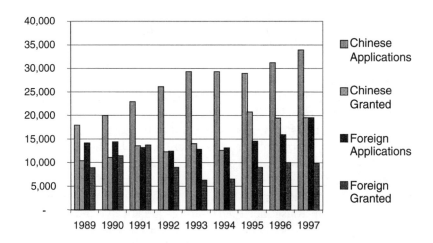

Figure 8d. Patents applied for and granted

THE INTEGRATED CIRCUIT LAYOUT PROTECTION LAW

Taiwan is seeking to develop its IC industry as one of the key new technologies and protection for overseas licensees of IC technology has been given high priority by the government. Taiwan's *Integrated Circuit Layout Protection Law* was promulgated in August 1995 and came into force in February 1996. The enforcement rules were also issued in February 1996.

Foreign nationals can apply for protection under the Law provided that their home country extends reciprocal treatment to ROC nationals. Protection can also be afforded on the basis of first commercial use in Taiwan. Protection can only be given to circuits and layout designs registered with the National Bureau of Standards, the body designated as the competent authority to administer the Law. An application for registration must be filed within two years of the first commercial use of the layout and protection is granted for a period of ten years thereafter.

The new Law provides protection of the rights of the designers and creators of circuit layouts that are incorporated into integrated circuits. In order to gain protection under the new Law, a circuit layout must be shown to be original. Considerable weight is given to creativity—at the time of its creation the key features of the layout must not have been in common use or widely known among the industry.

Once rights have been established, the circuit owner can exclude others from reproducing or importing any circuit which reproduces the protected layout in whole or in part. The only exceptions permitted under the Law are reproductions made solely for research, teaching or reverse engineering.

The *IC Protection Law* provides for civil remedies for transgressions but not criminal penalties. In this aspect it differs from the *Patent*, *Copyright* and *Trademark Law*s which provide both criminal penalties and civil redress. If a claim can be established under the Law the victim has a number of options for compensation including the award of damages of up to NT$5 million.

THE CONSUMER DATA PROTECTION LAW

All companies involved in the maintenance of databases relating to individuals are governed by the *Consumer Processed Personal Data Protection Law*. This Law and the accompanying enforcement rules are under the regulatory jurisdiction of the Ministry of Justice. *The Data Protection Law* seeks to balance the individual's right to privacy with the new emerging operating realities of the business environment. Any organisation within Taiwan that engages in the collection, storage, processing, use, transmission or distribution of information about any person (bearing any sort of relation to the organisation) is subject to the Law. The Law also specifies the conditions under which personal data can be exported to foreign countries.

Key articles of the *Data Protection Law* are:

- *Article 3: Definitions*—The Law defines the term 'personal data' to mean the name, date of birth, uniform number of identification card, special features, fingerprint, marital status, family, education, profession, health condition, medical history, financial condition, and social activities of a natural person as well as other data sufficient to identify the said person;

- *Article 4: Revision, Correction or Deletion of Personal Data*—The Law permits data subjects to request the revision, correction or even deletion of personal data should the validity of the data be in question or should the underlying purpose for collection no longer exist;

- *Article 18: Consent of Data Subjects*—Either the written consent of a person or a contractual relationship must exist before an organisation can collect and use personal data. However, when previously collected data is to be used beyond the confines of the originally specified purpose, fresh consent must be obtained. Generally, once properly collected, data should be freely transferable within the boundaries of the data's specific purpose;

- *Article 25: International Transmission of Personal Data*—The Law stipulates that in situations where data is to be transferred to other countries, the receiving country must have in place an adequate set of data protection laws.

As the Law has only recently been promulgated, the Ministry of Justice (MoJ) is still formulating the precise operating guidelines. While a number of local companies have run foul of the Law, the MoJ is reputedly sympathetic to any problems the Law may present to MNCs (such as international and *bona fide* credit companies) that are required to transmit data internationally as part of their normal business operations.

It is relevant to note that the insurance industry can freely gain access to medical records of applicants for life insurance without running foul of the *Data Protection Law* as the 'need to know' has been recognised by the Ministry of Justice.

KEY GOVERNMENT AGENCIES

Ministry of Justice
130 Chungking South Road, Taipei
Tel: (02) 2314 6871
Fax: (02) 2331 9102

Ministry of Economic Affairs
15 Foochow Street, Taipei
Tel: (02) 2321 2200
Fax: (02) 2391 9398

Fair Trade Commission
8F, 150 Tunhwa North Road, Taipei
Tel: (02) 2351 7588
Fax: (02) 2397 4997

Consumer Protection Commission
1 Chung Hsiao East Road, Section 1, Taipei
Tel: (02) 2356 6600
Fax: (02) 2321 4538

Environmental Protection Administration
41 Chunghwa Road, Section 1, Taipei
Tel: (02) 2311 7722
Fax: (02) 2311 6071

National Bureau of Standards (MOEA)
3F, 185 Hsinhai Road, Section 2, Taipei
Tel: (02) 2738 0007
Fax: (02) 2735 2656

Patent Office
Tel: (02) 2735 2743
Fax: (02) 2377 1820

Trademark Office
Tel: (02) 2735 2530
Fax: (02) 2378 0998

Ministry of the Interior
   5 Hsuchow Road, Taipei
   Tel: (02) 2356 5000
   Fax: (02) 2356 6201

Copyright Committee
   Tel: (02) 2356 5042
   Fax: (02) 2397 6967

CHAPTER 9

WORKING WITH THE MARKET

Taiwan is now a consumer society. The change in living and lifestyle patterns that has taken place during the past decade, especially in Taipei, has been close to revolutionary. Much of this change has been brought about by the exposure Taiwanese now have to the outside world.

Travel has played a large part in bringing about the consumer revolution. It is barely ten years since the restriction on international tourist travel was lifted for Taiwanese (the restrictions being a measure introduced during the martial law period to conserve precious foreign exchange). In 1982 there were only some 641,000 outbound departures of Taiwanese nationals travelling overseas of which less than 300,000 were related to leisure purposes. By 1996, the number of departures had increased to more than 5.7 million—the vast majority travelling overseas as tourists.[1] There are very

---

[1] Collection of departure statistics relating to purpose of journey was discontinued in 1994. In the previous year there were a total of 4.6 million departures of which 4.0 million were tourism related.

few who have not had at least one overseas tour, but those who do not travel now have access to cable television and, for younger people especially, the Internet, as a means of keeping in touch with the world. Taiwanese have tasted the good life. Not only are they demanding more of their government in terms of seeking improvement in the quality of life, they have the money to acquire it for themselves.

Any person who has been a regular visitor to Taipei will be aware of the rapidity with which the city is changing in response to the demands of the consumer. Fashionable boutiques are no longer confined to the immediate vicinity of the international hotels but are now spread throughout the city. Younger people congregate in stylish coffee shops, pubs and restaurants while parents with young children can dine out at the full range of international family food chains. Despite earlier predictions to the contrary, Chinese of all ages have taken to pizza and hamburgers with alacrity.

Taiwanese increasingly shop in world-class department stores, supermarkets or hypermarkets. They drive new cars, take overseas holidays and watch movies in modern air conditioned entertainment complexes. All of this is a product of the 1990s.

Profiling the Consumer

Consumption patterns in Taiwan are most clearly differentiated by age. Those in middle age and the elderly grew up and prospered in difficult times and frugality is deeply embedded within them. The good life has largely passed them by. Taiwan's younger generation, on the other hand, has never known hunger and their parents seem to be content to let their children enjoy the fruits of their labour. They are free spenders who will have, and use, at least one credit card.

Consumption patterns are differentiated by locality. In terms of lifestyles and associated spending patterns, Taipei leads the way. A trend that begins in Taipei will then spread to the other major urban centres of Kaohsiung (in the south) and Taichung (in the centre of the island). Outside the major urban centres the pace of change is still much slower. Most of rural Taiwan is still awaiting the consumer revolution but then very few younger people (of working age) live in the countryside these days.

Taiwanese have high disposable incomes, a consequence of lifestyles that for many are still centred on the extended family. It is rare for Taiwanese young people to move out of the family home before marriage unless dictated by necessity, such as a move from a rural to an urban location for employment. Although tradition is slowly breaking down, it remains common for several generations to live in one house.

A 1995 government study into family income and expenditure patterns showed that on average disposable income of Taiwanese accounted for almost 80% of the total gross available personal income of NT$5,898 billion (US$179 billion approx.). Perhaps of equal interest is that, in terms of income sources, salary and wages accounted in aggregate for only 55% of the total. Entrepreneurial income from business activities accounted for 18%, while property rentals accounted for a further 15%. The remainder came from transfer receipts from other parties. These figures underscore the entrepreneurial nature of Taiwan's society and the fact that many such income recipients are business people and property owners with a propensity to spend and to invest. Almost 66% of all income earners are below the age of 45 years and 34.5% of them are female.

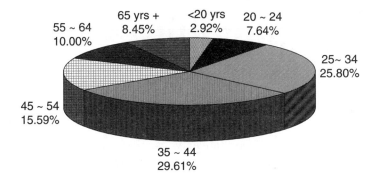

Figure 9a. The percentage of income recipients by age group (1995)

Lifestyles are changing too. A greater proportion of the population is either remaining single or marrying later in life and those who are marrying are now choosing smaller families. While Taiwan remains fundamentally a young society, changing lifestyles have resulted in an ageing of the income-earning population. Prior to 1992, the largest single income group was the 25- to 34-year-old age group whereas it is now the 35- to 44-year group. Children are staying at school longer and the proportion of the workforce below 20 years has declined dramatically as a result. Yet the under-20 age group has a high spending power, thanks to access to family incomes and allowances, and much marketing activity is aimed at this group.

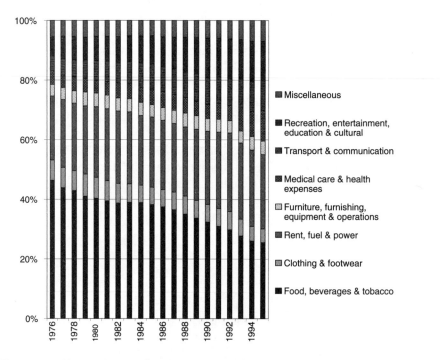

Figure 9b. Percentage distribution of total expenditure

Taiwanese are spending proportionately less on food, beverages, tobacco, clothing and footwear and spending more on medical and health care, transportation, recreation and education.

Households in the Taipei metropolitan area enjoy levels of disposable income and discretionary expenditure well above the national average. According to the 1995 survey, Taipei residents had disposable incomes that were almost 40% above the national level. They spent 50% more than others on clothing and footwear, 96% more on furniture and appliances, 85% more on recreation and 180% more than others in Taiwan on travelling. The only segment of the market where they fell below the national average was in relation to tobacco products. Discretionary savings were also higher for Taipei residents but overall they spent more and saved less. This consumption pattern can be expected to slowly work its way into other areas of Taiwan.

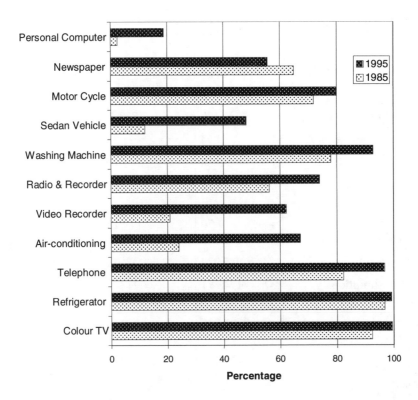

Figure 9c. Percentage of households with equipment and appliances: 1985 and 1995

In part, the trend of the 1990s towards consumer spending has been accelerated by the property boom of the late 1980s. Because of current high and stagnant property prices, Taiwanese are no longer investing in property to the extent they did previously. Since those owner-occupiers are now choosing to renovate rather than move, sales of kitchen appliances and home furnishings are booming. Conspicuous consumer durable items such as automobiles are seen as an alternative investment for many middle and higher income earners as well as being a status symbol of the *nouveau riche*. The booming leisure and travel market is also a reflection of the changed lifestyle patterns that cuts across all age groups.

Table 9.1. 1995 national expenditure survey

Survey Area	National Average	Taipei Municipality	
		Amount	%
Number of households	**5,731,179**	**838,551**	
# Persons per household	**3.94**	**3.73**	
# Adults per household	**2.58**	**2.54**	
# Employed persons per household	**1.71**	**1.58**	
# Income recipients per household	**1.70**	**1.67**	
A Total Receipts	**985,929**	**1,326,036**	**34.50%**
B Non-Consumption Expenditure	**174,591**	**213,231**	**22.13%**
C Consumption Expenditure	**591,035**	**852,811**	**44.29%**
Food	139,736	162,088	16.00%
Beverage	6,046	6,454	6.75%
Tobacco	4,950	3,315	-33.03%
Clothing and footwear	27,213	40,742	49.72%
Rent and water charges	130,722	212,774	62.77%
Fuel and light	16,506	22,318	35.21%
Furniture and family facilities	15,823	31,033	96.13%
Household operations	11,215	20,648	84.11%
Health care and medical	61,271	60,472	-1.30%
Transport and communications	59,089	68,882	16.57%
Purchase of transport equipment	15,453	11,110	-28.10%
Operation of transport equipment	25,020	29,206	16.73%

Table 9.1 cont'd

Purchased transportation	8,880	16,143	81.79%
Other communications	5,819	7,362	26.52%
Insurance of transport equipment	3,917	5,061	29.21%
Recreation, education and culture	77,519	143,583	85.22%
Travelling	24,041	67,527	180.88%
Recreation services	7,752	11,758	51.68%
Books and stationery	5,124	6,875	34.17%
Recreation facilities	7,719	12,562	62.74%
Education and research	32,884	44,861	36.42%
Miscellaneous	40,945	80,502	96.61%
Disposable Income	**811,338**	**1,112,806**	**37.16%**
Final Consumption Expenditure	**591,035**	**852,811**	**44.29%**
Savings	**220,303**	**259,994**	**18.02%**
Current Receipts	**1,029,053**	**1,401,261**	**36.17%**

RETAILING IN TAIWAN

The retailing industry in Taiwan has undergone a rapid transformation in recent years in line with the rising affluence and demands of the population. At the basic level, the traditional base of wet markets and general provision stores has, in the major cities at least, been eroded by a shift to modern retail chains supported by sophisticated warehousing and efficient distribution networks. This trend started in Taipei, which is the most sophisticated of Taiwan's urban areas, and has now spread to Kaohsiung and Taichung. While modern retailing outlets and methods are not yet island wide, the compact nature of Taiwan and heavy population densities (along the western corridor at least) ensure that the trend will continue across the island.

Unlike countries such as Korea, which have placed draconian restrictions on the development of retail chains by foreign companies, there are no such restrictions in Taiwan. The Japanese were the first to enter the market in Taiwan with modern supermarket retailing methods but the Japanese sophistication did not sit comfortably at first with the Taiwanese and it was the Hong Kong supermarket chains—with many years of experience in catering to Chinese tastes and requirements—that really changed the way people shop.

The Japanese have, however, had greater success in general merchandising and dominate the department store sector of retailing. Not surprisingly, Japanese products tend to feature prominently in these stores.

In the last six years, the growth of modern food retail outlets—supermarkets, convenience stores and hypermarkets—has been explosive and the trend is expected to continue. Modern chains offer economies of scale, which translate into cost advantages for consumers. National legislation has encouraged the development of modern, hygienic and efficient food retailing outlets. Sales from hypermarkets now outpace supermarket sales by a growing margin.

Changing Consumption Patterns

As the Taiwanese become more affluent there has been a noticeable shift in both consumption patterns and associated retailing methods:

- Taiwanese are now travelling internationally in large numbers. Not only has this created a demand for more variety, including Western foods and international brand names, but it has also influenced the manner in which many people now shop;
- The greater number of women in the workforce has dramatically increased the demand for convenience foods and products which cut down on domestic labour;
- Greater awareness of health and sanitation has increased the demand for 'nutritious' foods and at the same time has influenced the packaging and labelling of products;
- As consumers, the Taiwanese remain price sensitive in their daily consumption choices, however price sensitivity is thrown to the wind when it comes to purchasing items that provide a recognisable status image; here 'branding' is paramount.

Trends in Retailing Methods

Taiwan's retailing market represents an industry valued at NT$2.7 trillion in sales value and is currently growing overall at around 8% per annum. Overseas developers are now entering in increasing numbers and with ambitious projects in the hope of capturing a slice of the burgeoning market. Led by the hypermarkets and warehouse clubs, the size of retail outlets has been growing. The shopping complexes and associated malls so common elsewhere have come late to Taiwan, in part because of the scarcity of large tracts of land close to large urban neighbourhoods. However, highway improvements and the new mobility of the population is set to change the face of retailing further. A number of foreign and domestic developers have recently announced plans to build new shopping complexes, to the extent that if they all go ahead, Taiwan would rapidly reach a point of over-saturation. The TaiMall Development Company appears to be first in the race to bring in this new age with an NT$6.7 billion project for Taoyuan County, south of Taipei, which is due to be completed in late 1998. The seven floors of shops and associated parking lot for 3,600 cars will be strategically located within 30 minutes drive of an estimated 4.8 million consumers. The Core Pacific Group has announced plans to build a NT$12 billion shopping complex in Eastern Taipei while Taiwan's President Group will spend NT$80 billion building four large shopping and entertainment complexes in Taipei, Taichung, Tainan and Kaohsiung. These are just a few of the projects currently announced or under way.

The Major Retail Chains

Provision of food and food services is a major industry in Taiwan. Food and associated dry goods accounts for the largest retail sector and nowhere have the changing consumption patterns had more influence than in this sector. Although there is no publicly available official information on the segmentation of purchasing patterns, discussions with those engaged in the industry suggest the following:

- The majority of food purchased continues to be for private consumption and in the last six years modern retailing stores have made significant inroads into traditional distribution outlets. This trend is expected to continue;
- Younger people are tending more towards Western-style food while middle-aged and older people still prefer traditional Chinese and Japanese foods;
- One aspect of the accelerated trend towards modern distribution methods, designed to preserve the livelihoods of the traditional retailers, is the conversion of a number of former traditional markets into retailing cooperatives. Local government funds are made available to build large-

scale modern supermarkets on the former market sites. Government retains ownership of the land and building but operating control is in the hands of the cooperative;

- Disposable incomes are highest in the north of Taiwan and in the Taipei area. Taipei is the most sophisticated market area and the key to successful retailing; people in the rest of Taiwan tend to follow trends set in Taipei.

The food industry as a share of total GNP has continued to expand in recent years by a little over 1% per year. Government figures suggest the population spent a total of NT$1,265 billion on food in 1995 representing a 27.1% share of total consumption and a 15.8% share of total GNP. By far the greatest proportion of sales was at the retail level. Sales in the food service industry amounted to NT$107 billion or around 8.5% of total consumption.

Major retailing chains in Taiwan include convenience stores (52% of the food market), supermarkets (20%) and a sub-segment consisting of hypermarkets, warehouse clubs and government provision stores.

Table 9.2. Major retailers

Dominant Retailer	Market Segment
7-Eleven	Convenience
Wellcome	Supermarket
Carrefour	Hypermarket
Makro	Warehouse club

Convenience Stores

Since their introduction in the mid 1980s, the number of convenience stores has grown rapidly. Most operate on a 24 hours a day, 365 days a year basis. There are more than 3,500 convenience stores island-wide with 65% of them in northern Taiwan. The 7-Eleven Group, which is a joint venture with President Enterprises, is the largest convenience store chain with more than 1,500 outlets, double the number of its nearest rival, the 3Q Shop. 3Q is also owned by President but is a wholly domestically owned operation. Both 7-Eleven and 3Q tend to carry President brand products to the exclusion of other competitors and the holding company for the 7-Eleven chain has recently failed in its bid for a public listing because of its restrictive purchasing policies.

The rapid growth of convenience stores despite a very restricted range of products is a direct reflection of changing lifestyles. Cigarettes and soft drinks comprise the largest selling items of these stores (around 14% each of total sales) while food products account for only 10% of total sales. Not surprisingly, sales volume is seasonal with higher turnover achieved in the warmer months between April and October. The differential can be as high as 20% between summer and winter.

Supermarkets

Current industry figures show that there are only around 30 independently operated supermarkets in Taiwan. Independent operators are finding it hard to survive in the more liberalised market which has been dominated by Hong Kong interests and, more recently, a return of the Japanese to supermarket retailing which began with operations in the basement of Japanese-owned department stores. Wellcome (Dairy Farm Group) has dominated the supermarket segment since entering the Taiwan market in 1990 in Taipei and has steadily extended its operations to the centre and south of Taiwan. In recent years, however, the number of Wellcome stores has actually declined in the face of pressure from other (local) supermarket chains and the hypermarkets.

As for many of the larger supermarket chains that rely on highly diverse product ranges, problems of warehousing and distribution require a measured approach to expansion. Since Taipei is the most cosmopolitan of all Taiwan's cities, it is the logical place to commence operations. Once success has been achieved in the Taipei market, other areas of Taiwan will more readily accept change. Despite their centralised purchasing and distribution arrangements, supermarkets cannot compete with the hypermarkets when it comes to price and therefore tend to rely on the segment of the market that values convenience.

Another Hong Kong retailer, Park'N'Shop, also entered the Taiwan market at the same time as Wellcome but adopted a strategy of opening first in Kaohsiung in the south with the intention of moving northward. However, for one reason or another, Park'N'Shop did not prove to be successful and has since closed its local supermarket operations. Its associated retail pharmacy and personal store chain, Watsons, continues to do well.

Over 70% of supermarket stores continue to be in northern Taiwan although the number in the centre and south is slowly increasing as warehousing and distribution channels improve. Because most goods are hand-carried, purchasing continues to follow the Chinese trend of daily shopping in small quantities rather than the Western custom of a weekly shop. Trading hours are generally from 9 a.m. to 10 p.m. seven days a week. Most supermarkets only close for the Chinese New Year holiday.

Hypermarkets and Warehouse Clubs

Hypermarkets and warehouse clubs are the most recent trend in the food retailing industry and the most exciting in terms of their development. Hypermarkets are the largest of the food retailing outlets with typical floor areas of around 15,000 square metres and between 10,000 and 15,000 product lines. Because of their size they are generally found in urban areas and many offer parking facilities at their site. They tend to carry bulk items and have fewer problems with distribution than the supermarkets.

In addition to handling a variety of supermarket lines, such stores also carry clothing, household items and electrical and white goods. Carrefour, which is a joint venture between the French parent company and the President Group, adopted an early strategy of incorporating traditional wet markets into its food retailing area and this—and its bulk pricing—has accounted for a large part of its ready acceptance in Taiwan. The Formosa Plastics Group is the latest entrant to the hypermarket industry with plans to open an island-wide chain over the next three years as a means of utilising vacant land owned by the group.

Warehouses are technically opened only to licensed traders but this is not enforced and in practice there is little difference between the warehouses and the hypermarkets. Makro is the acknowledged market leader in the warehouse clubs and at present is dominant in this sector.

Commissaries and PX Stores

Commissaries and PX stores pre-date the rise of modern retailing and are a legacy of the martial law period when military personnel and government officials were accorded certain privileges in terms of tax relief and purchasing. Such stores would outnumber Wellcome in terms of total outlets by a factor of four but are often small in size. Many are to be found on military bases and associated with government agencies such as schools and hospitals. Management is highly conservative and reflects more a government bureaucracy than a company organisation. They do not import directly nor do they have a centralised warehousing and distribution system.

PX stores have until recently been exempt from charging VAT on purchases. Although technically confined to government employees, many non-government personnel in fact have access to such stores through family connections and friends.

An anachronism in modern-day Taiwan, PX stores are slowly being converted to regular supermarkets; however without an injection of modern management and capital, they do not appear to be growing and may decline in the future.

A 1994 study by the American Chamber of Commerce in Taipei suggested that government-run commissaries and PX stores controlled up to 40% of Taiwan's retail sales in the categories of food and beverages in which they dealt. Numbers remain static and may actually shrink in coming years. Their central organisation remains bureaucratic and often appears unable to adapt to modern market competition. Product access is tightly controlled and based on annual tender arrangements. Foreign companies report that they have virtually no access to product placement in PX stores without a well-placed local agent (often a retired general) who can make the necessary arrangements and 'considerations'.

The Department Stores

Collectively, department stores account for around 40% of all retail sales. The most successful department stores in Taiwan are those that are owned either in whole or in part by Japanese retailers and the pattern of department store retailing tends to follow the Japanese model. Hong Kong-based department stores appear to have fared less well in Taiwan. Aside from the Asia World and Far Eastern Groups, there are no major domestically owned department stores in Taiwan[2] although both the President Group and Formosa Plastics are moving aggressively into general retailing. As already noted, a number of domestic construction groups are engaged in the building of shopping complexes although management will be left to others.

The Japanese Sogo Group is the acknowledged market leader in the department store sector of the market, followed by the Mitsukoshi Group, which in Taiwan is in joint venture with the local Shin Kong Insurance Group. Not to be left behind in the retailing boom, Sogo has announced plans to build up to 10 more stores in Taiwan within the next five years while Mitsukoshi, which opened its third Taipei store in the new Hsinyi

---

[2] Asia World is actually owned by Filipino Chinese.

District of Taipei in late 1997, plans to build additional stores in Hsinchu, Changhwa and Taichung.

Table 9.3. Taipei's top ten department stores

Store	Income NT$ billion	% of Total	Annual Growth
Sogo (Chung Hsiao East Road)	10.10	19.56	16.7
Mitsukoshi (Chung Hsiao West Road)	4.43	8.58	16.7
Mitsukoshi (Nanking West Road)	4.07	7.88	11.4
Takashamaya (Tien Mu)	3.94	7.63	110.2
Far Eastern (Shimenting)	3.11	6.02	10.7
Asia World (Nanking East Road)	2.79	5.79	16.3
Ming Yao (Chung Hsiao East Road)	2.29	4.43	5.8
Printemps (Chung Hsiao East Road)	2.11	4.08	–
Far Eastern (Panchiao)	2.10	4.06	20.2
Rebar (Shimenting)	1.99	3.85	34.9

THE COMPLEXITIES OF DISTRIBUTION

The complexities of Taiwan's distribution system would require a volume of their own to cover properly. Again, the changes in consumption patterns which have brought about the retailing revolution have also in turn changed the distribution patterns, especially for imported goods.

For domestically produced products, factories generally deal directly with wholesalers and distributors, and in areas such as the fashion garment industry, enterprising middlemen often buy quantity export over-runs for sale to the domestic market. In the food industry, the major processing companies, such as the President Group, I-Mei and Shin Tung Yang, have developed vertically integrated sales and distribution networks which make penetration from outside difficult or impossible unless one or other of these groups are the local import and/or distribution agent for an imported product (or allied to them).

The Agricultural Sector

Taiwan's protected agricultural sector has a separate distribution system, which remains the most traditional, and the one that is dominated by the agricultural products wholesale markets. With Taiwan's forthcoming entry to the World Trade Organisation and the liberalisation of the import regime for agricultural products, penetration of Taiwan's agricultural distribution network will present a major challenge for overseas agricultural suppliers or marketing companies seeking to take advantage of the new opportunities.

Overseeing Taiwan's wholesale markets is the Provincial Food Bureau, an arm of the Taiwan Provincial Government. The markets themselves can be either privately owned and operated (i.e. a corporate structure) or operated by the network of farmers' or fishermen's associations and cooperatives. Regulation of the markets is governed by the *Agricultural Products Market Transaction Law* and the *Regulations of Wholesale Management of Agricultural Products in Taiwan.* Foreign investment into the market management companies is not prohibited but so far none has occurred.

By regulation, only one such market is allowed in each prefecture, city and township. There is currently a total of 148 wholesale markets in Taiwan consisting of 65 fruit and vegetable markets, 23 livestock (meat) markets, 59 fish markets and one composite market (in Tainan). The livestock markets concentrate on hogs which (despite the foot and mouth epidemic of 1997) remain the primary domestic meat produced. Transactions can be on the basis of auction or price negotiation with each market determining its own procedures.

Although current import restrictions severely limit the level of foreign agricultural products allowed into Taiwan, those products that do enter the market in bulk form are, for the most part, sold on in bulk by the importer to one of the wholesale markets. Chilled and frozen products are usually handled by wholesalers and distributors with the experience and equipment to handle such goods although many of the larger retailers are now establishing such facilities themselves. According to industry sources, there is an increasing tendency for such chains to purchase imported fruit direct from the importer while they rely on the wholesalers and wholesale markets for vegetables that are less temperature and time-sensitive. In general terms, the volume and the value of unprocessed food products passing directly from importers to retailers is increasing and will continue to do so.

Specialty processed agricultural products such as wines and cheeses would only be sold to distributors or wholesalers either for retail sale in selected supermarkets and other retail outlets or for institutional users such as hotels and restaurants.

A number of the more commercially minded agricultural distributors have already sensed the winds of change and are ready to seek alliances with foreign suppliers in anticipation of the expected adaptations that will be necessary once Taiwan joins the WTO. Now is the time for a foreign agricultural supplier to seek a long term strategic position.

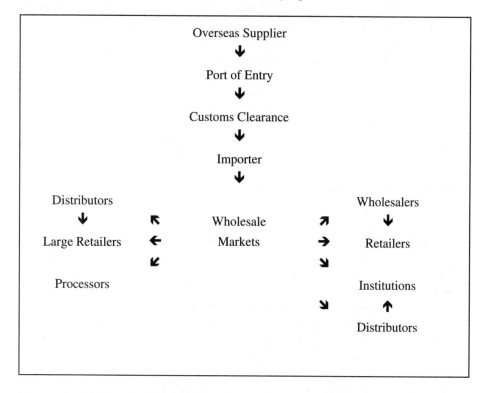

Figure 9c. Taiwan's distribution system for imported agricultural products

Processed Food and General Merchandise

The distribution system for processed items and general merchandise goods is equally complex but again the import agent has a key role to play in dealing with distributors and wholesalers. In many instances the importer will also be either a distributor, wholesaler, or both, and will deal directly with key accounts such as the major supermarkets and hypermarkets.

For many products the availability of warehousing and storage facilities (including cold storage) will be another major factor influencing the distribution channel. Fortunately, the development of modern retailing facilities has brought with it centralised warehousing facilities. This means that distribution is less of a problem unless a product is destined for sale through the more traditional retail outlets.

A number of the major retail chains are now bypassing the local distribution network and undertaking direct importing, although in the case of processed foods, more than 80% of the market is still supplied from import agents.

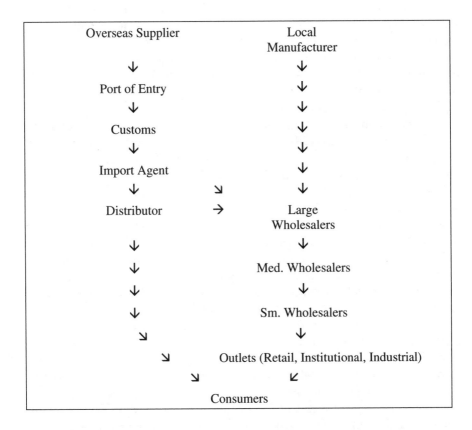

Figure 9d. Distribution system for processed foods and other items

While vertically integrated domestic companies dominate much of the food retailing industry, in the area of brand name fashion goods, it is the foreign companies that have led the way in establishing their own retail chains. A number of the department stores, especially, have opened in-house brand name boutiques and, as the development of integrated shopping complexes accelerates, a greater degree of vertical integration within the distribution chain appears inevitable—especially for foreign products seeking a coordinated approach to development of the market.

MARKETING FOR SUCCESS

Affluence has brought with it a desire, especially on the part of younger people, for an upmarket image and a whole advertising and marketing industry has grown around the need for companies to achieve name recognition. Yet, while the market desires sophistication, Taiwan is by no means a sophisticated market. While generalities can sometimes be dangerous, the Taiwanese consumer tends to lack discrimination. The intrinsic quality of a product is often of less importance than the packaging or the hype of the marketing.

Foreign companies seeking to influence the purchasing patterns of consumers need effective advertising and promotional campaigns carefully orchestrated by seasoned professionals if they are to have any chance of gaining—and keeping—a foothold in the market.

Possibly the one defining characteristic of the market is that of price sensitivity. Consumers like to have a brand name product but many are unwilling to pay a brand name price. This has at least two consequences. On the one hand, any product that does well in Taiwan will quickly spawn imitations. The *Fair Trade Law* has gone some way to protecting companies from imitation in name, design or packaging but the onus is on the aggrieved party to initiate and demonstrate harm. Secondly, the success of any brand name will invariably lead to attempts at parallel importing. Indeed, a number of the more successful marketing and distribution companies in Taiwan started life in this way and were so successful they either took over the franchise for the product or, having established a viable distribution network, were approached by a rival company seeking quick access to the market. Vigilance is the name of the game.

Perhaps the second aspect of the market is its fickleness. Taiwanese are quick to latch onto a fad, especially if it is one associated with status, but will equally easily turn away without constant reinforcement or reason for purchase.

224

Name recall is especially important and quite often will require a change or adaptation from the English (or other foreign language) into Chinese. In the booming credit card industry for example, one reason for the Visa Card's popularity over its rival, MasterCard, is the simple fact that the word 'Visa' is not only easy to pronounce in Chinese but has instant name association whereas 'MasterCard' is both difficult for many Chinese to pronounce and has no such recognition.

Once a brand is established and accepted, however, the rewards can be considerable; designer labels for example retail for around three times the price of a similar quality non-branded product.

Promotion and awareness campaigns can take a number of forms and will depend on the product. Most foreign suppliers will appoint a merchandising company specifically to organise brand promotion and familiarisation campaigns.

Promotional Methods

Advertising is the traditional and most common form of sales and product promotion but can be quite costly unless high sales are anticipated. Television advertising on the three government-controlled broadcast channels is extremely expensive, typically running at more than NT$33,000 (US$1,000) for a ten-second time slot at peak viewing times. Rates on the local cable network are less expensive and have the advantage of targeting local areas where advertising can be most effective. The cable network also carries several home shopping channels which are especially popular for marketing such items as skin care products. [3]

While newspaper circulation in Taiwan has been declining in recent years, publishing generally is booming, as are sales of magazines catering to the new upwardly mobile consumer class. Advertising rates are generally expensive. Not unexpectedly, newspapers tend to be dominated by time-specific advertising whereas the magazines cater more to brand awareness.

Food Products

In regard to the marketing of food products, most supermarkets and other chain outlets in Taiwan charge listing fees to ensure that a product is

---

[3] Amazing as it may seem to foreigners, Taiwan has one cable TV channel totally dedicated to the advertising of bust enlargement products.

displayed on shelves. Some also charge an advertising contribution fee. These fees can often be quite high but are a necessary part of doing business with the major retail food chains. Because of the importance of in-store promotions to attract customers, suppliers will be expected to participate in regular promotional campaigns throughout the year. The most common types of promotion include in-store tastings (especially popular to introduce new products and for meats, biscuits and wines) and straight price discounts as well as multiple packaging whereby items are packaged together at a specially discounted price. In view of the price sensitivity displayed by consumers when purchasing household necessities, these latter forms of promotion are widespread in Taiwan.

General Merchandising

Taiwan offers considerable potential in a whole range of consumer products and the demand for imported consumer items has grown rapidly. Areas most tapped by foreign suppliers include fashion garments, skin care products, furniture and furnishings and domestic household appliances.

In the fashion industry, by way of example, the annual growth rate for garment imports has exceeded 25% on average over recent years. With the rapid growth of demand for overseas products and an end to export quotas for domestically produced products scheduled for the year 2005, more and more domestic manufacturers are forging alliances with European and US brand labels in order to produce high value fashion goods domestically for the local market while at the same time shifting their traditional low-end product lines to elsewhere in Asia.

In some areas, especially in the realm of appliances, product demonstration as well as detailed instructions in Chinese are often essential if Taiwanese are to understand the product let alone create a desire to purchase. Chinese noodle-making machines (when they are used at all—Chinese noodles are usually made by hand) are very different from the Italian variety.

In the area of general merchandising, a foreign supplier must usually be prepared to compete either on the basis of price or spend the necessary time, effort and money to create and maintain brand recognition and a dedicated retail network. Led by the cosmetic industry and clothing chains, such brand-name marketing is now extending to include a full range of products including giftware, toiletries and household items. Even so, the full potential for this type of promotion in Taiwan remains to be exploited.

Direct Marketing

In recent years a number of direct sales companies have established themselves in Taiwan as an alternative means of reaching the consumer. Such companies thrive on the appeal of being able to provide a distributed sales force at minimal cost. Many otherwise non-working women have been attracted to such companies by the opportunity to earn a part-time income. The most successful of the direct marketing companies are those that have been established from overseas. Less successful have been the operations of a number of local entrepreneurs seeking to enter this new industry, often with great enthusiasm but with little experience and even less capital. The situation with regard to direct marketing has become of sufficient concern to force the government to introduce stringent controls on this form of marketing activity. Many companies openly continue to flout the regulations, however. Since it is only a matter of time before they are brought under control, foreign companies seeking to enter this market are well advised to seek proper commercial checks followed by professional advice before engaging a local company as an agent in this area.

Direct mailings are a further popular means of promotion, and a number of companies in Taiwan specialise in offering direct mail lists including both consumer and business information. In spite of passage of the *Computer Processed Consumer Data Protection Law*, such businesses appear to be unaffected provided the information used in compiling the lists is obtained from public sources.

CHAPTER 10

WINNING FRIENDS AND INFLUENCING PEOPLE

Dale Carnegie had it right. Much in business, as in life in general, gets down to the personal touch. Many foreign companies, large and small, have sought to carve a niche in the Taiwan market. Some prosper, some quickly wither. Having the correct distribution and marketing strategies are of course essential ingredients for business survival but there is a flip side: adaptation either of products, of approach, or both is often equally necessary to achieve a lasting place in the Taiwan market.

In Taiwan, pizza chains offer fried rice (and that travesty to the true pizza aficionado, the apple pizza), and burger franchises offer vegetarian alternatives. Some French winemakers repackage their product into screw-top bottles since few Taiwanese own a cork-screw, and foreign manufacturers of shutter-doors increase the gauge of their steel simply to cater to the security concerns of Taiwanese. All these companies and others recognise that an understanding of cultural patterns and concerns is part and parcel of the business equation in Taiwan. Neither product nor management structures from overseas are necessarily transferable without taking such cultural factors into account.

Equally, no book on doing business in Taiwan would be complete without at least flagging some of the more important of these considerations that need to be borne in mind. This is the purpose of this chapter. The advice may appear simplistic to some, but experience has shown that many companies often fail in Taiwan simply because of their wrong approach or belief that they can transport an American or European regional sales centre into the Taiwan environment and make it work. Wrong!

BEFORE YOU BEGIN

Proper groundwork is an essential part of planning for any new business activity. Even if involvement with the Taiwan market is to be purely a transactional buy-sell arrangement, the wise company that is seeking long term business will benefit from a market entry strategy. If involvement is to be more substantial and entail monetary investment, such a strategy becomes essential.

Market research is where most companies begin. Yet many smaller companies, looking for quick profit—and believing that they are immune from the problems faced by others—neglect this most basic business tool. Researching the market will lay the foundation for a full market entry strategy if one is needed. Furthermore the cost of a preliminary research report is often much less in pure dollar terms than that of sending a senior executive to Taiwan, let alone the opportunity time cost factor.

There are a number of companies, our own included, which specialise in both consumer and industrial market research and in the development of market entry strategies for foreign corporations. As a first stage a market research report would typically include a number of basic elements, such as:

- The current demand for product and market trends;
- Segmentation of the market between locally produced and imported product;
- Impediments to market access (import tariffs, quotas and other aspects of the trading regime);
- Identification of brands in the market and an assessment of market share;
- Product assessment;
- Issues relating to marketing and distribution;
- Identification of potential agents and distributors;
- Pricing information.

A market research company will often be in a position to assist further in arranging appointments or product trials. Otherwise there are local trade offices that can assist with this function. 'Cold calling' is not a recommended approach in Taiwan and seldom leads to a business relationship of any substance.

Any preliminary visit to Taiwan should not be rushed and should include meetings with home country representatives, chambers of commerce, banks, accountants and legal firms. Above all, take time to understand the culture and the local business etiquette.

If you are to appoint an agent in Taiwan, then ensure that you have more than one target in mind. Get to know them all and let them know you. Wherever possible, obtain an independent third-party credit check on your prospective business associates.[1] On-line checks via the Internet cost much less than US$100 but can save considerable time and expense later. Check out their network of contacts and existing business relationships claimed by potential partners. Bear in mind that it is common for businesses in Taiwan to register multiple companies, each of which can then be appointed as an 'exclusive agent' for a product. A proper computerised credit check can often unearth such 'associated' businesses.

Above all, do not confuse hospitality with friendship. Taiwanese are among the most hospitable (and friendly) people in the world but business entertaining is done for a business purpose and has nothing to do with friendship. Friendship will come, but only once business has been established.

NURTURING THE RELATIONSHIP

It is an accepted maxim that the Chinese do not do business with people they do not trust. Family and kinship groups play an important role in the local business scene, far more than outsiders generally realise, and much more than are common in a Western country. It is not uncommon for business relationships to be based, if not on family, then on high school, college or connections forged during military service (which is compulsory for young men in Taiwan and acts as a bonding agent for many). Large companies can be especially difficult to approach without inside connections and often the best means of making contact, initially at least, is through third parties. Often these will be local trading houses that have already established connections.

---

[1] A list of companies providing these services is provided in Chapter 5.

It follows that any foreign company or organisation seeking to do business in Taiwan needs not only to forge relationships but also to nurture them. Once a representative or agent is appointed, time will need to be spent to ensure that the agent understands and is committed to the product and to building the business network. Maintaining independent contact should not undermine the agent but should provide a safeguard so that should the relationship go wrong for any reason, contact with end-users and others in the network is not lost.

The Issue of 'Face'

Good manners and decorum are very important. Chinese are very sensitive to atmosphere, and harsh or abrasive attitudes do not sit well. Equally, foreigners need to be sensitive to the Chinese concept of 'face'. The importance of this cultural facet cannot be over-emphasised. Any criticism should always be offered privately and not in the presence of others and is often best done through an intermediary.

The same concept works in reverse. Simply because a Chinese person is polite and praises your product does not mean it is acceptable and he is happy. He is giving you 'face'. Either use a third party to check independently or seek to engage the person privately to ascertain whether there are any likely problems arising. Also bear in mind that such criticism may be offered obliquely rather than directly. Be alert for any signals.

Language Skills and Pointers

English is widely spoken among the business community but a knowledge of Chinese is a useful asset when doing business in Taiwan. Even a small smattering of Chinese will take a foreigner a long way in a social environment.

Mandarin Chinese is the official language and is used in most major business houses and at all levels of government, but in the countryside and in the south of Taiwan, Taiwanese is prevalent. The written form of the language uses the full form character, which is different from that used in Hong Kong and different again from the PRC. When preparing Chinese language material for use in Taiwan it is much better to have this done locally or at least by someone conversant with the form of the language used in Taiwan.

In some quarters, to hand out material prepared for use on the Mainland can still cause offence and complicate a business relationship. It is not a good way to start.

Name cards are used extensively in Taiwan and should specify clearly the name and position of the holder, in Chinese if possible. Most hotels will provide a service for the quick preparation of business cards if needed.

THE ART OF NEGOTIATION

The Chinese have a reputation as tough negotiators. Negotiation style is very different from the usual Western approach and careful preparation for the initial meeting is of utmost importance. Even before negotiations begin, a company entering the local market should have prepared and distributed a proper profile both of the product and of the company itself. Furthermore, all essential material should be in Chinese. In this regard it is not necessary to reproduce full glossy brochures simply for the local market but any foreign language brochure should include at the very least a good quality, black and white, Chinese language insert. Preferably this should be prepared locally.

Common tips and pointers in relation to local negotiation style include the following:

- Be prepared for detailed questioning. If possible have product samples or videos available (in NTSC/VHS format) and if the product has a technical characteristic, ensure that a technical representative is on hand or can at least be contacted overnight to answer any points of detail;

- Do not force the pace of negotiations and be prepared for preliminary meetings to be informal. For reasons already stated, Chinese will usually wish to get to know their prospective business colleagues both socially and as business people before entering any serious arrangement;

- In any complex negotiation involving a team approach, the Chinese side will usually speak in both English and Mandarin. In such circumstances always make sure you deal with the chief negotiator and talk directly to him—even if through an interpreter. Unless an open discussion forum has been signalled, to talk directly to another member of the team will often cause the team leader to lose face to the detriment of the negotiation;

- The Chinese side will generally speak among themselves in Chinese. Westerners should not feel intimidated by this. If possible have at least one Chinese-speaking staff member on your own team. If you need to break for private consultations, do so. The Chinese side will understand this;

- Prepare for long negotiations and be prepared to walk away from a bad deal. Just because you are a visitor; do not allow pressure of time to force you to make unnecessary concessions. Chinese will often play a waiting game just to determine your 'bottom line';
- The Chinese view of a legal agreement is very different from the view taken by Westerners, and you should not expect Western views to prevail. Any formal agreement reached represents an intention of both parties to use their best endeavours to bring about the events specified in the agreement. It should be considered as a working document and as such should be short, easy to understand and broadly phrased; as a general rule do not expect points of detail. If the relationship is successful, negotiation and renegotiation will be an ongoing process.

Of course, where negotiations are especially complex or involve foreign investment such agreements take on an added dimension. Even so, they will still be drawn up and played out according to local rules. For any agreement of substance, proper (and local) legal advice should be considered, especially in situations where intellectual or movable property (such as dies and moulds) are involved. There are a number of international law firms in Taiwan that have considerable experience in these areas, though for the most part, companies will prefer to have their lawyers operating behind the scenes and not at the negotiating table.

Price Negotiations

In any trading arrangement, before any local company will discuss pricing issues, the *bona fides* of the enquirer as a future supplier or customer have to be established. There is an etiquette to pricing issues in Chinese companies that should be noted and understood:
1. Before prices are discussed, the business relationship has to be established. This can involve several meetings and social occasions. A Chinese company will wish to weigh up the seriousness of the other party, its capability and its reliability before discussing price;
2. Prices are never discussed at initial meetings and never over the telephone. If the Chinese company wishes to do business then it will usually signal that the time has come to get down to business;
3. Generally speaking, a Chinese company will never give the first price but will wait for the other party to make an offer. This waiting game can be a frustrating experience for foreigners but is a customary part of doing business. A Chinese company will never show its impatience or

the necessity to trade; it will always be put in the context that they are doing you a great favour by dealing with you;

4. Initial prices discussed are never, ever, the final price negotiated. Nor is the final price negotiated the true final price. Even after an agreement is reached (and, often, signed) the Chinese party will usually come back seeking some improvement in the terms. This can be frustrating to Westerners not used to oriental business practices. Flexibility and manoeuvrability are the keys to establishing long-term business relationships;

5. Once the relationship has been established, Chinese business partners can be fiercely loyal and will often defend their overseas partner should the terms of trade move the other way. But this can take a long time and many Western companies are not prepared to wait for this 'bonding' to occur;

6. As already noted, Chinese have scant regard for legal contracts; everything comes down to personal trust.

The same considerations apply to payment practices and often price and payment terms can be linked to produce an attractive package. For small trade-related orders, cash payment is usual in Taiwan (and Taiwanese have special regard for cash). For larger orders, payment terms are usually negotiable but between three- and six-month payment terms seem common in much of industry.

Finally a word should be written regarding promptness. Business runs at a fast pace in Taiwan and any correspondence should be followed up immediately. Many business opportunities are lost to competitors by the failure of overseas parties to respond quickly and effectively. Australians are especially notorious in this regard and have lost out in the market because of it.

SOME SIMPLE RULES FOR GAINING MARKET SHARE

There are at least four key factors influencing long term purchasing arrangements of Taiwanese companies: product, price, image and service.

For any overseas supplier wishing to enter the Taiwan market or improve its market share, there are a number of steps to be taken into consideration. While the following guidelines have been drawn up with industrial products in mind, the same rules are generally applicable in other areas.

Firstly, an overseas supplier will need to ensure that both the company name and the product are well known throughout the industry. A local representative office established independently of any local import agent (or multiple agents) is often useful as an independent point of contact for the local industry and demonstrates a commitment to the market. It is the usual approach adopted by Japanese companies, and one which Western suppliers could well emulate more readily. A local representative office will be able to step in and ensure continuity of business should the local agent terminate the business at some point.

It is no good for out-of-country salespeople to visit Taiwan spasmodically and expect business to flow as a result. Again this is a common complaint made of Western companies as compared to their Japanese counterparts. Often the local industry does not have the same personal warmth in its relationship with a Western supplier as it does with Japanese suppliers for precisely this reason.

Delivery times need to be considered along with quality and price. Delivery times from Europe can be especially long and products can take up to a month to reach Taiwan whereas products from Japan can reach Taiwan in three days. Maintaining inventory within the Asian area is one means of overcoming this problem. Actually investing in a manufacturing facility for the Asian region is another. Taiwan offers real opportunity in this regard.

Processing and tooling can also sometimes influence purchasing decisions. Much of the equipment used in Taiwanese factories originates from Japan and is designed to process Japanese-sourced materials. Problems can arise in the processing cycle when local companies switch their sourcing from Japan to other countries. Ensuring that precise specifications and processing requirements are in the Chinese language is often one way around this problem. The availability of technical back-up can also go some way to overcoming this type of problem.

Often when an overseas company is facing difficulties in Taiwan the fundamental issues to be addressed are not so much technical in character but relate to management of the relationship with its customers. Most Western companies will never be able to match the market share gained by Japanese companies but with proper attention they should be able to compete more vigorously with non-Asian suppliers and against the Japanese companies that dominate much of the market.

The following simple rules apply to any non-Asian company seeking to access the growing Asian market and considering its options for Taiwan in a regional context.

Recommendation 1: Maintaining an Image

To be successful in the long term an overseas supplier needs to pay attention to its image in the market as a serious and competitive manufacturer. There are companies that will undertake this work for a fee but a company can begin with a little self-help before it brings in outside professionals.

Targeted information

A supplier should prepare summary information on the company and its products, in the Chinese language, for distribution to all major trading companies and potential end-users (industrial) or retailers (consumer items) of its product in Taiwan.

Targeted visits

A supplier needs to establish good personal relationships with its potential customers. This should be done in the first instance by a structured and regular visit program either from head office or from a regional headquarters centre. Such visits should take place at least every three months initially and senior management in the home country must recognise that relationships will often need to be nurtured for some time before orders appear. The focus in the first instance should always be on obtaining a detailed understanding of customer requirements and addressing any concerns. A problem solving phase then needs to be initiated, supported from headquarters, should any supplier-side problems be found to be impeding market access.

Recommendation 2: Maintaining Regional Technical Capabilities

Chinese technical staff

For products of an engineering or technical nature, an overseas supplier can do a great deal to demonstrate its *bona fides* by employing a competent sales engineer fluent in the Chinese language. Sales engineers are commonplace in the Asian environment and are trained as such at the outset in contrast to the Western approach whereby engineers are often called upon to perform a sales role without specialist training. It would be the duty of a sales engineer to establish peer-to-peer contact with the engineering departments and project managers of major corporations, and to reinforce at the technical level the work being done by corporate executives at the management and purchasing levels. A competent Chinese sales engineer would be able to establish relationships and obtain the detailed technical feedback sought by the company to develop a product specifically for the local market. He or she would also be able to gain valuable market intelligence about the activities of competing companies that can only be gained in a peer-to-peer environment.

Recommendation 3: Improving the Corporate Presence

As part of its broader strategy in the Asian region, foreign companies seeking long term business in the region should consider the establishment of a regional office based on two distinct types of presence:

In-country representative office

Foreign suppliers should consider the establishment of small in-country representative offices in key target markets in order to promote the supplier's product. Such an office would also provide technical support and be able expedite orders placed through local trading companies. A representative office would follow the Japanese model and would not compete with existing trading companies, who would open Letters of Credit direct to the supplier's home base. Local companies appear familiar with this practice.

Regional sales office

Technical support as well as sales support should be maintained at a regional sales office established in order to coordinate supplier activities throughout the Pacific Rim region. The objective would be to have one key experienced executive permanently stationed in the region. For many companies this can be a more cost-effective alternative to separate in-country home executive presence. A major role of a regional sales office would be to coordinate tendering for major contracts such as power stations, petrochemical plants and the like. This is best done on a regional basis rather than on a country-by-country basis.

Recommendation 4: Maintaining Regional Reserves

Where necessary, a supplier should give consideration to establishing its own strategic reserves within the region, or arranging with one or more suppliers to have stock shipped on a consignment basis and made readily available, should delivery times be identified as one of the problems impeding sales. Giving extended trading terms to existing suppliers—perhaps those who agree to maintain a specified minimum level of stock—is another option that a number of companies have used with success. A third option would be to enter into a joint venture with an existing manufacturer and transfer the necessary technology to actually manufacture product within the Asian region.

DEALING WITH GOVERNMENT

Often the need to develop sustainable business relationships will include dealing with government, either directly or through one or other of the government enterprises. The successful business person will recognise the value in dealing not only with the Central Government but at all levels. If involvement with Taiwan includes investment into a factory or other facility then contact with—and cultivation of—the local council members is a prudent course to follow. Local elections are closely fought in Taiwan and not for altruistic reasons. Rather, local council members expect to benefit from any new business generated in their locality. Local corporations involved in the building of power and petrochemical complexes will admit (off the record) that up to 5% of the cost of a major project goes into pay-offs to local officials. This is no longer done directly; such activities are of course illegal. Rather, such payments are in the form of contracts let to companies with which the official is associated through friends or family members.

The Government Tendering Process

For any overseas company seeking to participate in ROC government contracts, an understanding of the tendering system in Taiwan is essential.

Major purchasing decisions at both the national and provincial government levels are based on a complex tendering process. Within the basic tendering framework, different government agencies adopt different approaches to tenders, and any overseas company seeking to access ROC government projects must understand the tendering requirements of the specific agencies involved.

Every tender is initiated by the end-user agency of government and a prime focus of any company, whether local or overseas, seeking to tender is often the middle management of the agency responsible for writing the tender specifications. The Japanese, with their long-standing influence in Taiwan, are said to be especially adept at having tender specifications tailored to Japanese products. The United States also fares well because of the large numbers of engineers and professionals in government who have been educated and trained in the United States and who are familiar with US equipment and standards. Many of the codified specifications—such as those in civil aviation and pharmaceuticals—are based on US requirements, although the *Fair Trade Law* has done much to curtail this practice.

Aside from the end-user agency, three other government agencies are also involved in the overseeing and screening of tenders:

- **The Central Trust of China (CTC):** The CTC is the central government agency administering the tender system for the purchase of equipment and supplies on behalf of all other central government ministries and departments. All purchases with a value in excess of NT$50 million (US$2 million approx) must be made through the CTC tender system. Purchases below this amount can be handled directly by the office placing the order. Regulations governing procurement now allow State-owned corporations to undertake direct purchasing if they so wish;

- **The Taiwan Provincial Government Supply Bureau (TSB):** The TSB is the counterpart agency to the CTC handling procurement on behalf of the Taiwan Provincial Government and its agencies. Its operations at the provincial level mirror those of the CTC. According to those with experience of the tendering process, there is said to be greater 'flexibility' shown in provincial government contracts and generally the end-user agencies make their own on- and off-shore procurements, bypassing the TSB in the process;

- **Ministry of Audit (MoA), Control Yuan**: The Ministry of Audit is responsible for auditing State-owned enterprises and public institutions owned by government or in which the government has greater than a 50% shareholding. The Taiwan Provincial Audit Division within the Ministry of Audit is responsible for auditing provincial government agencies and the Taiwan Supply Bureau. Under ROC law the role of the Ministry of Audit is also to ensure that all government agencies and departments comply with the relevant laws and regulations in the award of contracts. It is the Ministry that establishes the procurement rules, has the right to be present at the opening of bids and which should be informed of contract ceiling prices prior to the opening of bids. The MoA also supervises price negotiation with the bidders as well as any ongoing price adjustments which may be necessary throughout the contract. While both the CTC and the TSB are administrative agencies, the Ministry of Audit is more closely linked to the political process and is said to be more open to political leverage.

Types of Tender

Under ROC law, all public works are subject to open bidding from at least three bidders. Under certain circumstances, direct procurement by price negotiation with one bidder is permitted. The tenders themselves normally fall into one or other of three categories:

1. *Open Tender:* These tenders are advertised in the local press. Local bidders may or may not have been pre-qualified to bid prior to the bid announcement;
2. *Restricted Tender:* The pre-qualification requirements are advertised in the local press but the tender itself is not advertised. Only those bidders who have pre-qualified are invited to submit for tender;
3. *Negotiated Tender:* The tender is not advertised. Prospective bidders are generally well known to the agency undertaking the procurement and are invited to negotiate directly for the project. Many companies believe that under both the negotiated tender process and the direct procurement procedures, financial inducements to accept certain bids are common practice.

Many tenders in the ROC are not open to foreign companies as prime contractors. Yet, in many such instances the tender may include a substantial foreign component either in goods or services required. In such instances, foreign companies often enter into joint venture arrangements with suitable local firms in order to undertake bidding. Local firms can also play an essential role in some of the 'grey areas' of the underground economy, which are a necessary part of doing business in Taiwan but which are best avoided by foreigners unfamiliar with the local environment.

CHAPTER 11

THE ROC TAX SYSTEM

Taiwan has a complex taxation system with 23 separate revenue-raising items. In keeping with Taiwan's three-tier government system, separate taxes are levied at each level of government: national, provincial and local/municipal. In fact six major tax groupings contribute the bulk of the total revenue gathered by government. There are at present two forms of income tax, personal and business, although it is intended to combine these into a consolidated income tax in the future.

The personal tax system, including its application to foreign nationals, is discussed in Chapter 12 while business taxation is discussed in Chapter 13. This chapter is meant to provide a general outline of Taiwan's taxation system.

OVERVIEW

The authority to raise taxes for budget revenue is vested in the *Law on the Distribution of Financial Revenues and Expenditures*. This Law, promulgated in 1981, is reviewed annually by the *Executive Yuan* as the body that decides the proportion of tax revenues to be raised by each government authority. The *Self-Governance Law for Provinces and Counties* and *the Self-Governance Law for Special Municipalities (Taipei and Kaohsiung)* provide the authority for governments at the provincial level and below to levy additional taxes and charges for specific purpose revenue raising.

According to the 1981 Law, current taxes are defined under four different categories as follows:

1. **National taxes** consist of income tax (individual income tax and profit-seeking enterprise income tax), estate and gift tax, customs duties, commodity tax, securities transaction tax and mining lot tax. Of these, estate and gift tax is apportioned such that, in the case of a province, 10% of the total revenue gathered shall be allocated to the province and 80% to the prefectures (cities and municipalities). In the case of the special municipalities, 50% of the revenue gathered is allocated to the municipality;

2. **Provincial and City taxes** consist of a business tax, stamp tax and vehicle licence tax. Of these, both business tax and stamp tax shall, in the case of a province, have 50% of their total revenues distributed according to an overall plan among its prefectures (cities and municipalities), and in the case of a city, belong entirely to the city;

3. **Prefectural and Municipal taxes** consist of land taxes (land value tax, agricultural land tax, and land value increment tax), house tax, deed tax and amusement tax. Of these, land value increment tax shall have 20% of its total revenue allocated to the province and 20% distributed by the province among the prefectures (cities and municipalities) according to an overall plan. In the case of a city under the Central Government, city taxes are in place of the prefectural and municipal taxes and the total revenue of city taxes shall go to the city government;

4. **Monopoly revenues:** Article XXI of the *Law Governing the Allocation of Government Revenues and Expenditure* allows the Central Government to monopolise certain specified commodities and control their manufacture with a view both to increasing government revenue as well as controlling consumption. These monopoly provisions are the basis of a number of important government-owned enterprises including petroleum, sugar and salt.[1]

---

[1] As noted earlier in this book, these monopolies are now being phased out.

Separate regulations, in place since 1953, govern the state monopoly of tobacco and wine. Customs duties and commodity taxes on tobacco and wine (defined to include all alcoholic beverages) are incorporated into monopoly revenues and are not levied separately.

Of the monopoly revenues collected, 65% are allocated to the Central Government and 35% to the Taiwan Provincial Government which may, at its discretion, allocate part of its revenue to the special municipalities of Taipei and Kaohsiung.

Government Revenues

Total government taxes (including monopoly revenues) in 1996 amounted to NT$1,171 billion (US$35 billion). Taxes on income (personal and business) contributed almost 30% of the total and have been increasing both in absolute terms and as a percentage of total tax gathered in recent years, due in large measure to improved efficiency in tax collection procedures.

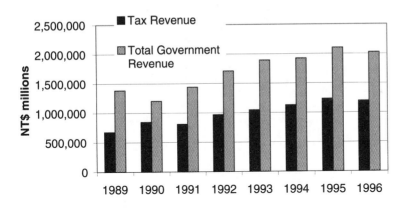

Figure 11a. Tax and total government revenues

During the period 1989–96, government tax revenues rose by an average of 11% per year. The business tax (VAT) has become the next largest item at 18% of the total while the various forms of land tax contributed 13% in 1996.

Efforts are under way to reform the tax system and to reduce the plethora of separate taxes levied in Taiwan. For instance, neither Harbour Construction dues nor the 'slaughter tax' on animals have been collected since 1991, although they remain on the books.

245

The Business Guide to Taiwan

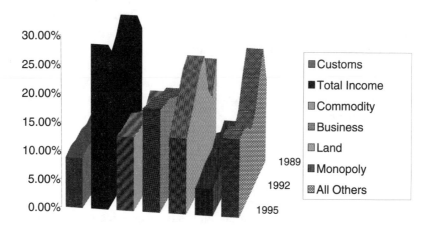

Figure 11b. Tax gathering share of major items

Table 11.1. Net revenues of government by source

Fiscal Year	Total	Tax and Monopoly Revenues			Gov't Enterprises	Public Bonds	Income from Loans	Other Income
		Sub Total	Tax	Monopoly				
1989	1,382,533	677,419	629,753	47,666	128,210	117,397	313,138	146,369
1990	1,203,171	847,733	794,812	52,921	121,418	15,831	72,886	145,303
1991	1,484,990	854,925	794,812	60,113	94,835	145,003	136,605	253,622
1992	1,550,200	807,022	748,508	58,514	141,045	312,903	89,133	200,097
1993	1,820,092	971,219	909,110	62,109	166,471	340,886	99,609	241,907
1994	1,845,106	1,048,090	983,387	64,703	184,914	108,327	231,135	272,640
1995	1,994,658	1,124,186	1,062,778	61,408	141,956	75,104	389,432	263,980
1996	2,052,995	1,226,815	1,170,856	55,959	181,094	115,769	249,676	279,641

Total government revenue in 1996 totalled more than NT$2,000 billion (US$61 billion). Tax (including monopoly revenues) as a percentage of total income of government has increased from 49% in 1989 to more than 59% in 1996. Net income from public enterprises contributed only NT$181 billion (US$5.5 billion) or around 9% of the total.

NATIONAL TAX POLICY

National tax policy has generally emphasised direct taxes as being at the core of the revenue raising system. Direct taxes as a percentage of revenue raised have increased steadily over the years and has roughly reached parity with indirect collections since 1990. Income and business tax collections have also increased in importance as primary means of generating revenue. Total income tax collections amounted to 16.7% of all government revenue in 1996 and 28.7% of all taxes gathered. Business tax (VAT) accounted for a further 181% of tax and 10.6% of total revenue.

National policy is now to maintain a balance between direct and indirect taxes in order to avoid the direct (and progressive) taxation burden adversely affecting the inclination to work or to invest.

There is no single tax code in Taiwan and each tax is based on a separately legislated code which consists of both substantive and procedural laws. Collection procedures are contained in the *Tax Collection Law* of 1976. Among its more important provisions are the following.

The obligation to pay tax

The 1976 Law lays down general rules relating to the obligations of taxpayers: in the case of jointly owned property, the manager shall in the first instance have the obligation to pay the taxes and where there is no manager the co-owners shall share the obligation to the extent of each person's ownership share in the property. If the property is held in joint names, each of the joint owners are considered liable.

Should a juristic person, partnership or non-corporate body be dissolved and liquidated the liquidator is obligated to pay off all taxes (according to the order of priority contained in the Law) before distributing the assets. Where this is not done, the liquidator becomes liable for the tax obligation.

Where a profit-seeking enterprise ceases to exist through merger, the successor enterprise assumes the obligation to pay any residual taxes owing by the defunct enterprise.

Tax notification

Except for property taxes, taxpayers voluntarily report their taxes through filing a return, making payment of the calculated due amount to the public treasury and submitting the return to the tax collection authority within the time specified under the specific tax code.

In the case of property tax and other taxes assessed by the collection authorities, the Law provides that a notification of collection is to be issued and delivered to the taxpayer. Such notification is to provide the name and address of the taxpayer, the type of tax levied, the amount of tax, the tax rate and deadline for payment.

Filing of tax returns and payment

The time allowed for filing a return and for paying taxes due are prescribed in the various tax codes (see below). The relevant tax collection authority may, at its discretion, extend the payment period should special circumstances warrant. Taxes lawfully levied but not paid are enforceable by a court of law upon application by the collection authority.

Taxpayers who have overpaid on account of an error by the tax office in the original assessment may apply for a refund within five years from the date of payment. Should the claim of the taxpayer be upheld, any outstanding taxes (under any item) are deducted before the balance is refunded.

The tax assessment period

Under the Law, any tax found to be leviable during a specified period of assessment can be collected retroactively and any tax not found to be leviable cannot be levied subsequently. The period of retroactive assessment varies according to circumstances: generally the period is five years where no evidence of fraud or evasion is imputed and seven years where it is determined that there was a deliberate attempt to evade taxes by fraudulent or other illegitimate means.

The tax collection period

Where a tax levied by law becomes overdue because the whereabouts of the taxpayer is unknown or through other circumstances, the taxation authority has the right to claim a tax debt within a seven-year time limit specified under the *Tax Collection Law*. Any leviable tax that is not levied within seven years from the date of determination can no longer be levied unless it has been referred to a court of law for enforcement prior to the expiry of the seven-year period.

Taiwan operates a non-discriminatory tax regime in that foreign corporations operating in Taiwan and foreign individuals residing in Taiwan are afforded national treatment. Both corporate and personal taxes are broadly consistent with regional standards.

THE TAXATION ADMINISTRATION

The Ministry of Finance (MoF) under the direct control of the *Executive Yuan* is the Central Government's highest administrative body in relation to revenue and tax collection. While the responsibility for broader monetary policy generally lies with the Central Bank of China (CBC), it is the Ministry that defines taxation policy, enacts and administers the tax laws and oversees the collection of taxes.

National taxes are levied in two broad categories: inland taxes and customs duties. Within the Ministry, the Department of Taxation is charged with the drafting, enactment, interpretation and collection of all inland tax codes while a separate Department of Customs Administration oversees the collection of customs duties. The National Tax Administration of Taipei and the National Tax Administration of Kaohsiung are separately maintained offices of the Ministry charged with the local collection of national taxes. Within Taiwan province, the provincial government acting as the agent of the Ministry of Finance collects national taxes.

The Taiwan Provincial Department of Finance is the counterpart body to the MoF within the provincial government, charged with the levying of all provincial taxes. Under the Department is the Taxation Bureau, in charge of the planning, supervision and collection of provincial taxes as well as acting as the agent of the MoF in the collection of national taxes. City tax bureaux are the counterpart organs of the special municipalities in charge of the levy and collection of city government taxes.

At the local level, prefectural and municipal governments under the Taiwan Provincial Government maintain their own local tax offices while also acting as agents for the collection of national and provincial taxes.

INTERNATIONAL TAX AGREEMENTS

General bilateral agreements relating to double tax avoidance currently exist with Singapore, South Africa, Paraguay, Indonesia, Australia and Fiji.

Discussions relating to further such agreements are currently under way with Poland, Hungary, Malawi, Belgium, the UK, New Zealand, Germany, the US, Malaysia, Vietnam, Thailand and the Philippines.

Tax agreements relating to air traffic and shipping have been signed with the Republic of Korea and Japan and a further five agreements relating to air only have been signed with Singapore, South Africa, Thailand, Luxembourg and the US.

It must be stressed that the above information is only an overview, and cannot be considered a substitute for professional advice. A number of first- and second-tier international accounting firms have established offices in Taiwan to service the needs of the international business community. Some of these are detailed below.

INTERNATIONAL ACCOUNTING FIRMS IN TAIWAN

Chiang, Lai, Lin, Tu, Chang & Wu, Touche Ross
7F, 102 Kuangfu South Road, Taipei
Tel: (02) 2741 0258
Fax: (02) 2773 3833

Coopers & Lybrand
12F, 367 Fuhsing North Road, Taipei
Tel: (02) 2545 5678
Fax: (02) 2514 0248

Diwan, Ernst & Young
9F, 333 Keelung Road, Section 1, Taipei
Tel: (02) 2720 4000
Fax: (02) 2757 6050

KPMG Peat Marwick
6F, 156 Ming Sheng East Road, Section 3, Taipei
Tel: (02) 2715 9999
Fax: (02) 2715 9888

Price Waterhouse
27F, 333 Keelung Road, Section 1, Taipei
Tel: (02) 2729 6666
Fax: (02) 2757 6371

T N Soong & Co (Arthur Anderson)
12F, 156 Minsheng East Road, Section 3, Taipei
Tel: (02) 2545 9988
Fax: (02) 2545 9966

KEY GOVERNMENT AGENCIES

The Ministry of Finance (MoF)
2 Aikuo Road, Taipei
Tel: (02) 2322 8000
Fax: (02) 2321 205

Directorate General of Customs
85 Hsinsheng South Road, Section 1, Taipei
Tel: (02) 2741 3181
Fax: (02) 2711 4166

National Tax Administration of Taipei
2 Chunghwa Road, Section 1, Taipei
Tel: (02) 2311 3711
Fax: (02) 2389 3311

National Tax Administration of Kaohsiung City
148 Kwangchou 1st Street, Kaohsiung
Tel: (07) 2725 6600
Fax: (07) 2711 5784

Taipei Tax Bureau, Taipei City Government
7–2 Peiping East Road, Taipei
Tel: (02) 2720 8898
Fax: (02) 2759 8799

Tax Administration of the Taiwan Provincial Government
Chunghsing Village Nantou Hsien
Tel: (049) 332 121
Fax: (049) 335 025

China External Trade Development Council
4–7F, International Trade Building
333 Keelung Road, Section 1, Taipei
Tel: (02) 2725 5200
Fax: (02) 2757 6653

CHAPTER 12

INDIVIDUAL INCOME TAX IN THE ROC

OVERVIEW

Individual income tax is levied by calendar year on all ROC-sourced income of both residents and non-residents unless exempted in accordance with the provisions of the law. The tax rate is progressive and personal tax rates on earned income currently range from 6% on income of less than NT$370,000 to a maximum of 40% on income earned in excess of NT$3.7 million.

In recent years, the government has attempted to reduce the taxes of low- and middle-income families through a range of deductions and standard concessions. For tax purposes residents are those people who either maintain a domicile in the ROC, i.e. hold an 'alien residence certificate' (see Chapter 16) and who are ordinarily resident in the ROC, or who reside in the ROC for 183 days or more in a taxable year even if no domicile is maintained. Non-resident foreigners who extend their visitor visas beyond 90 days must also file returns before leaving the ROC or requesting a further extension.

253

For tax purposes it is important to note that any foreign individual who resides in the ROC for 183 days or more in a taxable year is regarded as a resident while individuals who stay less than 183 days are regarded as non-resident. This has important implications for claiming deductions and allowances.

Table 12.1. Current rates of progressive personal income tax (1997 reporting year)

Tax Bracket (Unit NT$)	US$ Equivalent	Tax Rate
0 – 330,000	0 – 10,000	6%
330,001 – 890,000	10,001 – 26969	13%
890,001 – 1,780,000	26,970 – 53,939	21%
1,780,001 – 3,340,000	53,940 – 101,212	30%
3,340,001 and over	Over 101,212	40%

Foreign individuals domiciled or resident in Taiwan for 183 days or more per year are subject to taxation on income from Taiwan sources, but they are not liable for tax on income earned outside Taiwan. Residents—whether Chinese or alien—are entitled to certain exemptions and deductions which reduce the overall tax burden.

It is also important to be aware that foreign individuals who report their income as residents in the preceding year, but who do not depart from the ROC until the following year, are still regarded as residents for tax purposes up until the time of their departure irrespective of whether their stay in their year of departure amounts to 183 days or more.

Non-resident aliens residing in Taiwan for 90 days or less within the same calendar year are liable for payment of withholding tax on ROC-sourced income at a rate of 20% on wages and salaries, commission payments, rental received or interest earned. Dividends are subject to a 20% withholding tax (withheld at source) if the investment was approved under *the Statute for Investment by Foreign Nationals* or the *Statute for Investment by Overseas Chinese* otherwise a rate of 35% applies.

Non-resident aliens who reside in the ROC for more than 90 days but less than 183 days in any tax year are required to consolidate and report any income received in the ROC (including that received from foreign employers) and are taxed at the relevant withholding rates. Foreigners receiving income in the ROC or expecting to receive income should apply for a taxpayer's code number irrespective of the class of entry visa held. Taxpayers' code numbers are obtained from the National Tax Bureau at the address listed below. Counter staff speak English. A taxpayer's code number consists of eight numerals and two alphabetic characters derived from the taxpayer's date of birth and the first two letters of their English name as it appears on their passport. Thus a Jacqueline Smith born on 10 December 1967 would be given the taxpayer's code 19671210JA. In theory two taxpayers could have the same number but, apparently, it has not been a problem until now.

Income tax need not be withheld on salaries paid to employees of Taiwanese companies employed outside of Taiwan. Non-residents are not entitled to any exemptions or deductions.

TAXABLE INCOME

The gross income of an individual is considered to be the aggregate of salaries and wages plus other income which is classified into eight categories as follows:
1. Business income: cash or stock dividends declared and distributed, distributed profits;
2. Income from professional practice;
3. Interest income;
4. Rentals and royalties received;
5. Income received from self-employment in primary activities (agriculture, forestry and fishing);
6. Income from the sale, exchange or disposal of property;
7. Income from contests and games (including frequent-flyer and similar awards);
8. Miscellaneous income.

'Salary and wages' includes all income received for services rendered or work performed including allowances, annuities, bonuses, retirement benefits, pensions, and other similar compensation. Income received overseas for work performed in the ROC for more than 90 days in a taxable year is also regarded as income derived from ROC sources and should be declared as part of the tax assessment.

For the purposes of calculating tax liability, the income of a spouse and dependants within the household is consolidated and reported together. However, taxpayers may choose to calculate the tax due on a spouse's salary separately. In such cases only the exemption and special deduction (see below) for the spouse's salary can be claimed in calculating the spouse's tax due. All other income, exemptions and deductions (excluding those claimed by the spouse) are included with the main taxpayer's assessment. The spouse's tax is then combined with that of the taxpayer to calculate the total tax liability of a family unit.

METHOD OF ASSESSMENT

There are a number of standard deductions designed to reduce the overall tax burden which are available to residents but not to non-residents. ROC *Income Tax Law* also prescribes a number of exemptions related to income received from business operations, professional services, wages or interest on capital as well as tax credits applicable to certain situations. Not all of these will generally be applicable to foreigners unless the foreigner has a Chinese spouse and is living permanently in the ROC. For the sake of completeness, the full list of deductions, exemptions and credits is described below.

Exemptions

The allowed personal exemption on earned income for the 1997 tax year is NT$72,000 (US$2,182) for the taxpayer, spouse and each dependant (including children over the age of 20 supported by the taxpayer because of continuing education, physical or mental disability, or inability to earn a living). In addition, for the parent or any lineal ascendant of the taxpayer or his/her spouse aged over 70, an additional exemption of NT$108,000 can be claimed in respect of each. These exemptions are adjusted annually for inflation.

Deductions

In addition to the exemptions, there are also a number of allowable deductions and taxpayers can choose one of two methods for calculating their deduction entitlements.

Standard deduction

A taxpayer can choose to take a standard deduction currently amounting to NT$43,000 for a single person (NT$65,000 for a married couple) or, as an alternative, a taxpayer can claim itemised deductions.

Itemised deductions

A taxpayer choosing this option can itemise six areas of claim:

- Donations to officially registered educational, cultural, charitable or public welfare organisations, up to 20% of consolidated income before deduction of the donation;
- Insurance premiums can be deductible to the extent of NT$24,000 per person;
- Medical and childbirth expenses (less any insurance reimbursement);
- Disaster losses due to *force majeure* where not covered by insurance payments or other compensation;
- Mortgage interest on owner-occupied residences up to NT$100,000 per family;
- Campaign expenses of those running for office (not applicable to non-citizens).

Taxpayers claiming itemised deductions are required to furnish original receipts to justify the claim.

Special deductions

A number of special deductions may also be claimed irrespective of whether a taxpayer chooses to take the standard or itemised deductions listed above. Some of these are not generally applicable to foreigners but the list of special deductions includes the following:

- Losses from property transactions may be deducted from any gains for property transactions in the same year; if the deductible amount exceeds the gain then the difference may be carried forward for up to three years;
- Salary and wage earners may claim a special deduction for salary up to a maximum of NT$60,000;
- To encourage private deposits and thereby increase the supply of capital, there is also a special tax deduction for interest income received from bank deposits (including short term commercial paper), bonds (government and private), trust funds and for dividends and interest from registered stocks and shares. The maximum allowed deduction under this category is NT$270,000;
- There is a special deduction of NT$72,000 for people with disabilities provided such persons are in possession of a Handicapped Registration Certificate;

- A further special deduction for tuition fees up to NT$25,000 can also be claimed on behalf of children of taxpayers who are attending college or university.

Penalties for Non-Compliance

Penalties apply for tax avoidance or for late payments. Any omission or under-reporting of taxable income is subject to a fine of no more than twice the tax avoided. Where an individual fails to file an annual income tax return and is found to have had taxable income the applicable fine is up to three times the amount of tax evaded.

INDIVIDUAL INCOME TAX FILINGS FOR FOREIGNERS

Individual income tax returns are due by 31 March and are filed with the tax authority located in the district in which you live:

Taipei City

Foreign Affairs Office, National Tax Administration of Taipei
#2, Section 1, Chunghwa Road, Taipei
Tel: (02) 22311 3711 Ext: 1116 8

Kaohsiung City

Foreign Affairs Office, National Tax Administration of Kaohsiung
#148 Kwang Chou 1st Street, Kaohsiung
Tel: (07) 725 6600 Ext: 8102, 8210

Taiwan Province

Taxes can be paid at any service centre or branch office of the National Tax Administration.

Any tax balance due can only be paid by cash or cheque. Tax self-assessment forms are available in both English and Chinese. Separate tax forms apply to single taxpayers and to those with dependants. If an extension of time is required then such an application must be made prior to the deadline. The maximum allowed extension is 30 days.

Tax Liabilities of Non-Resident Foreigners

Individual income tax is levied at a flat rate. Salary or wages income, commissions, interest, rental income and income from awards or prizes shall be taxed at a flat rate of 20%.

Dividends shall be taxed at the rate of 35% unless the dividend relates to an investment made under the *Statute for Investment by Overseas Chinese* or the *Statute for Investment by Foreign Nationals* in which case a rate of 20% applies.

Income from property transactions and profit from occasional trade is taxed at the rate of 35%.

Miscellaneous income is taxed at the rate of 20%.

Tax Credits

Tax credits are available to certain designated share purchases or underwriting activities. Where registered share certificates are held for a period of at least two years, individuals may claim an amount of up to 20% of the price paid to offset their income tax payable for the year in which the two-year holding requirement is met. Circumstances where this credit applies includes:
1. Those who subscribe to or underwrite registered share certificates on the original issue for the establishment or expansion of government designated 'important scientific technological enterprises' or 'important investment projects';
2. Those who subscribe to or underwrite registered share certificates on the original issue for the establishment or expansion of venture capital enterprises.

If the deductible amount exceeds the amount of income tax payable in the year of assessment, the balance may be carried forward for up to four years provided the deductible amount in any year does not exceed 50% of the income tax payable in those years. This limit does not apply, however, in the final year of the four-year period.

Tax credits are also available in relation to the income earned from the sale of a property in which the taxpayer was residing. If such a residence is sold and the gain from the sale is consolidated and taxed and, within a two-year period, another residence is purchased at a price exceeding the sale price of the former residence, then the taxpayer may claim a credit or a refund on the income tax payable in the year in which registration of the purchase is made. This credit also applies in situations where a taxpayer purchases another property first and sells the original property later.

Application of the *Statutes for Investment by Foreign Nationals* to Individual Taxpayers

In a situation where an individual makes an investment in Taiwan in accordance with the *Statute for Investment by Overseas Chinese* or the *Statute for Investment by Foreign Nationals*, and where the taxpayer concurrently acts as the chair, supervisor or manager of the company in which the investment is made, then—provided the 183 day residence requirement is met—any dividends received from that company may be taxed at the withholding rate of 20%.

CHAPTER 13

CORPORATE, BUSINESS AND OTHER TAXES

Taiwan's business tax laws are complex. Many—such as the land tax laws—derive from customary Chinese practice developed over the centuries. There is no consolidated tax code and each tax is levied under a separate law or regulation.

Businesses and individuals face more than sixteen forms of tax with which to contend, including three variants of land tax.

Business taxes in their various forms currently account for around 85% of all tax revenue raised (83.7% in 1996). Among the more important of these taxes are the Business Income Tax, the Business Value-Added Tax (VAT) and the Commodity Tax. These three together account for more than 50% of the total. Customs duties raise a further 10%. Also of importance to business enterprises that hold real property in Taiwan are the taxes on land sales. The agricultural land tax is no longer of significance but because of the rapid appreciation of land values in recent years, profits derived from the sale of commercial land contribute a further 15% to government tax revenues.

It is important to note that business taxes apply not only to corporations but can also—as is the case with the house tax—extend to individuals who trade any item or service for profit.

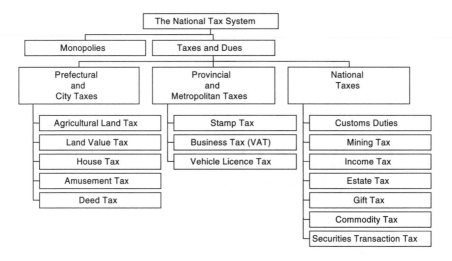

Figure 13a. Taiwan's taxation system

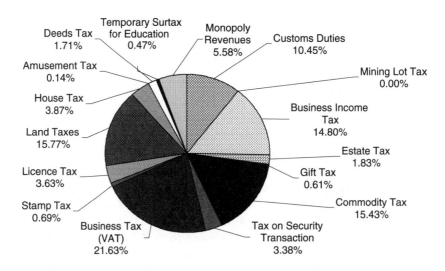

Figure 13b. Business tax collections 1996

THE PROFIT-SEEKING ENTERPRISE INCOME TAX

Corporate income tax (or 'profit-seeking enterprise income tax') is levied by the national government on all registered profit-seeking enterprises including companies, sole proprietors, partnerships and other forms of business organised for profit. The authority to apply this tax rests with the *Profit-Seeking Enterprise Income Tax Law.*

For such business organisations, taxable income is generally defined as worldwide gross revenues minus allowable deductions. For ROC companies conducting business overseas (either through branch companies or agents) any tax levied abroad and paid in accordance with the tax law of the country concerned can be deducted from the ROC tax liability. The amount deducted can be up to but not exceeding the tax liability that would have been due had tax not been paid offshore.

Any business with its head office located outside the Republic of China but which maintains a business office within the ROC is liable for income tax on that part of its business income derived from local sources. If an overseas business has no fixed place of business or business agent within the ROC then the tax liability is in the form of a withholding tax at a rate of 25% withheld at source (or 20% if the investment was approved under the *Statute for Investment by Foreign Nationals* or the *Statute for Investment by Overseas Chinese*).

Both foreign and locally owned firms operating within Taiwan and which are classed as profit-seeking enterprises are subject to the following rates of tax:

- for taxable incomes up to NT$50,000 no income tax liability is incurred;
- for incomes between NT$50,000 and NT$100,000 the tax payable is 15% of total taxable income to a maximum not exceeding 50% of the portion of taxable income in excess of NT$50,000;
- for taxable incomes above NT$100,000 the portion in excess of NT$100,000 is taxed at 25%.

The maximum income tax rate for scientific industries operating in the Science-Based Industrial Park is 20%. This is allowed for under the *Statute for the Establishment and Administration of Science-based Industrial Parks.*

In addition to the above taxation liability incurred on the basis of an annual tax return and settlement, a number of taxes are withheld at source as withholding taxes. Tax is levied on the basis of income received in any fiscal year. The fiscal year is usually the calendar year. Annual returns are filed between February 20 and March 31 of each year but may be extended where an accountant has been entrusted to prepare the return. Taxable income is calculated according to the formula:

Taxable Income	=	Income for the whole year	−	deductions for any losses in the past five years	−	various tax exempt incomes

Foreign branch offices with a fixed place of business in Taiwan are only subject to payment of tax on local operations in the same manner and at the same rate as local companies. If there is not a fixed place of business, a withholding tax on ROC sourced income, usually of 20%, is assessed. All accounting is on an accrual basis.

Income tax regulations divide revenue and expenses into operating and non-operating items. In the case of application for exemptions, only net operating income is exempt from tax. Non-operating income (including investment income, exchange rate gains/losses and inventory gains/losses) may be taxed if it exceeds a certain percentage of the total. Any capital gains achieved as a result of revaluation of property in accordance with government regulations are tax exempt.

In addition to the usual deductions for normal business expenses and depreciation, other items which may be deducted when calculating taxable income include premiums from stock issues set aside as capital reserves and all research and development expenses.

Retained earnings cannot normally exceed 100% of a company's paid in capital. If retained earnings exceed the applicable limit, a company can elect to pay a 10% surtax on the excess and then retain the excess indefinitely. Alternatively, the earnings can be allocated to the shareholders as taxable dividends.

Depreciation may be based on either market value or replacement cost. A firm may opt for the straight-line, declining-balance or working-hours method, subject to the approval of local tax authorities. Taxpayers who do not apply for permission to use another method must adopt the straight-line method. Any switch from one depreciation method to another must be filed with the tax authorities six months in advance.

TAXATION BENEFITS AVAILABLE UNDER THE STATUTE FOR UPGRADING INDUSTRY

Various laws have been enacted over the years to encourage industrial development, the latest of which is the *Statute for Upgrading Industry* (SUI). Introduced in 1991, the current Statute will remain in force until

31 December, 1999 and will probably be extended beyond this date.

The SUI and the related *Enforcement Rules* specify a number of tax benefits related to the encouragement of investment. The more important provisions include the following.

Acceleration of depreciation for upgraded equipment

Under the SUI, the service life of certain fixed assets can be accelerated. Included in this provision are instruments and equipment used for research and development in QC and inspection procedures as well as energy saving equipment.

Tax credits on upgraded equipment

A company may credit against its income tax liability between 5% and 20% of the funds disbursed for specified purposes relating to upgrading and deductible amounts can be carried forward for up to four years. Included in this provision are:
1. Funds invested in equipment for production automation;
2. Funds invested in equipment or technology for pollution control;
3. Funds used in research and development;
4. Funds used for investment into energy saving and re-use of waste water.

Regional tax credits

Up to 20% of the total investment amount can used as a tax credit against income tax for companies that relocate to designated areas deemed to be under-developed. For all intents and purposes this means the eastern seaboard of Taiwan.

'Important' and 'venture capital' enterprises

For stocks subscribed or underwritten and held for two years, in relation to those areas designated by the government as 'important technology-based enterprises', 'important enterprises' or 'venture capital enterprises', investors may credit up to 20% of the acquisition price against their business income tax.

Tax benefits for investors in venture capital funds

Any company making an investment into a venture capital enterprise may exclude 80% of the income derived from its investment from its income tax in the current year.

Exemption of income tax on salaries of foreign personnel

Where a foreign company—which has made an investment under either the *Statute for Investment by Foreign Nationals* or the *Statute for Investment by Overseas Chinese*—sends senior administrative or technical personnel to the ROC to perform temporary work related to its investment in the ROC, then provided that the period of residence in any one tax year is less than 183 days in aggregate, no tax liability within the ROC is incurred in relation to salaries paid outside the ROC.

SCHEDULE FOR PAYING TAXES

Between 1 July and 30 July, companies must pay half of the preceding year's tax. A penalty is incurred for understatement of tax. The balance of corporate taxes on the preceding calendar year's income is officially due at the end of March, but various procedures permit payment to be delayed until the end of May.

Dividends received by a company from portfolio investments are normally exempt from taxes up to 80% of their value. Stock dividends received by shareholders (corporate or individual) as a result of an expansion are not taxable until transferred. Dividends derived from securities exchange transactions conducted by a venture-capital company are tax exempt during the period of suspension of the securities exchange income tax.

Translated copies of the two main tax return forms, the profit and loss statement and the balance sheet are included at the end of the chapter below.

BUSINESS TAX (VAT)

A business tax (VAT) exists, with payments due once every two months. The *Business Tax Law* and accompanying *Enforcement Rules* were last amended in 1995. The tax extends to any transaction of goods or services within the territory of the ROC. Importantly, liability for the tax is incurred once an invoice is issued rather than when it is paid. Any transaction involving either the export or the import of goods is considered under *Article 4* of the Law to be a transaction within the ROC. The tax is also applicable to situations involving overseas transactions where services are provided or utilised within the ROC. For example, the purchase of a trademark from an overseas company to be used within the territory of the ROC falls within the scope of the *Business Tax Law*.

For most enterprises subject to business tax, the applicable rate for VAT payments is 5%. If a credit exists, the company may apply for a refund or carry the credit forward. Imports are subject to VAT calculated on the landed price, including duties, commodity taxes and harbour construction dues (although the latter is no longer collected). Penalties for evasion are a fine of between five and twenty times the tax evaded and, for three violations in a single year, a suspension of business for two weeks.

A zero VAT rate applies to exports, to items sold by duty-free shops, to goods sold to export-oriented entities within a tax-free export zone or the Hsinchu Science-Based Industrial Park and to goods sold to a bonded factory or warehouse. Exempt status applies to health care services, land sales, and approved textbooks and academic writings. A total of 31 specific goods and services are exempt from VAT.

Left outside the scope of VAT are banking, insurance, securities brokerage, pawnshops and dealings in short term commercial paper, all of which are subject to a business receipts tax of 5%; reinsurance, subject to a 1% tax; and bars, clubs, restaurants and entertainment establishments, subject to separate taxes of between 15% and 20%.

In July 1995, *Article 8* of the *Business Tax Law* was amended to remove the VAT from certain inter-bank transactions such as derivatives trading, corporate bonds, inter-bank borrowing and bond financing provided commissions and bank charges were deducted (i.e. commissions and bank charges remain taxable).

Zero-Ratings and Exemptions from VAT

A 'zero-rating' is designed as an exemption with credit for input tax previously paid. Taiwan accords a zero-rating to a limited range of goods and services including:
1. Exported goods;
2. Export-related services or services supplied domestically but used abroad;
3. Goods supplied to departing passengers or passengers in transit by duly organised duty-free shops;
4. Machinery, equipment, material, supplies, fuel or semi-finished products supplied to export enterprises located in the tax-exempt export zones, manufacturing enterprises within the science-based industrial parks or customs-supervised bonded factories or warehouses;
5. International transportation subject to reciprocity by the foreign country in which a foreign transport enterprise engaged in international

transportation within the ROC is incorporated;
6. Ships and aircraft engaged in international transportation as well as ocean-going fishing boats;
7. Goods or repair services supplied to ships or aircraft used in international transportation or ocean-going fishing boats.

An 'exemption' is defined as an exemption without credit for business tax previously paid. Since an input tax on purchases in not creditable by an exempt business entity, an exemption is not as advantageous as a zero-rating. The *Business Tax Law* provides 31 categories of exemptions including:
1. The sale of land;
2. Water supplied to farmland for irrigation;
3. Medical services provided by hospitals, clinics and sanatoriums;
4. Services offered by nursing homes for children, the elderly or handicapped;
5. Educational services offered by educational and cultural institutions;
6. School textbooks and specialised academic writings;
7. Newspapers and magazines;
8. Animal feed and unprocessed products of the agricultural, forestry, fishery and livestock industries;
9. Rice and wheat flour and the service of husking rice;
10. The sale of fixed assets not regularly traded;
11. Certain insurance services;
12. Government bonds and securities;
13. Interest on the flow of funds between head and branch offices of financial institutions.

COMMODITY TAX

A commodity (sales) tax is levied *ad valorem* on certain types of goods, whether locally made or imported. Items to which the tax is applied are specified in the *Statute for Commodity Tax*, last substantially revised in 1990. For domestically produced goods, the tax liability is incurred by the manufacturer at the time goods are despatched from the factory. For imported goods, it is incurred at the time of import with the consignees or holders of bills of lading being liable for the tax payment.

A total of eight commodity groups are subject to commodity tax with varying rates of tax being applied to individual items within each group. The major groups subject to tax are as follows:

1. **Tobacco and wine:** Since items in this category are currently sold under the monopoly system, the application of commodity tax on items in this category is temporarily suspended;
2. **Rubber and tyres:** Rates vary from 10% to 15% with exemptions applied to inner tubes and rubber tyres used on farming vehicles and those which are man- or animal-powered;
3. **Cement:** The rate varies from a low of NT$280/MT for slag cement to a high of NT$600/MT for white or coloured cement;
4. **Beverages:** A rate of between 8% and 15% is applied with pure natural juices and certain other concentrated or natural juices being exempt from the tax;
5. **Flat glass**: A general tax rate of 10% is applied;
6. **Oil and gas:** The highest tax rate is applied to gasoline which is taxed at a rate of NT$6,500/KL. Fuel oils carry the lowest rate at NT$100/KL;
7. **Electric appliances**: A tax of between 10% and 20% is applied to a range of white goods and audio/video equipment;
8. **Vehicles:** A progressive rate of tax is applied to automobiles ranging from 25% on sedans below 2,000cc cylinder volume to 60% for sedans above 3,601cc.

For domestically manufactured items, the applicable tax rate is computed according to the formula:

$$\textbf{Taxable Value} = \frac{\textbf{Ex-factory price}}{\textbf{(1 + tax rate + 12\%)}}$$

For the purposes of calculating the tax, goods are assigned a taxable value equal to the average ex-factory selling price divided by the sum of 1 plus the tax rate plus 12%; thus, for a domestic product with a value of NT$500 and a rate of 10%, or 0.1, the taxable value is NT$500 divided by 1.22 (NT$410). For imported commodities, the taxable value is equal to the total amount of customs duty.

Exemptions from the tax are generally allowed in circumstances where the commodity is used as a raw material for production of another taxable item; where goods are manufactured for export and in certain other circumstances. However, in order to obtain a refund of the levy on exports, firms must go through a lengthy and complicated application process.

Exemptions and Deductions

A business enterprise may apply for exemption from payment of the commodity tax where:

- Commodities are used as a raw material for the manufacture of another taxable commodity; except for flue-cured leaf tobaccos;
- Commodities are exported for overseas sale;
- Commodities are supplied for exhibition purposes only;
- Commodities are supplied for military morale purposes or for military use and approval has been obtained from the Ministry of Defense.

In addition to those circumstances leading to an exemption from commodity tax, an application may be made for a refund or an off-set of tax previously paid where:

- Goods are exported;
- Goods are used as input for the manufacture of export items;
- Goods are unsaleable and are returned to the factory;
- Goods become unsaleable due to damage or destruction.

CUSTOMS DUTIES

Although not a member of the Customs Cooperation Council, since 1989 the ROC has adopted the *Harmonised Description and Coding System* (HS) as the basis of its Customs Import Tariff. While remaining an important source of tax revenue, the government has progressively lowered import tariffs as a means of reducing industrial inputs to domestic industry as well as to bring Taiwan into line with current international efforts to expedite trade liberalisation. It is stated government policy to continue to lower tariffs as circumstances require. The average real tariff (i.e. the weighted average of goods actually traded) fell to an effective rate of around 6% in 1996.

The government has also brought into effect an automated cargo clearance system through the computer linking of customs offices, brokers, warehouses, banks and other agencies concerned with cargo clearance. Automated air cargo clearance was introduced in 1992 and sea cargo clearance has been in effect at all major ports since June 1995.

Tariffs are generally measured *ad valorem*, with the transaction value taken as the basis for customs valuation purposes. The transaction value is defined in Section 1 of *Article 12* of the *Customs Law*. It replaced the earlier CIF valuation in 1986 in order to bring Taiwan into line with the 1979

GATT Customs Valuation Code.

Where the customs value cannot be determined from the transaction value, as with re-imported goods, goods on which only a rental or royalty has been incurred or goods imported at less than market price, the *Customs Law* provides a number of alternative means of valuing goods for customs purposes, including the transaction value of identical goods sold for export, the value of similar goods imported into the ROC or other means.

Information on specific tariffs may be obtained from the Directorate General of Customs, a body under the authority of the Ministry of Finance. Copies (in English) of Taiwan's Customs Import Tariff and Classification Schedule may be obtained from the China External Trade Development Council.

Privileged customs treatment in terms of exemption of customs duty, deferred payment, duty bonding or duty refund is afforded in a number of situations:

* Machinery and equipment imported for oil exploration in accordance with the *Statute for the Exploration of Oil in Seabeds* is exempt from customs duty;
* Companies manufacturing 'sophisticated' products for export in accordance with the *Statute for Upgrading Industry* can have the duty deferred for five years on machinery and equipment imported for their own use;
* Export processing factories may be registered as bonded factories and imported goods may be re-exported within prescribed time limits, free of customs duty.

THE SECURITIES TRANSACTION TAX

The Securities Transaction Tax (STT) is imposed upon all securities exchange transactions in accordance with the *Statute for Securities Transaction Tax* (1990). Securities are defined in the Statute as being:
1. Shares or share certificates issued by companies;
2. Corporate bonds;
3. Any securities offered to the public which have been duly approved by the government;
4. Government bonds.

The current tax rate is 0.3% of the shares or share certificates issued by companies or 0.1% of the value of corporate bonds or any other securities

271

offered to the public and duly approved by government. Government bonds and treasury bills are currently exempt from application of the STT as are:

- Any shares issued by a new company or by an existing company in connection with a capital increase;
- Any initial issue of corporate bonds offered to the public which have been duly approved;
- Any securities which have been acquired by succession or donation.

The seller of the security incurs the tax liability, however, due to the large number of share transactions taking place, STT is usually withheld and paid by the tax-collecting agent.

LAND TAXES

The *Land Tax Law* of 1977 provided the first unified code on land tax consolidating various rules and regulations governing the collection of **land value tax** (tax on land based on an assessed value), **agricultural land tax** (assessed on farming land) and **land value increment tax** (levied on the capital gain realised upon the sale of land). Land value tax is assessed only on non-farm land and is the most important. Generally, the taxpayer is the owner of the land title deed. The formula for assessing the tax is complex and based on six classes of land to which different formulas apply. Special privileged rates apply to residential land in urban areas of less than 300 square metres and to industrial or public land.

The land value increment tax is designed to curb speculation and monopolisation of land. The tax is collected on the total incremental value at the time of transfer of the title to the land with 'total incremental value' assessed according to prescribed formulas.

A special levy is applied to vacant lots to which access roads and other services have been provided. The levy is another means of discouraging speculation and, in a country where land is a scarce commodity, of ensuring the effective use of available land.

The means of assessing agricultural land tax is based on the same principles in use within China for more than four thousand years and involves a combination of payment in kind (a proportion of the crop) or monetary substitution. Now considered obsolete, the collection of agricultural land tax has been suspended, although there seems to be a great reluctance to throw out a tax that has been on the books throughout four millennia. It is in fact the world's oldest recorded tax.

BUILDING (HOUSE) TAX

The house tax is levied on all houses and related buildings attached to land. It is one of the main sources of revenue to local governments. Collection of house tax is based on the *House Tax Act* of 1967, which replaced a previous Act. The Act provides for maximum and minimum rates of tax to be applied but leaves it up to local government authorities to set the actual rate within these limits.

OTHER TAXES

Deed Tax

Article 2 of the *Statute on Deed Tax* provides that for transactions involving the purchase, sale, bestowal or partitioning of immovable property, a deed tax shall be paid. Immovable property includes both land and fixtures. In its application to the land component of any transaction, deed tax is only assessed in situations where land increment tax is not levied. For all practical purposes in Taiwan, the latter has replaced the deed tax that is now collected only on houses, buildings or other fixtures.

Amusement Tax

An amusement tax is levied on the price of tickets sold or the fees collected by amusement businesses which provide on-site equipment or activities for entertainment. Where no ticket price is involved but drinks or entertainment is provided to customers (such as nightclubs), the tax is levied on the total charge.

Stamp Tax

Since 1986 only four items have remained subject to stamp tax and there are indications that the tax is being phased out.

Vehicle Licence Tax

Under the 1979 *Vehicle License Tax Law* responsibility for levying and collecting vehicle licence taxes was transferred to the provincial and municipal governments. The tax is progressive according to vehicle size and since 1995 no tax has been payable on motorcycles below 150cc engine capacity. At the same time, the tax on private passenger vehicles and larger motorcycles has been increased.

Current annual licence plate tax rates (in NT$) on small passenger vehicles (seating nine persons or fewer) are reproduced in the accompanying table (Table 13.1).

Table 13.1. Annual tax rates for motor vehicles(small passenger vehicles seating 9 or fewer

Cylinder Displacement (CC)	Vehicle Type and Rate (NT$)	
	Private	Commercial
500cc and below	1,620	900
501–600	2,160	1,260
601–1,200	4,320	2,160
1,201–1,800	7,120	3,060
1,801–2,400	11,230	6,480
2,401–3,000	15,210	9,900
3,001–4,200	28,220	16,380
4,201–5,400	46,170	24,300
5,401–6,600	69,690	33,660
6,601–7,800	117,000	44,460
Over 7,801cc	151,200	56,700

Mining Lot Tax

The imposition of a tax on mining concessions is an integral part of the customary Chinese taxation system that has carried over into Taiwan. However, as mining is not a major industry, the effects of the tax are minimal. The *Mining Industry Statute* was enacted in 1930 at a time when the ROC was governing the Chinese mainland. According to the Statute there are two different mining taxes; mine concession tax and mineral tax. However, collection of the latter has been suspended since 1950. Income from the remaining concession tax is minimal.

Estate and Gift Tax

The current *Estate and Gift Tax Law* dates from 1973 and was revised in 1981 and again in 1995. Estate and gift taxes currently generate only around 2.4% of total tax revenue.

Estate tax is payable on property left as part of a deceased estate and is applicable to all ROC citizens normally residing in the ROC, irrespective of whether the property is located within the ROC or overseas. Property of ROC citizens not normally resident in the ROC or of non-citizens is subject to estate tax only on property located in the ROC. 'Estate' also includes movable and immovable objects with a market value.

The definition of 'constant residence' defined in the Law is taken to mean a person who maintains a domicile in the ROC within two years prior to death and has stayed within the territory of the ROC for at least 365 days within those two years. An exception is made for deceased foreigners who were under a service contract to the ROC government and who had only stayed for the period of time specified in their contract.

Tax liability in such situations is incurred by (in order of priority) the executor of the will, heirs and legatees, and an administrator appointed under the Law in the absence of an executor or heir.

A number of exclusions, deductions and exemptions apply to deceased estates of which the most important are listed below.

Exclusions

A total of twelve categories of exclusions are listed of which the most important are:
1. Property inherited by the deceased within five years of death provided that estate taxes had been paid on the property;
2. Insurance payments to a beneficiary maturing at the time of death.

Deductions

A total of eleven categories of deduction are allowed of which the most important are:
1. NT$4 million for a surviving spouse;
2. A deduction of NT$400,000 for each lineal descendent of the deceased plus a further deduction of NT$400,000 for each year from the current age of such dependents up to the age of 20 years;
3. A deduction of NT$1 million for each surviving parent;
4. A deduction of NT$5 million for any handicapped or mentally ill heirs;

5. A deduction of NT$400,000 for each sibling of the deceased, plus a further deduction of NT$400,000 for each year from the current age of such siblings up to the age of 20 years;
6. A deduction of NT$400,000 for each surviving grandparent of the deceased;
7. A standard deduction of NT$1 million for funeral expenses.

Exemptions

A general exemption of NT$7 million can be claimed. However, this amount is doubled in relation to ROC citizens who are normal residents of the ROC and who are soldiers, police, civil servants or teachers.

After allowing for exclusions, deductions and exemptions tax is payable on deceased estates at a progressive tax rate.

A gift tax is payable in situations where a donor transfers property *gratis* to a donee. The most common example of a gift tax is related to property where the transfer of property between family members as well as the holding of property in the name of nominee owners has been a common means of reducing the tax liabilities of an owner. Any property donated in this form is assessed for tax purposes against its market value and not the government rateable value (which is usually less than market value).

The donor is generally liable for payment of the gift tax although the obligation can revert to the donee if the tax is not paid within a certain time limit.

Exclusions exist in relation to transfers between spouses and marriage gifts to the value of NT$1 million. An annual exemption is also available of up to NT$1 million for each donor.

Table 13.2. Estate taxes: progressive tax rates

Level	Net Estate in NT$	Tax Rate %
1	0–600,000	2%
2	600,001–1,500,000	4%
3	1,500,001–3,000,000	7%
4	3,000,001–4,500,001	11%
5	4,500,001–6,000,000	15%
6	6,000,001–10,00,000	20%
7	10,000,001–15,000,000	26%

Table13.2 cont'd

8	15,000,001–40,000,000	33%
9	40,000,001–100,000	41%
10	Over NT$100,000,000	50%

Table 13.3. Withholding tax rates applicable in the ROC

Type of Income	Withholding Rate of Tax	
	Profit-Seeking Enterprise with a permanent establishment	*Profit-Seeking Enterprise with no permanent establishment*
Dividends distributed by companies and profits distributed by cooperatives	15%	25%; or 20% if the investment was approved under the *Statute for Investment by Foreign Nationals* or the *Statute for Investment by Overseas Chinese.*
Commission	10%	20%
Interest Income	10%; or 20% taxed separately from ordinary income on interest from short term commercial paper	20%
Awards or prizes obtained from participating in contests, games or lotteries, etc.	15% if the amount exceeds NT$4,000; or 20%, to be taxed separately, for a prize received from lotteries sponsored by the government, if the prize exceeds NT$2,000 per ticket.	20%; or 0% if the prize received is from lotteries sponsored by the government and below NT$2,000 per ticket.
Rental	10%	20%
Royalties	15%	20%

Table 13.3 cont'd

International transportation and other contracted projects in which income has been permitted to be calculated at a fixed rate according to *Article 25* of the *Income Tax Law*		25%
Income derived from property transactions		25% of the reported amount
Foreign motion picture enterprises in which income has been permitted to be calculated by a fixed rate according to *Article 26* of the *Income Tax Law*		20%
Other income		20%

SAMPLE BUSINESS INCOME TAX DECLARATION FORM (31)

[Income Year: from: 01 January _____ to 31 December _____.]

(Date of commencement of business :   )

Business Title				
Business Address				
Person in Charge		Identity Card #		
Residential Address				
Business Uniform #		Tax Registration #		
Residential Tax Code #		Standard Code #		
Type of Organisation		Type of business		

Subjects of Profit and Loss [Business Net Profit]		Closing Amount (in NT$)	Value Self-adjusted (in NT$)
01	Sales Turnover (including export income)		
02	Minus sales return		
03	Sales concession		
04	Net business income		
05	Business operating costs		
06	Gross business profit (04–05)		
07	Gross profit rate [(06/04) x 100]		
08	Total business expenses and loss (10 to 32 in total)		
09	Expenses rate [(08/04) x 100]		
10	Salary and Wages		
11	Rent payments		
12	Stationery		
13	Travel expenses		
14	Shipping and freight		
15	Postage and telecommunications		
16	Repairs		
17	Advertising		

Sample Business Income Tax Declaration Form cont'd

18	Water and electricity		
19	Insurance		
20	Entertainment		
21	Donations		
22	Taxation		
23	Loss through bad debts		
24	All depreciation		
25	Amortisation		
26	Foreign loan exchange losses		
27	Meals allowance		
28	Employees welfare		
29	Research allowance		
30	Commission payments		
31	Occupational training		
32	Miscellaneous expenditure		
33	**Net Profit from Business Operations**		
104	Business Operations Net Profit Rate (33/04)		
[Non Business Income]		**Value Accounted (in NT$)**	**Value Self-adjusted (in NT$)**
34	Total non-business income		
35	General dividends and bonuses		
36	Dividends (according to *Article 42* of *Income Tax Act*)		
37	Registered stock exemption		
38	Interest income		
39	Rental income		
40	Capital gains from property sales		
41	Commission income		
42	Merchandise inventory profit		
43	Exchange profit		
44	Other miscellaneous income (incl. 1997 tax return)		
[Non Business Loss]			
45	Total non-business losses and expenses (46 to 52 in total)		
46	Interest paid-out		
47	Investment loss		

Sample Business Income Tax Declaration Form cont'd

48	Loss from trading properties		
49	Loss from disasters		
50	Merchandise inventory loss		
51	Exchange loss		
52	Other miscellaneous losses		
[Profit/Loss and Income Taxable]			
53	**Total Income for the Year (33+34-45)**		
54	Net profit rate [{53/(04+34)} x 100]		
55	Approved deductable losses for the last 3 years		
56	Interest from tax exemption (see *Bond Act*)		
57	Exempt (tax free) income		
58			
59	**Taxable Income (53 - 56 -57 -58)**		
[Tax Calculation]			
60	(1) Income Taxable NT\$ x Tax Rate **25%** - progressive difference NT\$10,000 = Tax Payable NT\$		
	(2) If business operation is less than one year, the total income of the year should be converted into [NT\$ x 12/ x % -]x /12 = Tax Payable for the Year *(Blank)*		
61	Tax Deductibility (15% of Tax Payable) applies under the *Encouragement of Investment Act, Articles 24* and *40*		
95	Tax Deductibility applies under the *Encouragement of Investment Act, Articles 10, 20, 20-2* and *34-1*		
96	Tax Deductibility applied under the *Encouragement of Investment Act, Article 34-1*		
62	Temporary tax payable for this year or revised temporary tax payable		
63	Withheld tax yet to be deducted for this year		
64	Supplementary Business Income Tax to be paid to the authority for this year		
65	Business Income Tax applied for refund this year		
[Reasons and Instructions for Adjustment]			

Sample Business Income Tax Declaration Form cont'd

66	In relation to the *Income Tax Act, Article 76-1*, 2nd Item, only those Profit and Loss Declared Items which are over the specific standard, which have legitimate certificates and have normal reasons can be listed and declared: NT$*(blank)* (in a manner of self-adjustment or prepared by a Certified Public Accountant)
[Instructions for Adjusting Business Income]	
01	NT$_____ (sales turnover declared and settled this year differs from:
68	NT$_____ (total value shown on the uniform invoices issued by the Head and its branches) at a value of:
69	NT$_____ details of which are given as follows: Total Value shown on the Uniform Invoices issued:
[Plus]	

70	Pre-collected money transferred from last term	
71	Money receivable this term without issue of uniform invoices	
75	Others: Sales return (_____) and Depreciation (_____)	

[Minus]		
76	Pre-collected money this term	
77	Money receivable as shown on the uniform invoices this term	
78	Value to be regarded as sales shown on the uniform invoices	
79	Value over-drafted on the uniform invoices	
80	Income from commissions	
81	Income from rentals	
82	Sales of waste materials	
83	Sale of assets and property	
84	Money collection	
87	Others	
88	**Number of employees at the end of this year**	

Paid temporarily this term (or revised estimation) dated:_____ and filed

105	Temporary tax paid	
106	Investment tax exemption	
107	Tax deductible	
108	Self-paid tax	
98	Interest income from short term notes which is not included in income taxable	

Sample Business Income Tax Declaration Form cont'd

99	Stock exchange income which has ceased to be collected		
100	Dividends not regarded as income (according to the *Income Tax Act Article 42*)		
101	Capital gains from land sales on an income tax exemption basis		
	Standard Code #	**Business Type**	**Enlarged Auditing Net Profit Rate**	**Value (NT$)**
89				
91				

Manner of Tax Return: ( ) Return by mail or ( ) Return to savings account at:

This company has been using money collection machines since the date of:

Taxation Representative Practising License #:
Identity Card of the Representative:

Officially recognised uniform invoice chop was given by _____ and other official seals were given at the bottom of this Form as follows:
Person in Charge   : (with officially recognised seal)   Legal
Representative: *(blank)*
Receipt Number of Collection Office _____
(The above information has been declared to the _____ *on* _____ *with official filing chop)*

SAMPLE BALANCE SHEET

[Income Year: 31 December 19___]
(Date of commencement of business : _____)

Business Title	
Business Uniform #	
Business Tax Code #	

Assets		Sub Total (in NT$)	Total (in NT$)
1100	**CURRENT ASSETS**		
1111	Cash		
1112	Deposits in bank		
1113	Marketable securities		
1115	Minus: loss allowance for marketable securities		
1114	Short term investment		
1121	Notes receivable		
1122	Minus: bad debts allowance		
1123	Accounts receivable		
1124	Minus: bad debts allowance		
1129	Other accounts receivable		
1130	**INVENTORY**		
1131	Merchandise		
1132	Finished products		
1133	Manufacturing products (or processing projects)		
1134	Raw materials		
1135	materials		
1136	Products sold on behalf of others		
1138	Others (residual raw materials)		
1140	**ADVANCE PAYMENTS**		
1141	Prepaid charges		
1142	Goods inventory		
1143	Advance Charges		
1149	Other prepayments		
1190	**OTHER CURRENT ASSETS**		

Sample Balance Sheet cont'd

1191	Temporary debt		
1192	Current shareholders		
1193	Current business associates		
1194	Tax on items purchased		
1199	Others (tax return)		
1200	Funds		
1300	Long term investments		
1400	**FIXED ASSETS**		
1410	Land		
1421	Mineral Resources		
1422	Minus: accumulated depreciation		
1431	House and building		
1432	Minus: accumulated depreciation		
1441	Machinery and equipment		
1442	Minus: accumulated depreciation		
1451	Transportation equipment		
1452	Minus: accumulated depreciation		
1461	Furniture and fixtures		
1462	Minus: accumulated depreciation		
1470	Unfinished construction		
1480	Pre-paid purchasing equipment charge		
1491	Other fixed assets		
1492	Minus accumulated depreciation		
1510	Intangible assets		
1520	Minus: accumulated depreciation		
1900	Other assets		
1910	Guarantee deposits and margins paid		
1920	Organisational costs		
1930	Guarantee notes receivable		
1940	Undespatched expenditure		
1950	Accounts paid on behalf of others		
1990	Others		
1000	**TOTAL ASSETS**		

Liabilities		Sub Total (in NT$)	Total (in NT$)
2100	**CURRENT LIABILITIES**		

Sample Balance Sheet cont'd

2110	Short-term loans		
2111	Bank overdrafts		
2112	Loans from bank		
2113	Commercial notes payable		
2119	Other short-term loans		
2120	**ACCOUNTS PAYABLE**		
2121	Notes payable		
2122	Accounts payable		
2123	Expenses payable		
2124	Tax payable		
2125	Dividends payable		
2129	Other accounts payable		
2130	**PRE-COLLECTED ACCOUNTS**		
2131	Pre-collected charges		
2139	Other pre-collected accounts		
2190	**OTHER CURRENT LIABILITIES**		
2191	Temporary credit		
2192	Current shareholders		
2193	Current business associates		
2194	Tax for selling items		
2195	Others		
2200	**LONG-TERM LIABILITIES**		
2210	Corporate bonds payable		
2220	Long-term loans		
2290	Other long-term liabilities		
2900	**OTHER LIABILITIES**		
2910	Guarantee deposits and margins received		
2920	Allowance for capital gain from land		
2930	Allowance for foreign debts and exchange losses		
2940	Allowance for retirement		
2950	Allowance for export losses		
2960	Guarantee notes payable		
2970	Entrust sales		
2980	Tax collection deputy		
2990	Collections		
2999	Others		

Sample Balance Sheet cont'd

2000	**TOTAL LIABILITIES**		
3100	**CAPITAL**		
3110	Capital received		
3120	Capital not received		
3200	**LEGAL SURPLUS AND PROFIT**		
3210	Legal surplus		
3220	Capital surplus		
3230	Special surplus		
3240	Allowance for value added up		
3250	Accumulated profit		
3260	Profit and loss of this term		
3000	Total amount of net worth		
9000	**TOTAL LIABILITIES AND EQUITY**		

Person in Charge: (with officially recognised seal)
Chief Accountant: (with officially recognised seal)
Chartered by: (with officially recognised seal)
(The above information has been declared to the   on   with official filing chop)

CHAPTER 14

MONEY AND BANKING

Taiwan is in the process of transforming from a manufacturing to a service-based economy. It is national policy to develop Taiwan as an economic hub for the Greater China region. Within this national objective, the ROC Government accords a high priority to the establishment of Taiwan as a regional financial centre within East Asia.

Progressive financial liberalisation has been under way since 1987 although reform was slow in the early years. Recent and more rapid changes are now creating many new opportunities for the banking and financial services community and for those companies that provide value-added services to this sector.

MONETARY POLICY AND PERFORMANCE

Responsibility for monetary policy rests with the Central Bank of China which, together with the Ministry of Finance, shares overall responsibility for the regulation of Taiwan's financial markets and financial service industries. While both are committed to an opening of the local financial market to international competition and the development of Taipei as a financial centre, it is generally believed that the Central Bank adopts a more cautious approach than those agencies directly under the direct and daily control of the ROC Cabinet. The Central Bank is primarily responsible for regulating the money supply and foreign exchange market while the Ministry of Finance supervises and regulates the financial market as a whole.

Money Supply

In recent times the growth of Taiwan's broad-based money supply (M2) has been slow—tending towards the lower end of the 10% to 15% annual growth range set by the Central Bank since 1994 (and more recently dropping below this range). Domestic capital experienced a massive outflow in late 1995 and early 1996 following the PRC's military exercises off the coast of Taiwan, pulling the annual rate of growth for the first quarter of that year down to a historic low of 7.27%. As the situation recovered during the year capital returned, the trade surplus grew and Taiwan's stock and bond markets slowly revived, reversing the decline. Yet the investment climate in 1996 remained sluggish throughout the year, with the result that demand for money remained weak. M2 grew for the whole year by only 8.12%—a full 2% less than in 1995.

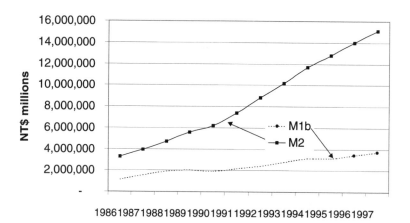

Figure 14a. Growth in money supply 1986–1997

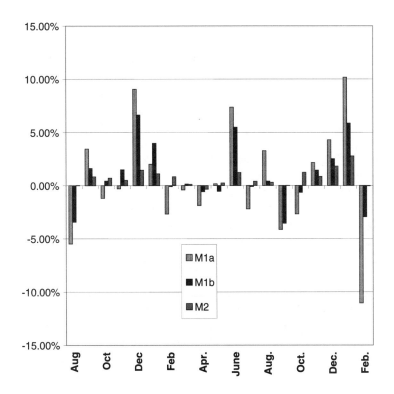

Figure 14b. Monthly changes in money supply July 1996 to Feb 1998

In January 1997, the Central Bank redefined broad-based money (M2) to include deposits within the postal savings system as well as repurchase transactions. The change has not had any noticeable impact on the market. Indeed, as of December 1997 (and based on preliminary data) the growth in broadly defined money (M2) increased only 6.89% over the previous year—well below the government's target range. M1A (currency in circulation, chequeing accounts and demand deposits) increased by only 2.7% in the same period while M1B (M1A plus passbook savings deposits) grew by almost 4.3%. Up until September 1997, the M1 indicators had been performing more strongly (9.85% and 13.59% YOY); a reflection of the active conditions in the stock market earlier in the year in contrast to the slow growth of bank credit that affected M2 (5.96% to September). The Asian currency meltdown and the drop of the local dollar during the final quarter influenced the year-end figures.

Interest Rates

Since 1989 banks have generally been allowed to determine their own interest rates for both deposit and loan activities. There is no true base rate for transactions and the overnight interbank rate generally fulfils this role. The Interbank Call-Loan Rate is determined by the Interbank Money Center while the Treasury Bills Rate is the responsibility of the Central Bank of China. Treasury bills are of declining importance in the money market (see below), largely due to the slow growth of the money supply and the consequent lack of any surplus liquidity to mop up.

Banks involved in consumer lending set their own prime lending rates on the basis of the overnight rate plus a margin, which can vary considerably between banks. Those banks that do not engage in lending set their rates against the deposit rate. The spread in rates can be quite wide. In February 1998 the weighted overnight rate stood at 7.222%, although between the different banks the rate varied from 9.300% to 6.000%.

In the face of economic stagnation, the Central Bank progressively eased back on its monetary policy during 1996 and early 1997. In order to stimulate recovery the rediscount rate was lowered twice in 1996 while the deposit reserve ratios of the banks were also lowered. Despite these measures, demand for capital remained weak and interest rates generally fell across the board.

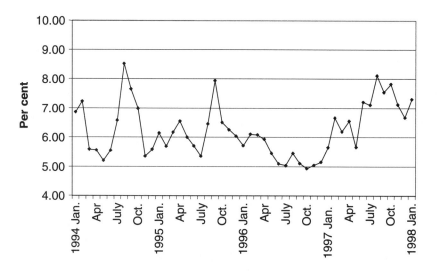

Figure 14c. Interbank call loan rates

Table 14.1 Rates of accommodation to banks by the Central Bank

Effective Date	*Rediscounts*	*Accommodation Against Secured Loans*	*Temporary Accommodation*	*Accommodation in Foreign Exchange*
February 1995	5.80	6.00	9.625	Libor[1] + 6 month USD
July 1995	5.50	5.875	9.625	Libor + 6 month USD
May 1996	5.25	5.625	9.625	Libor + 6 month USD
August 1996	5.00	5.375	9.625	Libor + 6 month USD
August 1997	5.25	5.625	9.625	Libor + 6 month USD

Short-term interest rates have generally been increasing throughout 1997, a consequence of rapidly rising stock market activity creating demand for funds. Between January and July 1997, the value of Taiwan's general stock index increased by more than 45% and many investors withdrew their funds from the banks to invest in stocks, thereby boosting short term interest rates. The overnight interbank rate climbed as high as 13% in June 1997, but the range has generally been around the 7% level.

As of January 1998 the base lending rates of the domestic banks were generally in the range between 7.15% and 8.7%, but there is a general expectation that rates will rise in keeping with the need to attract funds both into Taiwan and into the banking system.

Currency Outlook

For the greater part of 1996 and well into 1997, the Taiwan dollar was stable and trading within a narrow range between 27.15 and 27.85 to the US dollar. The general policy adopted by the Central Bank was to allow a slow depreciation of the currency in order to stimulate export growth. During early 1997, and in spite of a strengthening US dollar, the local currency

---

[1] London Interbank Rate.

retained its value, bolstered by increasing activity on the stock market and strong demand from overseas investors remitting funds into Taiwan.

In the third quarter of 1997 Asia generally was starting to feel the impact of the currency crisis affecting a number of key economies. Yet Taiwan weathered the initial storm rather well. In the third quarter the local dollar dropped from 27.8 at the end of June to 28.7 three months later. Aided by a strong reserve position of more than US$85 billion, the Central Bank Chairman went on the record with a vow to defend the local currency. Although supposedly independent of government, the public declaration of support may have been motivated, in part at least, by political concerns. Year end elections were looming and a sharp drop in the currency would have caused problems for the stock market and for interest rates generally—problems the government was anxious to avoid. In September 1997, in an effort to bolster the local financial market, the reserve requirements were cut on a wide range of deposits. Exhortations to exporters to off-load their foreign exchange hoardings in an effort to ward off currency pressures went unheeded, and the Central Bank was reportedly spending more than US$1.5 billion a month during this period to defend the local dollar.

Typhoon Ivan hit Taiwan in mid-October 1997 and as it approached the shore it was upgraded to the status of a 'strong' typhoon. Ivan was a harbinger of the maelstrom that was shortly to hit Taiwan's financial market. Faced with the mounting cost of defending the currency—more than US$5 billion in the third quarter alone—the Central Bank finally withdrew its support. The slide was rapid, with a loss of more than NT$1 in one day at one stage. To make matters worse, the initial slide occurred only one day after the Central Bank Governor, SHEU Yuan-dong[2] announced to the media that the dollar would remain unchanged over the next three months. His credibility and that of the Central Bank suffered as a result. By October's end, the dollar was nudging the 31.0 mark and by year-end had fallen to around 32.6. A further fall in January 1998 saw the dollar break the 34.0 mark and there were fears that it would fall to below 35. So far this has not happened.

---

[2] Sheu was tragically killed in the February 1998 China Airlines Crash at Taipei International Airport. He was replaced by PERNG Fai-nan, former Chairman of the International Commercial Bank of China. Perng has a reputation for taking a tough line against currency speculators.

The January 1998 fall—each successive month in the final quarter of 1997 being the 'lowest in ten years'—may have been an overshoot. With the Chinese New Year looming, demand for US currency was particularly high, and since the New Year a small correction appears to have taken place. Fundamentally, Taiwan's currency remains sound. At US$100 million, Taiwan's external debt position is among the lowest in Asia. The great strength of the local market has been that it is better regulated than many other Asian financial markets and does not suffer from the massive asset inflation that has beset a number of financial institutions elsewhere. There have been no bank failures in Taiwan as a result of the turmoil and none are expected. While bad debt is a growing problem in Taiwan it appears to be confined to the small and medium enterprises and is nowhere near the epidemic proportions seen elsewhere in the region such as in Korea.

The general outlook for the currency as of early 1998 is that unless there are further major falls in other regional currencies that will force a response from Taiwan to remain competitive, there is room for a slight appreciation of the local dollar in the months ahead.

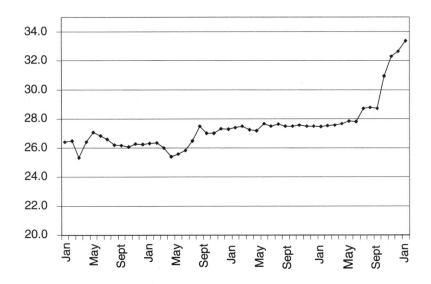

Figure 14d. Interbank closing rate against the US dollar (Jan 1996 to Jan 1998)

Forward contracts for foreign exchange transactions have been permitted since 1991 and provide an important edge for exporters and others involved in foreign exchange transactions, especially during times of exchange rate volatility. Swap transactions and margin trading have also been permitted since 1991 although pre-export loans, whereby loans are granted on the basis of projected foreign exchange income, are generally preferred. NT dollar to foreign currency forward contracts are also permitted.

Foreign Exchange Transactions and Remittances

In preparation for its entry to the World Trade Organisation, Taiwan is progressively easing those regulations relating to capital flows. Indeed, there are few remaining restrictions on foreign exchange-related activities in Taiwan. The individual ceiling for both inward and outward remittances converted into NT dollars without prior approval from the Central Bank is US$5 million for each Taiwan national or resident alien and US$10 million for corporations. If the remittance is not converted into the local currency then no ceiling applies. Individual outward remittances do not need to be reported unless the amount exceeds NT$500,000. Money can be remitted on the day of application.

There are no restrictions imposed on trade-related remittances and for investments made under the *Statute for Investment by Foreign Nationals,* 100% of total invested capital can be repatriated after one year from the commencement date of operations. Capital invested into machinery, raw materials and intellectual property can only be repatriated in the currency of original approval. Dividends and net profits from *SIFN* approved businesses can also be freely remitted.

Similarly, there are no restrictions imposed on the payment of interest and principal of foreign loans nor on income from royalties or licensing agreements.

Monetary Instruments

Taiwan's money market includes the interbank call loan market and short-term accommodation markets as well as securities with a maturity of less than one year that are transacted on the primary and secondary markets. Instruments transacted include government and corporate bonds, financial securities and negotiable certificates of deposit.

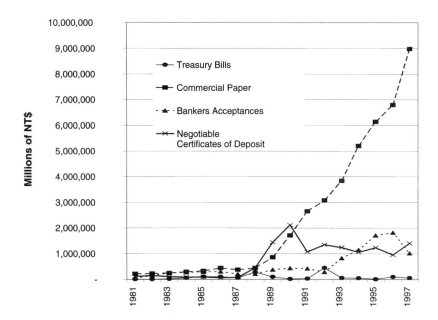

Figure 14e. Issue of money market bills

Commercial Paper (CP) is the most popular short-term financing technique in the formal money market, followed by Bankers Acceptances (BAs) and Negotiable Certificates of Deposit (NCDs). Among many companies credit against post-dated cheques is also very common and is often part of the terms of trade—payment terms can sometimes be as long as three to six months using this means of settlement.

Total issue of CPs in 1997 stood at NT$8,976 billion[3] while BAs amounted to NT$1,019 billion (US$31 billion) and NCDs NT$1,401 billion (US$42.5 billion). Gross issues in 1997 represented a more than ten-fold increase over the value in 1987 when liberalisation first began (see Figure 14f).

Interest rates on the various instruments are volatile and fluctuate in line with the interbank call loan rate. Commercial paper generally attracts a higher interest rate than either NCDs or BAs, although only the larger firms generally have access to this market. Many smaller firms remain reliant on

---

[3] Unless otherwise indicated, all US dollar figures quoted in parentheses are based on a notional exchange rate of 33.0.

the unorganised and traditional money markets which continue to thrive alongside the banking industry and which (in keeping with tradition) are often organised either through jewellery shops or through local savings syndicates (known as *hweis*). Interest rates in this market are considerably higher than those of the banks and are generally quoted in per cent per month. The interest on loans against post-dated cheques currently varies between 1.46% and 2.7% per month. Other rates are quoted for unsecured loans (1.79%–2.85%) and for deposits with companies (1.22%–2.19%).

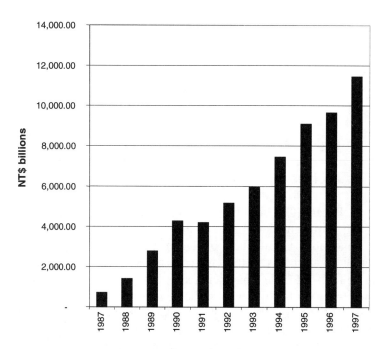

Figure 14f. Total issues 1987–1997

Table 14.2. Issue of money market bills

Year	T-Bills	CP	BA	NCD
1987	99,300	374,525	204,167	78,562
1996	98,650	1,816,546	1,816,546	955.042
1997	57,320	1,018,731	1,018,731	1,400,707
			Units: millions of New Taiwan Dollars	

TAIWAN'S MONETARY INSTITUTIONS

Financial institutions are generally organised and registered according to the *Banking Law* or other government laws and regulations. Within this definition are the 'monetary institutions' (those able to create money) and 'other financial institutions'. Taiwan's monetary institutions consist of the Central Bank, the deposit-taking banks (domestic commercial banks, medium business banks, and the local branch operations of foreign banks) and the community-based financial institutions consisting of the various rural credit departments and cooperative associations of farmers and fishermen. Until recently these were regulated separately from the banks and under provincial government control.

A series of financial scandals in 1995 which primarily affected the credit cooperatives highlighted the lack of accountability of these community institutions. A review of the regulatory procedures has brought about change with the cooperatives and credit departments now being forced to comply with the standards of the Central Deposit Scheme. Those who do not meet current standards have been given three years in which to adjust or be phased out.

Other financial institutions include the postal savings system (which is in reality a specialised deposit-taking bank), the investment and trust companies and life insurance companies. Property and casualty insurance companies as well as the bills and securities finance companies are not regarded as financial institutions but as part of the private sector.

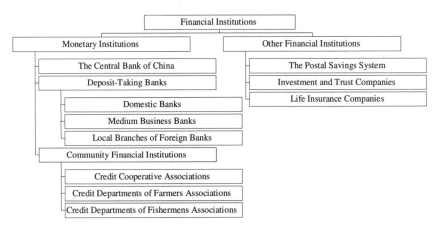

Figure 14g. Schematic of the ROC financial system

The Central Bank of China

The Central Bank of China was founded in Canton in 1924 and relocated to Taiwan in 1949. It is a government bank and an agency directly responsible to the *Executive Yuan* (Cabinet). In accordance with its charter, it deals only with government agencies and financial institutions. Its role is to promote financial stability, ensure the maintenance of sound banking practices, maintain the stability of the currency and to foster economic development. The CBC determines the rediscount rate as well as other interest rates and deposit reserve ratios and acts as a lender of last resort to other banking institutions. CBC holds Taiwan's international monetary reserves and the overall management of foreign exchange and acts as the fiscal agent of the ROC Government.

The Central Trust of China

The Central Trust of China is a specialised bank which is wholly government-owned and which carries out a range of government-related operations including the handling of government tenders and procurement, specialised trading in commodities where import or other restrictions preclude trading through normal commercial channels, warehousing and transportation and insurance operations on behalf of government employees. It is generally classified for statistical purposes as a domestic commercial bank but, like the Central Bank, acts as an instrument of government policy and does not deal with the general public as a rule.

THE DEPOSIT-TAKING BANKS

As of December 1997 there were a total of 39 domestic banks with a combined total of 1,5685 branches. Twelve of these banks, including the largest domestic banks, have significant government ownership and control, although some degree of privatisation is in progress for all of them. The medium business banks are all government-controlled and concentrate on corporate and business services. New banks which opened during the course of 1997 were the Sunny Bank, Bank of Panhsin, Lucky Bank and Kao Shin Commercial Bank.

Despite the changes taking place in Taiwan's financial market, the banking sector remains dominated by the traditional domestic deposit banks, many of which remain partially or wholly government-owned. In the case of the International Commercial Bank of China (ICBC), the ruling Kuomintang Party is one of the major stockholders and has many of the characteristics of the government banks.

Table 14.3. Growth of the deposit-taking banks in Taiwan

Year	Local Banks				Local Branches of Foreign Banks	
	Deposit Banks		Medium Business Banks			
	Total	Branches	Total	Branches	Total	Branches
1989	16	692	8	261	33	38
1990	16	721	8	275	35	43
1991	17	756	8	290	36	47
1992	32	897	8	315	36	50
1993	33	1030	8	352	37	55
1994	34	1174	8	403	37	57
1995	34	1361	8	446	38	58
1996	34	1464	8	472	41	65
1997	39	1,685	8	491	45	69

Until recently these banks enjoyed a privileged position in the market. Their primary business was focused on servicing the requirements of corporate clients and such consumer banking business as existed was largely restricted to deposit taking and provision of mortgage financing.

This situation is rapidly changing. Amendments to the *Banking Law* in the early 1990s, which relaxed restrictions on the operation of foreign banks as well as the creation of new privately owned domestic banks, have served to introduce new elements of competition into the financial services sector.

It is the new private domestic banks that have largely driven the emerging consumer banking market in Taiwan. With the need to carve out a new market niche, the new banks have aggressively entered the area of consumer financing. Credit cards have led the way but automobile and general unsecured personal loans are rapidly gaining a foothold in the market.

The traditional banks have adapted to changing conditions more through necessity than through enthusiasm. As the local financial market matures, so corporations are becoming more sophisticated in their financial transactions. Corporate treasuries are increasingly turning to the money market for their financing and cash management and away from the formal banking sector. The major banks, many of which are in the process of being privatised by the government, are being forced to adopt new strategies in order to remain competitive. The problem of adaptation for many banks is compounded by the fact that over the last six years the number of bank branches in Taiwan has doubled. At the middle management level there is a serious dearth of experience leaving many banks poorly equipped to handle the banking revolution that is under way.

With the exception of Citibank, the foreign banks have not usually offered general retail banking services but have sought out niche markets, especially in areas of trade finance, loan syndication. This is now also changing. While foreign banks are only permitted to open one new branch office per year, the advent of electronic banking has, to a large extent, levelled the playing field for them. Bank of America, Standard Chartered, ABN-AMRO and the Hong Kong Bank are all aggressively moving into consumer banking with both credit cards and consumer loans.

Alongside the traditional banking sector, general finance and leasing companies are now emerging in the market. Chailease Finance, part of the China Trust Group, is the largest of these with more than 60% market share. At present, ROC law precludes the offer of leasing contracts to individuals, but this is expected to change. Leasing companies expect that consumer-leasing will be a larger market than the current corporate leasing market within five years.

While the consumer loan market has grown quickly in recent years in both size and in product (and there is every expectation that it will continue to grow), Taiwan is not yet a mature market by any means. The need for growth and market share has, more often than not, outstripped the ability of many financial institutions to develop the sophisticated management systems necessary to ensure sustainable profitability. For reasons already mentioned, the problem is often compounded by a lack of skill and experience at the middle management level.

Table 14.4. Taiwan's top 20 local banks (measured by capital)

1996 Rank	Bank	1994 Rank	Global Rank	Net Worth (US$ millions)	Assets	Pre Tax Profits (%)	Return on Assets
1	Bank of Taiwan	1	100	3,598	60,055	531	0.89
2	Land Bank of Taiwan	3	205	1,495	40,584	302	0.74

Table 14.4 cont'd

3	Fubon Commercial Bank (FCB)	2	224	1,355	33,008	255	0.77
4	Hua Nan Commercial Bank (HCB)	4	226	1,353	32,266	229	0.71
5	Chinese Commercial Bank (CCB)	5	228	1,348	29,759	204	0.69
6	Co-operative Bank of Taiwan	12	241	1,272	54,908	258	0.47
7	International Commercial Bank of China	7	255	1,176	19,942	212	1.06
8	Taiwan Business Bank	9	266	1,122	25,502	164	0.64
9	China Trust Commercial Bank	8	274	1,100	15,442	132	0.86
10	United World Chinese Commercial Bank	6	284	1,064	15,021	167	1.11
11	Chiao Tung Bank	10	297	987	16,086	114	0.71
12	Taipei Bank	11	335	852	17,252	121	0.70
13	Farmers Bank		348	818	15,421	59	0.38
14	Shanghai Commercial and Savings Bank	13	382	747	7,458	198	2.66
15	Taipei Business Bank	15	319	658	8,564	112	1.31
16	Taichung Business Bank		435	634	7,877	104	1.33

Table 14.4 cont'd

17	Chung Shing Commercial Bank	14	493	553	3,683	38	1.03
18	Grand Commercial Bank	16	516	511	4,447	43	0.96
19	Union Bank of Taiwan	18	530	494	4,204	31	0.73
20	Cosmos Bank	19	541	482	4,671	29	0.63

The Domestic Commercial Banks

The domestic commercial banks continue to dominate both the savings and loan business. The domestic banks consist of the 'traditional' banks and the 'new' banks. The traditional banks are those that were in existence prior to 1992 and which remain for the most part under full or partial government control. There are a total of nine traditional commercial banks as well as more than twenty 'new' commercial banks established since 1992. There are also eight business banks that are limited in their operations to a specific county or geographic area of Taiwan. An additional four banks fulfil a developmental role in channelling government funds into specific sectors and programs as discussed further in this chapter.

The Deposit Structure

Total monetary deposits within the banking sector as of June 1997 amounted to NT$12,103 billion (US$367 billion approx.) of which 74.7% was held within the local commercial banks (the domestic commercial banks accounted for 63.7% of total deposits while the medium business banks accounted for a further 11.0%.) The community-based financial institutions held a further 23% and the balance was held by the local branches of foreign banks.

Over the last ten years there has been a noticeable shift away from demand deposits and into fixed time deposits, the latter now accounting for almost 65% of total funds on deposit within the banking sector. Time 'savings' deposits (held by individuals) account for 68.9% of this total while general commercial time deposits account for 28.1%. Negotiable Certificates of Deposit account for the balance.

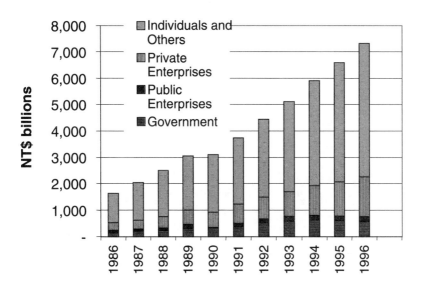

Figure 14h. Deposits with domestic commercial banks

Table 14.5. Growth in deposits by type 1987–1997 (NT$ millions)

Year	Total	Monetary Deposits (as % of total)	Fixed Time Deposits (as % of total	F/E Deposits (as % of total	Government Deposits (as % of total
1987	3,073,905	1,283,261 (41.75%)	1,557,482 (50.67%)	13,275 (0.43%)	219,887 (7.15%)
1988	3,824,661	1,629,849 (42.61%)	1,908,064 (49.89%)	30,145 (0.79%)	256,603 (6.71%)
1989	4,730,019	1,720,343 (36.37%)	2,626,781 (55.53%)	41,877 (0.89%)	341,018 (7.21%)
1990	5,203,804	1,577,240 (30.31%)	3,200,200 (61.50%)	74,052 (1.42%)	352,312 (6.77%)
1991	6,179,342	1,777,564 (28.77%)	3,945,262 (63.85%)	56,372 (0.91%)	400,144 (6.48%)

Table 14.5 cont'd

1992	7,429,514	1,998,335 (26.90%)	4,790,647 (64.48%)	82,881 (1.12%)	557,651 (7.51%)
1993	8,744,802	2,336,003 (26.71%)	5,654,447 (64.66%)	111,289 (1.27%)	643,063 (7.35%)
1994	10,039,213	2,641,523 (26.31%)	6,569,393 (65.44%)	127,475 (1.27%)	700,822 (6.98%)
1995	10,868,579	2,656,407 (24.44%)	7,320,199 (67.35%)	215,535 (1.98%)	676,438 (6.22%)
1996	11,743,252	2,927,545 (24.93%)	7,857,957 (66.91%)	309,854 (2.64%)	647,896 (5.52%)
June 1997	12,102,565	3,209,813 (26.52%)	7,838,565 (64.77%)	349,962 (2.89%)	704,225 (5.82%)

Table 14.6. Growth in deposits by institution 1987–1997 (NT$ millions)

Year	Total	Domestic Banks			Foreign Banks	Community Financial Institutions		
		Domestic Commer-cial Banks	Medium Business Banks	Sub Total		Credit Co-ops	Farmers and Fishermen Assoc.	Sub Total
1987	3,073,905	2,042,532	217,233	2,259,765	41,925	410,210	362,005	772,215
1988	3,824,661	2,506,648	315,890	2,822,538	52,428	526,686	423,009	949,695
1989	4,730,019	3,038,254	448,083	3,486,337	56,706	693,361	493,615	1,186,976
1990	5,203,803	3,225,168	516,218	3,741,386	77,224	806,034	579,159	1,385,193
1991	6,179,342	3,712,749	676,187	4,388,936	75,736	988,339	726,331	1,714,670
1992	7,429,514	4,445,288	785,323	5,230,611	102,728	1,208,288	887,887	2,096,175
1993	8,744,802	5,102,430	967,787	6,070,217	122,456	1,493,538	1,058,591	2,552,129
1994	10,039,203	5,907,824	1,110,538	7,018,362	148,322	1,650,984	1,221,535	2,872,519
1995	10,868,579	6,580,107	1,226,045	7,806,152	188,725	1,620,175	1,253,527	2,873,702
1996	11,742,999	7,318,876	1,288,041	8,606,917	238,982	1,622,250	1,274,850	2,897,100
June 1997	12,102,565	7,718,718	1,326,325	9,045,043	256,548	1,495,565	1,305,409	2,800,974

LENDING ACTIVITIES

Total outstanding loans as of June 1997 stood at NT$1,307 billion (US$40 billion approx.) of which 64% was accounted for by the domestic commercial banks, 44% was in the form of loans to individuals, a further 36.5% was taken up by private enterprise and the balance by government agencies and enterprise.

Over the past five years, overall loan activity by the domestic banks has grown by more than 15% per annum with government borrowing increasing on average by 25% per annum; private enterprise by 13.4% and individuals by 16.6%. Worrisome to the government in terms of investment is the recent slowdown in loan activity by private enterprise. Recorded growth in 1995 from this sector was only 4.5% and in 1996 loans actually declined by 3%. This trend may have been reversed in 1997 with figures to June 1997 showing a 4.4% increase over the previous 12 months. It remains low by historic standards.

Of the NT$8,549 billion in outstanding loans as of June 1997, 34.5% was in the form of short-term loans and overdrafts while 65.4% were classified as medium- and long-term loans. Advances on imports and discounts accounted for the remainder.

Lending policies are generally conservative and for the most part secured against real assets. Furthermore, because of the way in which small and medium enterprises are structured in Taiwan, many of the loans classified as 'individual' are in reality supporting business activities.

Although banks are now free to set their own loan rates there is no standard credit rating system in Taiwan. The major financial institutions undertake limited 'in-house' consumer credit assessment but generally recognise the inadequacies of their present evaluation systems. For commercial loans not secured by real assets, properly audited accounting records are the normal yardstick.

At the national level, consumer credit reporting is almost entirely undertaken by Taiwan's central credit bureau, the Joint Credit Information Center (JCIC), which to all intents and purposes is an agency of the Ministry of Finance. For many of the smaller local banks this is the only independent source of credit information. The product currently available from JCIC is considered to be good by Asian standards but does not meet market expectations. There is a growing problem of bad debt in Taiwan which indicates a market need for better credit reporting and credit management techniques.

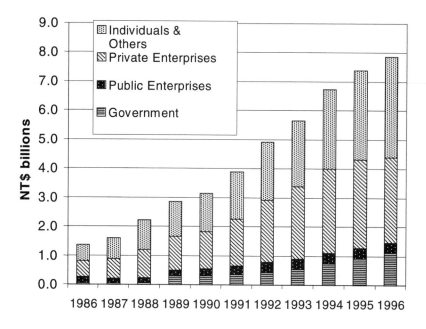

Figure 14i. Loans of the domestic banks

The Bank of Taiwan

The Bank of Taiwan was founded in 1946 and until the re-activation of the Central Bank of China (CBC) in 1961 it performed the role of a central bank. Since the change in its charter it has operated as a commercial bank but one with special links to the CBC. The New Taiwan Dollar continues to be issued in the name of the Bank of Taiwan. It is the largest of Taiwan's banks as measured by asset value.

Initially, establishment capital was provided by the government treasury and subsequent capital increases were funded through asset revaluation and accumulated surpluses. Originally standing at NT$5 million (following the 1949 currency reform on Taiwan), the capital base of the Bank has stood at NT$22 billion since December 1994.

The Bank of Taiwan remains the largest of the commercial banks and is wholly government-owned although some measure of privatisation is expected in the foreseeable future. It is one of a number of banks under the control of the Taiwan Provincial Government and reports directly to the Banking Committee of the TPG. Other banks with similar status include the

Land Bank of Taiwan; the Taiwan Co-operative Bank; 1st Commercial Bank; Hua Nan Commercial Bank; Chang Hwa Commercial Bank and Taiwan Business Bank.

The Bank of Taiwan is a major shareholder in the Medium Business Bank of Taiwan (42% of stock) and the Hua Nan Commercial Bank (49%) and retains smaller shareholdings in a number of other banks.

Total funds on deposit with the Bank of Taiwan at the end of 1996 (excluding interbank deposits) stood at NT$1,211,580 million (US$37 billion at current rates of exchange), an increase of 6.03% over the previous year. Within the total, time deposits accounted for NT$745,149 million (+13.9% increase), government treasury deposits accounted for NT$316,765 million (-10.6%) and demand deposits NT$149,630 million (+11.7%).

Lending policies of the Bank of Taiwan are weighted in favour of activities that directly support the economic and financial goals of the government. At the end of 1996 loans to government agencies accounted for 40.8% of all outstanding loans (much of which is in the form of long-term loans for public construction) while loans to government enterprises accounted for a further 13.1% (including loans for plant modernisation). Loans to private enterprise amounted to 25.5% (including preferential loans for small and medium enterprises), private individuals and non-profit organisations accounted for a further 18.5% and the balance went in loans to banks and other financial institutions.

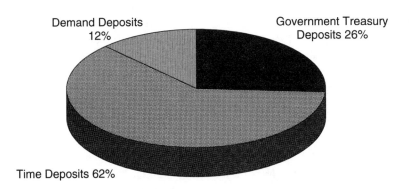

Figure 14j. Bank of Taiwan deposit structure 1996

The Bank of Taiwan maintains 99 domestic branches as well as an Offshore Banking Unit. Overseas, it maintains branches in New York, Amsterdam,

Los Angeles, Hong Kong, Singapore and Tokyo as well as representative offices in London and Amsterdam. It also owns two subsidiary Banks: the Bank of Taiwan (South Africa) Ltd in Johannesburg and the Bank of Taiwan (Europe) N.V. in Amsterdam.

Chinatrust Commercial Bank

Chinatrust is one of the newer privately-owned banks in Taiwan and is part of the Koo Financial Group. It is generally regarded as one of the most aggressive of Taiwan's banks and an acknowledged market leader, especially in the growing consumer market. Although relatively new as a bank, having been established only in 1992, it has a long history—at least in local terms. Chinatrust commenced business in 1966 as a securities trading and underwriting company during the period when Taiwan was seeking to rationalise its nascent capital market. It was reorganised as the China Trust Company in 1971 with a charter to promote capital formation and to provide medium- and long-term loans to the rapidly growing business sector. Over the following years, and guided by an innovative management, it became the largest trust company in Taiwan with over one third of all aggregate trust funds under its management.

With the liberalisation of the banking sector in 1992, Chinatrust became a commercial bank. It has emerged as the largest private bank in Taiwan and is ranked at No. 266 globally. The Bank has pursued an aggressive and innovative policy targeting younger, well-educated consumers. It was one of the first banks in Taiwan to issue credit cards (even before it became a bank) and is now the largest local card issuer. The bank offers a special 'WoFe' card targeted at professional women as well as a variety of co-branded cards in association with universities, department and chain stores. Motorists who are holders of Chinatrust credit cards can also participate in a 24-hour road side service that provides many of the services of motorist organisations in other countries.

Chinatrust has invested heavily into automated banking, ATM cash cards and point-of-sale (POS) equipment. Chinatrust is the first issuer in Taiwan of IC ATM cards that meet international EMV[4] standards.

Chinatrust was one of the first to pursue the consumer loan business with Easy-Access Personal Loans, Second Mortgage Loans and Refinance Option Loans. Individuals now account for 44.5% of all outstanding loans while

---

[4] Europay-MasterCard-Visa.

310

loans to enterprises account for 51.9%. The balance is made up of all other forms of loan. The bank also offers guarantees including those to corporations for commercial paper, corporate bonds, bid and performance bonds and stand-by letters of credit. Total guarantees in 1996 amounted to almost NT$53 billion—a 71% increase over the previous year.

Foreign exchange deposits totalled US$542 million and foreign exchange trading exceeded US$6.3 billion in 1996. Chinatrust is also one of Taiwan's leading banks for derivatives including NDF (Non Deliver Forward), IRS (Interest Rate Swap) and CCS (Cross Currency Swap).

Chinatrust maintains 34 branches island-wide as well as a network of 24-hour automated service centres. Internationally the bank maintains representative offices in London, Tokyo, Hong Kong, Jakarta, Bangkok and Manila as well as branches in India and in Paraguay. In the US, the Chinatrust Bank of California and the Chinatrust Bank of New York have recently merged into a single US-owned subsidiary and Chinatrust has announced that it plans further acquisitions in the US with the aim of becoming the largest Chinese bank in America by 2002.

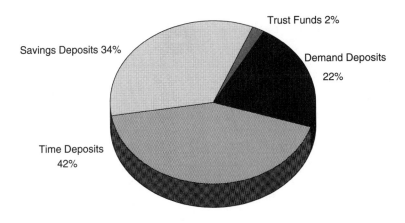

Figure 14k. Chinatrust Bank deposit structure

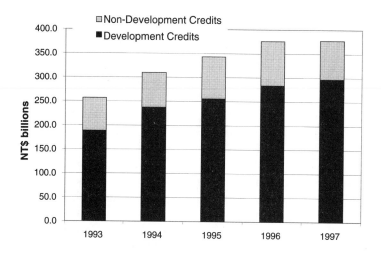

Figure 14l. Total loan program by loan type

DEVELOPMENT BANKS

Taiwan has four government-controlled banks that provide concessional and development loans to the private sector in support of government policies. They are part of the domestic commercial banking system but perform a specialised role within it.

The Chiao Tung Bank

Formerly known as the Bank of Communications, the Chiao Tung Bank traces its origins back to 1907. Established during the last years of the Chi'ing dynasty, the bank relocated to Taiwan in 1949. It is a specialised bank whose charter is to provide funds required for the development of the transportation, telecommunications and shipping industries. In the early years of the Republic (circa 1911), the Bank of Communications and the Bank of China were the two agents of the national treasury authorised to issue legal tender. That role has now disappeared.

In 1979, the *Bank of Communications Act* was revised and the newly named Chiao Tung bank was reclassified as a 'development bank' with a charter to assist in the development of Taiwan's industrial, mining, transportation and public utility services. An amendment to the Act in 1991 increased the capital base to NT$20 billion (US$600 million approx.) and its charter was extended to encompass the service industry. Its shares have been traded on the Taiwan Stock Exchange since 1996 although the government retains a majority shareholding. A further public share issue is planned for 1988 which, if implemented, will reduce the government's share of capital from the current 88.8% to 60.48% of the issued stock.

Concessional Loans

As a development bank, the Chiao Tung Bank is a major source of medium- and long-term concessional financing for strategic industries as determined by the *Statute for Industrial Upgrading* and other government programs. As of 30 June 1997, total credit extended amounted to NT$364 billion (US$11 billion) of which 78% was in the form of development credit. Current concessional loan programs operated by the bank (and utilising the development fund of the Executive Yuan) include the following:

(a) **Procurement of Automatic Machinery:** Three concessional loan funds have so far been launched for the purchase of domestic machinery and six funds have provided loans for imported automatic machinery. Total funds committed so far amount to NT$216 billion (US$6.5 billion) of which 67.5% has been allocated to overseas purchases. A total of 3,678 applications had been approved as of 30 June 1997. The program is ongoing;

(b) **Procurement of Pollution Control Equipment by Private Enterprise:** Chiao Tung is one of five local banks participating in this program.[5] So far a total of NT$39 billion has been made available since 1989 with the Chiao Tung Bank approving NT$28 billion (US$850 million) within this overall amount;

(c) **Procurement of Business Automation Equipment:** This program is aimed at upgrading the wholesale and retail industries (and increasing the effectiveness of tax collection mechanisms in the process). Eligible items include point-of-sale equipment, automation of commodity selection, auto-accounting, loading and unloading, forwarding storage and inventory management. Total funds committed are small, only amounting to NT$243 million (US$7.4 million);

(d) **Procurement of Energy Conservation Equipment:** The scope of loans available under this program has recently been extended to include the

---

[5] The others being the Medium Business Bank of Taiwan, the First Commercial Bank, Chang Hwa Commercial Bank and the Hua Nan Commercial Bank.

accelerated replacement of old vehicles. Alongside the Chiao Tung Bank, this program is also available through the Medium Business Bank of Taiwan. As of June 30 1997, a total of NT$3.8 billion (US$115 million) had been loaned under this program;

(e) **Production of Military Matériel and Equipment:** Since 1994, concessional financing has been available to the private sector for investment into production facilities and technology related to the manufacture of military matériel and equipment. For this purpose a special Defense Industries Development Fund has been established with NT$1.5 billion (US$45 million) available, of which only some NT$286 million in loan applications has so far been approved;

(f) **Relocation of Industries to Eastern Taiwan:** Since 1994, concessional loans have been made available to assist corporations that are prepared to move their facilities to eastern Taiwan. A total of NT$2.6 billion has been allocated to the program, of which so far only NT$654 million has been utilised.

Other Loan Activities

Other loan activities of Chiao Tung Bank include general purpose medium- and long-term development finance, working capital term loans and loans for shipbuilding.

Equity Investments

Since 1982, the Chiao Tung Bank has made equity and venture capital investments into selected enterprises that are either highly technology intensive or which promise potential for development. Total equity placements as of mid-1997 amounted to NT$11.882 billion (US$360 million) of which 66% had gone into technology enterprises (with the electronic component industry alone accounting for 31% of total placement). A further 15% had gone to support venture capital investments with the balance going towards 'policy oriented investment'—chiefly into the financial, transportation, storage and construction industries.

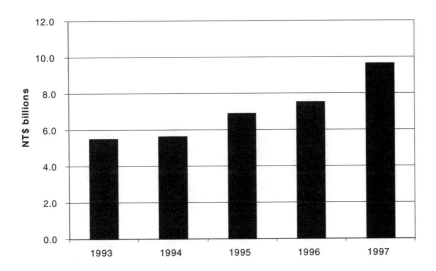

Figure 14m. Equity investments

The Land Bank of Taiwan

The Land Bank of Taiwan is the designated bank for handling real estate and agricultural credits associated with national development. As such it is an important instrument in the realisation of the government's housing, agriculture and land-use policies. The Land Bank was established in 1946 as the successor to the Nippon Kangyo Bank. In its early years it was instrumental in implementing the government's agricultural reform programs of the 1950s. It remains 100% owned by the Central Government.

The Land Bank maintains a diverse deposit structure with deposits as of June 1996 (latest available data) totalling NT$931 billion (US$28 billion approx.) Almost 80% of all deposits were in the form of time savings deposits with other financial institutions providing 36% of funds on deposit followed by individuals with 24% and government agencies at almost 16%.

In terms of its loan structure, the Land Bank deals primarily in specialised loans for financing property and land purchases and for agricultural development. The totality of specialised loans in 1996 amounted to NT$1,153 billion as against NT$124 million extended as general loans. Individual real estate and agricultural loans accounted for 58.5% of all loan activity in that year.

315

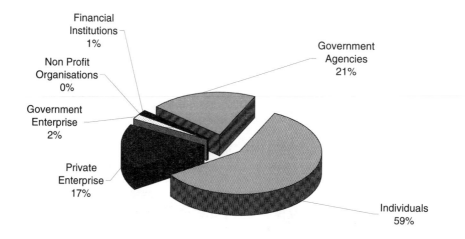

Figure 14n. Land Bank: structure of loans 1996

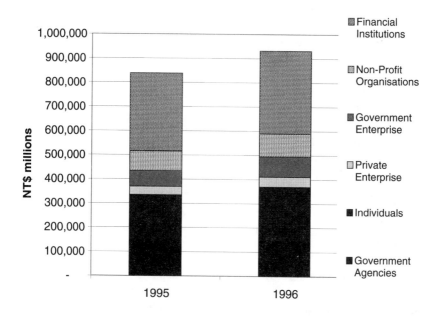

Figure 14o. Land Bank: deposits by source

In addition to general commercial banking activities the Land Bank also acts on behalf of the Central Government in the handling of payments and commissions due from public sector enterprises such as the Taiwan Tobacco and Wine Monopoly Bureau and the Chinese Petroleum Corporation, as well as the leasing of publicly owned land and management of State-owned real assets.

The Taiwan Co-operative Bank

Rural-based cooperative organisations were established in the early years of the 20th century during the period of the Japanese occupation of Taiwan. In 1923, this loosely knit group was formalised into an organisation through the Taiwan Co-operative Association, which acted both as a central institution to assist the development of cooperatives and as a central treasury for cooperative funds. In 1946, after the return of Taiwan to Chinese Control, the Taiwan Co-operative Bank was established as the successor to the central cooperative treasury organisation. The bank's present name dates from 1989 and it remains jointly owned by the Taiwan Provincial Government (60%), the Farmers and Fishermen's Associations (23%) and the credit cooperatives (17%). Total capital now stands at NT$15.12 billion (US$460 million approx.).

The Bank retains a central banking function on behalf of the cooperative organisations by accepting surplus funds for deposit and making loans to these organisations. However, in 1996 and in the wake of a series of loan scandals affecting the cooperatives (see below), its power to examine and inspect the credit cooperatives and the credit departments of the local Farmers and Fishermen's Associations was ceded to the Central Deposit Insurance Corporation in line with the regulatory arrangements for the domestic banking industry as a whole.

Alongside the Land Bank and the Farmers Bank, the Taiwan Co-operative Bank is at the forefront in providing agricultural loans and cooperative financing.

In recent years, and in line with government liberalisation policies, an increasing proportion of loans is now going to support the development of small and medium business enterprises (SMEs). Total outstanding loans in 1997 amounted to NT$1,087 billion (US$362 million) of which 53% was accounted for by SMEs and only 20% of loans went to the cooperatives and to support agriculture and fisheries industries.

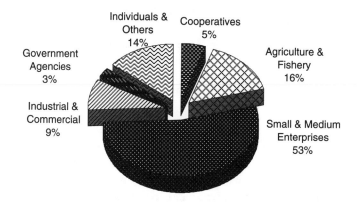

Figure 14p. Taiwan Co-operative Bank: 1997 loan structure

The Farmers Bank of China

The Farmers Bank of China began in 1933 on the Chinese Mainland and although it relocated to Taiwan in 1949 with the ROC Government it did not resume its operations until 1967. Reactivated by the Government with an initial capital of NT$150 million, by June 1997 the capital base had increased to NT$9 billion (US$272 million). The Central Government, through the Ministry of Finance, still retains 59.65% of the issued capital although a partial privatisation is under way.

In contrast to the Co-operative Bank, which is under the control of the Taiwan Provincial Government, the Farmers Bank of China is the principal vehicle through which national government assistance programs to farmers are implemented. Total loans outstanding as of 30 June 1997 stood at NT$329 billion (US$ 10 billion approx.) of which 61% were in the form of agricultural loans. General purpose agricultural loans used for general farm credit (associated with production, processing and marketing) totalled NT$8.986 billion while special project agricultural loans amounted to NT$52.436 billion. Special purpose loans carry preferential conditions and relate to development and modernisation activities including activities associated with a special Sino–US fund.

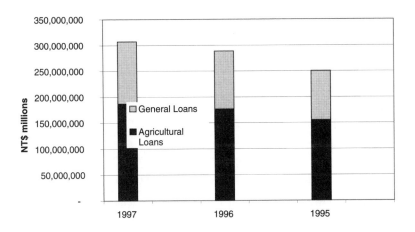

Figure 14q. Farmers Bank: loan structure 1995–1997

THE FOREIGN BANKS

A total of 44 foreign banks have established full branch operations in Taiwan and total assets of the foreign banking sector as of June 1997 stood at NT$788 billion (US$24 billion). Until recently, because of restrictions on branch operations, foreign banks had concentrated on wholesale and trade-related operations. This is now changing. The growing consumer market and the introduction of automated banking has seen a number of the foreign banks aggressively target the consumer banking segment of the market.

With the new aggressiveness of the market, many of the foreign banks are facing problems with market share, which has been declining in recent years. Total domestic lending by the foreign banks as of June 1997 stood at NT$358.3 billion. In fact between 1986 and 1991 loan activity on the part of such banks grew by an average of more than 24% per year. Yet since 1992, there has been a marked slowdown in this growth to less than 10% per annum. The aggressiveness with which the foreign banks are approaching the consumer loan and credit card markets is a reflection of the new competitive environment. Foreign banks now control less than 3% of the domestic loan market.

By contrast, and not unexpectedly, the foreign banks have a much larger share of the foreign currency loan market—around 25%. As of June 1997

319

total foreign currency loans of the foreign banks amounted to NT$134 billion, representing 24.3% of all foreign currency loans.

A number of other foreign banks maintain representative offices in Taipei but cannot conduct any commercial activity.

Table 14.7. Foreign banks in Taiwan

Dai-Ichi Kangyo Bank	Credit Agricole Indosuez
Citibank N.A.	Standard Bank of South Africa Ltd
Bank of America N.T. & S.A.	National Australia Bank
Bangkok Bank	Bank of Nova Scotia
American Express Bank Ltd	Union Bank of California N.A.
Metropolitan Bank & Trust Company	Union Bank of Switzerland
Chase Manhattan Bank	Ing Bank N.V.
Bank of New York	Canadian Imperial Bank of Commerce
Toronto-Dominion Bank	Corestates Bank N.A.
International Bank of Singapore	Australia & New Zealand Banking Group Ltd
Bank Boston	Bank of Tokyo-Mitsubishi Ltd
Deutsche Bank A.G.	Norwest Bank Minnesota N.A.
Société Générale	Kredietbank N.V.
Banque Paribas	Tokai Bank Ltd
ABN AMRO Bank	United Overseas Bank Ltd
Bankers Trust Company	State Street Bank & Trust Company
Development Bank of Singapore Ltd	Bank of Hawaii
Royal Bank of Canada	Fuji Bank Ltd
Hong Kong & Shanghai Banking Corporation	Nationsbank N.V.
Credit Lyonnais	Republic National Bank of New York
Banque Nationale de Paris	Sanhwa Bank Limited
Standard Chartered Bank	Bank of East Asia Ltd

OFFSHORE BANKING UNITS

As part of efforts to promote Taipei as a regional banking centre and to expand the domestic interbank and foreign currency call-loan markets, both domestic and foreign banks have been encouraged to operate offshore banking units (OBUs) that are exempt from domestic tax regulations. A foreign bank wishing to operate an OBU need only remit US$2 million to finance the operation and does not need to conduct domestic branch operations.

OBUs handle a range of foreign currency operations including the management of foreign exchange deposits of behalf of both companies and individuals, including ROC citizens. Foreign currency loans are an important part of OBU activity and total outstanding loans to non-financial institutions as of June 1997 stood at US$10.002 billion dollars. Other activities include the raising of offshore funds through the international financial markets. The offshore banking units also provide a means for direct commercial transactions with banks on the Chinese Mainland.

A total of 68 banks currently offer offshore banking facilities. Thirty-six of these are operated by the domestic banks and the balance by the foreign banks in Taiwan. As of June 1997 the combined assets of the OBUs totalled US$36.3 million. This represents an increase of 13.6% on the corresponding period in 1996.

Table 14.8. The offshore banking units (OBUs)

Domestic Banks	*Foreign Banks*
Bank of Kaohsiung	ABN AMRO Bank
Bank of Overseas Chinese	American Express Bank Ltd
Bank of Taiwan	Australian & New Zealand Banking Group Ltd
Bank Sinopac	Bangkok Bank
Baodao Commercial Bank	Bank Boston
Central Trust of China	Bank of America NT & SA
Chang Hwa Commercial Bank	Bank of New York
Chiao Tung Bank	Bank of Nova Scotia
Chinatrust Commercial Bank	Bank of Tokyo-Mitsubishi Ltd
Chinese Bank	Bankers Trust Company

Table 14.8 cont'd

Chung Shing Bank	Banque Nationale de Paris
Co-operative Bank of Taiwan	Banque Paribas
Cosmos Bank	Canadian Imperial Bank of Commerce
Dah An Commercial Bank	Chase Manhattan Bank
E. Sun Commercial Bank	Citibank N.A.
Entie Commercial Bank	Credit Agricole Indosuez
Export-Import Bank of the ROC	Credit Lyonnais
Far Eastern International Bank	Dai-Ichi Kangyo Bank
Farmers Bank of China	Deutsche Bank AG
First Commercial Bank	Development Bank of Singapore Ltd
Fubon Commercial Bank	Hong Kong & Shanghai Banking Corporation
Grand Commercial Bank	Ing Bank N.V.
Hsinchu Bank	Kredietbank N.V.
Huan Nan Commercial Bank	National Australia Bank
International Commercial Bank of China	Norwest Bank Minnesota N.A.
Land Bank of Taiwan	Royal Bank of Canada
Pan Asia Bank	Société Générale
Shanghai Commercial & Savings Bank	Standard Bank of South Africa Ltd
Ta Chong Commercial Bank	Standard Chartered Bank
Taichung Business Bank	Tokai Bank Ltd
Taipei Bank	Union Bank of California N.A.
Taipei Business Bank	Union Bank of Switzerland
Taishin Commercial Bank	
Taiwan Business Bank	

Table 14.8 cont'd

Union Bank of Taiwan	
United World Chinese Commercial Bank	

COMMUNITY-BASED FINANCIAL INSTITUTIONS

The community-based financial institutions originate from a time when Taiwan was largely an agrarian society. The credit cooperatives in fact date back to the Japanese colonial period. They were formed in 1908 and modelled on the Japanese system as a means of organising capital and resources at the local level. The Farmers and Fishermen's Associations date from 1952, following the relocation of the ROC Government to Taiwan, and were intended to provide an overlay of central government control on the local population and to weaken the influence of the cooperatives. Nowadays they coexist side by side. Both interact with the formal banking system through the Co-operative Bank. While from an economic perspective they have for the most part outlived their purpose as financial institutions, the network of cooperatives and associations are part of the grass-roots political structure and are not easily removed. Among all the ROC financial institutions, because of the political base they provide, they are also the most vulnerable to corruption and influence peddling.

The most celebrated financial scandal in Taiwan of recent times occurred in July 1995 following the embezzlement by the General Manager of Changhua's 4th Credit Co-operative of US\$107 million of depositors' money. A run ensued in which depositors withdrew more than US\$385 million. This compounded and the run spread to other cooperative organisations. More than US\$1 billion was withdrawn from the system in a matter of days, prompting the central regulatory authorities to overhaul the cooperative management system and subject it to the same deposit insurance system as the general banking sector.

There remains a total of NT\$2,800 billion (US\$ 85 billion) deposited by members within the remaining 71 cooperative associations and the 312 Farmers and Fishermen's Associations. Since local businessmen who aspire to a political role are often elected as chairmen of the local cooperative or agricultural association, this nest-egg of funds goes a long way to explaining why local elections in Taiwan are so heavily contested.

OTHER FINANCIAL INSTITUTIONS

The Postal Savings System

The postal system in Taiwan is administered by the Ministry of Transportation and Communications although related savings and remittance operations are supervised by the Ministry of Finance. Classified as an 'other financial institution' for statistical purposes, the postal savings system is in reality a specialised bank which operates through a network of 1,276 post offices and 251 postal agencies. Business operations include savings deposits, postal giro, postal remittances and life insurance. Since 1992 the postal savings system has functioned as a domestic bank with the ability to redeposit and invest its surplus deposits. Since 1997, postal savings deposits have been included as part of the broadly defined money supply.

Total deposits as of June 1997 amounted to NT$2,292 billion (US$69.5 billion) of which 65.1% was in the form of time deposits, 33.7% was passbook savings deposits and the balance was in giro accounts. The postal savings system does not undertake commercial loan activity.

The Life Insurance Companies

There are a total of 30 life insurance companies in the Taiwan market that play a relatively small role in the loan market. Total loans made by these companies as of June 1997 stood at NT$479.2 billion (US$14.5 billion).

The Central Deposit Insurance Corporation

A government re-insurance fund was established in 1956 and reorganised as the Central Deposit Insurance Corporation in 1985. Established in accordance with *Article 46* of the *Banking Law*, the CDIC is the sole agent in charge of deposit insurance. The board of directors is appointed jointly by the Ministry of Finance and the Central Bank of China. Until recently, while all financial institutions were eligible to apply for membership, the deposit insurance scheme was administered on a voluntary basis. As a result, many of the community financial institutions were outside the scope of the scheme and this was a contributing factor to the problems that engulfed a number of the credit cooperatives in 1995. As a result of these and other problems in the market which exposed the inadequacies of the regulatory arrangements, all financial institutions are now under the supervision of the CDIC.

CHAPTER 15

TAIWAN'S CAPITAL MARKET

T aiwan's capital market is generally defined as including all securities
with a maturity in excess of one year which are transacted on the open
market. Instruments currently transacted include government and
corporate bonds (including convertible bonds), financial securities and
shares.

Taiwan is committed to WTO-led national treatment and access principles
and it is stated policy to have a totally open market by the year 2000.
Foreigners are now allowed to operate securities, futures, securities
financing and trust investment businesses in Taiwan. In order to ease the
rules on local fund-raising for foreigners, the Security and Futures
Commission has recently relaxed the *Issuance Rules for Taiwan Depository
Receipts*; and is in the process of drafting new rules by which foreign firms
can apply to list their shares in Taiwan.

It has been announced that a Derivatives Market is to be established to
trade futures and other new financial products. In other liberalisation
measures, local firms are now allowed to cross list their shares abroad and

foreign firms can list in Taiwan.

Aside from the local stock indices, there is a Morgan Stanley Capital Taiwan Index listed on the Singapore Exchange (SIMEX) and Hong Kong has recently announced plans to list a Taiwan Futures Contract.

EQUITIES

As of December 1997 there was a total of 404 companies listed with the Taiwan Stock Exchange (TSE) and 470 listed stocks. Total par value of listed shares amounted to NT$2,025,467 million (US$61 billion). In August 1997 total market capitalisation broke the NT$10 trillion (US$360 million) level for the first time in its history although by December market capitalisation had been pared back from the August high and stood at NT$9,402.278 billion (US$285 billion).

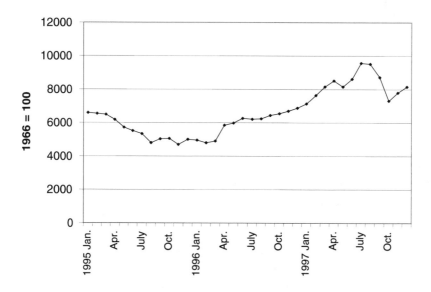

Figure 15a. Taiwan stock price index 1995–1997

Taiwan's stock market is the third largest in Asia and certainly the most volatile. It has been traditionally dominated by smaller investors who largely trade on the basis of emotion with short term concerns and expectations in mind. Accounts with local securities firms total more than six million, representing nearly 30% of Taiwan's total population. While almost 50% of all issued stocks are under the control of Taiwan's major corporations, institutional investors on the Exchange account for less than 20% of total traded stock. Even so, this is considered to be a substantial improvement on the situation which existed in the early 1990s when the small individual investors controlled 95% of all stock.

Local interest in Taiwan's stock market boomed in the late 1980s, and between 1987 and 1990 Taiwan's general stock index (TSI) climbed from less than 2,500 to more than 12,000. The crash of 1990 (triggered by the Gulf War) was spectacular, with the index losing half its value. The market languished for a while although signs of recovery were emerging in 1993 and 1994. However, problems with Mainland China in 1995 and 1996 prevented prospects of any real and sustained recovery. The market settled down in 1996 and the pace of growth quickened in the first half of 1997.

The Taiwan Weighted Stock Price Index[1] (TAIEX) closed at 6,933 points in 1996 and this represented a yearly increase of 35%. In the first half of 1997 even larger gains were posted with the index successively passing new benchmark levels. Warnings of the market becoming over-heated were largely ignored and many smaller investors—ignoring the lessons of 1990—borrowed again in order to finance speculative activities on the stock market.

Average daily trading values also hit new highs in 1997. The average daily trading value for the second quarter of 1997 increased to NT$159 billion ranking the local Bourse behind only the New York Stock Exchange and the NASDAQ. The single day trading record was broken on July 17 with a total of NT$297 billion (US$9 billion) traded. The financial crisis that was brewing elsewhere in Asia in the third quarter of 1997 and which had affected stock prices elsewhere was at first ignored by Taiwanese.

A bearish sentiment set in during late August and early September and the TAIEX generally followed other markets in a slow downward slide. The late October sell-off that sent Wall Street and Hong Kong's Hang Seng Index into a plunge also sent the TAIEX down by almost 6% in one day. By the end of October the index had dropped almost 30% below its August high and most of the gains for the year had been wiped out. Yet fears of a free-fall were unfounded. The government quickly intervened with the Securities and Futures Commission giving quick approval to a number of new funds in an effort to bring some liquidity back into the market. By the year's end the index had recovered somewhat and was again trading above the 7,000 mark. By February 1998 it was again approaching the 9,000 mark. Nevertheless, in

---

[1] Weight of Paid-in Capital x Price.

the face of all the uncertainties, most companies approached 1998 in a cost-cutting frame of mind.

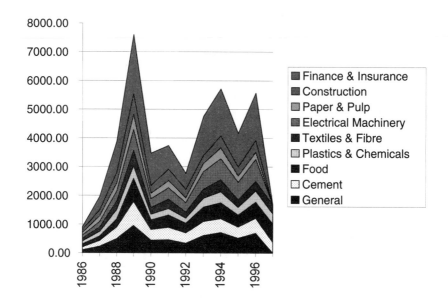

Figure 15b. Taiwan group stock indices (1986 = 100)

Table 15.1. 1998 TSE outlook by sector

Market Sector	Market Outlook
Cement	Demand for cement is likely to be boosted by increasing public and private infrastructure projects including the new power (IPP) generators. The government is relocating quarries away from the western corridor towards the East Coast of Taiwan and this will have implications for investment and transportation.
Chemicals	Only mild growth is anticipated in the short-term. There is growing public opposition, much of it politically motivated, to the construction of new chemical plants.
Electronics	Continued strong growth is expected. This is where the interest is at present. The electronics sector is vying with the financial sector in terms of market capitalisation.

Table 15.1 cont'd

Hotel and Entertainment Industries	Increased leisure time as a result of the introduction of a five-day alternate working week may have a marginal impact. Upgrading of existing entertainment facilities is likely but very few entertainment companies are publicly listed. There is plenty of opportunity for overseas investment into world-class facilities at present.
Financial	The older banks, especially the provincial banks, are trading at very high P/E ratios, because of land holdings that are carried at cost. Privatisation will improve their efficiency but the entrance of new banks has introduced fierce competition which many of the traditional banks are having difficulty in coping with.
Food	Fierce competition among the existing food companies has led to tighter profit margins and shrinking operating profits; very little new investment is anticipated. Many of the larger companies, especially those engaged in agribusiness, hold large tracts of land that will be progressively developed in coming years; future profits may therefore come from non-traditional activities.
Glass	Increases in domestic housing supply and public housing projects may see overall demand for glass products strengthen.
Pulp and Paper	Some improvement in prices could increase profit margins but overall this industry is slow and is increasingly moving offshore.
Retailing	Sales are currently stagnating and there is increasing competition with new entrants into the department store and hypermarket sectors.
Rubber	Synthetic rubber prices are falling and this will adversely affect natural rubber prices.
Steel	Increased efficiency from major performers should lead to better profit margins.
Transportation	There is a current oversupply in both the bulk and container markets and the entry of foreign shippers into the domestic transportation markets could further erode profits of domestic transport companies.

The TAIEX is a composite of 23 individual indices covering all aspects of the industrial and commercial sectors. In keeping with stock indices elsewhere, shares in electronics and electronic machinery have been among the strongest performers together with those in the finance and insurance industries. The pulp and paper sector has been the weakest performer of recent times.

Overall, the recent currency realignment is expected to improve the performance of export-oriented high-tech sectors such as the electronics industry. There will be both short-term and long-term gains for such companies. Short-term gains include the currency gains from their USD deposits and imported raw material inventories. The principal long-term gain is the enhanced export competitiveness which is expected to be more than enough to compensate for any increased production costs. While the Taiwan dollar has devalued much less than the Korean won, thereby creating a comparative advantage for Taiwan's chief rival in this sector, other problems of a more structural nature will prevent many Korean companies from taking advantage of the new environment. Other items currently traded on the TSE aside from listed stocks include beneficiary certificates, warrants and bonds.

THE OVER-THE-COUNTER MARKET

Before the establishment of the Taiwan Stock Exchange in 1961 all share trading was over the counter. The OTC market was reinstated in 1988 in order to provide small and medium enterprises with a forum for capital raising activities.

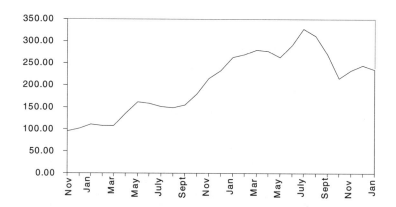

Figure 15c. OTC index performance (Nov 1995 to Jan 1998)

At the end of 1996 there were 79 companies quoted on the OTC exchange with a total capital value of NT$264 billion. Foreign investors have not yet played any significant or direct role in Taiwan's OTC market.

FOREIGN PARTICIPATION IN THE MARKET

At present foreign firms can only list on the TAIEX through Taiwan Depository Receipts (TDRs) which have been permitted since 1993 but have not proven popular. There has been only one TDR issued from a Singapore-domiciled, NASDAQ-listed affiliate of a local Taiwanese company. The reasons for listing as a TDR are obscure.

Qualified Foreign Institutional Investors (QFII) have been permitted to purchase shares in Taiwanese equity stocks since 1994. The qualifications necessary to obtain QFII status have been progressively expanded. QFII status is generally available to financial institutions that have at least three years' funds management experience. Once an application for QFII status has been approved by the Central Bank of China and the Securities and Futures Commission (SFC), a company with such status can invest directly in the market. The approval process for such investors has been progressively shortened from an average of 230 days in 1994, when the market was first opened, to 15 days in 1998. The maximum permitted investment quota is US$600 million and capital must be remitted into Taiwan within six months of approval. A QFII may obtain additional quotas upon application. Generally, one additional application from a pre-existing QFII is allowed once a year. Furthermore, there is no limit on additional quotas granted if a QFII has already met a number of requirements:

- The QFII must have already remitted into Taiwan the previous quota of US$600 million and such funds must have remained in Taiwan for at least one year;
- Over 70% of the remitted capital must have been invested into stocks;
- The QFII must not have violated any of the regulations relating to investment.

The percentage of shares that foreign investors may hold in a single listed local company was increased from 10% in 1994 to 25% in late 1996 and remains at this level although a further review is imminent. The intention is to fully open the market by the year 2000. No single QFII may hold more than 10% of the total. In situations where a locally listed company has acquired some foreign ownership through joint venture arrangements, up to a further 10% foreign ownership may be allowed through the QFII arrangement.

Individual foreign investors have been allowed to trade since March 1996. This category is also open to corporations and funds that do not qualify for QFII status. A non-QFII investor (also referred to locally as a GFII) may invest up to US$50 million and there is no deadline imposed on the inward remittance of capital.

As at December 1997 there were 367 listed institutional investors. Total approved funds applications amounted to NT$86,570 billion although only NT$29,473 billion had been remitted before the expiry term. Overall, foreign participation in Taiwan's stock market remains small at less than 4% of the total market share. In December 1997 QFII funds accounted for 3.32% of total market value, of which 78% was in equity stocks.

Investment principal from foreign investors may be freely repatriated without prior approval, however tax must be paid on earnings before being remitted overseas.

All applications for QFII or GFII status should be made to the Securities and Futures Commission in the first instance.

Table 15.2. QFII investment permit requirements

Banking Institutions	Total assets must rank within the top 1,000 worldwide; Experience in international finance, securities and trust business must be demonstrated
Insurance Companies	The value of securities held must exceed US$300 million; A minimum of three years' investment experience must be demonstrated
Fund Managers	Securities held must exceed US$200 million; A minimum of three years' investment experience must be demonstrated
Securities Companies	Net worth must exceed US$100 million; Experience in international securities investment must be demonstrated
Other Institutions	Must be either: 1. A foreign government investment agency; 2. A pension fund with at least two years' management experience; 3. A mutual fund (or similar) with more than US$200 million in assets and a minimum of three years' experience

THE BOND MARKET

Until the present decade, bond issues and trading were largely ignored in Taiwan. However, the government's need to raise capital to finance investment projects and the concurrent liberalisation of Taiwan's financial sector have both served to ensure a rapid growth of Taiwan's bond market and other fixed income securities.

In December 1992, total outstanding bonds were valued at NT$530 billion of which corporate bonds accounted for just 3.1% of the total. By December 1997, total bond issues had jumped to NT$1,075 billion of which government bonds still predominated—corporate bonds still only accounted for 3.8% of all outstanding issues.

Government bonds are issued at all levels of government although the Central Government accounts for the greater share of the total amount by far. Bond issues increased rapidly in the early 1990s, as a result of the government's need to finance major infrastructure investments, but have fallen off recently. Banks purchase many of the government issued bonds in order to meet their statutory reserve requirements and this in part accounts for their dominance in the market.

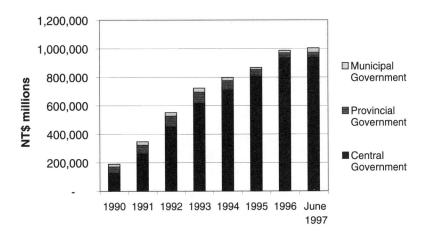

Figure 15d. Outstanding government bonds: 1990 to June 1997

The Government is actively encouraging the development of the commercial bond market as a means of reducing market volatility. While Taiwan's 'mom'n'pop' investors still prefer short-term investments into listed stocks, bonds are the preferred instrument of investment for many of the institutional investors. Many of the domestic and foreign banks, as well as the insurance companies, now trade in bonds—as do the bills–finance companies.

The market for corporate bonds has remained relatively weak until recently and has been largely confined to the domestic market. Since 1995, however, the growth of the corporate bond market has been more rapid. Many companies have taken advantage of lower interest rates to refinance their borrowings and lock in low borrowing costs through bond issues. Corporate bond sales in 1994 amounted to NT$20.7 billion and these increased by 87% in 1995 to NT$38.8 billion. This trend accelerated further in 1996 with corporate bond issues jumping to NT$162.85 billion—320% over the 1995 level. Within this total, there were 180 separate issues including eleven convertible bond issues plus nine issues of Global Depository Receipts (which in the SFC statistics are listed in with bonds rather than with equities).

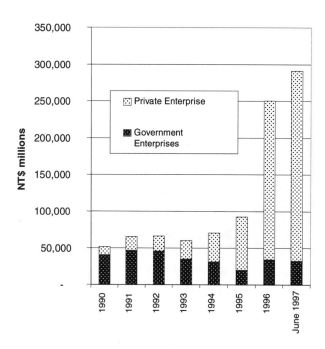

Figure 15e. Outstanding corporate bonds: 1990 to June 1997

Issuing activity in 1997 appears to have quietened down; as of 30 June 1997 there had been only a further NT$61 billion in corporate bond issues—less than the corresponding period in 1996 but still well above the totals of earlier years.[2]

The majority of corporate bonds are listed on the Centralised Bonds Exchange although most of the trading is done through over-the-counter trading among authorised dealers. Convertible bonds (bond issues whereby the debt can be traded for equity at some point) are becoming increasingly popular, both in local as well as in foreign markets.

MUTUAL FUNDS

Both closed-end and semi-open-ended funds are traded on Taiwan's stock market. The number of listed closed-end funds hit a high of 21 in September 1993 but has since declined. Changes made in April 1995 to the regulations regarding the opening of closed investment funds have resulted in a number of such funds being converted into open-ended funds. On the TSE, listed closed-end funds are usually traded at considerable discounts to their net asset values—often more than 20%.

Until 1993 four well-established and conservative Securities Investment Trust Companies (SITCs) dominated the fund market and during the early stages of market liberalisation these funds provided the only means for foreigners to invest in Taiwanese stocks through beneficiary certificates. A further eleven new SITCs were established in 1993, thereby creating a much more competitive market. Taiwanese mutual funds generally start with an initial market capitalisation of NT$5 billion. Closed-end funds traditionally trade at discounts and this provides subscribers with opportunities for arbitrage as soon as the fund is listed. Individual investors seldom paid attention to the funds due to their relatively quiet price movements as compared to stocks and such investors have little knowledge of arbitrage trading.

Fund management fees represent stable and substantial income for fund managers and as a result almost every listed closed-end fund in Taiwan has written into its charter tough requirements concerning its transformation to an open fund. Under new local rules relating to fund opening procedures (see

---

[2] Data on bond issues comes from three separate sources: the Ministry of Finance, the SFC and the Taiwan Stock Exchange. There is a slight variation within the data provided from each of these sources.

below), provided a fund has traded for two years, if its 20-day average market price is 20% below its 20-day average of net asset value (NAV) an application can be made to convert the fund from closed to open status. Since a rising market boosts the net asset values of companies, the discount between market prices and the fund's NAV increases, as prices of the closed-end funds are slow to respond to market changes. This mechanism has been used by a number of institutional investors seeking to convert their closed-fund investments into open status, thereby making a profit on the arbitrage.

In 1995, in order to reduce the large price discounts of the closed-end funds and eliminate what was seen to be unfair transformation requirements, the Ministry of Finance, acting on the advice of the Securities & Exchange Commission (SEC), amended the *Regulations Governing the Management of Securities Investment Trust Funds.* Under the rules as amended, any mutual fund is now allowed to purchase issues underwritten and may trade in OTC shares as well as the certificates of other listed funds. These changes also gave the SEC more direct authority over the SITCs by empowering the SEC to order SITCs to make any necessary changes where such changes would be to the benefit of certificate holders. These changes have dramatically altered the activities of the trust funds:

- Each fund can now purchase up to 1% of a company's total underwritten shares and each SITC can purchase up to 3% of total underwritten shares;

- Funds cannot purchase shares in other funds managed by its parent SITC, but can purchase shares in the funds of other SITCs where such funds are traded at more than a 10% discount to its NAV, provided that no more than 3% of a fund's NAV is used to buy other funds. Furthermore, a fund cannot receive any management fees for the proportion of its investment into other funds;

- The SEC has introduced a standard format for the charter requirements for holding beneficiaries' meetings and for transformation of a fund from closed to open status. If the 20-day average market price of a fund is 20% below its 20-day average NAV, then under the new rules, a beneficiaries' meeting must be called to vote on transforming the fund into open-ended status.

The new rules have made it more difficult for SITCs to manipulate fund prices and provide a greater chance for certificate holders to redeem at net asset value. As a result of these changes four closed-end funds have so far been transformed and were subsequently de-listed.

As of January 1998 there were only 18 closed investment trust funds remaining in the market. Of the remaining fund holdings, 38.3% are in electronics-related stocks. The total value of fund investments in bond and equity stocks at January 1998 stood at NT$498.961 billion.

OTHER FINANCIAL INSTRUMENTS

Financial reform has seen the emergence of a much wider range of traded securities in recent years. The passage of the *Futures Trading Law* paves the way for the opening of a separate futures exchange, to be named the Taiwan International Mercantile Exchange (TIME). Originally expected to be opened in October 1997, the opening has been progressively delayed and is now scheduled for some time in 1998. The first product to be traded will be a TAIEX-related index futures. It has been announced that futures trading will be exempt from the capital gains tax and that transaction tax on futures trading will not exceed 0.3%.

During 1997, the TSE announced new regulations covering the issue, listing and trading of warrants on TSE-listed stock, making these the first equity derivative in Taiwan. The warrants, which can be issued on a single underlying stock or on a basket of stocks, can be either European or American-style and with a duration of between one and two years. A transaction tax of 0.1% is applied to the seller and 0.3% is levied on the deliverer at the time the warrant is exercised.

In another noteworthy development, the SFC has published guidelines for the cross-border listing of shares in their original form. Under the new guidelines both TSE- and OTC-listed companies are eligible to float shares offshore and can list their shares in Taiwan either in original form or as Depository Receipts.

MARKET REGULATION

The three principal regulatory agencies regulating the capital and securities markets in Taiwan are the Ministry of Finance (MoF), the Securities and Futures Commission, and the Taiwan Stock Exchange. It is the MoF that is the primary regulator of the bond market with the Central Bank of China acting as the issuing agent for all government securities. The Securities and Futures Commission regulates and controls all publicly offered securities and in turn oversees the exchanges.

The Securities & Futures Commission

The Securities & Exchange Commission was originally established in 1960 as a body under the Ministry of Economic Affairs, and its establishment actually predates the enactment of the *Securities & Exchange Law* of 1961. Jurisdiction of the SEC (now known as the SFC) was transferred to the Ministry of Finance in 1981.

The Securities & Exchange Commission has been given a broad mandate to facilitate national development and investment protection within Taiwan's capital market and the securities service industry. The Commission also supervises and regulates certified public accountants. With the passage of the *Foreign Futures Trading Law*, promulgated in July 1997, the SEC was renamed the Securities & Futures Commission and its mandate was widened to include responsibility for the development, regulation and supervision of the new futures industry.

According to the *Guidelines for the Offering and Issuance of Securities by Publicly Held Companies*, all issuers must file registration with the SFC in order to commence the issuing and offering process.

All issuers are required to file quarterly reports with the Commission on the status of funds utilisation. In situations where funds have been used for other than the approved purpose, the SFC will determine the legality and the reasonableness of such a change. The track record on the use of proceeds is then used as a benchmark by the Commission to approve or disapprove future applications for cash offerings.

The SFC enforces a Full Disclosure Policy in relation to prospectuses and any other information that may affect shareholders' interests or stock prices.

Insider trading, although common, is strictly prohibited under the law. Any major shareholder, company director or senior staff member who indulges in such activities can face criminal and civil damage charges as well as a prison term. While the SFC has the regulatory authority over the market and its participants, any criminal matters are handled by the other relevant government authorities on the advice of the Commission.

Table 15.3. Summary of penalty provisions relating to securities trading

Violation	*Rule Violated*	*Penalty*
Failure to declare a transfer of a shareholding	*Article 22-2* of the *Securities Exchange Law*	NT$120,000
Failure to declare a change of shareholding	*Article 25* of the *SEL*	NT$60,000

Table 15.3 cont'd

Failure to maintain the minimum required shareholding	*Article 26* of the *SEL*	NT$60,000
Failure to declare acquisition of more than 10% of total outstanding shares	*Article 43-1* of the *SEL*	NT$60,000

The Taiwan Stock Exchange Limited

The Taiwan Stock Exchange was established in 1961 with 18 listed companies and a total market capitalisation of NT$5.4 billion. Establishment of the Exchange actually predated enactment of the associated regulatory framework, which was not introduced until the revision of the Securities & Exchange Law in 1968. A Central Depository was established in 1989 to handle the clearing and settlement of all securities transactions, except for large blocks, which remain with the Clearing Department of the Exchange.

The TSE is currently organised as a corporation with a capital base of NT$3.2 billion. Private institutions hold 61% of TSE ownership with the remaining stock controlled by government-owned banks and enterprises. The TSE is currently seeking ISO 9000 certification.

Under *Articles 139* and *141* of the *Securities Exchange Law*, the Taiwan Stock Exchange has the authority to review any listing applications subject to approval of the SFC, while it is the SFC itself that is responsible for supervising both the TSE and the underwriters in order to ensure compliance with listing procedures.

Amendments to the *Securities Trading Law* in 1997 now allow the establishment of new stock exchanges as well as ownership in the exchanges by foreign interests subject to approval from the Ministry of Finance. At present, however, the TSE is the only stock exchange in Taiwan.

The TSE has primary responsibility for reviewing listing applications and has recently amended the rules governing examinations and listing of securities with a view to bringing local listing rules and procedures into line with international practice.

The regulatory powers of the TSE are limited to the de-listing of companies and the making of recommendations to the SFC.

Taiwan Ratings Corporation

The Taiwan Ratings Corporation was established in May 1997 with an initial capital of NT$200 million. TRC is a joint venture between the TSE and

Standard & Poor's. Warrant issuers are to be the first to be subjected to credit rating procedures with other debt instruments following in due course.

UNDERWRITING, BROKERING AND TRADING

Only foreign listed companies and local public companies established under Chapter V of the ROC Company Code can apply for listing on the Taiwan Stock Exchange. All financial statements must be made available for public scrutiny. As noted above, primary responsibility for examination of the application rests with the TSE, but the SFC oversees the application process. Listing fees are negotiable and all underwriting is done on a 'best efforts' basis. The maximum underwriting commission available is 2% but in reality it is usually lower than this.

A number of large State-owned corporations are due to be privatised between 1998 and 2002, transferring a total of NT$929 billion in share values into private hands. In order to dilute the impact this could have on the local securities market the Ministry of Finance has announced that the underwriting process for the privatisation of public sector enterprises will be undertaken simultaneously in Taiwan and overseas.

Until 1997 there were four categories of listed shares. Category A, B and C stocks were traded as a group while Category D stocks were traded separately and required full delivery. The first three categories have now been simplified into a single category. As of December 1997 there were only three companies traded requiring full delivery.

Brokering

There are now more than 230 broking firms in Taiwan. The vast majority of these have been established since 1988 when the ban on the issue of new broking licences was lifted. The top ten brokers account for more than 30% of all business in Taiwan.

Rules relating to the operation of foreign brokers have recently been revised, and foreign broking firms may now open branches in Taiwan after maintaining a representative office for at least one year. Applications for broking licences are made to the SFC and an applicant must demonstrate the following requirements:

- For a Broking Licence, the paid-in capital of the Head Office must exceed NT$200 million (US$6.1 million);

- For a Dealing Licence, the paid-in capital of the Head Office must exceed NT$400 million;
- For an Underwriting Licence, the paid-in capital of the Head Office must exceed NT$600 million.

Trading

Most securities offered in Taiwan are common shares. A number of investment trust funds are also listed. The standard lot is 1,000 shares and 'block' trades involving more than 500 lots must be registered with and approved by the Exchange. All trading activities are computerised. Off-market dealing is prohibited.

Trading hours are from 9:00 a.m. to 11:00 a.m. from Monday to Friday and on alternate Saturdays. These hours are expected to be extended to 12 noon sometime during 1998. All settlement procedures are administered by the Clearing Department of the TSE. Settlement is by book entry.

Table 15.4. Dealing costs in Taiwan (b.p. = base points)

Government and Corporate Bonds	*Other Securities*
For transactions up to NT$5,000,000: 10 b.p. For the portion of transactions between NT$5,000,001 and NT$50,000,000: 7.5 b.p. For the portion of a transaction above NT$50,000,000: 5 b.p.	For transactions up to NT$10,000,000, 14.25 b.p. is charged for both the purchase and sale of stocks and funds; however if the brokerage charge is less than NT$20 then a minimum brokerage charge of NT$20 is applied. For that portion of a transaction between NT$10,000,001 and NT$50,000,000: 13.25 b.p. For that portion of a transaction between NT$50,000,001 and NT$100,000,000: 12 b.p. For that portion of a transaction between NT$100,000,001 and NT$150,000,000: 11 b.p. For that portion of a transaction above NT$150,000,000: 10 b.p. A transaction tax of 0.3% (30 b.p.) is applied to the sale of all stocks.

Table 15.5. Company statistics (monetary figures in NT$ billions) Source: Taiwan Stock Exchange

	Totals		*TSE Listed Companies*					*OTC Companies*		*Unlisted Co.s*	
Year	*Number*	*Reg'd Capital*	*Number*	*Reg'd Capital*	*Growth Rate (%)*	*Par Value*	*Market Value*	*Number*	*Reg'd Capital*	*Number*	*Reg'd Capital*
1994	488,804	6,127	313	1,099	21	1,071	6,504	14	10	917	1,205
1995	527,093	7,145	347	1,347	22	1,325	5,108	41	173	999	1,218
1996	545,977	8,225	382	1,661	23	1,627	7,537	79	264	1,110	1,345

Table 15.6. Issue of corporate bonds and global depository receipts (monetary units in billions)

	Corporate Bonds		*Convertible Corporate Bonds*		*Overseas Corporate Bonds*		*Global Depository Receipts*	
Year	*Issue*	*Amount*	*Issue*	*Amount*	*Issue*	*Amount*	*Issue*	*Amount*
1994	31	NT$24.35	2	NT$1.5	11	USD1.415	5	USD0.411
					3	SF0.173		
					1	JPY4.000		
1995	45	NT$39.39	2	NT$2.10	1	USD0.250	5	USD0.590
1996	169	NT$165.21	11	NT$25.15	15	USD1.295	9	USD1.860
					1	JPY20.000		

CHAPTER 16

LIVING IN TAIWAN

Whether here for a short-term business assignment or for an extended stay, living in Taiwan can be a memorable experience. Leaving politics aside, Taiwan is not China—although it is definitely Chinese. Neither does its society mirror the other centres of Chinese commerce and culture, Hong Kong and Singapore. Taiwan, and Taipei especially, is a modern dynamic society that is fast asserting its place in Asia and the world. The juxtaposition of traditional Chinese values with those of the global 'information' society creates tensions and idiosyncrasies that are unique.

MOVING TO TAIWAN

Immigration and Visa Information

Entry formalities into Taiwan are relatively relaxed. Border control staff are generally friendly and courteous and *bona fide* visitors and business people should not encounter any problems.

All visitors to Taiwan are required to hold valid entry visas. Visitor visas are normally valid for 60 days and can be extended twice without leaving the country. A visitor visa to Taiwan can be obtained from any diplomatic, consular or representative trade office which, despite the lack of formal diplomatic ties, Taiwan maintains in most countries.

Visitor visas to Taiwan can still be obtained in Hong Kong from the Chunghua Travel Service located at 89 Queensway in Admiralty. Chunghua Travel offers a same-day visa service for travellers to Taiwan. Passports lodged in the morning can be collected in the afternoon of the same day. The standard of service provided in Hong Kong is good. Business travellers often report encountering difficulties in other centres, especially in such places as Manila and Bangkok.

Normal visitor visas are for single entry. Multiple re-entry visas can be obtained for up to one year for business purposes by presenting a letter from an employer on company letterhead stating the purpose for which a multiple entry facility is sought. Multiple re-entry visitor visas still allow a 60-day stay on each visit.

If you are required to extend your stay beyond 60 days an application must be made to the authorities before expiry of the 60-day visa validity period. Applications in Taipei are made at the Foreigners Service Centre, Taipei Municipal Police Headquarters at 96 Yen Ping South Road.

Nationals of 17 countries: the USA, Japan, Canada, Australia, New Zealand, the UK, France, Germany, Austria, the Netherlands, Belgium, Luxembourg, Spain, Portugal, Sweden, Italy and Costa Rica are allowed visa-free entry for visits up to 14 days. In addition, nationals of Switzerland, Poland, the Czech Republic and Hungary can obtain landing visas upon arrival at Taipei airport.

If you intend to work in Taiwan and stay beyond six months you will be required to hold a work visa. In such circumstances you will also need to apply for an Alien Residence Certificate. The law requires that all foreigners holding resident visas apply for such a certificate within 20 days of arrival. Failure to comply will result in a fine and could delay your subsequent departure from Taiwan.

Students attending Mandarin Language classes in Taiwan generally apply initially for a 60-day visitor visa before arrival. Students may extend their visas in Taiwan provided they obtain a certificate from a government-approved school stating that they have attended classes for at least 10 hours per week. After 180 days, a student must either leave the country before returning to study (many choose to make a simple one-day trip to Hong Kong just to comply with the law) or apply for a resident visa. Overseas students attending a course at a recognised ROC college of university can apply directly for residence visas.

In order to obtain an Alien Residence Certificate as a student, you must have already studied for at least four months at a government-approved school and have proof of pre-paid tuition for at least three months.

Climate

Taiwan has a sub-tropical climate. Summers are hot and humid with temperatures generally between 23°C and 32°C. Afternoon rain showers are frequent during the summer, which is also the season for typhoons. Taiwan generally experiences at least two to three typhoons a year, usually between July and September.

The winter season lasts from November to April. Winters are generally mild with temperatures that can fall to around 12°C during the day in mid-winter and below 10°C at night. The hillier residential areas sometimes experience snow but this is a rarity (and something of a novelty for the local population). Generally Taipei winters mean drizzle and gusty winds.

Between these two main seasons are the short transitory seasons of Spring and Autumn (Fall) which many people regard as the best times of the year in Taiwan. Spring time is officially the May–June period but in reality is likely to occur in either May *or* June. Spring temperatures are generally mild and typically range between 17°C and 25°C. Humidity is often high at this time, especially at the time of the spring ('plum') rains. By contrast, clear sunny days and relatively low humidity mark the autumn season.

Dress codes at any time of the year are less formal in Taiwan than in Hong Kong or Singapore. While men commonly wear suits they are not regarded as mandatory except for the most formal business meetings. Open-necked and short-sleeved shirts are common in most offices during the hot summer weather. Entertaining is generally informal except for the 'ball season'. Even during the most formal black-tie events, the 'black tie' dress code is not considered mandatory and takes second place to conviviality. Taipei is, above all, an informal city and one to be enjoyed.

Central heating is not common in Taiwan and warm winter clothing and bed linen are advisable.

What to Bring

You can buy just about anything in Taipei—at a price. Retailing has undergone a dramatic transformation in recent years, although with Japanese retailing chains dominating the department store segment of the market, there is a trend towards more Japanese than Western-style goods, especially in the appliance sections and the supermarkets.

Household furniture and soft furnishings are in plentiful supply in Taiwan to suit all tastes and budgets. Some shopping around may be in order to get beyond the fake Rococo that appears to be flavour of the moment with many Taiwanese yuppies. Those into Chinese antiques will find Taipei to be a shopper's paradise although prices are high. Very little antique furniture on sale in Taiwan is sourced nowadays from the local market. Most of it comes in by the container load from China.

There is little necessity to bring heavy items to Taiwan. Indeed many apartments and houses are rented fully furnished and for those that are not, furnishing can often be negotiated with the landlord or obtained on the thriving second-hand market via one or other of the numerous bulletin boards.

Clothing

Most clothing in Taiwan is ready-to-wear and designed for Chinese body frames, which are generally smaller than the Caucasian. The standard of tailoring in Taiwan is indifferent with many expatriates still reliant on tailors in Hong Kong or Seoul for their made-to-measure clothes. With most entertaining centred around eating, and with the quality and richness of Chinese food, the expanding waistline is an occupational hazard for anyone working in Taipei.

For men, lightweight suits and jackets are required for all but the winter season where heavier weight dress is desirable. A medium weight topcoat is also needed for the winter and for any travel during these times to China, Korea or Japan.

Women require lightweight cotton clothing during the summer months and woollen suits, dresses and sweaters for the winter period.

Formal wear for both men and women is an asset if you intend to party at the various balls and other functions that liven up the expatriate social calendar during the gloomier winter months. Formal wear can be hired locally if desired. Generally though, most entertaining tends from informal to casual, even in the larger companies.

Casual gear abounds. Jeans, sweat suits and other everyday items are sold on just about every street corner and prices range from the ridiculously cheap to the ridiculously expensive. Designer labels (most of which are made in South-East Asia) dominate the latter segment of the market, but there is very little difference across the range apart from the label. Chinese yuppies favour the 'designer' end of the market but expatriates generally choose the utility models. The combination of grime and acid rain ensures that after two or three wearings, the two extremes are indistinguishable anyway.

Children's clothing

There is plenty available, although at the upper end of the market, clothing for young boys and girls tends towards 'prissiness'. Rough and tumble is not for the Taiwanese youngster—remember this is a society where it is considered chic to give a 5-year-old his or her own mobile phone. The best shopping for children's clothing is in the markets and back streets rather than in the boutiques and department stores.

Appliances

Electrical outlets in Taiwan are generally 110 volt, 60 Hz. Air-conditioners operate on 220/240 volt and have separate and distinguishable wall sockets. Plugs and sockets are of the American type. Light bulbs are universally of the screw-in type. Bayonet bulbs and sockets are not available anywhere. Transformers are available for the operation of small 240 volt appliances from 110 volt outlets and some of the more expensive apartments have outlets providing both voltages—especially in areas catering to expatriates—although this is not common.

Television and VCRs follow the American NTSC system. The majority of households are now connected to a cable TV service, but the quality is appalling. Many expatriates use their television solely as an off-line entertainment centre: videotapes and laser disks are in plentiful supply in Taiwan and the neighbourhood video store is commonplace. However, if you have a good collection of videos of your own, then it would be wise to bring them with you.

Small kitchen appliances are readily available in Taiwan but speciality appliances such as waffle irons, coffee percolators, etc. are hard to come by locally.

Except at the top end of the realty rental market, kitchens with full-range stoves are a rarity in Taiwan. Gas is always used for cooking; electric stoves do not exist and are not considered suitable for Chinese cooking. Most households rely on a simple two-ring burner. Baking (except on a commercial basis) is not part of the local culinary repertoire and as a consequence ovens are a rarity. Small steamer ovens are available locally and are fine for grilling, cake making or preparing small roasts but the Christmas or Thanksgiving turkey would need to be cut into six sections in order to make it to the table from one of these.

A microwave/convection oven is the obvious answer and although microwave ovens are now readily available in Taiwan, those with convection or browning capabilities are in short supply. Furthermore, the majority of microwaves on sale in Taiwan carry all instructions in either Chinese or Japanese. A large, American-style microwave would be a definite asset in any expatriate household.

Food processors are another item that is common enough in Western households but relatively unknown in Taiwan domestic kitchens, as are food mixers.

One word of caution: Taiwanese are relative newcomers to the convenience gadget and although they have taken to them with alacrity, the service and repair industry remains woefully under-developed. Whether it is a food processor that has lost its buzz or the clutch on your car, the tendency in Taiwan will be to say that it cannot be fixed and you must buy a new one. With perseverance things can be repaired but it is not always easy. Patience and a sense of humour (if not resignation) are necessary in this department.

Because of the constant turnover among expatriates there is a large informal market in second-hand appliances—many of which are relatively new. It is often wise to keep an eye on the community bulletin boards in supermarkets, at the American Club or in other places where expatriates gather. You may find just the thing you are looking for, and more easily than by hunting through the traditional retail maze.

Kitchen items

Most Chinese food is stir-fried or boiled and implements for other cooking methods are not always easy to find. This is especially true of bakeware, roasting pans and accessories such as rolling pins, meat thermometers, cutters, etc. Non-stick cookware is available but is expensive.

Silverware can be a problem in Taiwan, especially for those living in the Tienmou and Yangminshan areas, close to the hot springs and fumaroles. Brass and copper are similarly affected. As relaxing as the sulphur baths are, the sulphurous air can wreak havoc on your silver service. Silver needs to be kept under wraps in Taiwan. Silver polish can be found but supplies are sporadic and it is not always available. A good stainless steel cutlery canteen is a wise investment for your entertaining needs.

Linen items

Taiwan is a major textile producer and a wide variety of fabrics are available locally. Cotton is the exception. Cotton fabrics are expensive and not always easy to find.

Tablecloths and table linen are available in Taiwan but tend to be expensive, and the sizes, designs and styles do not always reflect Western tastes. Placemats, except for those made from cork, are not readily available. Imported placemats are available at the major department stores but the range is generally limited and prices are high.

Many expatriates choose to bring in the bedding items they require, since good quality cotton bed linen can be hard to find and is again expensive—even compared to Hong Kong prices. Local bed linen usually comes as a pre-packaged set and, although reasonably priced, the colours are often considered garish by foreigners.

Towelling is another area where the local product leaves much to be desired and imported items sell for a very high price. Bath sheets can seldom be found in Taiwan.

Food items

The range of food items available in Taiwan has increased remarkably in recent years and as Taiwan further liberalises its markets, so the range can be expected to improve. Almost any item of food can be found in Taiwan these days, but to say that all items are readily available is another story. In this area, Taipei lags far behind Hong Kong.

What you can buy locally depends very much on where you live. Those living in the Tienmou/Yangminshan areas of Taipei or in the Hsinyi area downtown will find the supermarkets and speciality grocery stores stocking a wide variety of familiar items. If you live outside these areas, though, the availability of overseas products will be severely limited.

In most areas the range of dairy products available is extremely small. Full cream and low fat milk are available everywhere these days, but butter and cheese (other than the processed, single sliced variety) can sometimes be hard to find. Take another quantum jump to the esoteric world of your favourite Stilton or Camembert and your choice narrows immeasurably.

The same is often true of vegetable and salad items. If sweet potato is your thing then you can be satisfied on any street corner but if you are looking for brussels sprouts and parsnips to have with your Christmas roast then disappointment is a certainty. Some of the specialist grocery shops and butcheries now carry a range of imported frozen vegetables but prices are extremely high. Generally speaking, the quality of local vegetables is adequate at best. Hydroponically grown tomatoes are starting to appear in some of the Taipei supermarkets; the local tomato is green and of indifferent quality. Capsicums and bell peppers are the same uniform green. Despite the improving situation, many expatriates still use their trips to Hong Kong to bring back fresh vegetables and gourmet items that cannot be found locally.

If you are into home cooking then a selection of spices, condiments and food flavourings should be included in your Taipei starter pack.

Toiletries and personal hygiene

The major retail pharmacy chains, Mannings and Watsons, have opened stores throughout the island and most basic health and hygiene products are available in Taiwan. Most also have at least one English-speaking staff member—usually the pharmacist—who can assist foreigners. Local pharmacies are plentiful although language can sometimes be a problem. It is not uncommon in Taiwan, as elsewhere in Asia, for the pharmacist to double as a kind of all-purpose physician and the preferred first port of call for anyone with an ailment.

A word of caution is necessary. Many drugs in Taiwan that would require prescriptions in other countries can be purchased over the counter in Taiwan. Furthermore, while all pharmacies have to be registered in the name of a licensed pharmacist, they are not all owner-operated. Many pharmacies are rented out to unqualified personnel who operate the business in the same manner as they would any other corner store. In such situations, the philosophy of 'buyer beware' should be paramount.

Speciality soaps, bath salts and the like are not readily available locally. Personal deodorants are becoming available but at exorbitant prices and many people prefer to purchase such items in bulk when they travel to Hong Kong. In regard to feminine hygiene, tampons are not often used by Chinese and consequently are not often found. There is only one brand of tampon ('o.b.') available locally.

Customs Formalities

Customs in Taiwan are relatively relaxed and straightforward provided you know the rules and obey them. Customs Declaration Forms must be completed by every passenger entering Taiwan. The 'Head of Household' may make a declaration on behalf of a family group. Items that must be declared for customs purposes include the following:

- Dutiable articles, new articles, samples, machine parts and accessories, industrial and other raw materials, etc;
- Gold, silver, foreign currencies and New Taiwan dollars above the specified amount;
- Arms and ammunition including fishing and air guns;
- Computer software and videotapes (beyond one copy for personal use);
- Drugs and medicines.

Declarations include both accompanied and unaccompanied baggage.

Exemptions are allowed by the ROC Customs Authority in relation to most items intended for personal use, including the following:

- Each person aged 20 years or over may bring in one bottle (1 litre or less) of alcoholic beverages plus 25 cigars, 200 cigarettes or 1 lb of tobacco;
- Personal/household belongings that are pre-owned and have been used by the passenger overseas and are of a quantity considered reasonable and appropriate for personal use.

While many items are in principle dutiable, duty payments are often not enforced.

In addition, a number of items are listed as prohibited imports into Taiwan. These include all restricted substances and non-prescriptive non-medicinal drugs, soils, plants and animal products from infected areas and endangered species of wildlife.

The scope of the Customs regulations and their enforcement is constantly changing and tending towards more liberal attitudes except in matters affecting trademarks and copyright protection or where trade is restricted by international convention. Any international moving and freight forwarding service will be able to advise in relation to the importation of specific items.

No pets can be brought into Taiwan without a valid import permit issued by the Bureau of Commodity Inspection and Quarantine (BCIQ). An application for an animal import permit can only by made by persons with a valid work permit. In order to import an animal into Taiwan the following details must be supplied together with the application covering letter:

- A photocopy of the information and visa pages of the owner's passport;

- A copy of the owner's work permit issued by the ROC government as well as the work certificate issued by the owner's employer;
- An official certificate of animal health issued by the appropriate authority in the home country;
- An official declaration of rabies immunity;
- Four 4 x 4 inch full-body colour photographs of the animal.

All animals permitted entry to Taiwan are subject to quarantine for a 63-day period. The quarantine period starts from the day of arrival at the quarantine station (not the day of arrival of the animal into Taiwan). Pets are normally quarantined at the National University Veterinary Hospital, 142 Chow Shan Road, Taipei and can be visited daily.

SETTLING IN

Hotels

Most foreigners when arriving in Taipei reside initially at one of Taipei's major hotels in the downtown city area. Living in a hotel for any length of time can, however, prove a costly and debilitating exercise, in spite of the five-star comforts, and most expatriates seek to move out as quickly as possible.

Choice of hotel will most likely be governed by proximity to office premises. In a city where the traffic situation is more often than not chaotic, this can often be the overriding consideration.

If expense is no object then either the Grand Hyatt or the more sedate Far Eastern Plaza is the obvious choice. Both are located in the new Hsinyi business district (south-east) of Taipei close to the Taipei World Trade Centre. The Grand Hyatt is as expansive as it is expensive, with a lobby the size of an aircraft hangar (although the sheer volume of human traffic leaves more the impression of Grand Central Station). Where the Grand Hyatt spreads out, the Far Eastern towers upwards, providing a more intimate and less bustling atmosphere. Personal preference aside, both are not only comfortable but world-class.

In this area of Taipei, the Howard Plaza Hotel is the other alternative and, because of its proximity to the new Fushing MTR line, is often considered more convenient for moving about Taipei.

In the Chungshan (north-east) area near the domestic airport and main north-south freeway, the Sherwood Hotel is the clear favourite, although rooms tend towards the small size. The Sherwood is an intimate hotel for those of sophisticated tastes.

The Ritz, by contrast, appeals to the pure sybarites. One of the older hotels in the north-west quarter of the downtown area, the Ritz is pure understated elegance. Those old-timers who have seen it all claim that the Ritz beats all others hands down. Certainly its Paris–1940 Restaurant, home to the Taipei Chapter of the Chaine-de-Rotiserres, is fine European dining at its best.

Moving westward, on the Chungshan Road area of Taipei the President Hotel—long a firm favourite with many short term visitors because of its proximity to the entertainment areas of Taipei—has recently closed as it is scheduled for demolition. Taking up the slack within the same area is the newly renovated Imperial Hotel, now managed by the Intercontinental Group. The 'new' Imperial is very comfortable and equally convenient. Also on Chungshan Road is the Grand Formosa Regent Hotel; very large and very stylish, the Grand Formosa Regent offers space above all else.

Completing the circle, in the south-west area of the central business district are the Hilton and Lai Lai Sheraton Hotels. Both are older, well established hotels which have honed their service to perfection over the years and which remain firm favourites among seasoned travellers and the local business population.

Alongside the major flag carriers are an ever increasing number of four-star and business hotels, all of which offer reasonable standards of comfort at prices that are much more user-friendly. Anybody contemplating an extended hotel stay in Taipei should consider that a suite in one of these smaller hotels can be had for much less than the price of a single room in the major chain hotels. While catering and recreation amenities in such establishments tend to be simpler than in the five-star hotels, unless one is really stuck on a 24-hour room service regimen, the trade-off is often worthwhile. Taipei is not short of places to eat, whatever your taste and whatever the time.

Serviced apartments offer one cost effective option for an initial settling in period and allow an expatriate time to find the type of house or apartment they are looking for without the pressure of time or cost. The Howard Gardens serviced apartments operated by the Howard Plaza Hotel are among the most popular with the foreign community.

Housing

Housing for expatriates is generally regarded as expensive compared to home country standards but less so by comparison with neighbouring countries such as Hong Kong. The majority of expatriates live in apartment buildings rather than in single-family houses and if you choose to live in downtown Taipei, this is likely to be your only option.

There is a market, however, for all budgets and tastes. Students and those on limited incomes generally opt for shared apartments close to the university. At the other end of the spectrum, villas set in their own grounds are available—at a price—in the foothills surrounding Taipei.

Generally, 'villas' (or what most American or Australians would regard as ordinary houses) are most often found on the outskirts of Taipei and usually as part of residential communities with controlled access and other measures to ensure security.

Choice of residence and residential area can make all the difference to whether or not your time in Taipei is an enjoyable one. Taking the time to get to know the city and your own requirements while living here is the single most important factor to consider. You are unlikely to find your dream residence in Taipei; it is a city built for money rather than dreams and as a result, whatever decision you take regarding your housing, you will quite likely have to compromise.

Most of the expatriate community lives in one or more of the following areas:

Tienmou

Tienmou in the northern suburbs of Taipei, and adjacent to the northern foothills is the site of the old American army camp. The US Army is long gone but Tienmou remains the focus for the foreign community in Taipei, and especially the English-speaking foreign community.

Tienmou is, above all else, convenient. The American, Japanese and British schools are all in the area and for those with children this is often the prime consideration.

Tienmou is fashionable. The supermarkets are stocked with imported wines and food (by comparison with other areas of Taipei at least) and speciality groceries and Western-style butcheries ensure that if you can buy it in Taipei, you can buy it in Tienmou. The area is well serviced by buses to all the downtown areas, but commuting at peak times can be troublesome because of the limited access routes into and out of the area.

Housing in Tienmou is generally modern and of good quality. Prices can range from NT$35,000 per month for a basic three-bedroom furnished apartment to upwards of NT$200,000 per month at the upper end of the market. Many of the more expensive have swimming pools and other recreation facilities on the grounds. Freestanding houses are rare.

Peitou

Adjacent to Tienmou, although a little farther out, is the suburb of Peitou and, beyond Peitou, Tamshui. These areas are also becoming popular especially with the more price-conscious end of the market. The recent opening of the Tamshui/Peitou MTR line has made commuting to and from these (essentially dormitory) suburbs much easier. Above Peitou, the community of Wellington Heights is a favourite for those with the budget to afford their own residences, although most of the houses appear to be quite old and maintenance on some can be a problem.

For those choosing to live in Wellington Heights, a car is essential.

Yangmingshan

Above Tienmou and Peitou is Yangmingshan (Yang Ming Mountain). This is considered to be the prestige area of Taipei in which to live and has much of the hype that surrounds the 'Peak' area in Hong Kong, probably for the same reason. While being able to retreat from the squalor of the city to the cool mountain breezes may have made good sense in days gone by, these days Yangmingshan is quite impractical for all but the diplomatic corps and those who can afford to be chauffeured from one coffee morning to the next.

However, Yangmingshan does have its good points. If you are really after a house with its own grounds, you are most likely to find this in the Yangmingshan area. But on the down side is the isolation of the area; for those living in the foothills, even buying milk from the convenience store involves a car drive and the weekly shopping involves a trip to Tienmou or downtown.

Hsinyi

Expatriates in Taipei definitely fit into one of two categories. On the one hand are those who live in the suburbs and could not stand to live among all the noise and pollution of downtown Taipei. On the other are those who like the convenience of city living and who are quite content to close the door, turn up the air-conditioning and the music and tune out the world.

Certainly, for those without children to consider, living in the main metropolis has a lot going for it. If inner city living is your style then you will probably want to check out the Hsinyi area of Taipei. Apartments here tend to be either smaller or higher priced. An older one-room bed-sitter will rent for around NT$20,000 per month while a modern three-bedroom apartment may rent for around NT$200,000 a month. Generally, rents in the Hsinyi area are roughly 50% above the Tienmou price.

While rental costs may be the down side, convenience is the big plus. Not only are commuting times reduced to the minimum, you are close to all the 'in' places to while away the nighttime hours. Needless to say, Hsinyi is often the place preferred by the young, single set.

Other areas

If you are a rugged individualist and not afraid to get away from the pack, then Taipei offers many other options. Outside the fashionable areas, rental prices drop dramatically. Neihu on the northern side of Taipei and Hsintien in the south are two suburbs in the foothills that offer good accommodation for much more modest outlays. The catch, of course, is that while you may be able to get away with public transport for your commuting to and from work, you will definitely need a car in order to retain any kind of social life—unless of course you own a local taxi company. The choice is yours.

Using a Realty Agent

Some of the best residences in Taipei have been found from the Bulletin Board at the Taipei American Club or by word of mouth from friends and business associates, but for most people, there is little choice but to use a local realty agent.

The two English language daily newspapers, *China News* and *China Post*, both carry daily realty classifieds. Their pages carry advertisements for properties for rent and from some of Taipei's leading real estate companies that cater to expatriates.

Bear in mind that the system in Taiwan ensures that the real estate agent receives a commission from both parties. Both the landlord and the lessor are each expected to pay one half month's rent as a success fee to the real estate agent introducing the parties. Transport costs to inspect the premises are often your responsibility. It is rare for an agent to offer to provide transport.

It is a wise precaution to make initial contact with two or three agents and then choose to deal with the person you feel most at ease with. Make sure you have written down your specific requirements and be aware that prices are always negotiable. Other points to bear in mind include the following:

- Check the condition of the premises. If repairs need to be made make sure this is done before any payment is made; it is sometimes a problem for a tenant to have the landlord effect necessary work after the lease has been signed;
- Unfurnished premises often mean just that. In such circumstances you will more than likely have to take responsibility for putting in the stove, hot water system, etc;
- Check all plumbing and drainage carefully before moving in. Plumbing and sanitation problems can often be major headaches—even in the newer buildings. It is not unknown for tilers and other workers to flush excess cement down the toilet bowl when work on an apartment is supposedly finished;
- Check on security and access control to the premises. What security (guard) fees are payable in addition to the monthly rent? Bear in mind that at the time of the lunar New Year, such fees double in order to cover bonuses to staff. If you decide to move in, then change the locks when you do so;
- Find out what parking facilities are available. Never assume that because there are empty parking spaces in the streets during the day, the same will be true after hours; cars can be double- and even triple-parked in some areas at night. If you intend to own a car in Taipei, make sure you have an apartment with a garage.

Above all else, if you see something you like then be prepared to negotiate but remember that negotiation is a matter of give and take on both sides. Generally, you will get far more from your landlord if you indicate you are prepared to give something yourself.

Household Staff

Live-in household staff is becoming a rarity in modern Taiwan. Very few Chinese *amahs* are prepared to live on the premises and even those who work full-time will choose to return to their families at the end of the day's work. Filipino *amahs* generally work full-time and live with the family employing them. Generally, they are less expensive to employ than Chinese *amahs*. If you choose to employ a Filipina then you should ensure that she has entered Taiwan legally and holds a work visa. Filipino *amahs* are generally paid at the basic rate of NT$15,800 per month plus board and lodging.

Expected salary levels for Chinese *amahs* depend upon the neighbourhood and on supply and demand. A part-time *amah* will generally cost between NT$1800 and NT$2000 per day. A workday is considered to be the hours between 9 a.m. and 5 p.m. with an hour off for lunch. An *amah* will expect to use your rice to cook lunch with. Whether full-time or part-time you will be expected to pay a bonus equivalent to one month's salary at the lunar New Year festival and to provide a small gift at Christmas time.

Furthermore, although part-time, an *amah* regards her employment as permanent part-time work and if you take home-leave during the year you will be expected to pay your *amah*'s salary during your absence. Many *amahs* will continue to work during this time and will come to your house during your absence to undertake the type of major cleaning that cannot be done when people are living on the premises on a daily basis.

It is imperative that you work out and agree the range of duties expected before any contract—verbal or written—is entered into. It is also a good idea to write down the agreement, even if it does not constitute a formal contract, so as to avoid any later misunderstandings.

Schools

The growing foreign community in Taiwan has put increasing pressure on educational services catering to the children of foreign families. The majority of these schools are located in the Tienmou/Shihlin area.

The Taipei American School is often the first choice for many expatriate families and offers an American curriculum. Enrolment at the school is open to all children of families carrying foreign passports.

All tuition and other fees charged by the American School are set in New Taiwan dollars but can be paid in US dollars at the official exchange rate applicable at time of payment. Tuition fees for the 1997–98 academic year are reproduced below and are indicative of the charges of other foreign schools in Taiwan.

Table 16.1. Taipei American School 1997–98 semester and fee schedules

Application Fee	NT$5,000
Registration Fee	NT$25,000
Tuition Fees (per semester):	

Table 16.1 cont'd

Kindergarten	NT$119,500
Grades 1–5	NT$129,800
Grades 6–12	NT$149,300
ESL[1] Charges (if applicable)	
Grades 1–5	NT$37,500
Grades 6–10	NT$44,750

Many wealthy Chinese families have obtained overseas residence passports in order that their children may benefit from a Western-style education and for this reason the Taipei American School has a high proportion of children who are from local Chinese families. This is good from the viewpoint of exposing children to cross-cultural differences but it does mean that services are often strained.

Other options for expatriate families seeking an English language education are the Taipei British School and the Morrison Academy, which follows a non-sectarian Christian educational philosophy.

There are a number of preschools and kindergartens offering English language programs and several in the Tienmou area that cater specifically to the needs of the foreign community. The Community Services Center in Tienmou can assist families to locate a suitable preschool for their children.

Community Support Services

In addition to the business and social organisations organised around specific nationality groups, there are a number of social and non-profit community organisations that provide both support services as well as recreational outlets for the foreign community in Taipei.

The Community Services Center is a well-known and well-regarded non-profit registered organisation, which assists foreigners both in settling into the Taiwan environment and with any ongoing problems that might arise.

Programs offered at the centre include:

• Counselling Services for Individuals, Couples and Families;

---

[1] English as a Second Language.

- Adult Education Classes;
- Distance Learning Support;
- Newcomer Orientation;
- Cross-Cultural Training for International Businesses.

The Community Services Center maintains its own Internet website at http://community.com.tw and this site provides detailed information concerning the programs, publications and activities offered. For further information, English-speaking staff at CSS may be contacted at (Taipei) 2836 8134 (telephone) or 2835 2530 (facsimile).

Many expatriates in Taiwan choose to join the **American Club** to take advantage of its well-organised social and recreational facilities that are among the best in Taiwan. Membership fees are quite high and often preclude membership applications from individuals who are not supported by a company.

Membership involves payment of a refundable bond and a non-refundable initiation fee. There are also monthly dues and minimum billing charges to be met. Currently a corporate bond costs NT$250,000 for the first member and NT$215,000 for any subsequent members from the same organisation. The initiation fee is NT$98,000.

For individuals, the bond is set at NT$175,000 with the same initiation fee. Monthly dues currently stand at NT$2,500 and there is a minium billing fee of NT$4,750.

The American Club is located at 47 Pei An Road near the Taipei Grand Hotel and may be contacted at (Taipei) 2594 8260 (telephone) or 2594 8263 (facsimile).

RECREATION ACTIVITIES

Virtually all of Taiwan's expatriate business life is centred on Taipei. Expatriate communities in other major cities are considerably smaller and tend to be either teaching or missionary communities or individual technical experts assigned to manage a specific local project. Taipei, Kaohsiung and Taichung, in that order, all provide outlets for their local foreign communities although outside these centres the pickings are slim. Fortunately, the island is small enough that nobody need be isolated unless by choice.

Taipei's Social Scene

Taipei has changed much in recent years. Coupled with a more relaxed social environment, as memories of the martial law environment fade away, there is plenty to enjoy from any period of time spent living in Taiwan. Most activities are indoors—a factor of the climate, which for the most part is hot and/or wet—but for a price almost any activity can be accommodated.

Business etiquette in Taiwan, if not business survival, depends on networking. There is very little opportunity to opt out. Evening engagements invariably involve eating and drinking, making some form of exercise mandatory for those who wish to stay in shape. Golf is a firm favourite of the business set but many other sports and leisure activities are available. If you are not the type of person given over to the sporting life, you can always head for a hefty dose of aerobics at one or other of Taipei's discotheques.

Involvement in one or more of the foreign business associations is almost mandatory as a means of networking and making friends. The foreign community in Taiwan is still sufficiently small that you can pretty much cover the whole territory if you work at it. 'Out of sight is out of mind' may be a cliché but it is one that applies very much to the local business scene. If you are out for business you must be part of the pack. Image is very important; possibly more so than substance.

Both the American Chamber of Commerce and the European Council hold monthly business luncheons and have their own network of special interest policy committees which form the basic business and social structure for many in the foreign community. The Canadian Society welcomes non-Canadian and Canadian alike and is one of the most vibrant and welcoming of social groups on the Taipei scene. It organises regular evening and daytime (holiday) functions for its members and friends. The Canadians also organise monthly business breakfasts.

The hills surrounding Taipei and the northern coastal areas offer plenty of opportunities for relaxation. While the northern foothills around Yangmingshan (including the Yangmingshan National Park) are well-known and well-travelled by the foreign community—largely on account of proximity to Tienmou—the southern foothills in the Mucha and Hsintien areas are much less travelled but can be even more delightful. An afternoon in one of the tea houses on Tea Mountain or a trip to the (Taiwanese) Aboriginal centre at Wulai are worthy target destinations to begin exploring this area.

On the northern coast, the once sleepy fishing port of Tamshui is rapidly becoming part of Taipei's urban area and, as one of the termini for the MTR line, can become excessively crowded at weekends and during holidays. Perseverance in negotiating the traffic can be rewarded however. A trip to the old fort (and one-time British Consulate) on the hill above the Tamshui river estuary affords not only a rare glimpse into Taiwan's past history but the opportunity afterwards to enjoy delightfully fresh seafood at any one of the waterfront restaurants on the quayside. The movie *The Sand Pebbles* was largely filmed on the Tamshui river. Take time to wander this area and you may discover some real gems.

The port city of Keelung, north-east of Taipei, became Taiwan's major seaport during the Japanese occupation period. Easily accessible by freeway or by commuter train from Taipei's Central Railway Station, Keelung offers all the bustle and tumble of any harbour city. Famous for its night markets, dinner *al fresco* at any of the roadside stalls is not only fun but can be amazingly inexpensive. Nearby is the old mining centre of Choufen, nestling in the hills and (on a clear day) offering superb views from any one of the tea houses and restaurants which take the visitor back to a bygone age.

Arts and Entertainment

Outside the formal business associations, Taipei offers a lot by way of entertainment. Long famous for the quality of its Chinese food, which is quite different and more pungent than that found in Hong Kong, Taipei now truly caters to all tastes.

Popular with visitors who wish to try something a little out of the ordinary, the Mongolian Barbecue is probably the most fun, delicious and reasonably priced option. If you opt for this style of eatery, then expect to prepare you own concoction of meats, vegetables and sauces. In former days, you would have cooked your meal on a shield above the open flames. Nowadays whatever combination you throw together will be expertly cooked for you by the in-house chefs who appear to be chained to their massive firepots. The Shann Garden in the mountains overlooking Peitou is probably the best spot for enjoying this type of food and the set-price meal charge (including a buffet and dessert) is very reasonable at around NT$500 per person.

Looking for still more local flavour? Then try the beer houses on Sungchiang Road, Fu Yuan Street (near the intersection of Nanking and Keelung roads), Ah Ho Road in Taipei or on Chung Cheng Road in Tienmou. With this style of eating, you can see the food (suitably refrigerated) outside the restaurant and then choose both the food you want to eat and the manner in which it is to be cooked. The food is usually eaten

362

at low tables sitting on stools and washed down with jugs of very cold draught beer. Noisy, yes, but delicious, friendly and heaps of fun.

Complete books have been written about dining out in Taipei. This is just to whet the appetite (so to speak).

After dinner, or before if you are meeting friends, you can relax at one of Taipei's many pubs. Pubs and bars come in many varieties but the expatriate crowds tend to follow a well-trodden path to a few regular watering holes. In the Tienmou area, the British-style Pig and Whistle has been a firm favourite for many years—but always check your bill before you pay; the staff are well-known for making mistakes. Downtown in the Hsinyi area, most people head for the Malibu on the intersection of Jen Ai and Tun Hwa roads.

If you are really dedicated to a night out on the town then you have a whole street of bars at your disposal. Te Wei Street, near the Imperial Hotel, has been affectionately known as the 'Combat Zone' since the days of the Vietnam conflict. Here you can find between 20 and 30 bars to satisfy the most acute of thirsts. The Hsiaoling Pub is generally regarded as one of the best with fair prices and good service.

For those seeking more cultural pursuits, Taipei will not disappoint —provided you do not set your sights too high, that is. Regular orchestral concert performances and recitals are staged at a number of locations around Taipei and a free monthly program is available in English from most bookstores and ticket outlets. The English newspapers also cover 'what's on' on a weekly basis and more often for major events.

The National Palace Museum holds the world's finest collection of Chinese antiquities. The Taiwanese claim the collection covers 5,000 years of Chinese history and they are probably correct if you count the Chinese version of the Stone Age. Pomposity aside, the collection is remarkable and vast with only around 1% on display at any one time. The sheer magnitude of the offering makes it essential that you schedule more than one visit.

By contrast, the government gives scant attention to modern artistry, which is a pity because Taiwan is producing some fine modern artistic works. The Taipei Modern Art Museum leaves much to be desired although it is worth a visit. Much of the modern artistry is to be found in private galleries and in the myriad of art shops which abound in Taipei.

Finally, mention should be made of the weekend markets that open in the carpark under the ChienKuo Expressway around the Jen Ai Road area. There are two main markets—the flower market and the jade market—but there is much else in this area to see besides. Coins, antiques and bric-a-brac are all to be found in this market but as always, haggle over the price; it is expected and is part of the fun.

Travelling Around Taiwan

Both of Taiwan's English language newspapers contain regular articles extolling the virtues of some of the lesser known scenic spots, and those wishing to see the 'real Taiwan' will find these articles a useful reference for exploration of the island.

A trip down the eastern coast is one of the 'must do' adventures for anybody spending any significant time on the island and it is worthwhile to make the journey at least twice—once by car and once by train. Each is equally spectacular but from a different point of view. While not a long journey in terms of road miles, it is wise to plan ahead for such a trip. Chaotic weekend traffic conditions could well turn a pleasant afternoon drive into an all day bumper-to-bumper nightmare if you pick the wrong day for your trip.

The east coast as far as Hualien is the most travelled part of the area and the most spectacular, especially when taken in combination with a visit to the adjacent Taroko Gorge and its cliffs of pure marble. Completion of the southern portion of the east-west rail link and improvements to the national highway have made a complete around-the-island tour, by car or by train (car is recommended), a worthwhile experience. Forget the west coast on this occasion; unless you are planning to spend a week at it, the journey between Taipei and Kaohsiung can be accomplished as quickly as possible on the freeway (actually a tollway). If you are heading in an anti-clockwise direction, then the adventure really begins south of Kaohsiung as you travel to the resort area of Kenting and the adjacent national park.

Besides the resort hotels, Kenting offers bargain accommodation especially during weekdays and out of tourist season. Many expatriates visiting the area choose to stop off at Amy's Cucina, a delightful Italian-style restaurant on the main drag of Kenting town. If you fancy a spot of game fishing, the management will assist you to hire an air-conditioned motor cruiser for the day and the restaurant staff will also cook your fish for the evening meal.

Kenting National Park is worth at least half a day of your time—more if you can afford it and the weather permits. From here you can travel to the southern-most tip of the island. Before heading over to the east coast, take time to stop off in the market town of Hungchuan and take a stroll along the old city wall that has been recently restored.

Taitung used to be a sleepy backwater but has become the centre of some major tourist developments in recent years. Close to Taitung City are the Chihpan Hot Springs. Hotels in this area range from five-star luxury

364

accommodation to basic European *pension* style but, if you have the time, an evening spent at the hot springs can relax and invigorate you after a hard day of sightseeing.

Other areas where you have the chance to get away from the crowds and enjoy the pure tranquillity for which Taiwan was famous in past times include Sun Moon Lake, Mount Alishan (ride the mountain railway from Chiayi) and the forests of Hsitou. If you have the inclination and the patience, you will discover that Taiwan has much more to offer than Asia's largest trade mart.

PERSONAL MATTERS

Medical and Health

Few expatriates experience serious medical problems induced by the local environment and provided a few simple precautions are taken the chances of serious illness are slight. However, skin irritations and infections resulting from the high humidity are common.

While local medical services are quite good they are often overcrowded with long waiting times at local surgeries and clinics. Most expatriates choose to go to Hong Kong or return to their home country if serious medical problems are encountered.

Local (private) medical insurance is available to those with Alien Residence Certificates. Otherwise you are expected to pay in full at the time of treatment.

The Veterans General Hospital in Shihpai District, adjacent to Tienmou, is often used by expatriates in the area for emergency treatment and offers first class facilities, as do the Taiwan Adventist Hospital and the Chungshan Hospital in downtown Taipei.

Ambulance services are available but English is not widely spoken among paramedical staff.

Utilities Services

Despite an infrastructure that is comparatively sophisticated by regional standards, utilities services, while good, still leave much to be desired. Although Taipei is laying claim to becoming an international city, the billing and payment procedures for utilities charges are relatively cumbersome. A complex bi-monthly billing system with accounts only in the Chinese

365

language can cause difficulties for newcomers to Taipei who are unfamiliar with the system. The problem becomes progressively worse outside the main metropolitan area. While you can pay your charges through the banking system, each service provider makes life interesting for you by using a different bank.

Electricity

Electricity charges are billed bi-monthly and, prior to the due date, accounts can be paid by bank transfer through the Co-operative Bank of Taiwan. Electricity charges are high and the charge increases with the volume consumed. Brownouts and blackouts caused both by overloaded systems and by typhoons are not uncommon in Taipei. Sensitive electrical equipment such as computers should always be connected through uninterruptable power supplies and a supply of candles as well as a flashlight should always be on hand. Most blackouts last only a few minutes but occasionally can last for several hours.

Gas

The use of gas for cooking is universal in Taiwan. Domestic water heating is almost always by gas also. Most buildings in the main metropolitan area and in Tienmou are connected directly to the town gas supply. Again, meters are read bi-monthly and a representative of the local gas company will call to collect payment. In most apartment buildings, a notice is posted several days prior to the reading and if you are not home when the Gasman Cometh, you are invited to read your own meter and record it on the notice. If no reading is made, you will be charged a notional amount based on past patterns of usage. Similarly with payment, if you are out when the collector calls, the onus is on you to pay the charge in person at the local gas office or through the Medium Business Bank of Taiwan. Disconnection for non-payment is swift.

For buildings without town gas, the only option is bottled gas which is available from neighbourhood suppliers. Usually you will require at least two cylinders—one connected to your gas range and another connected to your hot water heater. Gas distributors charge a 'deposit' of around NT$1,000 per canister. Do not expect a receipt for your deposit and do not expect a refund when you leave. This is a rip-off, pure and simple.

Water

Although the local water supply is considered potable, many people use bottled water for cooking and drinking purposes and there are a large number of companies that deliver bulk drinking water. Payments for general tap-water services can be made through the Taipei City Bank or at any branch of the local water company.

Sanitation and waste disposal

Foreign residents are sometimes appalled to learn that less than 3% of all effluent in Taiwan is treated before being discharged into local waterways. Toilet paper and sanitary napkins are not flushed down the toilet but placed in a container for separate disposal. As antediluvian as this practice is—arising from the lack of enforcement of provisions relating to the minimum diameter of effluent pipes in the construction industry—the penalty for non-compliance may be severely blocked drainage outlets.

Solid garbage collection arrangements, at least in the Taipei area, have improved markedly in recent years. Garbage collection vehicles do their rounds of the city streets every evening and residents dispose of their garbage directly into the truck. Apart from the dumpsters that are scattered randomly around the city, it is no longer acceptable to leave garbage on the streets for collection.

Telephone services

The local telecommunication provider has recently been privatised and services are slowly improving, although the local phone service leaves much to be desired. Almost all buildings in Taipei are already wired for phone connections and it is possible that you may be able to take over an existing number provided by your landlord. If not, or if you want additional phone lines, application must be made to the local office of Chunghwa Telecom. Most offices have at least one person who can speak English. You will need to produce your passport when applying for a wired phone line. If you wish to have a mobile phone you will need to produce an Alien Residence Certificate to obtain a personal number. If you do not have an ARC you can register the number in the name of a Chinese friend, or through a local company, if you have one with which you are associated.

Telephone accounts are billed monthly and may be paid at any bank provided payment is made prior to the due date. Be warned that the phone company is tardy with its postage and often there are only a few days between receipt of the bill and the date for payment. Phone lines are disconnected swiftly if the account is not paid within 14 days. Beware, many expatriates have returned from home leave to find themselves cut off from the world.

Internet

The Internet is rapidly growing in popularity in Taiwan as a means of communication, although investment in infrastructure by the national service provider has not kept pace with demand. Many people who want a low cost connection apply through either Seednet or Hinet, both of which are quasi-government controlled. Seednet services are available through Chunghwa Telecom.

Quality of service provided by the major national Internet service providers (ISPs) leaves much to be desired and most professionals opt for a service with one of the smaller independent ISPs. The Transend Internet Company specialises in providing full function Internet services to the foreign business community and is a joint venture between American and local interests. Transend maintains its own leased lines providing international connectivity independent of the main trunk operators, thereby improving bandwidth for its customers. The company charges NT$10,000 per year for a full Internet account, which includes unlimited access to ftp, homepages, e-mail, the world wide web, and training classes. Transend may be reached on the web at http://www.transend.com.tw or more conventionally at (Taipei) 2706 9089 (telephone) or 2706 3384 (facsimile).

THE EXPATRIATE WOMAN

Many single expatriate professional women find that working as a professional in Taiwan is sometimes easier than in their home countries. Taiwan is an Asian society where Confucian values, hierarchy and respect of title, as well as of knowledge and education, still prevail. All of this translates into an environment that gives respect to a woman who likes to deal in or lead a business—not because she is a woman but because she is a professional. In this respect, Taiwan is a gender-neutral society. The woman who asserts herself in a positive fashion will be given respect because of her rank in the organisation.

Nevertheless, 'glass ceilings' do exist and family-operated organisations still tend to be patriarchal in nature with the top positions reserved for the elder males in the family. If there are no blood male leaders they will go to the spouses of the female children. Expatriate women of course do not generally encounter such problems, simply because they are expatriate and therefore working (usually) for large international corporations or running their own businesses.

In general, hard work and ambition are rewarded in Taiwan and there is no real barrier for an ambitious and assertive female. However, many women—especially among the Chinese—do not have such qualities, by choice. Family values are still extremely important throughout much of society and many women choose not to use their power for fear of alienating their male counterparts. Unfortunately, many Chinese professional women still choose to play a subservient role within the office. It remains a fact that few oriental men are willing to date, let alone marry, a woman who is above his educational or societal level.

Sexual harassment is generally not a problem for expatriate professional women simply because they are assertive and thus command respect. It is more of a problem for those who have chosen subservience. Although officially frowned upon it is understood that sexual harassment continues to be a real problem within many companies for women who are not in executive positions.

In social activities, single expatriate women probably have less choice than their male counterparts. Unlike foreign men, who have a large pool of women to choose from as friends, a foreign woman is much more limited in her social choices. Often this is for no other reason than that stated above: oriental males will give respect to a more senior female within the work environment, but would lose face by befriending a woman who may lay claim to an equal or higher status.

There is an active Women's International Network in Taiwan which is open to both expatriate and Chinese women. Many prominent women within Taiwan are members and this is said to be one of the best means for an expatriate woman to network in the local society. Contact can perhaps best be made through the American Chamber of Commerce in Taipei. Activities are also advertised in the major daily newspapers on a regular basis.

CHINESE LANGUAGE SCHOOLS IN TAIPEI (A Partial Listing)

The Mandarin Training Centre
National Taiwan Normal University
162 Hoping East Road, Section 1, Taipei
Tel: (02) 2391 4248

Tamkang University Public Service Centre
18 Lishui Street, Taipei
Tel: (02) 2321 6320

Chinese Culture University Mandarin Centre
321 Chienkuo South Road, Section 2, Taipei
Tel: (02) 2700 5858

National Chengchi University
64 Chihnan Road, Section 2, Wenshan District, Taipei
Tel: (02) 2938 7102

Fu Jen Catholic University
510 Chungcheng Road, Hsinchuang City, Taipei County, Taiwan
Tel: (02) 2903 1111

Mandarin Daily News Language Center
2F, 2 Fuchow Street, Taipei
Tel: (02) 2392 1133

Taipei Language Institute
50 Roosevelt Road, Section 3, 4Fl, Taipei
Tel: (02) 2367 2112
Fax: (02) 2363 4857
Email: tli@transend.com.tw

China Language Institute
1F, 4, Lane 90, An-Ho Road, Section 1, Taipei
Tel: (02) 2707 2812
Fax: (02) 2708 7157

INTERNATIONAL SCHOOLS IN TAIWAN

Taipei Area

Deutsche Schüle, Taipei
731 Wenlin Road, Taipei
Tel: (02) 2832 6538
Fax: (02) 2834 4789

Dominican International School
    76 Tahchih Street, Taipei
    Tel: (02) 2502 8451
    Fax: (02) 2504 2914

École Française de Taipei
    731 Wenlin Road, Taipei
    Tel: (02) 2834 5221
    Fax: (02) 2834 5223

Morrison Academy, Bethany Campus
    P.O. Box 30–134 Taipei, 100
    Tel: (02) 2365 9691
    Fax: (02) 2365 9696

Overseas Korean Primary School in Taipei
    1, Lane 68, Chingnien Road, Taipei
    Tel: (02) 2303 9126
    Fax: (02) 2309 7780

Taipei American School
    800 Chungshan North Road, Section 6, Taipei
    Tel: (02) 2873 9900
    Fax: (02) 2873 1641

Taipei English School
    731 Wenlin Road, Taipei
    Tel: (02) 2834 1654
    Fax: (02) 2832 7464

Taipei Japanese School
    785 Chungshan North Road, Section 6, Taipei
    Tel: (02) 2872 3801
    Fax: (02) 2873 6744

Taiwan Adventist Elementary School
    64, Lane 80, Chuang Ting Road,
    Yangmingshan, Taipei
    Tel: (02) 2861 6400

Taichung Area (Central Taiwan)

Morrison Academy, Taichung Campus
P.O. Box 27–24, Taichung 400
Tel: (04) 292 1171
Fax: (04) 295 6140

Lincoln American School
P.O. Box 27–111, Taichung 40719
Tel: (04) 568 2387
Fax: (04) 568 0337

Hsinchu International School
Yen Ping Road, Sec 1, #212, Hsinchu 300
Tel: (035) 267 837
Fax: (035) 248 261

Kaohsiung Area (Southern Taiwan)

Dominican School
37 Chung Hua 1st Road, Kaohsiung
Tel: (07) 581 2989

Kaohsiung American School
123 7 Taipei Road, Niaosung Hsiang, Kaohsiung
Tel: (07) 731 5565
Fax: (07) 731 5565

Morrison Academy, Kaohsiung Campus
P.O. Box 52 43, Kaohsiung
Tel: (07) 371 8043
Fax: (07) 372 1354

INTERNATIONAL BUSINESS ASSOCIATIONS IN TAIWAN

American Chamber of Commerce in Taipei
Room 1012, 96 Chungshan North Road, Section 2, Taipei
Tel: (02) 2581 7089
Fax: (02) 2542 3376

Australia New Zealand Business Association
8F, 44 Chungshan North Road, Section 2
Tel: (02) 2568 3352
Fax: (02) 2222 1232

British Chamber of Commerce of Taiwan
7F, 99 Jen Ai Road, Section 2, Taipei
Tel: (02) 2356 0210
Fax: (02) 2356 0211

Canadian Society
c/- The Canadian Trade Office in Taipei
13F, 365 Fu Hsing North Road, Taipei
Tel: (02) 2514 9477
Fax: (02) 2712 7244

European Council of Commerce and Trade
11F, 285 Chunghsiao East Road, Section 4, Taipei
Tel: (02) 2740 0236
Fax: (02) 2772 0530

A LIGHT-HEARTED LOOK
AT SOME OF THE MORE ENDEARING
FEATURES OF TAIPEI LIFE

There are two kinds of expatriates in Asia. There are the 'one-timers'—those on a single assignment who see the chance to save some money before returning to the fold. Such people are rarely seen around town; their sole social outlet seems to be a weekly run to the local video store. Then there are those intrepid souls who are in it 'for the term of their natural life' and would not have it any other way. These people love the challenge and survive in good measure because of a lively sense of humour.

To finish this book on an up-beat note, a small group of fellow travellers got together one evening to put together a list of the things they love to hate about Taipei, plus some insights into getting along with local people that really did not fit anywhere else. My thanks to Nigel Page, Brian Asmus, Lee Ting, Jessica Lu and Keelee Chen for their inspiration. The following is an alphabetic list of the things the other business guides will not tell you.

A is for **art and culture** which can be found in Taiwan if you look hard enough. Taipei is hardly the cultural capital of the world but it does house what is arguably the world's finest collection of Chinese antiquities in the National Palace Museum. Unfortunately, for many, Chinese culture ended with the Ch'ing Dynasty. For most of the period of the Chinese Republic the country was engaged in civil war, and artistic development was one of the casualties. Things are slowly changing although most 20th century fine art is in private collections and galleries and not generally on public display. The Taipei Fine Arts Museum on Chung Shan

North Road has the occasional exhibition but overall the standing collection is disappointing. A similar situation prevails in the performing arts although local standards are steadily improving. Taipei has some fine concert halls, including the Sun Yat-Sen Memorial Hall and the National Concert Hall and Opera House at the Chiang Kai Shek Memorial Park. Monthly programs in both English and Chinese are available from major ticket outlets (including major bookstores in Taipei) and feature regular performances by international artists, orchestras and soloists.

A is also for **auspicious days**. These are very important if you live by the lunar calendar. Do not be surprised if business negotiations, contract signing, funerals, weddings, house moving, etc. are postponed for seemingly unknown reasons. The probable fact is that the day is not listed as being lucky for that particular event. You will therefore have no option but to wait until a more auspicious moment.

B is for **betel nuts**, known affectionately as Chinese Chewing Gum, and less affectionately as the 'Big Spit'. Betel nut growing is a traditional industry in Taiwan, especially in mountainous areas where it is the major cash crop available to communities. While officially discouraged because of the adverse medical side effects induced by chewing betel nuts, the industry has a powerful lobby not only among rural constituencies but also among the general betel nut chewing population. No reliable statistics are readily available but in the central and southern parts especially, its use is widespread—particularly, although not entirely, among the less well-educated population. Betel nut chewers can be readily identified by brown teeth and inflamed gums and a tendency to spit a brown slime at regular five-minute intervals. Pity the poor foreign students who in their effort to blend into the local scene have taken to the habit. They would be better off with a Camel.

B is also for **blood types**. As a Westerner, you may know your blood type but consider it of no importance in your daily life. Not so for many Taiwanese. Like the Zodiac calendar that many live by, blood types are considered to determine your personal characteristics. There are four blood types: A, AB, B and O. Chinese do not distinguish between O+ and O-. If you are the boss of a company and your blood type is O then you may wish to employ only people with blood type B because Type O people can control these people while O itself is controlled by Type A. People with blood type A are supposedly good accountants while B make good sales people. There is more but you get the drift.

C is for **compensation**, a magic word among the local populace which through some mystic form of transcendentalism is supposed to right all wrongs—real and imaginary. If a motor bike runs a red light and smashes into your Volvo, you must give him (or her) compensation. Why? you might ask. Well, the logic of the situation goes like this: if you are driving a Volvo you are obviously better off than the bloke on the Vespa and you can make him feel better by compensating him (or her) for the hurt that person has inflicted on himself (or herself). If a business deal goes bad—for whatever reason—forget about what is written in the agreements (assuming you have a written agreement) or a negotiated settlement; more often than not, the cry will go up for compensation. It is supposed to make the other party feel better about breaking up the relationship.

C is also for **con-job**. By the way, it does not work in reverse. If you are the person on the Vespa running into a Volvo then you are a stupid foreigner who got what you deserve.

D is for **driving** in Taiwan, a hazardous occupation at the best of times. Roads are generally good in Taiwan—it's just that there are not enough of them for the volume of traffic. Driving tends to follow the 'law of the unoccupied space'—namely, if you see an empty car length in front of you (even if it several car lengths in front of you), then go for it and damn the consequences. Concepts such as 'defensive driving' and offering the 'courtesy of the road' are unknown in Taiwan. Driver education seems to follow basic Confucian principles insofar as driving schools train people to pass tests and not necessarily to drive on roads. If you do intend to drive in Taiwan you should be totally familiar with the local highway code:

- Red traffic lights are advisory only and can be ignored if you can get away with it by driving across an intersection at high speed;
- Turn signals are not to be used—even when executing a left hand turn from a right hand lane;
- If possible do not use headlights either at nights or in tunnels as their use increases your fuel consumption;
- Young children need plenty of air when in a car and can best be positioned standing on the centre arm rest between the front seats with their head poking through the retractable roof;
- Normal speed limits do not apply if you are driving on the shoulder or in the emergency lane of a highway;

- Pedestrians give way to scooters; scooters give way to cars; cars give way to buses and everything gives way to gravel trucks. If you plan to ignore this rule go back and check the C-word;
- When driving long distances or in heavy traffic, relieve boredom by placing a television in front of the steering wheel—but make sure it is tuned to your favourite program;

D is also for **death wish** which appears to be common among many drivers, particularly those on motor bikes and scooters.

E is for **eating**; some say it is what Taiwanese do best. For Chinese gourmands, Taipei has long been known for its fine culinary traditions, epitomised in the recent movie *Eat, Drink, Man, Woman* (highly recommended). Food from every province of China is available in Taiwan and most Chinese still buy much of their produce at the traditional local markets (which increasingly are being modernised and air conditioned, without losing any of their character—just improving their hygiene standards). Local Taiwanese food tends to be quite pungent with lots of seafood dishes and one of the true delights of local eating is to try one of the many so-called 'beer houses'. These run the full gamut of style from simple outdoor eating establishments where patrons sit on stools at small tables, to the up-market places on An-Ho road which resemble hotel restaurants. Go for simplicity: you can usually choose your food straight from the refrigerated trays and often tell the staff how you want it cooked. Swig it down with a two litre pitcher of Taiwan Beer which, since they removed the formaldehyde, has become quite drinkable. Beware though: in many establishments the idea of a cold beer is to fill your glass with ice cubes. We have tried to explain that in Australia to put ice in a person's beer is a capital offence but they don't believe us.

Generally when eating out, Taiwanese do not split the bill but take it in turns to pay. When friends dine together, there will often be a 'fight' over who is going to pay for the meal. All this is ritual. Custom dictates that the host pays, but equally that there is a fight over the bill before (s)he does so. Remember too that many Taiwanese are vegetarian and it is always wise to include one or more vegetarian dishes in a meal or enquire whether anybody wishes to have vegetarian food.

F is for **freeways**, or rather the lack of them. The sole north-south freeway which runs from Keelung in the north to Kaohsiung in the south is woefully overcrowded, since for most of its length it is only a two-lane affair, and as Taiwanese love to speed, pile ups—often fatal—are common. Impatient drivers then clog the shoulders preventing rescue trucks and emergency vehicles from getting to the scene and traffic can be held up for hours. Once you are stuck in this situation there is no way out. The freeways in Taiwan are not free but are in fact tollways. The basic toll for a private car is NT$40 and there are ten stops on the 300 km+ length of highway. A new highway has been opened between Hsinchu and the southern parts of Taipei and a new connecting road connecting to the Taipei international airport has just been completed. Once the remaining interchanges around Taipei are opened (due to be sometime in 1998) traffic should ease. Actually, Taiwan is developing quite a good secondary highway system which is not only free but less congested than the freeways proper. If you must drive around Taiwan, allow for plenty of time and give the toll freeways a miss.

F is also for **face**. We've already mentioned this in the text but not the official explanation for it. Face is a concept invented by Chinese to explain why they can act in front of Western people in ways that would never be tolerated by other Chinese.

G is for **gravel trucks**, usually overloaded, the horsemen of the apocalypse which descend daily on local roads hell bent on leaving behind trails of destruction. Gravel trucks account for an alarmingly high proportion of road deaths in Taiwan. Give them a wide birth and never, ever, challenge them to a game of chicken or you will be the one cooking your goose.

G is also for **gifts**. Giftgiving is common in Taiwan and always practised when invited to a home. Often, the host will thank you for the gift but initially refuse to accept it until you persist. This can go on for several minutes before the host finally (and reluctantly) succumbs. This is all ritual. He or she will be most offended if you take the gift back. Unlike Western custom, gifts are usually not opened in the presence of the giver. This is viewed as greedy behaviour.

H is for the **Hash House Harriers**, that civilising influence imported from the West (not too far west; the Hash originated in Malaysia according to popular lore). These uncaped crusaders can be seen each weekend cavorting through the hills of Taipei; robust and not-so-robust Western guys yelling their cry of 'on, on' and pursued by the groupie girls at whom the cry is addressed. If you want to join, rumour has it that members can usually be found of a Sunday afternoon, swigging the odd ale or three at the Post Home in Tienmou.

I is for the **Internet** in Taiwan which, thanks to an overloaded system, goes off the air with depressing regularity. Taiwan is a sink for information, so we are told, which means getting information out of the country over the Net is relatively easy. Importing information is another matter. In Taiwan, despite the much-vaunted opening up of the telecommunications market, the government has the Internet by the proverbials. Two government-owned corporations control the overwhelming majority of access to the high-bandwidth overseas lines and retain a virtual monopoly position. It beats us why they have never been taken to the Fair Trade Commission. HINET and SEEDNET, the government agencies who were not supposed to be ISPs but in fact have collared 95% of the market, are woefully oversubscribed. Customers of these organisations are being serviced by only a 150:1 bandwidth availability, when the desired industry ratio is around 30:1. If you are a serious surfer, go for a private provider.

J is for the **Jade Market** to be found each weekend operating from a city carpark underneath the Chienkuo expressway, near the intersection with Jen-Ai Road. We can't comment on the quality of jade, nor the prices, but there are certainly a lot of people doing business, not only in jade but in a wide variety of collectibles. One of the fun things to do on a wet Sunday afternoon in Taipei is to visit the Jade Market and the associated flower and bric-a-brac markets. But do not expect to park your car close by; it's best to use public transport. Not a place for small children, owing to the crowds.

K is for **kickbacks**, said to be part of the local business scene but we would not know about these things. All we know is there are a lot of people being arrested around town who claim to have never heard of the word.

L is for **landlords** and, more often than not, landladies—since it is often the women of Taiwan who control the purse strings. Many are quite reasonable. Some are not. Beware of the variety who seem to think that all Western people are generous to the point of foolhardiness.

M is for **massage** which comes in a number of varieties in Taiwan. Not surprisingly, many so-called massage parlours and barber shops were fronts for prostitution (surprise, surprise!) but most of these have been closed down by the incumbent Taipei mayor. However, it is still possible to get quite a good Japanese-style massage, complete with the hot towel compresses and back-walks. We have always wondered about just how well some of these girls are trained and would recommend caution if she offers to walk on your back—especially if she is on the heavy side. As a rule of thumb, there appears to be an inverse correlation between the degree of prettiness of the masseuse and the level of expertise of her service. Prices are around NT$1200 for 90 minutes. Afterwards you will either feel like a million dollars or like spending the same amount on a chiropractor.

M is also for **money**, which you will have in your pocket if you stay away from the massage parlours. Chinese have a special affection for money (don't we all?). In business, expect Chinese to argue over every penny. Tell them you have an excellent investment that will bring them a 20% annual return guaranteed over five years and they will not trust you. Tell them you have illegal connections to corrupt politicians and all you need is US$1 million for one day to get them a return of US$1 billion and the money will be on the table in a flash.

N is for the **National Palace Museum** which houses the world's largest collection of Chinese collectibles spanning the full five millennia (so they say) of Chinese recorded history. Given the recent Australian archaeological finds tracing human habitation back 125,000 years, the Aussies might yet knock the claim by 100,000 years or more. Not that it matters. The museum collection is among the world's finest and traces every aspect of Chinese culture through the ages. The items housed are so vast that it takes 10 years for all items to be cycled through the display halls. Rumour has it that somewhere in the museum archives is the original pizza recipe which some claim Marco Polo stole from the Chinese and took back to Italy. It has not been put on display for fear of provoking an international crisis.

O is for **opera** which in Taipei is mostly of the Chinese variety. Indeed, the cable television operators have whole channels devoted to this art form. Chinese opera tends to follow the classic 'Peking Opera' format though the potted versions you can see on the box are no substitute for a live performance.

P is for **public transportation**. Taiwan has a relatively good public transportation system. Taipei buses are clean and air conditioned, albeit sometimes slow and crowded. An English-language route guide can be found in a number of Taipei book stores. Government and private bus companies offer an island-wide service to almost all towns throughout the island. Government buses are non-smoking but smoking is permitted by most private operators. Trains have special smoking compartments. Domestic air services are all non-smoking. Taipei is building a rapid transit system consisting of both light and regular rail services. Although considered to be the most expensive in the world it is not yet finished and the short stretch that is working has been plagued by construction and operational problems.

Q is for **'quakes**, although for the most part those experienced in Taiwan are merely tremors. Taiwan is a mountainous country with volcanic activity evident in many places throughout the island. These are nothing to worry about although you will certainly notice them from time to time. There are no active volcanoes as such although fumaroles abound, many of which can be seen in the Yangminshan National Park area just north of Taipei.

R is for the Taiwan **railway** network which one local publication claims is 'vast'. We would be less expansive in our praise and believe the local rail system can best be described as 'adequate'. Although Taiwan plans to develop a high speed rail link to service the main north-south trunk route (taking some pressure off of the main freeway) this is still in the planning stage. In the meantime, rail travellers must make do with a network that dates from the era of Japanese occupation. The present rail system is narrow gauge and for a considerable portion of its length the main trunk route is still only single tracked. Still, as long as you take one of the express trains, the rolling stock is modern, comfortable, and relatively safe. The East Coast line is not yet electrified but the train journey to Hualien is well worth making once during a stay in Taiwan, as is the mountain line between Chiayi and Alishan. In short, if you are a train aficionado, you will find some real gems on and off the Taiwan tracks. If you are looking for speed, jump a jet.

R is also for **rings**. Chinese love to wear rings, preferably gold and often lots of them. To Western tastes it all looks terribly ostentatious, but read on. The rings are meant to cover cracks in the fingers which, if not covered, would allow money to flow away. Buying and wearing rings not only plugs the holes but ensures a prosperous future.

S is for **singing**, a pastime indulged in by many; not alone and under the shower but usually in the company of friends and, often, alcohol. More commonly known as Karaoke or KTV, the Chinese like nothing more than to spend their evenings crowded into a dark room with an oversized television and a bottle of Scotch for companionship. Many company outings follow the same format. Company buses drive through Taiwan's scenic areas with the curtains drawn while those inside sing their hearts out.

S is also for the **sirens** of the fire trucks that can often be heard racing through the city; KTV parlours tend to catch fire with depressing regularity—often tragically with loss of life.

And **S** is also for **superstition**. Chinese generally are a very superstitious people. The number 4 in Chinese sounds similar to 'death' and is therefore to be avoided. In most buildings, the 5th floor comes directly after the 3rd floor. Similarly the number 13 is also to be avoided. The number 8 is considered lucky as it sounds similar to 'prosper' in Chinese. In regard to colour, white is the colour of death. Wearing white shirts or blouses is fine in everyday life but should be avoided on social occasions, especially joyous ones like wedding banquets.

T is for **transvestites** who, we are told, are quite commonly found in the clubs and discos around the university area in Taipei. Although Chinese are usually quite conservative in matters of sex, younger Chinese are slowly coming out of the closet and alternative lifestyles, while not yet generally accepted in Taiwan, are at least acknowledged as such. As meeting places for this genre, saunas are passé. Taipei now has a number of gay and lesbian bars for meeting, some of which advertise as such in the daily papers.

T is also for **toilets**. Not a subject often discussed, but it is necessary to point out that public conveniences in Taiwan are next to nonexistent except along the main north-south freeway. Thankfully, in recent years Ronald McDonald has stepped in to solve the problem.

U is for the **underworld**, not that place between Scilla and the Charybdis, but rather the more sinister one that tends to manipulate construction contracts and build mass transit systems with sea sand in the supporting pillars. Taiwan has recently begun a concerted crackdown on organised crime, and a number of gangland leaders are now incarcerated on Green Island prison. However, there is a long way to go if the system is really to be cleaned up.

V is for **vandalism**, of which there is very little in Taiwan compared to that found in most Western cities. One particularly quaint local social custom however is the pastime known as car scratching. This is no longer a matter of the 'have-nots' waging war on the 'haves'. Rather, it reflects a city with too many cars competing for too few spaces. Consequently, many locals take rather a territorial view of the public roads, especially outside their residences or places of business, and the adjacent parking space is often considered to be personally owned. Park there at risk! There is no logic to any of this of course. How can you tell whether you have intruded another's space? You cannot. But if you return to your brand new car and find deep scratch marks over the bonnet and along the doors (usually rendered by another set of car keys), you will know that somebody has objected to you using 'their' space and you should park somewhere else next time. Spray painting is a thriving industry in Taiwan. Not on walls, but on car panels.

W is for **weddings**, which in Taiwan are still quite popular and which have some interesting local variants. Firstly, if invited to a Chinese wedding, do not go shopping for gifts. The only thing appreciated is money! The amount to be given will vary according to your relationship with the bride or groom and you should check with your Chinese colleagues if confronted with this situation. As a rough estimate think of at least NT$1,200 for starters, to be given in a red envelope otherwise known as *hung pao*. Secondly, do not expect a ceremony or speeches. Taiwanese actually marry at the local district office where they simply register the fact that they have closed the nuptials. The actual celebration can take place weeks and sometimes months later—often all these dates are decreed by a local fortune-teller. Expect to drink and eat a lot. Taiwanese enjoy both with alacrity and there is no better time than a wedding. Country weddings were also well known for their entertainment, which often included strippers, but this custom is now frowned upon. If you are a male contemplating marriage to a local—be warned. Chinese girls, (so we are told) irrespective of age, act like 16 year olds before marriage and 50 year olds thereafter.

X is for **X-rated** television in Taiwan. Do not expect to see it on the government channels but flick to cable (as most Chinese do, precisely because rediffusion services are government-owned or government-backed channels) and you will find it. When cable TV started it was an illegal but tolerated industry that went largely unregulated. As a consequence, the different operators vied with one another to bring adult movies to the public. Much of the hard-core material was only available for an added monthly subscription and most of it was kinky Japanese stuff.

Since the government started to regulate the industry a lot of it has disappeared. Under the current licensing system there is now only one cable operator in each area who bids for the licence to operate the service. With the element of competition gone from the market, so has a lot of the programming. In sheer numbers, you may be getting 60 or more channels for your viewing pleasure but most of them are, ahem, a tad boring. Still, for those who care, you can still get almost everything in Taiwan for a price, even—well, let's leave it at that.

X is also for **X-rays**. These come free in many buildings in downtown Taipei—a consequence of an entrepreneur in the 1980s buying up a job-lot of irradiated steel cheaply and selling it to local construction companies. Everybody is still arguing over the C-word but those involved in the deal have long since emigrated to Canada and are reluctant to return. When searching for your dream apartment, it may be worthwhile to take along a Geiger counter.

Y is for **yachts and yachting**. Until a couple of years ago, sailing in Taiwan was a complete no-no. Apparently the local military feared that watersports might encourage the PLA on the Mainland to take to the sea in Laser dinghies and somehow infiltrate the island through the local yacht clubs. Things are now a bit more relaxed and sailing is starting to grow in popularity. There are a few clubs around, most started by foreigners.

Z is for the Combat **Zone**, otherwise known as Te Wei Street, near the Imperial Hotel. The Zone is a well known and much loved area of Taipei city. It can be a lot of fun and is frequented by both resident foreigners and the fly-in laptop brigade alike. It is a good place for business networking and far cheaper than the various business clubs around town. If you are a newcomer, pick up a copy of *This Month in Taiwan* for details of the various bars. A word of advice: The Zone is a safe and fun area frequented by most expats at some time or another. Beer prices are generally around NT$120 + 10%. Some pubs have hostesses who will drink with you, and some do not. Beware of places with touts outside trying to lure you inside with all sorts of promises. As a general rule of thumb, if the girl sitting with you has a drink for under NT$200, she is probably a student seeking some spare cash and wanting to brush up her English. Do not insult her and embarrass yourself by expecting more. On the other hand, if the lady orders drinks for NT$400 or more, then she is most likely a professional and anything goes. Our advice: put NT$1,000 in your pocket and have a good night out on the town, but leave your credit cards behind in a safe place.

READER REPLY COUPON

Valid until 31 December 1998

As a purchaser of the *Business Guide to Taiwan* you are entitled to access the Virtual Taiwan website to obtain new or additional information or to access other services available. Please complete the coupon below and send to: P.O. Box 81–738, Taipei, Taiwan, ROC.

Reader details

Name (Family Name <u>Last</u>):	
Email:	
Country of Purchase:	

Reason for purchase

Personal Use:		Business Use:	
Corporate Research:		Academic:	

Your password access to the members' area at http://virtualtaiwan.com will be sent to the email address nominated above.

INDEX

A

A to Z of Taiwan, 375–385
accounting firms, international, 251
ACP (Asian Company Profiles), 137
acquisitions, corporate, 184–185
advertising, 225
agricultural sector, 60, 63–64, 221–222
airports, 36–37
Alien Residence Certificate, 344, 345
American Chamber of Commerce, 361, 372
American Club, 360
amusement tax, 262, 273
animal import permits, 351–352
anti-competitive practices, 183–189
appliances, 347–348
area, geographic, 4
Arts, 363, 375
Asian Company Profiles (ACP), 137
Asian Pacific Regional Operations Centre (APROC), 19, 33–35
Australia, 96

B

balance sheet sample, 284–287
Bank of Taiwan, 308–310

Bankers Acceptances (BAs), 297, 298
banks
    central, 300
    deposit structure, 304–306
    deposit-taking, 300–304
    development, 312–319
    domestic commercial, 304, 305, 308–312
    foreign, 301, 302, 319–320
    interest rates, 292–293, 297–298
    loans *see* loans
    medium business, 301
    OBUs, 321–323
    privatisation, 43
    State involvement, 44–45
    top 20 local, 302–304
bars, 363
beer houses, 362–363
bond market, 333–335, 341
Branches, 134–135
brokering, 340–341
building (house) tax, 262, 273
business associations, 361, 372–373
business cards, 3, 233
business culture, 135
business hours, 2
Business Income Tax, 261, 262
'business investigation' services, 137–138
business tax (VAT), 247, 261, 262, 266–268
businesses *see* enterprises

C

cable television industry, 41–42
Canadian Society, 361, 373
capital market
    defined, 325–326
    foreign participation, 331–332
    regulation, 337–340
Central Bank of China (CBC), 300
Central Deposit Insurance Corporation, 324
Central Government, 15–16

Central Trust of China (CTC), 240, 300
CETRA (China External Trade Development Council), 138
Chiang Ching-kuo, 9, 10
Chiang Kai-shek, 9, 10
Chiao Tung Bank, 312–315
China, Mainland *see* Mainland China
China Credit Information Services, 137–138
Chinatrust Commercial Bank, 310–311
climate, 345
clothing, 345, 346–347
club memberships, 142
Combat Zone, 385
Commercial Papers (CPs), 297, 298
commissaries, 218–219
Commodity Labelling Law, 193
commodity tax, 261, 262, 268–270
Community Services Center, 359–360
community support services, 359–360
companies *see* enterprises
Companies Limited by Shares, 126–129
consumer data protection, 203–204
Consumer Protection Law (CPC), 191–192
consumption patterns, 208–214
convenience stores, 216–217
cooking appliances, 347–348
copyright protection, 198–200
corporate bonds, 334, 342
corporate tax
    benefits under SUI, 264–266
    exemption on salaries, 266
    formula, 264
    overview, 261–262, 263–264
    payment schedule, 266
    sample declaration form, 279–283
    tax credits, 265
    withholding rates, 277–278
cost of living adjustment, 141
credit reporting, 136, 137–138, 307
crime, 20–21
cultural pursuits, 363, 375

currency
  depreciation, 52, 53
  exchange rate movements, 32–33
  foreign exchange, 13, 39, 296
  national, 5
  outlook, 293–296
currency markets, 39
customs regulations, 262, 270–271, 350–352

D

data protection, consumer, 203–204
decentralisation, 146
deed tax, 262, 273
Democratic Progressive Party (DPP), 9–10, 25, 29
department stores, 219–220
Derivatives Market, 325
diplomatic recognition, 21–22
direct marketing, 227
directors roster, 133
disputes, industrial, 172–174
distribution systems, 220–224
dividend tax, 259, 266
dress codes, 345
Dun & Bradstreet Taiwan, 138

E

ECCT (European Council of Commerce and Trade), 99, 361, 373
Economic Development Plans, 83–91, 99–102
economy
  annual growth, 24
  basic indicators, 12
  export-driven, 55
  foundation, 11–15
  revival, 31–33
  State role, 42–46
  transition period, 24–25
education, 142, 161
Edwards International Limited, 138
'Eight Major Key Technologies', 103
electricity, 152–153, 347, 366

employee checks, 136
employment *see* labour market
enterprises
  capital requirements, 128–129
  definitions, 125–128
  documentation, 129–133, 284–287
  forms of presence, 133–135
  getting started, 121–123
  improving presence, 238
  total registered, 122
  venture capital, 261, 262
environmental legislation, 195
Environmental Protection Administration (EPA), 193–196
estate tax, 262, 275–277
European Council of Commerce and Trade (ECCT), 99, 361, 373
European Union, 70
expatriates
  housing, 354–356
  women, 368–369
  working conditions, 140–143
Export Processing Zone Administration (EPZA), 74
export processing zones (EPZs), 74
Export-Import Bank of the ROC (Exim Bank), 71–74
exports
  basic rules, 78–79
  EPZs, 74
  European Union, 70
  Japan, 69
  major items, 64–66
  markets, 66–67
  patterns, 63–66
  trade imbalance, 59
  United States, 68–69
  value, 13, 52, 53
  WTO rankings, 56–57

F
'face', 232, 379
factories
  bonded, 75–76

licences, 131
rental space, 148–149
total registered, 132
Fair Trade Commission, 180–183
Fair Trade Law, 180–182, 183–191
Farmers Bank of China, 318–319
financial institutions
banks *see* banks
community-based, 323
defined, 299
deposit growth, 305–306
finance and leasing companies, 302
life insurance companies, 324
postal savings system, 324
financial market, 38–40
fiscal year, 5
food
availability, 349–350
dining options, 362–363
distribution, 222–224
marketing, 225–226
retail services, 215–216
Taiwanese style, 378
foreign exchange, 13, 39, 296
foreign investment
application process, 112–113
incentives, 107–110
in/out flow, 97–99
legal requirements, 123–125
loans and subsidies, 110–112
origins, 95–96
policy reforms, 34–35
restrictions, 119–120
role, 94
by sector, 96–97
value, 95
foreign policy, 21–22
founding fathers, 10–11
Four-Year Plan for National Development, 99–100, 104–106
freight

air, 37, 38
  sea, 35–36
futures exchange, 337

G
gas, 366
GDP (gross domestic product), 11, 85
GFII (non-QFII investor), 332
gift tax, 262, 275, 276
gift giving, 379
Global Depository Receipts, 334, 342
GNP (gross national product), 12, 84, 91
government
  bureaucratic reform, 14
  corporate investments, 44–46
  key agencies, 18, 47–49
  levels, 15–17
  official title, 4
  procurement practices, 189–191
  revenues, 245–247
  tendering process, 239–241
  trade practices, 189–191
government bonds, 333
gross domestic product (GDP), 11, 85
gross national product (GNP), 12, 91

H
health services, 365
holidays, national, 3
home help, 142, 357–358
Hong Kong, 67, 70–71, 95
hotels, 352–353
house tax, 262, 273
household expenditure, 211–213
household staff, 142, 357–358
household taxation, 255–256
housing, 14, 141, 354–357
Hsinyi, 355–356
hypermarkets, 218

I

image, business, 237
immigration, 343–345
imports
  basic rules, 79–80
  major items, 61–63
  origins, 68, 69, 70
  patterns, 60–63
  prohibited, 76
  restricted, 76–77
  taxes and tariffs, 54
  trade imbalance, 59
  value, 13, 52, 53
  WTO rankings, 56, 58
income tax, individual
  business taxes, 262
  deductions, 256–258
  exemptions, 256
  filing returns, 258
  gross income, 255–256
  non-residents, 254–255, 256, 259
  overview, 253–255
  penalties, 258
  rates, 254
  tax credits, 259–260
incomes, 158, 165–168, 209
in-country representative offices, 238
Industrial Development and Investment Center, 107, 119
Industrial Development Bureau, 107
industrial parks, 35, 103–104
industrial relations, 171–174
infrastructure development, 104–106
insurance
  plant and equipment, 150–151
  unemployment, 170–171
  workers', 169–170
integrated circuit layout protection, 203
intellectual property protection, 196–204
interest rates, 292–293, 297–298
Internet, 368, 380

investment, foreign *see* foreign investment
Investment Commission, 107, 113

J

Jade Market, 380
Japan, 69, 95, 96
Joint Credit Information Center (JCIC), 307
Joint Venture Companies, 135

K

kitchen items, 347–349
Kuomintang Party (KMT), 8–9, 10, 25, 29

L

Labor Standards Law, 162–163
labour disputes, 172–174
labour market
   age distribution, 159
   average monthly earnings, 166
   dismissals, 170
   females, 158, 159, 164–165, 170
   foreign nationals, 174–177
   insurance provisions, 169–170
   legal framework, 162–163
   overview, 155–157
   part-time workers, 168–169
   remuneration levels, 165–168
   retirement benefits, 171
   skills, 160
   structure, 158–160
   temporary workers, 168–169
   welfare funds, 171
   working conditions, 163–165, 168
Land Bank of Taiwan, 315–317
land taxes, 262, 272
language, 4, 7, 232–233
leave entitlements, 142, 165, 167
legislative reform, 91
'letters of intent', 113, 114–118
Liaison Offices, 133

licences
  business, 129–131
  factories, 131
  professional, 132
life insurance companies, 324
lifestyles, 209–211
Limited Companies, 126–129
linen items, 349
loans
  activity, 307–308
  concessional, 313–314
  Exim structure, 73
  preferential, 111–112
Local Government, 16–17

M

Mainland China
  divided country, 19
  ROC exports, 67, 70–71
  ROC relations, 26, 27, 30–31
  WTO membership, 54
manufacturing, 35, 89–90, 131, 158
market research, 230–231
market share, 235–239
marketing, consumer, 224–227
media, 41–42
medical services, 365
mergers, 184–185
mining lot tax, 262, 274
Ministry of Audit (MoA), 240
Ministry of Finance (MoF), 249, 337
monetary institutions *see* financial institutions
monetary instruments, 296–298
monetary policy
  currency outlook, 293–296
  foreign exchange, 296
  money supply, 290–291
  responsible bodies, 289–290
monopolies, 184
monopoly revenues, 244

mutual funds, 335–337

N
name cards, 233
names, importance of, 3
National Development Plan (1997–2000), 99–100
national development targets (1997–2006), 100–106
National Palace Museum, 381
National tax policy, 247–249
natural gas, 153–154
Negotiable Certificates of Deposits (NCDs), 297, 298
negotiated tenders, 241
negotiations, 233–235
networking, 361
New Party, 27, 29

O
office accommodation, 143–148
offshore banking units (OBUs), 321–323
open tenders, 241
Organisation for Economic Cooperation and Development (OECD), 19
outwards investment, 97–99
Over-The-Counter Market (OTC), 330–331

P
pass-offs, 186–189
patent protection, 202
Peitou, 355
personal hygiene items, 350
pet entry permits, 351–352
pharmacies, 350
politics
  1995 elections, 25–27
  foundation, 8–10
  hoodlum element, 20–21
  parties, 29
  transition period, 22–23
pollution, 194, 195, 196
population
  age distribution, 7

  ethnic groups, 6–8
  total, 4
ports, 36, 102
postal information, 3
postal savings system, 324
power sector, 43, 46
preferential loans, 111–112
presence, corporate, 238
price fixing, 185–186
price negotiations, 234–235
privatisation, 43, 102, 340
profit-seeking enterprise income tax *see* corporate tax
property market, 13, 77, 143–148, 151
Provincial/Municipal Governments, 16
pubs, 363
PX stores, 218–219

Q
Qualified Foreign Institutional Investors (QFII), 331–332

R
railway network, 382
R&D *see* research and development
realty agents, 356–357
recreational activities, 360–365, 382–383
regional reserves, 238–239
regional sales offices, 238
regulatory agencies, 206–207
relationships, business, 231–232, 235, 237, 239
religion, 4
rental costs, 144–145, 147–148, 149, 150
Representative Offices, 133, 134, 238
research and development
  approved, 93
  expenditure, 89, 92
  GNP, 91
  minimum levels, 93
  sources, 91–92
  White Paper blueprint, 93–94
Responsible Person, 127

restricted tenders, 241
resumés, 136
retail chains, major, 215–216
retailing industry, 213–220
roads, 378–379
ROC Company Laws, 126–128

S
sanitation, 367
savings, 84, 85
schools
   American School, 358–359, 371, 372
   Chinese language, 369–370
   international, 370–372
Securities and Futures Commission (SFC), 337, 338–339
Securities Investment Trust Companies (SITCs), 335, 336
Securities Transaction Tax (STT), 271–272
service sector, 158
serviced apartments, 353
settlement, origins of, 5–6
shareholders, 123–124, 133
Singapore, 95, 96
SITCs (Securities Investment Trust Companies), 335, 336
small business sector, 157
social scene, 361–363
sole proprietors, 125–126
spending patterns, 208–214
stamp tax, 262, 273
stock market *see* Taiwan Stock Exchange
stock reserves, 238–239
'strategic alliance' program, 113
STT (Securities Transaction Tax), 271–272
Sun Yat-sen (Dr), 10
sunrise/sunset industries, 89, 90, 91
supermarkets, 217–218
superstition, 383

T
TAIEX (Taiwan Weighted Stock Price Index), 327
Taiwan Co-operative Bank, 317–318

Taiwan Depository Receipts (TDRs), 331
Taiwan International Mercantile Exchange (TIME), 337
Taiwan Provincial Government Supply Bureau (TSB), 240
Taiwan Ratings Corporation, 339–340
Taiwan Stock Exchange Limited (TSE)
  1998 outlook by sector, 328–329
  background, 326–330
  company statistics, 342
  organisation, 339
  trading, 341
  warrants, 337
Taiwan Weighted Stock Price Index (TAIEX), 327
Taiwan's general stock index (TSI), 327
tariffs, 270–271
taxation
  administration, 249
  agencies, 252
  assessment and collection, 247–249
  categories, 244–247
  corporate *see* corporate tax
  foreign investment, 108–110
  government revenues, 245–247
  individual *see* income tax, individual
  international agreements, 249–250
  national policy, 247–249
  overview, 243–244
  system chart, 262
TDRs (Taiwan Depository Receipts), 331
technical capabilities, regional, 237–238
Technology Transfer Service Center, 107
telecommunications, 40–41, 43, 46
telephone services, 3–4, 367–368
television, 41–42, 46, 347
'Ten Emerging Industries', 103
tendering process, 239–241
Three Principles of 'Nationalism', 10–11
Tienmou, 354–355
TIME (Taiwan International Mercantile Exchange), 337
time zone, 5
toiletries, 350

touring, 364–365
trade
  1985–1997 growth, 52
  basic rules, 78–80
  changing, 59–66
  controls, 76–77
  imbalance, 59
  incentives and restrictions, 71–76
  key agencies, 81
  patterns, 66–71
  surplus, 52, 56
  value, 52
  WTO rankings, 56–58
trade secrets, 198
trade unions, 171–172
trademarks, 200–202
transportation
  air, 36–38
  personal, 142
  public, 381–382
  sea, 35–36
travel, overseas, 207–208
Treasury Bills, 297, 298
TSB (Taiwan Provincial Government Supply Bureau), 240
TSE *see* Taiwan Stock Exchange
TSI (Taiwan's general stock index), 327

U

unemployment, 156, 157, 170–171
unfair trade practices, 183–189
unions, trade, 171–172
United States, 54, 68–69, 95
utilities, 152–154, 365–368

V

VAT (business tax), 247, 261, 262, 266–268
vehicle licence tax, 262, 273–274
venture capital enterprises, 261, 262
visas, 142–143, 343–345

W

wages, 158, 165–168, 209
warehouse clubs, 218
warehouses, bonded, 75–76
warrants, 337
waste disposal, 367
water supply, 153, 367
weddings, 384
welfare funds, 171
White Paper on Science and Technology, 93–94
workforce *see* labour market
working conditions, 140–143, 163–165, 168
World Trade Organisation, 13, 53–55

Y

Yalta Agreement, 8
Yangmingshan, 355, 361

Z

zero-rating, 267
Zone, The, 385